Fifth Edition

JUVENILE JUSTICE

A Guide to Theory and Practice

Steven M. Cox
John J. Conrad
Jennifer M. Allen

Boston Burr Ridge, IL Dubuque, IA Madison, WI New York San Francisco St. Louis
Bangkok Bogotá Caracas Kuala Lumpur Lisbon London Madrid Mexico City
Milan Montreal New Delhi Santiago Seoul Singapore Sydney Taipei Toronto

McGraw-Hill Higher Education
A Division of The ***McGraw-Hill*** *Companies*

JUVENILE JUSTICE
Published by McGraw-Hill, a business unit of The McGraw-Hill Companies, Inc., 1221 Avenue of the Americas, New York, NY, 10020.

This book is printed on acid-free paper.

2 3 4 5 6 7 8 9 0 FGR/FGR 0 9 8 7 6 5 4 3

ISBN 0-697-35617-5

Editorial director: *Phillip A. Butcher*
Senior sponsoring editor: *Carolyn Henderson Meier*
Senior marketing manager: *Daniel M. Loch*
Media producer: *Shannon Rider*
Project manager: *Jill Moline*
Production supervisor: *Carol A. Bielski*
Senior designer: *Jenny El-Shamy*
Photo research coordinator: *Alexandra Ambrose*
Photo researcher: *Christine Pullo*
Supplement producer: *Nate Perry*
Cover design: *Crispin Prebys*
Cover photograph: *Getty Images/Rex Ziak*
Typeface: *10/12 Times Roman*
Compositor: *Shepherd Incorporated*
Printer: *Quebecor World Fairfield Inc.*

Library of Congress Cataloging-in-Publication Data

Cox, Steven M.
Juvenile justice : a guide to theory and practice/Steven M. Cox, John J. Conrad, Jennifer M. Allen.—5th ed.
p. cm.
Includes index.
ISBN 0-697-35617-5 (alk.paper)
1. Juvenile justice, Administration of—United States. I. Conrad, John J. II. Allen, Jennifer M. III. Title.
HV9104 .C63 2003
364.36'0973—dc21 2002024636

www.mhhe.com

Contents

Preface

Major changes have been proposed and are occurring in the juvenile justice network. Those who believe the network "coddles" juveniles have been successful in convincing legislators in a variety of jurisdictions that juveniles who commit serious offenses should be treated as adults. At the same time, those who believe that treatment and education are better alternatives for most juveniles with problems have established restorative justice programs as alternatives to, or additions to, official processing. Serious violent crime committed by juveniles has been less frequent over the past five years than in the prior ten, yet juvenile gangs seem to be proliferating. New programs, promising to be more effective and efficient, are initiated while older programs disappear from the scene. Can we make sense of these rapidly occurring changes?

As both practitioners in the juvenile justice network and instructors in criminology, criminal justice, and sociology courses, we have time and again heard: "That's great in theory, but what about in practice?" We are convinced that a basic understanding of the interrelationships among philosophy, notions of causation, and procedural requirements is a must, if one is to understand, let alone practice, in the juvenile justice network.

With these concerns in mind, we decided some 25 years ago to write a text that was student and instructor friendly, comprehensive, yet concise. As we revised the text for this new edition, these concerns remain, though we have expanded discussions where necessary and updated reference and legal materials throughout the text.

Approach

In this text, we integrate juvenile law, theories of causation, and procedural requirements while examining their interrelationships. We have attempted to make our treatment of these issues both relevant and comprehensible to those actively employed in the juvenile justice network, to those who desire to become so employed, and to those whose interest in juvenile justice is more or less academic. We address the juvenile justice network as a composite of interacting individuals whose everyday decisions have very real consequences for others involved in the network. The day-to-day practical aspects of the network are discussed in terms of theoretical considerations and procedural requirements.

- The network approach allows us to examine the interrelationships among practitioners, offenders, victims, witnesses, and others involved with delinquency, abuse, neglect, and other varieties of behavior under the jurisdiction of the juvenile court.
- The roles of practitioners in the network are discussed in relationship to one another and with respect to discretion, politics, and

societal concerns. Thus the police, juvenile probation officers, and social service agents all have roles to play in providing services for juveniles with problems. Unless each contributes, the network is likely to be ineffective in dealing with these problems.
- The law, of course, plays a key role in juvenile justice and we have attempted to present the most recent and important changes in juvenile law based upon an overview of a number of states.
- What we know about theories of behavior should dictate the procedures and treatments employed in dealing with juveniles. To ignore theory is to ignore possible explanations for behaviors and treatment is likely to be ineffective if explanations of behavior are lacking; as such, we spend time discussing theories of behavior and their importance in juvenile justice.

In the following pages, we have attempted to define technical terms clearly where they are presented, and we have included numerous practical examples—which we call "In Practice" sections—in an attempt to present students with a basic understanding of both the theoretical and practical aspects of the juvenile justice network. These real-world "In Practice" boxes are designed to help students connect theory and practice and include discussion of such critical issues as these:

- In Chapter 1, *Juvenile Justice in Historical Perspective*—"The 'adult time law' for juveniles hasn't fulfilled its backers' promises"
- In Chapter 3, *Characteristics of Juvenile Offenders*—"Racial inequities in America's criminal justice system start early"
- In Chapter 5, *Purpose and Scope of Juvenile Court Acts*—"Observers decry approach to delinquent girls"
- In Chapter 6, *Juvenile Justice Procedures*—"Defense asks judge to exclude juvenile's statements to police"
- And in Chapter 11, *Child Abuse and Neglect*—"In molestations, mothers often defend perpetrators; lack of belief hurts the abuse child deeply, experts say"

The Fifth Edition

In addition to the new "In Practice" highlights identified above, we have made numerous other changes to this edition:

- updated references
- coverage of current concerns and recent trends in juvenile justice
- coverage of restorative justice programs
- expanded discussion of theory
- discussion of recent changes in juvenile codes from a variety of states
- expanded discussion of gangs
- a new look at the future of juvenile justice

Pedagogical Aids

To enhance learning, we have included the following devices in every chapter:

- chapter-opening vignettes to capture student interest
- chapter outlines to provide a road map to reading each chapter
- in-chapter "In Practice" boxes to help students see the practical application of what they are reading
- "Career Opportunities" boxes in each chapter
- end-of-chapter "Internet Activities" to encourage students to use the net as a research and learning tool
- end-of-chapter summaries and key terms lists to help students prepare for exams
- end-of-chapter "Critical Thinking Exercises" to encourage students to go beyond memorization of terms and concepts in their learning

INSTRUCTOR SUPPLEMENTS

As a full service publisher of quality educational products, McGraw-Hill does much more than just sell textbooks. The company creates and publishes print, video, and digital supplements for students and instructors as well. This particular text is accompanied by the following instructor supplement:

- Instructor's Manual/Testbank—chapter outlines, discussion questions, a complete testbank, and more.

The Instructor's Manual/Testbank is provided free of charge to instructors. Orders of new (versus used) textbooks help McGraw-Hill defray the substantial cost of developing supplements like this. Please contact your local McGraw-Hill representative for more information on the supplements available with any of our texts.

Acknowledgments

In Appreciation

A number of people have helped in the preparation of this book. For their encouragement and assistance, we would like to thank, Dr. William P. McCamey, Dr. Gene Scaramella, Dr. Michael H. Hazlett, Dr. Giri Raj Gupta, Professor Dennis C. Bliss, Professor Terry Campbell, and Chief Probation Officer Courtney Cox.

We also want to thank the reviewers of the fifth edition manuscript for their many helpful suggestions:

Alejandro del Carmen—University of Texas at Arlington

Stephan D. Kaftan—Hawkeye Community College

Anne T. Sulton—New Jersey City University

Donna Massey—University of Tennessee at Martin

John E. Holman—University of North Texas

Greg Scott—DePaul University

William Kelly—Auburn University

Janet McClellan—Southwestern Oregon Community College

Stephanie R. Bush-Baskette—Florida State University

We welcome your comments concerning the text.

SM-Cox1@wiu.edu
JM-Allen@wiu.edu

CHAPTER

Juvenile Justice in Historical Perspective

Chapter Learning Objectives

Upon completion of this chapter, students should be able to:

Understand the history of juvenile justice in the United States

Understand contemporary challenges to the juvenile justice network

Discuss the controversy between due process and informality in juvenile justice

Recognize discrepancies between the ideal and real juvenile justice networks

Key Terms

Age of responsibility
Common law
Mens rea
Chancery courts
Parens patriae
In loco parentis
Houses of refuge/reform schools
Humanitarian era
Cook County Family Court
Era of socialized juvenile justice
Holmes *case*
Kent *case*
Gault *case*
Winship *case*
Breed v. Jones *case*
McKeiver *case*
Legalistic v. therapeutic approaches

The juvenile justice network in the United States grew out of, and remains embroiled in, controversy (see In Practice 1.1). More than a century after the creation of the first family court in Illinois (1899), the debate continues as to the goals to be pursued and the procedures to be employed within the network, and a considerable gap between theory and practice remains. Meanwhile, concern over delinquency in general, and

First Juvenile Court Building, Ewing and Holsted, Chicago, 1899.
Chicago Daily News/Chicago Historical Society

In Practice 1.1

WHAT IS JUVENILE JUSTICE?

More than 100 years ago, reformers pushed for the creation of a juvenile justice system that treated children involved in criminal behavior differently than adults. It focused on rehabilitation and reform rather than punishment and incarceration.

So why did the nation just witness the sentencing of a sobbing 14-year-old boy to life in prison without parole for murdering another child in Florida when he was 12? In this particular case, there were all sorts of complicating factors, including the amazing fact that Lionel Tate's mother and attorneys stupidly refused a deal that would have sent the boy to juvenile detention for three years, followed by counseling and probation. At that point, the judge imposed the state-mandated sentence.

However, there's a larger point to ponder—the increasing propensity of states to enact statutes that require the waiving of youthful offenders to adult court for trial and sentencing in capital crimes, part of the get-tough-on-criminals movement. Indeed, this very cry was raised last week in California when a 15-year-old opened fatal fire in his high school.

Clearly, if a juvenile commits murder, stronger action must be taken than that for burglary or other lesser offenses. Some experts have suggested juvenile boot camps, which would be tougher than most current juvenile institutions. And certainly, counseling and probation should be in order.

But discretion on the part of the judge, who can benefit from information provided by psychologists and therapists, also should be part of the equation. That discretion could include, particularly in cases involving older teens, a referral to adult court. But for younger miscreants, separation from the community in strictly run juvenile facilities can reinforce or introduce positive behaviors. Trying offenders as young as 10 in adult court—theoretically allowed in Wisconsin—could condemn them to a life beyond horror and without hope.

To be sure, the crime Lionel Tate committed was beyond horror, and the state needed to act. Fortunately, Florida Gov. Jeb Bush seems likely to intervene, offering clemency so that the teenager, who has the mental capacity of an 8-year-old, can be referred to an appropriate juvenile facility.

Still, the larger question looms. Consider the perspective of Amnesty International, which has monitored this case and others like it in the United States. "The fundamental principle at stake here is that children are capable of change and growth and should not be denied that opportunity," according to William Schultz, the group's executive director.

That was what the reformers thought 100 years ago. It's not too late to learn from them now.

Editorial. (2001, March 15). What is juvenile justice? *Milwaukee Journal Sentinel,* p. 18A.

violent delinquents in particular, continues to grow while confidence in the juvenile justice network continues to erode. As Bilchik (1999a, p. 1) indicates, "the reduction of juvenile crime, violence, and victimization constitutes one of the most crucial challenges of the new millennium."

The juvenile court was supposed to have provided due process protections along with care, treatment, and rehabilitation for juveniles while protecting society. Yet there is increasing doubt as to whether the juvenile justice network can meet any of these goals. Violence committed by juveniles, particularly in schools, has attracted nationwide attention and raised a host of questions concerning the juvenile court, even though such violence has actually declined considerably over the past five years. Can a court intended to protect and care for juveniles successfully deal with youth that, seemingly without reason, kill their peers and parents? Is the juvenile justice network too "soft" in its dealings with such youth? Isn't a "get tough" approach what's needed to deal with violent adolescents? Was the juvenile court really designed to deal with the types of offenders we see today?

While due process for juveniles (discussed in detail later, but consisting of such things as the right to counsel and the right to remain silent), protection of society, and rehabilitation of youthful offenders remain elusive goals, frustration and dissatisfaction among those who work in the juvenile justice network, as well as among those who assess its effectiveness, remain the reality. Some observers have called for an end to juvenile justice as a separate system in the United States. Others maintain that the juvenile court and associated agencies and programs have a good deal to offer youth in trouble. For example, recent evidence from a survey of Tennessee residents indicates that, in that state at least, the public believes that rehabilitation should still be an integral goal of the juvenile justice network (Moon, Sundt, Cullen, and Wright 2000). In a similar vein, in the 1997 legislative session in Maryland, the legislature revised the Juvenile Causes Act with a focus on balanced, restorative, and victim-centered justice. The revised act emphasizes prevention through development of programs for at-risk youth and also focuses on improving the network's response to offenders by providing a continuum of sanctions and treatment alternatives (Simms 1997, p. 94).

Can the reality and the ideal of the juvenile justice network be made more consistent? What would have to occur before such consistency could be realized? Why does the disparity exist and why is it so difficult to remedy? A brief look at the history of juvenile justice and a detailed look at the network as it now operates should help us answer these questions.

JUVENILE JUSTICE HISTORICALLY

The distinction between youthful and adult offenders coincides with the beginning of recorded history. Some four thousand years ago, the Code of Hammurabi (2270 B.C) discussed runaways, children who disowned their parents, and sons who cursed their fathers. Approximately two thousand years ago, both Roman civil law and later canon (church) law made distinctions between juveniles and adults based upon the notion of "**age of responsibility.**" In ancient Jewish law, the Talmud specified conditions under which immaturity was to be considered in imposing punishment. There was no corporal punishment prior to puberty, which was considered to be the age of twelve for females and thirteen for males. No capital punishment was to be imposed for those under twenty years of age. Similar leniency was found among Moslems, where children under the age of seventeen were typically exempt from the death penalty (Bernard 1992).

By the fifth century B.C., codification of Roman law resulted in the "Twelve Tables," which made it clear that children were criminally responsible for violations of law and were to be dealt with by the criminal justice system (Nyquist 1960). Punishment for some offenses, however, was less severe for children than for adults. Thus, theft of crops by night was a capital offense for adults, but offenders under the age of puberty were to be flogged. Adults caught in the act of theft were subject to flogging and enslavement to the victim, but youth received corporal punishment at the discretion of a magistrate and were required to make restitution (Ludwig 1955). Originally, only those children who were incapable of speech were spared under Roman law, but eventually immunity was afforded to all children under the age of seven as the law came to reflect an increasing recognition of the stages of life. Children came to be classified as "infans," "proximus infantiae," and "proximus pubertati." In general, "infans" were not held criminally responsible, but those approaching puberty who knew the difference between right and wrong were held accountable. For much of Roman history, "infantia" meant the inability to speak, but in the fifth century A.D. this age was fixed at seven years and children under that age were exempt from criminal liability. The legal age of puberty was fixed at fourteen for boys and twelve for girls, and youth above these ages were held criminally liable. For children between the ages of seven and puberty, liability was based upon capacity to understand the difference between right and wrong (Bernard 1992).

Roman and canon law undoubtedly influenced early Anglo-Saxon **common law** (law based on custom or usage), which emerged in England during the eleventh and twelfth centuries. For our purposes, the distinctions made between adult and juvenile offenders in England at this time are most significant. Under common law, children under the age of seven were presumed incapable of forming criminal intent and therefore were not subject to criminal sanctions. Children between seven and fourteen were not subject to criminal sanctions unless it could be demonstrated that they had formed criminal intent, understood the consequences of their actions, and could distinguish right from wrong (Blackstone 1803, pp. 22–24). Children over fourteen were treated much the same as adults.

The question of when and under what circumstances children are capable of forming criminal intent (**mens rea** or "guilty mind") remains a point of contention in juvenile justice proceedings today. In order for an adult to commit criminal homicide, for instance, it must be shown not only that the adult took the life of another human being without justification, but that he or she intended to take the life of that individual. One may take the life of another accidentally (without intending to) and such an act is not regarded as criminal homicide. In other words, it takes more than the commission of an illegal act to produce a crime. Intent is also required (and, in fact, in some cases it is assumed as a result of the seriousness of the act, e.g., felony murder statutes).

But at what age is a child capable of understanding the differences between right and wrong, or of comprehending the consequences of his or her acts before they occur? For example, most of us would not regard a four-year-old who pocketed some money found at a neighbor's house as a criminal, since we are confident that the child cannot understand the consequences of this act. But what about an eight- or nine- or twelve-year-old?

Another important step in the history of juvenile justice occurred in the fifteenth century when chancery or equity courts were created by the King of England. **Chancery courts,** under the guidance of the king's chancellor, were created to consider petitions of those who were in need of special aid or intervention, such as women and children left in need of protection and aid by reason of divorce, death of a spouse, or abandonment, and to grant relief to such persons. Through the chancery courts the king exercised the right of **parens patriae** ("parent of the country") by enabling these courts to act **in loco parentis** ("in the place of parents") to provide necessary services for the benefit of women and children (Bynum and Thompson 1992). In other words, the king, as ruler of his country, was to assume responsibility for all those under his rule, to provide parental care for children who had no parents, and to assist women who required aid for any of the reasons mentioned above. Although chancery courts did not normally deal with youthful offenders, they did deal with dependent or neglected youth, as do juvenile courts in the United States today. The principle of *parens patriae* later became central to the development of the juvenile court in America and today generally refers to the fact that the state (government) has ultimate parental authority over juveniles in need of protection or guidance. In certain cases, then, the state may act *in loco parentis* ("as a parent") and make decisions concerning the best interests of youth. This includes, for example, removing children from the home of their parents when circumstances warrant.

In 1562, Parliament passed the Statute of Artificers, which stated that children of paupers could be involuntarily separated from their parents and apprenticed to others (Rendleman 1974, p. 77). Similarly, the Poor Law Act of 1601 provided for involuntary separation of children from their impoverished parents, and these children were then placed in bondage to local residents as apprentices. Both statutes were based on the beliefs that the state has a primary interest in the welfare of children and the right to insure such welfare. At the same time, a system known as the "City Custom of Apprentices" operated in London. This system was established to settle disputes involving apprentices who were unruly or abused by their masters in an attempt to punish the appropriate parties. When an apprentice was found to be at fault and required confinement, he or she was segregated from adult offenders. Those in charge of the City Custom of Apprentices attempted to settle disputes in a confidential fashion so the juveniles involved were not subjected to public shame or stigma (Sanders 1974, pp. 46–47).

Throughout the 1600s and most of the 1700s, juvenile offenders in England were sent to adult prisons, although they were at times kept separate from adult offenders. The Hospital of St. Michael's, the first institution for the treatment of juvenile offenders, was established in Rome in 1704 by Pope Clement XI. The stated purpose of the hospital was to correct and instruct unruly youth so that they might become useful citizens (Griffin and Griffin 1978, p. 7).

The first private, separate institution for youthful offenders in England was established by Robert Young in 1788. The goal of this institution was "to educate and instruct in some useful trade or occupation the children of convicts or such other infant poor as (were) engaged in a vagrant and criminal course of life" (Sanders 1974, p. 48).

In the early 1800s, changes in the criminal code that would have allowed English magistrates to hear cases of youthful offenders without the necessity of long delays were recommended. In addition, dependent or neglected children were to be appointed legal guardians who were to aid the children through care and education (Sanders 1974, p. 49).

These changes were rejected by the House of Lords due to the opposition to the magistrate's becoming "judges, juries, and executioners" and due to suspicion concerning the recommended confidentiality of the proceedings, which would have excluded the public and the press (Sanders 1974, pp. 50–51).

Meanwhile in the United States, dissatisfaction with the way young offenders were being handled was increasing. As early as 1825, the Society for the Prevention of Juvenile Delinquency advocated separating juvenile and adult offenders (Snyder and Sickmund 1999). Up to this point in time, youthful offenders had been generally subjected to the same penalties as adults and little or no attempt was made to separate youth from adults in jails or prisons. This caused a good deal of concern among reformers who feared that criminal attitudes and knowledge would be passed from the adults to the juveniles. Another concern centered around the possibility of brutality directed by the adults toward juveniles. While many juveniles were being imprisoned, few appeared to benefit from the experience. Others simply appealed to the sympathy of jurors in order to escape the consequences of their acts entirely. With no alternative to imprisonment, juries and juvenile justice officials were inclined to respond emotionally and sympathetically to the plight of children, which often caused them to overlook juvenile misdeeds or render lenient verdicts (Dorne and Gewerth 1998, p. 4).

In 1818, a New York City committee on pauperism gave the term *juvenile delinquency* its first public recognition by referring to it as a major cause of pauperism (Drowns and Hess 1990, p. 9). As a result of this increasing recognition of the problem of delinquency, several institutions for juveniles were established between 1824 and 1828. These institutions were oriented toward education and treatment rather than punishment, though whippings, long periods of silence, and loss of rewards were used to punish the uncooperative. In addition, strict regimentation and a strong work ethic philosophy were common.

Under the concept of *in loco parentis,* institutional custodians acted as parental substitutes with far-reaching powers over their charges. For example, the staff of the New York House of Refuge, established in 1825, were able to bind out wards as apprentices, although the consent of the child involved was required. Whether or not such consent was voluntary is questionable since the alternatives were likely unpleasant. The New York House of Refuge was soon followed by others in Boston and Philadelphia (Abadinsky and Winfree 1992).

"By the mid-1800s, **houses of refuge** were enthusiastically declared a great success. Managers even advertised their houses in magazines for youth. Managers took great pride in seemingly turning total misfits into productive, hard-working members of society" (Simonsen and Gordon 1982, p. 23). However, these claims of success were not undisputed and by 1850 it was widely recognized that houses of refuge were largely failures when it came to rehabilitating delinquents and had become much like prisons. As Simonsen and Gordon (1982, p. 23) indicated, "In 1849 the New York City police chief publicly warned that the numbers of vicious and vagrant youth were increasing and that something must be done. And done it was. America moved from a time of houses of refuge into a time of preventive agencies and reform schools."

In Illinois, in 1855, the Chicago Reform School Act was passed, followed in 1879 by the establishment of Industrial Schools for dependent youth. These schools were not unanimously approved, as indicated by the fact that in 1870 the Illinois Supreme Court declared unconstitutional the commitment of a child to the Chicago Reform School as a

Institutions for juveniles established between 1824 and 1828.
Stock Montage

restraint upon liberty without proof of crime and without conviction for an offense (*People ex rel. O'Connell v. Turner* 1870). In 1888, the provisions of the Illinois Industrial School Act were also held to be unconstitutional, although the courts had previously ruled (1882) that the state had the right, under *parens patriae,* to "divest a child of liberty" by sending him or her to an industrial school if no other "lawful protector" could be found (*Petition of Ferrier* 1882). In spite of good intentions, the new reform schools, existing in both England and the United States by the 1850s, were not effective in reducing the incidence of delinquency. Despite early enthusiasm among reformers, there was little evidence that rehabilitation was being accomplished. Piscotta's investigation (1982) of the effects of the *parens patriae* doctrine in the nineteenth century led him to conclude that while inmates sometimes benefited from their incarceration and that reformatories were not complete failures in achieving their objectives (whatever those were), the available evidence showed that the state was not a benevolent parent. In short, there was significant disparity between the promise and practice of *parens patriae.* "Discipline was seldom 'parental' in nature; inmate workers were exploited under the contract labor system, religious instruction was often disguised proselytization, and the indenture system generally failed to provide inmates with a home in the country. The frequency of escapes, assaults, incendiary incidents, and homosexual relations suggests that the children were not separated from the corrupting influence of improper associates" (Piscotta 1982, pp. 424–25).

The failures of reform schools increased interest in the legality of the proceedings that allowed youth to be placed in such institutions. In the last half of the nineteenth century there were a number of court challenges concerning the legality of failure to provide due process for youthful offenders. Some indicated that due process was required before incarceration (imprisonment) could occur and others argued that due process was unnecessary, since the intent of the proceedings was not punishment but treatment. In other words, juveniles were presumably being processed by the courts in their own "best interests."

In the post–Civil War period, an era of humanitarian concern emerged, focusing on children laboring in sweat shops, coal mines, and factories. These children, and others who were abandoned, orphaned, or viewed as criminally responsible, were a cause of alarm to reformist "child-savers." The child-savers movement included philanthropists, middle-class reformers, and professionals who exhibited a genuine concern for the welfare of children.

One of the outcomes of the *Zeitgeist* ("spirit of the times") of the late nineteenth century was the development of the first juvenile court in the United States. During the 1870s, several states (Massachusetts in 1874 and New York in 1892) had passed laws providing for separate trials for juveniles, but the first juvenile or family court did not appear until 1899, in Cook County, Illinois. "The delinquent child had ceased to be a criminal and had the status of a child in need of care, protection, and discipline directed toward rehabilitation" (Cavan 1969, p. 362).

By incorporating the doctrine of *parens patriae,* the juvenile court was to act in the best interests of children through the use of noncriminal proceedings. The basic philosophy contained in the first juvenile court act reinforced the right of the state to act *in loco parentis* in cases involving children who had violated the law or were neglected, dependent, or otherwise in need of intervention or supervision. This philosophy changed the nature of the relationship between juveniles and the state by recognizing that juveniles were not simply miniature adults, but children who could perhaps be served best through education and treatment. By 1917, juvenile court legislation had been passed in all but three states, and by 1932 there were over 600 independent juvenile courts in the United States. By 1945, all states had passed legislation creating separate juvenile courts.

The period between 1899 and 1967 has been referred to as the era of "socialized juvenile justice" in the United States (Faust and Brantingham 1974). During this era, youth were considered not as miniature adults, but as persons with less than fully developed morality and cognition (Snyder and Sickmund 1999). Emphasis upon the legal rights of the juvenile declined and emphasis on determining how and why the juvenile came to the attention of the authorities and how best to treat and rehabilitate the juvenile became primary. The focus was clearly on offenders rather than the offenses they committed. Prevention and removal of the juvenile from undesirable social situations were the major concerns of the court. As Faust and Brantingham (1974, p. 145) noted, "The blindfold was, therefore, purposefully removed from the eyes of 'justice' so that the total picture of the child's past experiences and existing circumstances could be judicially perceived and weighed against the projected outcomes of alternative courses of legal intervention."

The "new" reform schools of the 1850s did not live up to the expectations of enthusiastic reformers.
Courtesy of Massachusetts Department of Youth Services.

It seems likely that the developers of the juvenile justice network in this country intended legal intervention to be provided under the rules of civil rather than criminal law. Clearly, they intended legal proceedings to be as informal as possible, since only through suspending the prohibition against hearsay and relying upon the preponderance of evidence could the "total picture" of the juvenile be developed. The juvenile court exercised considerable discretion in dealing with the problems of youth and moved further and further from the ideas of legality, corrections, and punishment toward the ideas of prevention, treatment, and rehabilitation. This movement was, however, not unopposed. There were those who felt that the notion of informality was greatly abused and that any semblance of legality had been lost. The trial-and-error methods often employed during this era made guinea pigs out of juveniles who were placed in rehabilitation programs, which were often based upon inadequately tested sociological and psychological theories (Faust and Brantingham 1974, p. 149).

Nonetheless, in 1955, the United States Supreme Court reaffirmed the desirability of the informal procedures employed in juvenile courts. In deciding not to hear the **Holmes case,** the Court stated that since juvenile courts are not criminal courts, the constitutional rights guaranteed to accused adults do not apply to juveniles (*in re Holmes* 1955).

Then, in 1961, sixteen-year-old **Morris Kent, Jr.,** was charged with rape and robbery. Kent confessed and the judge waived his case to criminal court based upon what he verbally described as a "full investigation." Kent was found guilty and sentenced to thirty to ninety years in prison. His lawyer argued that the waiver was invalid, but appellate courts rejected the argument. He then appealed to the U.S. Supreme Court, arguing that the judge had not made a complete investigation and that Kent was denied his constitutional rights because he was a juvenile. The Court ruled that the waiver was invalid and that Kent was entitled to a hearing that included the essentials of due process or fair treatment required by the fourteenth Amendment. In other words, Kent or his counsel should have had access to all records involved in making the decision to waive the case, and the judge should have provided written reasons for the waiver. Although the decision only involved District of Columbia courts, its implications were far-reaching by referring to the fact that juveniles might be receiving the worst of both worlds—less legal protection than adults and less treatment and rehabilitation than promised by the juvenile courts (*Kent v. United States* 1966).

In 1967, forces opposing the extreme informality of the juvenile court won a major victory when the Supreme Court handed down a decision in the case of **Gerald Gault,** a juvenile from Arizona. The extreme license taken by members of the juvenile justice network became abundantly clear in the Gault case. Gerald Gault, a fifteen-year-old in 1964, was accused of making an obscene phone call to a neighbor who identified him. The neighbor did not appear at the adjudicatory hearing, and it was never demonstrated that Gault had, in fact, made the obscene comments. Still, Gault was sentenced to spend the remainder of his minority in a training school. Neither Gault nor his parents were notified properly of the charges against him. They were not made aware of their right to counsel, of their right to confront and cross-examine witnesses, of their right to remain silent, of their right to a transcript of the proceedings, or of their right to appeal. The Court ruled that in hearings that may result in institutional commitment, juveniles have all of these rights (*in re Gault,* 1967). The Supreme Court decision in this case left little doubt that juvenile offenders are as entitled to the protection of constitutional guarantees as their adult counterparts, with the exception of participation in a public jury trial. In this case, and in the Kent case, the Court raised serious questions about the concept of *parens patriae* or the right of the state to informally determine the best interests of juveniles. In addition, the Court noted that the handling of both Gault and Kent raised serious issues of fourteenth Amendment (due process) violations. The free reign of "socialized juvenile justice" had come to an end, at least in theory.

In the years that followed, the Court continued the trend toward requiring due process rights for juveniles. In 1970, in the case of **Samuel Winship,** the Court decided that in juvenile court proceedings involving delinquency, the standard of proof for conviction should be the same as that for adults in criminal court—proof beyond reasonable doubt (**in re Winship,** 1970). In the case of **Breed v. Jones** (1975), the Court decided that trying a juvenile, who had previously been adjudicated delinquent in juvenile court for the same crime, as an adult in criminal court violates the double jeopardy clause of the fifth Amendment when the adjudication involves violation of a criminal statute. The Court did not, however, go so far as to guarantee juveniles all of the same rights as adults. In 1971, in **McKeiver v. Pennsylvania,** the Court held that the due process clause of the fourteenth Amendment did not require jury trials in juvenile court. Nonetheless, some states have extended this right to juveniles through state law.

CONTINUING DILEMMAS IN JUVENILE JUSTICE

Several important points need to be made concerning the contemporary juvenile justice network. First, most of the issues that led to the debates over juvenile justice were evident by the 1850s, though the violent nature of some juvenile crimes over the last quarter of a century have raised serious questions about the juvenile court's ability to handle such cases. The issue of protection and treatment rather than punishment had been clearly raised under the fifteenth-century chancery court system in England. The issues of criminal responsibility and separate facilities for youthful offenders were apparent in the City Custom of Apprentices in seventeenth-century England and again in the development of reform schools in England and the United States in the nineteenth century.

Second, attempts were made to develop and reform the juvenile justice network along with other changes that occurred in the eighteenth, nineteenth, and early twentieth centuries. Immigration, industrialization, and urbanization had changed the face of American society. Parents working long hours left youth with little supervision, child labor was an important part of economic life, and child labor laws were routinely disregarded. At the same time, however, treatment of the mentally ill was undergoing humanitarian reforms as the result of efforts by Phillipe Pinel in France and Dorothea Dix and others in the United States. The Poor Law Amendment Act had been passed in England in 1834, providing relief and medical services for the poor and needy. Later in the same century, Jane Addams sought reform for the poor in the United States. Thus, the latter part of the eighteenth and all of the nineteenth century may be viewed as a period of transition toward humanitarianism in many areas of social life, including the reform of the juvenile justice network.

Third, the bases for most of the accepted attempts at explaining causes of delinquency and treating delinquents were apparent by the end of the nineteenth century. We will discuss these attempts at explanation and treatment later. At this point it is important to note that those concerned with juvenile offenders had, by the early part of the twentieth century, clearly indicated the potentially harmful effects of public exposure and were aware that association with adult offenders in prisons and jails could lead to careers in crime.

Fourth, the *Gault* decision obviated the existence of two major, more or less competing, groups of juvenile justice practitioners and scholars. One group favors the informal, unofficial, treatment-oriented approach, referred to as a *casework* or **therapeutic** approach; the other group favors a more formal, more official, more constitutional approach referred to as a **legalistic** or *formalistic* approach. The *Gault* decision made it clear that the legalists were on firm ground, but it did not deny the legitimacy of the casework approach. Rather, it indicated that the casework approach might be employed, but only within a constitutional framework. Thus, for example, a child might be adjudicated delinquent (by proving her guilt beyond a reasonable doubt) but ordered to participate in psychological counseling (as a result of a presentence investigation which disclosed psychological problems).

All of these issues are very much alive today. Caseworkers continue to argue that more formal proceedings result in greater stigmatization of juveniles, possibly resulting in more negative self-concepts and eventually in careers as adult offenders. Legalists contend that if formal procedures are not followed, innocent juveniles may be found delinquent, and that ensuring constitutional rights does not necessarily result in greater stigmatization, even if the juvenile is found to be delinquent.

In Practice 1.2

FIVE YEARS OF FAILURE THE 'ADULT TIME' LAW FOR JUVENILES HASN'T FULFILLED ITS BACKERS' PROMISES

Barbara White Stack
Post-Gazette Staff Writer

It would be a tough new era of cracking down on violent juvenile criminals, the politicians promised. No more would brutal teen-agers be coddled by juvenile courts.

Five years ago today, violent teens in Pennsylvania began serving "adult time for adult crime." Under the law, youths 15 and older charged with certain serious crimes go to trial in adult criminal court, unless a judge transfers the case to juvenile court.

The law is Pennsylvania's rivulet in a national torrent of such legislation. The "get tough" laws were prompted largely by a rapid increase in violent felonies by juveniles, particularly gun crimes, in the late 1980s and early 1990s.

Because the Pennsylvania statute stipulated that the teens either had to be repeat offenders or be charged with using a deadly weapon during the crime, the politicians said they'd be sentenced to at least five years in prison if found guilty—a year more than the maximum possible juvenile sentence to a reform school.

The longer sentences, the politicians said, would improve public safety and impose appropriate punishment.

From the day the law took effect in 1996, the Pittsburgh Post-Gazette began to track the 129 Allegheny County youths who would be charged as adults in the law's first year. The newspaper wanted to find out whether the reality of the law would live up to its rhetoric.

Now, five years later, after all of the teens except one have gone to trial, the Post-Gazette has compiled the stories and the statistics.

Some are sad. Some are startling. And all of them point to this conclusion: The law has proved to be both unfair and ineffective.

For instance:

- Black youths clearly suffered more under the new law. Three-quarters of those charged and kept in the adult

Similarly, the debate over treatment versus punishment continues. On the one hand, status offenders (those committing acts that would not be violations if they were committed by adults) have been removed from the category of delinquents, in part as a result of the passage of the Juvenile Justice and Delinquency Act of 1974 (Snyder and Sickmund 1999). On the other hand, beginning in the 1980s and continuing to the present, more severe punishments for certain violent crimes have been legislated, and waiver to adult court for such offenses has been made easier. The perceived (though mistaken) increase in the number of violent crimes perpetrated by youth has led many to ponder whether the juvenile court, originally established to protect and treat youth, is adequate to the task of dealing with

system were black, even though the number of juvenile offenders in the county is almost evenly divided between whites and blacks. Also, the median prison sentence imposed on black teens was twice as long as that given to whites. Despite politicians' claims that the law would send violent juveniles to prison for at least five years, most of the youths sentenced in adult court got less than a year. Such short sentences are served in county jails—not state prisons—so the majority of youths did not get the education, counseling or rehabilitative services that are available in a new prison Governor Tom Ridge built for these offenders. Ridge, who used "adult time" as a centerpiece in his first gubernatorial campaign, said he was unaware of the short sentences.

- When compared with the youths transferred to juvenile court and sent to reform schools, those who remained in criminal court and served time in jail were more likely to commit new crimes and more likely to commit more serious new offenses.
- Some of those new crimes were committed while the teens were out of jail on bond awaiting trial. There is no bond in the juvenile system, and most teens charged with serious crimes as juveniles are held in detention centers until their trials in juvenile court. The one Allegheny County youth arrested during the first year of the "adult time" law who hasn't yet been tried now faces trial on another charge: homicide, for killing a toddler while he was out on bail.
- Those charged with "adult crimes" in that first year included some of the most vulnerable teen-agers in the county. More than half had suffered abuse or neglect as children, and at least 40 percent were the children of criminals.

Today through Wednesday, the Post-Gazette will tell the stories of youngsters caught in the net of the new law and present the views of national experts who have studied the trend of prosecuting juveniles as adults.

The Post-Gazette does not usually withhold the identities of juveniles accused of crimes, but has made an exception for these stories.

In order to obtain some information about these teens that is normally confidential, the newspaper agreed not to disclose their full identities.

For that reason, and because those whose cases were transferred to the juvenile system do not have criminal records for those offenses, the newspaper is using only first names and last initials of those whose stories are told.

March 18, 2001, Sunday, Five Star Edition

modern-day offenders. At the same time, the concept of restorative justice, which involves an attempt to make victims whole through interaction with and restitution by their offenders, has become increasingly popular in juvenile justice (see chapter 10). This approach seems to emphasize a treatment philosophy as opposed to the "get-tough" philosophy so popular in recent years (see In Practice 1.2). Both of these approaches lead observers to believe that if the juvenile court survives, major changes in its underlying philosophy are likely to occur (Schwartz, Weiner, and Enosh 1998; Ellis and Sowers 2001).

Finally, the issue of responsibility for delinquent acts continues to surface. The trend has been to hold younger and younger juveniles accountable for their offenses, to exclude certain offenses from the jurisdiction of the juvenile court, and to establish mandatory or automatic waiver provisions for certain offenses.

There are a number of practical implications of the various dilemmas which characterize the juvenile justice network. Juvenile codes in many states have been changed in the 1990s to reflect expanded eligibility for criminal court processing and adult correctional sanctions. All states now allow juveniles to be tried as adults under certain circumstances. Because the juvenile justice network does not exist in a vacuum, laws dealing with juveniles change with changing political climates, whether or not such changes are logical or supported by evidence. Thus, the cycle of juvenile justice is constantly in motion. Disputes between those who represent the two competing camps are common and difficult to resolve. Finally, the discrepancy between the ideal (theory) and practice (reality) remains considerable. What should be done to, with, and for juveniles and what is possible based upon available resources and the political climate may be quite different things. Bilchik (1999b, p. iii) asks: "As a society that strives to raise productive, healthy, and safe children, how can we be certain that our responses to juvenile crime are effective? Do we know if our efforts at delinquency prevention and intervention are really making a difference in the lives of youth and their families and in their communities? How can we strengthen and better target our delinquency and crime prevention strategies? Can we modify these strategies as needed to respond to the ever-changing needs of our Nation's youth?" As we enter the twenty-first century, these are among the questions that remain unanswered in the field of juvenile justice.

Career Opportunities in Juvenile Justice

In each of the following chapters, look for the Career Opportunities Box which will provide you with information concerning specific occupations, typical duties, and job requirements within or related to the juvenile justice network. Keep in mind that different jurisdictions have different requirements, so we are presenting you with information that is typical of the occupations discussed. We encourage you to discuss career options with faculty and advisors and to contact the placement office at your university or college for further information. You might also seek out individuals currently practicing in the juvenile justice field to discuss your interest and concerns. Good hunting!

Summary

While the belief that juveniles should be dealt with in a justice system different from that of adults is not new, serious questions are now being raised about the ability of the juvenile justice network to deal with contemporary offenders, particularly those who engage in violent conduct. The debate rages concerning whether to get increasingly tough on youthful offenders or to retain the more treatment/rehabilitation-centered approach of the traditional juvenile court. The belief that the state has both the right and responsibility to act on behalf of juveniles was the key element of juvenile justice in twelfth-century England and remains central to the juvenile justice network in the United States today.

Age of responsibility and the ability to form criminal intent have also been, and remain, important issues in juvenile justice. The concepts of *parens patriae* and *in loco parentis* remain as cornerstones of contemporary juvenile justice, though not without challenge. Those favoring a more formal approach to juvenile justice continue to debate those who are oriented toward more informal procedures, though decisions in the *Kent, Gault,* and *Winship* cases have made it clear, in theory at least, that juveniles charged with delinquency have most of the same rights as adults.

While some (Hirschi and Gottfredson 1993) argue that the juvenile court rests upon faulty assumptions, there appears to be a renewal of the belief that the goals of the original juvenile court (1899) are still worth pursuing. It is becoming increasingly apparent that the political climate of the time is extremely influential in dictating changing, and sometimes contradictory, responses to juvenile delinquency.

INTERNET EXERCISES

In this chapter we discussed the history of the juvenile court. As was discussed, Illinois was the first state to create a separate court system for juveniles in 1899. Today, all states have separate juvenile or family courts that handle cases involving children. These courts rely upon the federal Juvenile Court Act and state-mandated Juvenile Court acts in order to incorporate the doctrines of *parens patriae, in loco parentis* and the best interests of the child into the rehabilitation and treatment of juveniles. In order to better understand how juvenile courts incorporate these philosophies into the treatment and rehabilitation of children, we encourage you to visit the website of the Illinois Compiled Statutes at http://www.legis.state.il.us/.

1. At the menu, click on Illinois Compiled Statutes under Legislation and Laws. From there, click on Chapter 705 Courts. From the Courts menu, click on Juvenile Courts, 705 ILCS 405/ Juvenile Court Act of 1987.
2. At the menu, click on and read Article I "General Provisions" of the Illinois Juvenile Court Act. Using Appendix A in the text and Article I, Sec. 1–2 "Purpose and Policy" of the Illinois Juvenile Court Act, compare the federal purpose of juvenile court to the purpose explained by the state of Illinois. What differences do you see? Do the state of Illinois and the federal government agree on the purpose of the juvenile court? Are the doctrines of *parens patriae* and *in loco parentis* apparent within both the state and federal Juvenile Court acts?
3. Using the Illinois Juvenile Court Act, find the section that discusses legal representation for juveniles accused of criminal offenses. Does this section adequately address the issues raised in *in re Gault?* If so, how does the Illinois Juvenile Court Act meet the requirements set forth in the *Gault* decision? If not, what is missing from the Illinois Juvenile Court Act that is necessary to meet the requirements of the *Gault* decision?
4. Using the menu of the Illinois Juvenile Court Act, click on Article 5, Part 7, "Proceedings after Trial, Sentencing." Read through the sentences available to the Illinois Juvenile Court. Are these sentences different than those discussed throughout the history of juvenile court in chapter 1? If so, how are the sentences different? Explain how the sentences provide for or do not provide for the best interests of the child.

USEFUL WEBSITES

The Juvenile Justice Clearinghouse—*http://www.fsu.edu/~crimdo/jjclearinghouse*

National Council on Crime and Delinquency—*http://www.nccd.com*

National Clearinghouse on Child Abuse—*http://www.calib.com/nccanch*

Children's Defense Fund—*http://www.childrendefense.org*

Office of Juvenile Justice and Delinquency Prevention—*http://ojjdp.ncjrs.org*

CRITICAL THINKING QUESTIONS

1. What do the terms *parens patriae* and *in loco parentis* mean? Why are these terms important in understanding the current juvenile justice network?
2. List and discuss three of the major issues confronting the juvenile justice network in the United States today? Are these new issues or do they have historical roots? If so, can you trace these roots?
3. What is the significance of each of the court decisions listed below?
    a. *Kent*
    b. *Winship*
    c. *Gault*
4. Discuss some of the historical events that have had an impact on the contemporary juvenile justice network in the United States. What do you think the long-term effects of these events will be on the juvenile justice network?

SUGGESTED READINGS

Bazemore, G., & Feder, L. (1997). Rehabilitation in the new juvenile court: Do judges support the treatment ethic? *American Journal of Criminal Justice, 21,* 181–212.

Bilchik, Shay. (1999a, December). Juvenile justice: A century of change. *Juvenile Justice Bulletin,* Washington, D.C.: U.S. Department of Justice.

Moon, M. M., Sundt, J. L., Cullen, F. T., & Wright, J. P. (2000). Is child saving dead? Public support for juvenile rehabilitation. *Crime and Delinquency, 46* (1), 38–60.

Reno, J. (1998). Taking America back for our children. *Crime and Delinquency, 44* (1), 75–82.

Schwartz, I. M., Weiner, N. A., & Enosh, G. (1998). Nine lives and then some: Why the juvenile court does not roll over and die. *Wake Forest Law Review,* 533.

Sprott, J. B. (1998). Understanding public opposition to a separate youth justice system. *Crime and Delinquency, 44,* 399–411.

CHAPTER

2 Defining and Measuring Offenses by and Against Juveniles

Chapter Learning Objectives

Upon completion of this chapter, students should be able to:

Understand and discuss the importance of accurately defining and measuring delinquency
Understand the impact of differences in definitions of delinquency
Discuss legal and behavioral definitions of delinquency
Discuss official and unofficial sources of data on delinquency and abuse and the problems associated with each

Key Terms

Legal definitions
Behavioral definitions
Age ambiguity
Unofficial/"hidden" delinquency and abuse
UCR (Uniform Crime Reports)
NIBRS (National Incident-Based Reporting System)
Offenses known to the police
Victim survey research
National Center for Juvenile Justice
Office of Juvenile Justice and Delinquency Prevention
National Center on Child Abuse and Neglect
National Children's Advocacy Center
National Crime Victimization Survey
Errors in juvenile justice statistics
Self-report studies
Police observational studies

One of the major problems confronting those interested in learning more about offenses by and against juveniles involves defining the phenomena. Without specific definitions, accurate measurement is impossible, making development of programs to prevent and control delinquency and offenses against juveniles extremely difficult.

There are two major types of definitions. Strict legal definitions hold that only those who have been officially labeled by the courts are offenders. Behavioral definitions hold that those whose behavior violates statutes applicable to them are offenders whether or not they are officially labeled. Each of these definitions has its own problems and implications for practitioners and leads to different conclusions about the nature and extent of offenses. For example, using the legal definition, a juvenile who committed a relatively serious offense but was not apprehended would not be classified as delinquent, while another juvenile committing a less-serious offense and being caught would be so classified.

Legal Definitions

Changing Definitions

A basic difficulty with legal definitions is that they differ from time to time and place to place. An act that is delinquent at one time and place may not be delinquent at another time or in another place. For example, wearing gang colors or using gang signs may be a violation of city ordinances in some places but not in others. Or the law may change so that an act considered delinquent yesterday is not delinquent today. For instance, the Illinois Juvenile Court Act of 1899 defined as delinquent any youth under the age of sixteen who violated a state law or city or village ordinance. By 1907, the definition of delinquency had changed considerably to include incorrigibility, knowingly associating with vicious or immoral companions, absenting oneself from the home without just cause, patronizing poolrooms, wandering about the streets at night, wandering in railroad yards, and engaging in indecent conduct. The current Illinois Juvenile Court Act more closely resembles the 1899 version except that the age for delinquency has been changed to seventeen, and attempts to violate laws are also included. Legal definitions are limited in their applicability to a given time and place because of these inconsistencies.

Age Ambiguity

Another problem with legal definitions has been the ambiguity reflected with respect to age. What is the lower age limit for a youth to be considered delinquent? At what age are children entitled to the protection of the juvenile court? While custom has established a lower limit for petitions of delinquency at about seven years of age, some states set the limit higher. For example, the youngest age for juvenile court jurisdiction for delinquency in several states is 10 (Bilchik 1999a, p. 9). Our thinking with respect to the minimum age at which children should be afforded court protection has changed with the emergence of crack cocaine and "crack" babies. Based upon an overview of current state laws dealing with this issue, it is clear that children are entitled to such protection from the time of conception (since pregnant women who use crack can now be prosecuted or committed to treatment programs involuntarily in order to help protect their unborn; see for example, *Illinois Complied Statutes (ILCS),* Ch. 705, Art. 2, Sec. 405/1–3: 1998. If there is any uniformity among the states regarding age limits, it rests in the establishment of an upper limit. There is, however, considerable diversity with respect to the upper age limit for specific categories of youth. The most frequently cited upper age limit for delinquency, for example, is eighteen (three-fourths of the states and the District of Columbia), but in three states it is sixteen years of age and in ten states it is seventeen years of age (Bilchik 1999a, p. 9). Some states set higher upper age limits for juveniles who are abused, neglected, dependent, or in need of intervention than for delinquents in an attempt to provide protection for juveniles who are still minors even though they are no longer subject to findings of delinquency. And, in most states, juvenile court authority over a youth may extend beyond the upper age of original jurisdiction.

An example of the confusion resulting from all these considerations is the Illinois Juvenile Court Act (*ILCS,* ch. 705: 1998). This act establishes no lower age limit, establishes the seventeenth birthday as the upper limit at which an adjudication of delinquency may be made, makes it possible to automatically transfer juveniles over the age of fifteen to adult court for certain types of violent offenses, and sets the eighteenth birthday as the upper age limit for findings of abuse, dependency, neglect, and minors requiring intervention. Adding to the confusion is the distinction made in the Illinois Juvenile Court Act between minors (those under twenty-one years of age) and adults (those twenty-one and over). This raises questions about the status of persons over the age of eighteen but under twenty-one. For example, a nineteen-year-old in Illinois is still a minor (although he or she may vote), but cannot be found delinquent, dependent, neglected, abused, or in need of intervention. Such ambiguities with respect to age make comparisons across jurisdictions difficult.

Inaccurate Images of Offenders and Victims

Yet another difficulty with legal definitions is that they lead to a highly unrealistic picture of the nature and extent of delinquency, abuse, neglect, and dependency. Since these definitions depend upon official adjudication, they lead us to concentrate on only a small portion of those actually involved as offenders and victims. Consider In Practice 2.1, which indicates a sizable increase in drug use by juveniles based upon official statistics (legal

Shoplifting is a common offense among juveniles.
Chuck Savage/corbisstockmarket

In Practice 2.1

YOUTH DRUG-ARREST RATE WORRIES OFFICIALS

Robynn Tysver

The 1999 crime statistics are out, and overall crime in Nebraska dropped 6 percent. However, drug-related arrests for youths rose by 12 percent. That didn't surprise one youth counselor. Therapist Bill Nelson, who has four years of counseling experience in Omaha, blamed the increase on an old culprit—marijuana. It's bigger than ever, he said. "It's probably bigger than the '60s. It's back, and everybody is using it, and it's OK," Nelson said Wednesday, the day the annual crime report was released by the Nebraska Crime Commission. The increase in drug-related arrests was of special concern to Governor Mike Johanns. He said that, if left unchecked, the trend could lead to larger problems in the future, noting that people who are forced to feed drug habits often turn to a life of crime. "We have to do a better job in that arena," Johanns said. Nelson said one of the biggest problems with marijuana is that it leads to more drug use. "It's a gateway drug. That makes it a big deal," he said. "You usually don't start out taking methamphetamine, acid or cocaine. You start out with marijuana and go on to the hard-core drugs." The overall drop in crime in Nebraska mirrors a national trend in which the crime rate was expected to drop by 7 percent, as it did in 1998. "Clearly, this is good news for our communities, big and small, as well as for law enforcement and criminal justice personnel," said Allen Curtis, executive director of the Crime Commission. "It appears the country and, hopefully Nebraska, is in the process of reversing upward trends." The City of Omaha reported a 1 percent drop in crime, while Lincoln recorded a 6 percent drop. The decline in small towns—those of 5,000 population or less—averaged 12 percent. A spokesman for the Omaha Police Department said it is not fair to compare a large, growing metropolitan area with the

definition). What are the implications of the In Practice article on the behavioral definition of delinquency?

Similar problems arise when considering abuse and neglect since only a small portion of such cases are reported and result in official adjudication. In short, most juvenile offenders and victims never come to the attention of the juvenile court and a strict legal definition is of little value if we are interested in the actual size of offender and victim populations. It may well be, for example, that females are more involved in delinquent activities than official statistics would lead us to believe. It may be that they are not as likely to be arrested by the police as their male counterparts. Not infrequently we have seen police officers search male gang members for drugs and/or weapons while failing to search girls who are with the gang members. It doesn't take long for the males involved to decide who should carry drugs and weapons. Similarly, blacks and other minority group members may be overrepresented in official statistics simply because they live in

state's more rural areas. "Omaha is a growing city, and we think a 1 percent decrease for a growing metropolitan area is significant," said Sgt. Dan Cisar, a police spokesman. Cisar noted that Omaha, as did the state, reported a 5 percent drop in violent crime. He said that statistic was as important as the overall numbers. "We think a 5 percent decrease in violent crime is very significant," Cisar said, "and we're happy with that." Johanns said crime statistics should be viewed cautiously and over a period of time. He said this was not the time to declare victory in the war on crime. "Today's numbers lead me to be optimistic that the good life is still a part of Nebraska," he said. "(But) this is no victory whatsoever, and I need to emphasize that. What we need to look at is a trend over time," he said, adding that statistics can fluctuate greatly from year to year. For example, 1998 crime statistics recorded a 2 percent increase in overall crime. Of the eight crimes included in the annual report, only two showed an increase for 1999: murder-manslaughter (11 percent) and arson (8 percent). The rise in the homicide rate was nothing to be particularly alarmed about, Curtis said, because it is traditionally a small number in Nebraska and fluctuates greatly year to year. The number of homicides increased from 53 in 1998 to 59 in 1999. Curtis also predicted that, despite several high-profile rural slayings this year, the number of homicides will be about the same in next year's report. "My guess is, our homicide rate is going to be about 50," he said. As for the increase in arson, Curtis said that also mirrored a national trend. The number of arsons reported in Nebraska increased from 459 in 1998 to 498 last year. "That's been going up every year," he said. Curtis said he has not determined why there was an increase in arson. The number of hate crimes reported in Nebraska decreased by 45 percent, from 51 in 1998 to 28 in 1999. It was only the second year that hate crimes have been reported. "There is simply no place in our state for the intolerance demonstrated by hate crimes," Johanns said. "This is the second year of voluntary reporting of this type of crime in Nebraska. We are pleased the number of law enforcement agencies participating rose from 65 percent to 85 percent, while the number of hate crimes decreased by 45 percent." (Tysver 1999)

high crime areas that are heavily policed and are therefore more likely to be arrested than those living in less heavily policed areas. For example, Chart 2.1 indicates that in 1999, blacks represented 15 percent of the overall juvenile population, but 41 percent of juvenile arrests for violent crime involved and 27 percent of property crime arrests involved black youth.

A final difficulty with legal definitions also characterizes behavioral definitions and results from the broad scope of behaviors potentially included. Does striking a child on the buttocks with an open hand constitute child abuse? What does the phrase "beyond the control of parents" mean? How is *incorrigible* to be defined? What does a "minor requiring authoritative intervention" look like? While all of these questions may be answered by referring to definitions contained in state statutes, in practice they are certainly all open to interpretation by parents, practitioners, and juveniles themselves. The broader the interpretation, the greater the number of victims and offenders.

Police search minority juveniles for drugs and weapons.
A. Ramey/Photo Edit

Chart 2.1 Juvenile arrests disproportionately involved minorities

The racial composition of the juvenile population in 1999 was 79% white, 15% black, and 5% other races, with most Hispanics classified as white. In contrast, 57% of juvenile arrests for violent crimes involved white youth and 41% involved black youth. To a lesser extent, black youth were also overrepresented in juvenile property crime arrests, with 27% of these arrests involving black youth and 69% involving white youth.

Most Serious Offense	Black Proportion of Juvenile Arrests in 1999
Murder	49%
Forcible rape	35
Robbery	54
Aggravated assault	35
Burglary	24
Larceny-theft	26
Motor vehicle theft	39
Weapons	30
Drug abuse violations	29
Curfew and loitering	25
Runaways	18

Data source: *Crime in the United States 1999,* table 43. In Snyder, H. N. (2000). Juvenile arrests 1999. *Juvenile Justice Bulletin,* Washington, D.C.: Office of Juvenile Justice and Delinquency Prevention, p. 4.

BEHAVIORAL DEFINITIONS

Focus on Behavior, Not Process

In contrast to legal definitions, behavioral definitions focus on juveniles who offend or are victimized, even if they are not officially adjudicated. Using a behavioral definition, a juvenile who shoplifts, but is not apprehended, is considered delinquent, whereas that juvenile would not be considered delinquent using a legal definition. The same is true of a child who is abused, but not officially labeled as abused. If we concentrate on juveniles who are officially labeled, we get a far different picture than if we include all those who offend or are victimized. Estimates of the extent of delinquency and abuse based on a legal definition are far lower than those based upon a behavioral definition. In addition, the nature of delinquency and abuse appears different depending upon the definition employed.

We might assume, for example, that the more serious the case, the greater the likelihood of official labeling. If this assumption is correct, relying upon official statistics would lead us to believe that the proportion of serious offenses by and against juveniles is much higher than it actually is (using the behavioral definition). Finally, relying on legal definitions (and the official statistics based on such definitions) would lead us to overestimate the proportion of lower social class children involved in delinquency and abuse. The reasons for this overestimation will be discussed later.

In general, we prefer a behavioral definition since it provides a more realistic picture of the extent and nature of offenders and victims. It may be applied across time and across jurisdictions since it is broad enough to encompass the age and behavioral categories of different jurisdictions and statutes. In addition, the broader perspective provided may help in the development of more realistic programs to prevent or control delinquency. In spite of its advantages, however, there is one major difficulty with the behavioral definition. Since it includes many juveniles who do not become part of official statistics, we have to rely upon unofficial, sometimes questionable, methods of assessing the extent and nature of unofficial or "hidden" delinquency and abuse.

OFFICIAL STATISTICS: SOURCES AND PROBLEMS

Official Delinquency Statistics

What do current official statistics on delinquency show? Despite a growth in the juvenile population over the past decade, crime and violence by youth have declined. In 1999, juveniles accounted for 16 percent of arrests for serious violent crimes, a 23 percent decrease from 1995. In fact, children are at a much greater risk of being the victims than the perpetrators of violent crime with an estimated 900,000 being victims of child maltreatment in 1999. Some 3,700 youth under the age of 19 were killed with handguns in 1998 (10 children per day) (Children's Defense Fund 2001). In spite of recent incidents, schools are one of the safest places for children (U.S. Department of Education 2000).

Black and Hispanic youth admissions into adult prisons have increased by six percent over the past twelve years, with black youth making up 15 percent of the population, 26 percent of those arrested, and 40 percent of those in residential placement (Bureau of Justice Statistic's February 2000). In 1997, Hispanic juveniles in residential programs were more likely than any other ethnic group to be behind locked doors (Snyder and Sickmund 1999). Over the past two decades, girls are the fastest growing segment of the juvenile justice population (American Bar Association & National Bar Association 2001).

Where do such varied statistics come from and how accurate are they likely to be? Official statistics on delinquency are currently available at the national level in *Crime in the United States*, published annually by the Federal Bureau of Investigation (FBI) based upon Uniform Crime Reports (UCR). Since 1964 these reports have contained information on arrests of persons under eighteen years of age. In addition, since 1974 the reports have included information on police disposition of juvenile offenders taken into custody, and urban, suburban, and rural arrest rates. In 1997, the FBI claimed that UCR covered roughly 95 percent of the total national population with the most complete reporting from urban areas and the least complete reporting from rural areas (FBI 1997, p. 1). Although the FBI statistics are the most comprehensive official statistics available, they are not totally accurate for several reasons.

First, since UCR are based upon reports from law enforcement agencies throughout the nation, errors in reporting made by each separate agency become part of national statistics. Sources of error include mistakes in calculating percentages and placing offenders in appropriate categories. Statistics reported to the FBI are based upon "offenses cleared by arrest" and therefore say nothing about whether the offender was actually adjudicated delinquent for the offense in question. These statistics become even more questionable due to the considerable disagreement among police officers (even those working in the same department) about what constitutes an arrest of a juvenile (booking, detention, recorded street contact). (See, e.g., Roberts 1989, pp. 98–99; Bynum and Thompson 1992, pp. 73–74; Empey, Stafford, and Hay 1999, p. 54).

Assuming that more serious offenses are more likely to lead to arrest (however defined) than less serious and more typically juvenile offenses, arrest statistics would show a disproportionate number of serious juvenile offenses. These types of cases actually account for only a very small proportion of all delinquent acts. Black and Reiss (1970) found that in urban areas only about 5 percent of police encounters with juveniles involved alleged felonies. Lundman et al. (1978) replicated the Black and Reiss study and also found a 5 percent felony rate, noting that only about 15 percent of all police-juvenile encounters result in arrest, leaving 85 percent of these encounters which cannot become a part of official police statistics. Empey, Stafford, and Hay (1999, p. 331) conclude: "We have seen that the police traditionally have been inclined to avoid arresting juveniles. Because they have been granted considerable discretion, however, the police continue to counsel and release many of those whom they have arrested albeit less frequently than in the past."

There are a variety of other difficulties with UCR data. If one wants to know the number of juveniles arrested for specific serious offenses in a given period of time in specific types of locations, UCR data are useful. But, if one wants to know something about the actual extent and distribution of delinquency, or about police handling of juveniles involved in less-serious offenses, UCR data are of little value. The FBI acknowledges most of these difficulties with UCR data in the preface to its annual editions.

In an attempt to combat some of the reporting problems found in UCR data, the FBI has been implementing an incident-based reporting system, a modification of the original UCR reporting system, since 1987 throughout the United States. Currently, eighteen states have been certified through the new system, eighteen states are working toward certification, and six states are developing the system with the help of the FBI (FBI 2000). The new system called the National Incident-Based Reporting System (NIBRS) was developed to collect information on each single crime occurrence. Under the new reporting system, policing agencies report data on "offenses known to the police" (offenses reported to or observed by the police) instead of only those "offenses cleared by arrest" as was done in the original UCR crime reporting process. Of all official statistics, "offenses known to the police" probably provide the most complete picture of the extent and nature of illegal activity, although there is considerable evidence from victim survey research (discussed later in this chapter) that even these statistics include information on less than 50 percent of the offenses actually committed (Johnson & DeBerry 1989).

Criminal justice agencies are also allowed to customize the NIBRS in order to meet agency statistical needs while still meeting the requirements of the UCR without biasing the data. Additionally, crimes that originally were not discussed in UCRs are included in the new reporting system, such as terrorism, white-collar crime, children missing due to criminal behaviors, hate crimes, juvenile gang crimes, parental kidnapping, child and adult pornography, driving under the influence, and alcohol-related offenses.

Data at the national level are also available from the National Center for Juvenile Justice that collects and publishes information on the number of delinquency, neglect, and dependency cases processed by juvenile courts nationwide. In addition, the Office of Juvenile Justice and Delinquency Prevention in the U.S. Department of Justice maintains and publishes statistics on juveniles. Unfortunately, much of the information available from these two agencies is out-of-date when published (two- to four-year time lags are not uncommon).

There are a variety of sources of official statistics available at local, county, and state levels as well. Many social service agencies, such as police departments, children and family services departments, and juvenile and adult court systems, maintain statistics on cases in which they are involved. These statistics are often focused on agency needs and are used to secure funding from local or private sources, the county, the state, and/or the federal government. The statistics may also be used to justify to the community or the media certain dispositions employed by the agency and to alert the community to specific needs of the agency.

Official Statistics on Abuse and Neglect

Official statistics on abused and neglected children are available from a number of sources, but are probably even more inaccurate than other crime statistics because of extreme underreporting, as In Practice 2.2 indicates.

Part II of the UCRs contains data on "offenses against family and children." The National Center on Child Abuse and Neglect, the National Children's Advocacy Center, and the National Resource Center on Child Sexual Abuse (all under the auspices of the U.S. Department of Health and Human Services, the American Humane Association, as well as the National Committee for the Prevention of Cruelty to Children) irregularly publish data on abuse and neglect of children. Ards and Harrell (1993) found that National Incidence Surveys on child abuse and neglect, upon which many of the agencies mentioned rely, are biased in terms of seriousness of offense and age of victim.

In Practice 2.2

How Much Child Abuse?

If the usual criminological sources of statistics on crime are questionable for estimating spouse abuse, they are useless for child abuse. Police statistics depend on a victim reporting the crime—something which is fairly rare in all sorts of family violence, but especially so when the victim is a child. Only when the abuse results in death can we trust police statistics to be accurate. The NCVS, our other national source of crime statistics, asks only about the victimization of household members age twelve and over. It does not even ask about assaults against younger children. Even for older children who are included, the survey will miss many cases of abuse because the person interviewed may wish to keep the abuse secret even from the interviewer.

Much of the data on child abuse come from other sources—social service agencies, hospitals, and doctors. In fact, the "rediscovery" of child abuse in the 1960s came about largely thanks to the efforts of pediatric radiologists, doctors who specialize in x-rays of children. Instead of accepting parents' statements about accidents or falls, the pediatric radiologists began to suspect that certain fractures and blood clots were the results of beatings or other deliberate assaults by parents. Social workers, pediatricians, and emergency room doctors and nurses quickly became more sensitized to the possibilities of child abuse, and the number of reported incidents rose rapidly. Still, hospitals and social agencies were not accurate sources for answering the question of how much child abuse there was. They could provide valuable information on the families in which abuse occurred or the circumstances which lead to abuse. But the number of cases they saw were only a small percentage of the real number. Who could guess how many cases, some perhaps not quite as severe, remained hidden? (Livingston 1996, pp. 210–11)

Data are also kept and periodically published by departments of children and family services of each state. Still, as Knudsen (1992) indicated:

> A significant source of bias in the identification of maltreated children is the inconsistent compliance with legal mandates to report suspected abuse or neglect to police or child protective agencies for investigation (30). . . . One of the important consequences of incomplete reporting is biased information regarding maltreated children based only on those who are reported (31).

The National Crime Victimization Survey (NCVS)

The U.S. Department of Justice (Bureau of Justice Statistics) and the U.S. Census Bureau annually provide us with official data on crime from the perspective of victims. The National Crime Victimization Survey (NCVS) involves interviews every six months with roughly one

TABLE 2.1 Percentage of Incidents Not Reported to Police by "Most Important Reason Not Reported" for Juvenile and Adult Victims

	Violent Crimes		Thefts	
Reason for Not Reporting to Police	**Juvenile***	**Adult***	**Juvenile***	**Adult***
Reported to another official	22%	11%	29%	9%
Private or personal matter	17	23	7	5
Minor or unsuccessful crime	20	16	30	31
Child offender(s), "kid stuff"	7	1	2	1
Not clear it was a crime	4	3	1	1
Police couldn't do anything	1	5	9	19
Police wouldn't think it was important enough	3	6	4	8
Police wouldn't help for other reasons	1	4	1	3
Did not want to get offender in trouble with law	2	3	1	1
Afraid of reprisal	4	4	0	1
Other reason (not specified)	16	22	11	16
Don't know	3	1	3	2
No one reason more important than another	1	2	2	4

*Percentages may not total 100 due to rounding.

Note: Adult = 18 + years; juvenile = 12–17 years.

Source: Bureau of Justice Statistics. 1998. *National Crime Victimization Survey.* Computer file, fifth edition. Survey conducted by U.S. Department of Commerce, Bureau of the Census. Ann Arbor, MI: Inter-University Consortium for Political and Social Research, p. 6.

hundred thousand individuals in fifty thousand households. These interviews allow us to estimate the amount of crime and the likelihood of victimization and to gain information about the characteristics of victims and their perceptions of offenders. When the data collected by NCVS are compared with the data from the UCR, we can make some rough estimates of the extent to which certain types of crime occur but are not reported. In general, these surveys indicate that only about one-third of the crimes occurring are reported to the police (Bureau of Justice Statistics 1995, p. 5). As noted in Table 2.1, the reasons for not reporting are diverse.

In addition to the NCVS, the Bureau of Justice Statistics has worked with the Office of Community Oriented Policing Services (COPS) to develop a statistical software program measuring victimization and citizen attitudes on crime. Local policing municipalities participating in community policing programs use the software program in conjunction with telephone surveys of local residents to collect data on crime victimization, attitudes toward the police, and other community issues. The results are used to identify which community programs are needed and where those programs should be located in the community.

Though victimization surveys would appear to be a better overall indicator of the extent and nature of crime, delinquency, and abuse, they too have their limitations. As is the case with all self-report measures (see the following section), there are serious questions about the accuracy and specificity of reports by victims. In addition, the surveys do not include interviews with children under the age of twelve and do not include questions about all types of crime (the NCVS primarily focuses on violent offenses).

Figure 2.1 **Some Sources of Error at Specified Levels in the Juvenile Justice System**

Data May Be Collected	Sources of Error in Official Statistics
Offenses known to police	All offenses not detected All offenses not reported to or recorded by the police
Offenses cleared by arrest	Errors from level 1 All offenses reported that do not lead to arrest
Offenses leading to prosecution	Errors from levels 1 and 2 All offenses that result in arrest but that do not lead to prosecution
Offenses leading to an adjudication of delinquency	Errors from levels 1, 2, and 3 All offenses prosecuted that do not lead to adjudication
Offenses leading to incarceration	Errors from levels 1, 2, 3, and 4 All offenses leading to adjudication but not to incarceration

Sources of Error in Official Statistics

While official statistics are collected at several different levels in the juvenile justice network, each level includes possible sources of error. Figure 2.1 indicates some sources of error that may affect official statistics collected at various levels. Each official source has its uses, but generally speaking, the sources of error increase as we move up each level in the network.

There are two additional sources of error that may affect all official statistics. First, those who are least able to afford the luxury of private counsel and middle-class standards of living are probably overrepresented throughout all levels. Thus official statistics may not represent actual differences in delinquency and abuse by social class but the ability of middle- and upper-class members to avoid being labeled (for a more thorough discussion see: Garrett & Short 1975: Empey & Stafford 1991, pp. 315–317; or Knudsen 1992, p. 31). Second, it is important to remember that agencies collect and publish statistics for a variety of administrative purposes (e.g., to justify more personnel and more money). This does not mean that all or even most agencies deliberately manipulate statistics for their own purposes. All statistics are open to interpretation and may be presented in a variety of ways depending upon the intent of the presenters (Fitzgerald & Cox 1994).

Unofficial Sources of Data

It is clear that relying upon official statistics on delinquency and abuse is like looking at the tip of an iceberg; that is, a substantial proportion of these offenses remain hidden beneath the surface. While it is certain that much delinquency and abuse is not reported to or recorded by officials, there is no perfect method for determining just how much of these behaviors remains hidden.

Self-Report Studies

Recognizing that official statistics provide a "false dichotomy" between those who are officially labeled and those who are not, a number of researchers have focused on comparing the extent and nature of delinquency among institutionalized (labeled) delinquents and noninstitutionalized (nonlabeled) juveniles. Short and Nye (1958) used self-reports of delinquent behavior obtained by distributing questionnaires to both labeled and nonlabeled juveniles. These questionnaires called upon respondents to indicate what types of delinquent acts they had committed and the frequency with which such acts had been committed. Short and Nye concluded that delinquency among noninstitutionalized juveniles is extensive and that there is little difference in the extent and nature of delinquent acts committed by noninstitutionalized and institutionalized juveniles. In addition, the researchers indicated that official statistics lead us to misbelieve that delinquency is largely a lower-class phenomenon, since few significant differences in the incidence of delinquency exist among upper-, middle-, and lower-class juveniles. Conclusions reached in similar studies by Porterfield (1946), Akers (1964), Voss (1966), and Bynum and Thompson (1992, pp. 78–79) generally agree with those of Short and Nye. Based upon these self-report studies, it is apparent that the vast majority of delinquent acts never become a part of official statistics (Conklin 1998, p. 67). This, of course, parallels information from victim survey research at the adult level.

More recent studies of self-reported delinquency have been conducted by Taylor, McGue, and Iacono (2000), Pagani, Boulerice, and Vitaro (1999), and Williams and Dunlop (1999) indicating that the technique is still in use. Self-report studies, however, are subject to criticism on the basis that respondents may under- or overreport delinquency or abuse, either as a result of poor recall or deliberate deception. To some extent this criticism applies to victimization surveys as well, even though victims are not asked to incriminate themselves. Mistakes in recalling the date of an incident, the exact nature of the incident, or the characteristics of the parties involved may occur. Or for reasons of their own, victims may choose not to report a particular incident. NCVS interviewers attempt to minimize these problems by asking only about crimes in the prior six months and by avoiding questions requiring personal admissions of offenses, but there are still no guarantees of accuracy and this is certainly the case when asking juveniles to report their own crimes or abuse. Hindelang, Hirschi, and Weis (1981, p. 22), for example, contend that illegal behaviors of seriously delinquent youth are underestimated in self-report studies because such youth are less likely to answer questions truthfully.

Some researchers have included "trap questions" to detect these deceptions. In 1966, Clark and Tifft used follow-up interviews and the polygraph to assess the accuracy of self-report inventories. They administered a thirty-five item self-report questionnaire to a group of forty-five male college students. The respondents were to report the frequency of each delinquent behavior they had engaged in since entering high school. At a later date, each respondent was asked to reexamine his questionnaire and to correct any mistakes, after having been told he would be asked to take a polygraph test to determine the accuracy of his responses. Clark and Tifft found that all respondents made corrections on their original questionnaires (58 percent at the first opportunity, 42 percent during the polygraph examination). Three-fourths of all changes increased the frequency of admitted deviancy, all respondents underreported the frequency of their misconduct on at least one item, and 50 percent overreported on at least one item. With respect to self-reported delinquency, Clark and Tifft conclude that "those items most frequently used on delinquency scales were found to be rather inaccurate" (28).

There are ways of attempting to improve the accuracy of self-reports. In a study of convicted child molesters, official records concerning the sexually abusive activity of the

Juveniles engaging in delinquent behavior. Would they self-report?
Richard Hutchings/Photo Edit

inmates could be compared with their self-reports of behavior. In some cases, it was also possible to confirm through official records the inmates' claims that they themselves had been abused as children (Rinehart 1991). Without some corroboration, however, the use of self-reports to determine the extent and nature of either delinquency or child abuse is, at best, risky. Nonetheless, self-report studies based upon either community or school samples have increased in number in recent decades. Empey, Stafford, and Hay (1999, pp. 73–89) conclude: "In short, self-report surveys, like other ways of estimating delinquent behavior, have their limitations. Nonetheless, they are probably the single most accurate source of information on the actual illegal acts of young people."

Consider In Practice 2.3 which indicates a decrease in crimes committed at school as reported by principals and students in public schools. Official statistics can sometimes create a perception of crime that is not supported by unofficial statistics (behavioral definitions of crime).

Police Observation Studies

Another method for determining the extent and nature of offenses by and against youth is observation of police encounters related to youth. Several studies over the years have found that most delinquent acts, even when they become known to the police, do not lead

In Practice 2.3

Children Safer at School, Says New Collection of Crime Statistics

Anjetta McQueen

Despite recent headline-making occurrences of school violence, the number of such incidents is falling and children are more likely to be hurt off-campus, the government reported Thursday. "America's schools are safe places," said Attorney General Janet Reno, releasing the report by the Education and Justice departments. It said schoolchildren are twice as likely to be victims of serious violent crime away from school. In the 1997–98 school year, 42 of the 3,000 children who were murdered or committed suicide, or 1.4 percent, died at school, the report said. In the same year, 253,000 students ages 12 to 18 were victims of serious crimes such as rape and robbery at school, compared with 550,000 children who were victims of such crimes away from school. "When we drop our children off at school or when we walk them to the school bus, we parents can know that our children are safer than they had been in the past," said Frank Holleman, a deputy to Education Secretary Richard Riley. The report uses information reported by students and principals to conclude that crime declined in the nation's schools since 1992. It is drawn from a variety of government statistics, and much of the information had been reported piecemeal in earlier studies. Worries about school violence were raised anew just this week with an incident Tuesday at Pioneer Elementary School in Glendale, Ariz. Nobody was hurt or killed when a 14-year-old boy carried a loaded 9-mm handgun into his former school and began a standoff in a classroom full of seventh- and eighth-graders that lasted about an hour. "Youth crime and violence are still one of the great challenges that we face," Reno said, adding that punishment of youth criminals must be "fair and firm." The drive for a greater federal role in making schools safer came amid deadlier incidents like the April 1999 Columbine High School shooting, in which two boys killed 12 schoolmates and a teacher before fatally shooting themselves. The new report was intended to create a national database to track school crime. Its veracity has come under some criticism from those who say students and principals alike might be unwilling to report all the troubles that occur in their schools. The percentage of children who reported they were victims of crime at school dropped from 10 percent in 1995 to 8 percent in 1999, the government said. About the same percentage of children reporting fights remained the same over that time period. Between 1993 and 1997, the proportion of high schoolers bringing in weapons dropped 25 percent, the report said. (McQueen 2000)

to official action and thus do not become a part of official statistics (Piliavin and Briar 1964; Terry 1967; Black and Reiss, 1970; Werthman and Piliavin 1967). These studies indicate that 70 to 85 percent of encounters between police and juveniles do not lead to arrest and inclusion in official delinquency statistics. The reasons given by the police for dealing informally with juvenile offenders are both numerous and critical to a complete understanding of the juvenile justice network. These reasons will be discussed in some detail in chapter 7. The point is that the number of juveniles who commit delinquent acts but do not become part of official statistics seems to be considerably larger than the number of juveniles who do become part of official statistics. Relying only on official statistics to estimate the extent and nature of delinquency can thus be very misleading. Morash (1984, pp. 108–109) concludes: "that youths of certain racial groups and in ganglike peer groups were more often investigated and arrested than other youths. Evidence of the independent influence of subject's race and ganglikeness of peers was not provided by the multivariate analysis, however. Thus, there is some question about whether race and gang qualities have an independent influence on police actions, or whether they are related to police actions because they are correlated with other explanatory variables. The multivariate analysis did provide evidence that the police are prone to arrest males who break the law with peers and who have delinquent peers. Alternatively, they are prone not to investigate females in all-female groups. These tendencies cannot be attributed to the delinquency of the youths or to correlations with other independent variables. There is, then, a convincing demonstration of regular tendencies of the police to investigate and arrest males who have delinquent peers regardless of these youths' involvement in delinquency."

Further, Frazier, Bishop, and Henretta (1992) found that black youth were more likely to receive harsher dispositions in areas where the proportion of whites was high, thus introducing another possible source of bias (relative proportion of whites and blacks in the community) in police statistics. Engel, Sobol, and Worden (2000, pp. 255–56) found that police action was affected by state of intoxication when combined with displays of disrespect on the part of the suspect. Overall, however, they conclude: "It appears that police officers expect their authority to be observed equally by all suspects, and do not make distinctions based on race, sex, location, and the seriousness of the situation."

Observation of police behavior with respect to abused children reflects a number of concerns. According to Peters (1991, p. 22), "As a result of insufficient investigation and unsophisticated prosecution, some innocent people have been wrongly charged [in child abuse cases]. More frequently, however, valid cases have not been charged—or were dismissed or lost at trial—because evidence was overlooked. While the police are mandated to report suspected cases of child abuse, they are frequently faced with determining where discipline ends and abuse begins." Bell and Bell (1991) found that the police often fail to take official action, preferring instead to handle incidents of domestic violence (involving child as well as adult victims) by referring the parties to another agency.

CAREER OPPORTUNITY—CHIEF JUVENILE PROBATION OFFICER

Job Description: Supervise juvenile probation officers as they supervise probationers, conduct presentence investigations, and hold preliminary conferences. Coordinate with police, judges, and other juvenile justice practitioners. Supervise probationers if dictated by caseloads.

Employment Requirements: A master's degree in social work, criminal justice, corrections, or a related field. Ten years of experience in juvenile justice with at least five years of direct service and casework experience.

Beginning Salaries: $30,000 to $50,000. Typically good retirement and benefits packages.

SUMMARY

Clearly, there are several potential problems arising from definitional difficulties. First, we need to keep in mind the fact that defining a juvenile as a delinquent is often interpreted as meaning a "young criminal." While some juveniles who commit serious offenses are certainly young criminals, it is important to note that others who commit acts which are offenses solely because of their age, or who are onetime offenders, may also be labeled young criminals. Yet these offenses would not have been considered criminal had they been adults (underage drinking, illegal possession of alcohol, curfew violations, and so on).

Second, rehabilitation and treatment programs are almost certainly doomed to failure if they are based solely on information obtained from officially labeled abused children and delinquents. Recognition of the wide variety of motives and behaviors that may be involved is essential if such programs are to be successful, particularly with respect to prevention.

Third, labels *(delinquent, abused child, minor requiring authoritative intervention)* tell practitioners very little about any particular juvenile. All parties involved would benefit far more from focusing on the specific behaviors that led to the labels.

There is no doubt that a good deal more delinquency and abuse occur than are reported, although the exact amount is very difficult to determine. There are scores of delinquent acts and abused children never reported. While it is tempting to divide the world into those who have committed delinquent acts and those who haven't, or those who have been abuse victims and those who haven't, this polarizes the categories and overlooks the fact there are many in the official nondelinquent, nonabused category who actually are delinquent or abused.

It is easy to perceive those who are delinquent or abused as if they were abnormal, when in fact the only abnormal characteristic of many of these youth may be that they were detected and labeled. In most other respects, except for extreme cases, they may differ little from their cohorts. With respect to delinquency, at least, there are reasons to be both optimistic and pessimistic based on this view. If most juveniles engage in behavior similar to that which causes some to be labeled *delinquent,* there is reason to believe there is no serious underlying pathology in most delinquents. Some types of delinquency occur as a "normal" part of adolescence. Activities such as underage drinking, curfew violation, and experimentation with sex and marijuana seem to be widespread among adolescents. While these activities may be undesirable when engaged in by youth, they are not abnormal or atypical. Reintegration or maintenance within the community should thus be facilitated.

Those viewing activities which are widespread among juveniles as atypical or abnormal are faced with essentially two choices. They can either define the majority of juveniles as delinquent, thereby increasing official delinquency rates, or they can reevaluate the legal codes which make these activities violations and remove such behaviors from the category of delinquent. Clearly many prefer to ignore the latter option and to continue to polarize "good" and "bad" youth.

To some extent, the same argument holds for abused and neglected youth. While those who are labeled are victims instead of perpetrators (as is the case with delinquents), they are not, in many cases, so terribly different from their peers either. If, as we suspect, the vast majority of abuse and neglect cases go unreported, many youth experience many of the same behaviors as those labeled abused or neglected. Thus, the way in which we treat those who are labeled may be crucial in determining the extent of psychological damage done. If we recognize them as victims, but also recognize that they are not abnormal, our efforts at reintegration and rehabilitation may be more effective.

Practitioners in the juvenile justice network, particularly juvenile court judges and those involved in prevention and corrections, may have a misleading image of delinquents and maltreated youth. Discussion with numerous practitioners at these levels indicate that many view the lower-social-class black male as the typical delinquent and the lower-social-class female as the typical victim of maltreatment. Some social science research perpetuates these mistaken impressions by focusing on labeled youth, but other research indicates that such youth are typical only of those who have been detected and labeled. Prevention programs and dispositional decisions based upon erroneous beliefs about the nature and extent of delinquency and maltreatment can hardly be expected to produce positive results.

Both legal and behavioral definitions of delinquency and child maltreatment present problems. Legal definitions assess more or less accurately numbers and characteristics of juveniles who become officially labeled. However, use of legal definitions can be misleading with respect to the actual extent and nature of offenses by and against youth. Behavioral definitions assess the extent and nature of such activities more accurately, but raise serious problems in the area of data collection. How do we identify those youth who commit delinquent acts or who are mistreated but not officially detected?

Official statistics reflect only the tip the iceberg with respect to delinquency and mistreatment and are subject to errors in compilation and reporting. The use of self-report techniques, victim survey research, and police observational studies helps us to better assess the extent of unofficial or hidden delinquency, abuse, and neglect, although each of these methods has weaknesses. Success in preventing and correcting offenses by and against youth depends upon understanding not only the differences between labeled and nonlabeled youth, but their similarities.

INTERNET EXERCISES

Chapter 2 addresses official and unofficial statistics in juvenile court. The chapter discusses the differences between these two types of statistics and the inherent problems of using official and unofficial statistics to explain the amount of crime present in society. In order to better understand the differences between and the problems apparent in official and unofficial statistics, you may need to read articles discussing these statistics. You may access articles discussing official and unofficial statistics by visiting the National Criminal Justice Reference Service (NCJRS) at http://www.ncjrs.org/.

1. From the homepage, click on Statistics. Review the titles of the articles provided. Focus on two or three articles and decide whether you believe the articles will provide official or unofficial statistics based upon the title of the article. What is apparent in the title of the article that is influencing your decision?

2. Next, open and read the articles. Based upon what you've read in the chapter and in the articles, do the articles provide official or unofficial statistics? Was your original assessment correct? Are there any apparent problems with the statistics used in the articles? What is or is not inherently lacking in the statistics?
3. After reading two or three articles using official statistics and two or three articles discussing unofficial statistics, explain the differences in crime rates based upon the type of statistics used. Do unofficial or official statistics provide the highest crime rates? Why? Which types of statistics are you more inclined to believe? Why? How can the statistics discussed in each of the articles you read influence the juvenile justice system's response to juvenile crime and to the rehabilitation of children?

You may also read about differences found in official and unofficial statistics by visiting the website of the Office of Juvenile Justice and Delinquency Prevention (OJJDP) at *http://ojjdp.ncjrs.org/* and clicking on JJ Facts and Figures. From the menu, click on Publications. Choose General (publications) and then click on the National Report found under the Juvenile Offenders and Victims Series. In chapter three of the national report, you will find information regarding official and unofficial statistics in juvenile court.

1. After reading the chapter, discuss what problems OJJDP points to with regard to official and unofficial statistics.
2. Why does the OJJDP believe that we should continue using official and unofficial statistics to determine crime rates?
3. Is the information provided in the OJJDP report what you expected or what you believed to be true about juvenile crime? Why or why not?

USEFUL WEBSITES

The National Institute of Justice—*http://www.ojp.usdoj.gov/nij*

Search—*http://www.search.org*

Sourcebook of Criminal Justice Statistics—*http://www.albany.edu/sourcebook*

U.S. Department of Health and Human Services, Division of Children and Youth Policy—*http://aspe.os.dhhs.gov/hsp/cyphome.htm*

Justice Information Center—*http://www.ncjrs.org/jjhome.htm*

CRITICAL THINKING QUESTIONS

1. What are the two major types of definitions of delinquency and child maltreatment? Discuss the strengths and weaknesses of each. How might legal definitions lead to mistaken impressions of delinquents and abused youth on behalf of juvenile court personnel?
2. What are the national sources of official statistics on delinquency? On child abuse? Discuss the limitations of these statistics.

3. What is the value of self-report studies? Of victim survey research? What are the weaknesses of these two types of data collection?
4. Compare and contrast the nature and extent of delinquency and child abuse as seen through official statistics on the one hand and self-report, victim survey, and police observational studies on the other.

SUGGESTED READINGS

America's Children. (2000). *http://www.childstats.gov/ac2000/highlight.asp.*

Maxfield, M. G. (1999). The national incident-based reporting system: Research and policy implications. *Journal of Quantitative Criminology, 15* (2), 119–149.

Puzzanchera, C. M. (2000, February). Self-reported delinquency by 12-year-olds, 1997. *OJJDP Fact Sheet.* Washington, D.C.: U. S. Department of Justice.

Wyatt, G. E., Loeb, T. B., & Solis, B. (1999). The prevalence and circumstances of child sexual abuse: Changes across a decade. *Child Abuse and Neglect, 23* (1), 45–60.

CHAPTER

3

CHARACTERISTICS OF JUVENILE OFFENDERS

CHAPTER LEARNING OBJECTIVES

Upon completion of this chapter, students should be able to:

Recognize differences between delinquency profiles based on official statistics and behavioral profiles
Recognize and discuss the multitude of factors related to delinquency
Discuss the impact of social factors (family, schools, social class) on delinquency
Discuss the effects of physical factors (gender, age, race) on delinquency

KEY TERMS

social factors
socialization process
broken homes
latchkey children
learning disabled (slow learners, low achievers)
drop outs
socioeconomic status
youth culture
criminal subculture
underclass
"meth" (methamphetamine)
"crack" (cocaine)

In any discussion of the general characteristics of juvenile offenders, we must be aware of possible errors in the data and must be cautious concerning the impression presented. In general, profiles of the juvenile offender are drawn from official files based on police contacts, arrests, or incarceration. Although these profiles may accurately reflect the

"Street-corner" juveniles.
© Tony Arruza/CORBIS

characteristics of juveniles who will be incarcerated or who have a good chance for an encounter with the justice network, they may not accurately reflect the characteristics of all juveniles who commit offenses.

Studies have established that the number of youthful offenders who formally enter the justice network is small in comparison to the total number of violations committed by youth. Hidden offender surveys, in which youths are asked to anonymously indicate the offenses they have committed, have repeatedly indicated that far more offenses are committed than are reported in official agency reports. In addition, even those juveniles who commit offenses resulting in official encounters are infrequently officially processed through the entire network. The determination of who will officially enter the justice network depends upon many variables that are considered by law enforcement and other juvenile justice personnel. It is important to remember that official profiles of youthful offenders may not actually represent those who commit youthful offenses, but only those who enter the system.

It is fairly common practice to use official profiles of juveniles as a basis for development of delinquency prevention programs. Based upon the characteristics of known offenders, prevention programs have been initiated that ignore the characteristics of the hidden and/or unofficial delinquent. For example, there is official statistical evidence indicating that the major proportion of delinquents comes from lower socioeconomic families and neighborhoods. The correlates of poverty and low social status include substandard housing, poor sanitation, poor medical care, unemployment, and so forth. It has been suggested that if these conditions were altered, delinquency might be reduced. The eradication of physical slums does not, by itself, eliminate or even substantially reduce delinquency rates (Gonzalez 1998, p. 24). (Recall our earlier comments on middle-class delinquency.)

In fact, officials in Saginaw, MI, discovered that the demolition of housing projects might be one cause for gang-related violence. The demolition of the Daniels Heights housing project resulted in youths and returning parolees being moved to different parts of the city, causing different alliances and violence between youths from various neighborhoods. According to W. F. Reynolds, supervisor of the Saginaw FBI office, "When they relocate, that can turn into a turf battle" (Associated Press, August 21, 1998). Even with the trend toward development of large mixed-income housing projects, Holzman (1996) suggests that big-city public housing will continue to suffer from crime. Venkatesh (1997) suggests that public housing projects are characterized by their own type of social support networks and that the move to scattered site housing destroys such networks, thus mixed-income developments, even large ones, may have something to offer.

The factors causing delinquency seem to be numerous and interwoven in complex ways. Multiple factors must be considered if we are to improve our understanding of delinquency. Unfortunately, simplistic explanations are often appealing and sometimes lead to prevention and rehabilitation efforts, which prove to be of very little value.

Most criminologists contend that a number of different factors combine to produce delinquency. With this in mind, let us now turn our attention to some of the factors that are viewed as important determinants of delinquent behavior. It must be emphasized once again that most of the information we have concerning these factors is based upon official statistics. For a more accurate portrait of the characteristics of actual juvenile offenders, we must also concentrate on the vast majority of youth who commit delinquent acts but are never officially labeled *delinquent.*

Numerous housing projects are now being demolished.
Dan Loh/AP/Wide World

SOCIAL FACTORS

Most authorities agree that social factors play a major role in delinquency, dependency, and abuse. As is shown in Chart 3.1, when social factors are ignored, increased health and behavior problems exist. Therefore, we must pay special attention to social factors in order to alleviate these conditions.

Family

One of the most important factors influencing delinquent behavior is the family setting. It is within the family that the child internalizes those basic beliefs, values, attitudes, and general patterns of behavior that give direction to subsequent behaviors. Since the family is the initial transmitter of the culture (through the socialization process) and greatly shapes the personality characteristics of children, considerable emphasis has been given to family structure, functions, and processes in delinquency research (Smith and Stern 1997). While it is not possible to review all such research here, we will concentrate on several areas that have been the focus of attention.

A great deal of research focuses on the crucial influence of the family in the formation of behavioral patterns and personality, as In Practice 3.1 indicates.

Chart 3.1 Risk Factors for Health and Behavior Problems

Risk Factor	Substance Abuse	Delinquency	Teenage Pregnancy	School Dropout	Violence
Community					
Availability of drugs	✔				✔
Availability of firearms		✔			✔
Community laws and norms favorable toward drug use, firearms, and crime	✔	✔			✔
Media portrayals of violence					✔
Transitions and mobility	✔	✔		✔	
Low neighborhood attachment and community organization	✔	✔			✔
Extreme economic deprivation	✔	✔	✔	✔	✔
Family					
Family history of problem behavior	✔	✔	✔	✔	✔
Family management problems	✔	✔	✔	✔	✔
Family conflict	✔	✔	✔	✔	✔
Favorable parental attitudes toward and involvement in the problem behavior	✔	✔			✔
School					
Early and persistent antisocial behavior	✔	✔	✔	✔	✔
Academic failure beginning in elementary school	✔	✔	✔	✔	✔
Lack of commitment to school	✔	✔	✔	✔	✔
Individual/Peer					
Rebelliousness	✔	✔		✔	
Friends who engage in the problem behavior	✔	✔	✔	✔	✔
Favorable attitudes toward the problem behavior	✔	✔	✔	✔	
Early initiation of the problem behavior	✔	✔	✔	✔	✔
Constitutional factors	✔	✔			✔

Source: Catalano and Hawkins, 1995; updated 1998–2000 by Developmental Research and Programs, Inc. In Wiebush, R., Freitag, R., and Baird, C. (2001). Preventing delinquency through improved child *Protection Services.* Washington, D.C.: office of Juvenile Justice and Delinquency Prevention, p. 4.

In Practice 3.1

Criminality runs in families. For many years, researchers have been trying to learn why that is so. Researchers have investigated how families with delinquent children differ from families in which children are not delinquent. They have found that parents of delinquent children often lack involvement with their children, provide poor supervision, and administer inadequate or erratic discipline. Some parents of delinquent youngsters are themselves not law-abiding, thus providing examples of deviant behavior and values that their offspring may imitate.

Many delinquent youngsters grow up in families that experience adversities, such as marital conflict, divorce, parental illness, poverty, or low socioeconomic status. Few families face all these difficulties, but many confront one or more. It may be that different combinations of family factors contribute to delinquency in offspring.

Being raised in poverty or being a child of criminal parents does not necessarily cause one to become a criminal. Nonetheless, there is substantial evidence that children raised in adversity are disproportionately likely to become delinquent. Although many individuals raised in adverse family circumstances are not criminals, overall, the chances for such children to become delinquent are greater than for children reared in happier settings. (Loeber, 1988)

Contemporary theories attach great importance to the parental role in determining the personality characteristics of children. Half a century ago, the Gluecks (1950) focused attention on the relationship between family and delinquency, a relationship that has remained in the spotlight ever since.

To the young child, home and family are the basic sources of information about life. Thus, many researchers and theorists have focused on the types of values, attitudes, and beliefs maintained and passed on by the family over generations. Interest has focused on the types of behavior and attitudes transmitted to children through the socialization process resulting in a predisposition toward delinquent behavior.

For example, research indicates a relationship between delinquency and the marital happiness of the children's parents. Official delinquency seems to occur disproportionately among juveniles in unhappy homes marked by marital discord, lack of family communication, unaffectionate parents, high stress and tensions, and a general lack of parental cohesiveness and solidarity (Wallerstein and Kelly 1980; Davidson 1990; Gorman-Smith, Tolan, and Loeber 1998; Fleener 1999; Wright and Cullen 2001). In unhappy familial environments, it is not unusual to find a lack of vicarious pleasure derived by the parents from their children. Genuine concern and interest is seldom expressed except on an erratic and convenient basis at the whim of the parents. Also typical of this familial climate are inconsistent guidance and discipline marked by laxity and a tendency to use children against the other parent. It is not surprising to find poor self-images, personality problems, and conduct problems in children of such families. If there is any validity to the adage "chip off the old block," it should not be surprising to find children in unpleasant family circumstances internalizing the types of attitudes, values, beliefs, and modes of behavior demonstrated by their parents.

It seems that in contemporary society, the family "home" has in many cases been replaced by a *house* where a related group of individuals reside, change clothes, and occasionally eat. It is somewhat ironic that we often continue to focus on broken homes (homes disrupted through divorce, separation, or desertion) as a major cause of delinquency rather than on nonbroken homes where relationships are marked by familial disharmony and disorganization. There is no doubt that the stability and continuity of a family may be shaken when the home is broken by the loss of a parent through death, desertion, long separation, or divorce. At a minimum, one-half of the potential socializing and control team is separated from the family. The belief that one-parent families produce more delinquents is supported both by official statistics and numerous studies. Canter (1982), for example, indicated that "youths from broken homes reported significantly more delinquent behavior than youths from intact homes. The general finding of greater male involvement in delinquency was unchanged when the focus was restricted to youths from broken homes. Boys from broken homes reported more delinquent behavior than girls from broken homes. Canter concludes, "This finding gives credence to the proposition that broken homes reduce parental supervision, which in turn may increase involvement in delinquency, particularly among males (164)." In the Pittsburgh Youth Study, Browning and Loeber (1999) found that the demographic variable most strongly related to delinquency was having a broken family.

There is also, however, some evidence that there may be more social organization and cohesion, guidance, and control in happy one-parent families than in two-parent families marked by discord. It may be that the broken family is not as important a determinant of delinquency as the events leading to the broken home. Disruption, disorganization, and tension, which may lead to a broken family or prevail in a family staying intact "for the children's sake," may be more important causative factors of delinquency than the actual breakup (Stern 1964; Emery 1982; Browning and Loeber 1999).

Not all authorities agree that broken homes have a major influence on delinquency. Wells and Rankin (1991), reviewing the relationship between broken homes and delinquency conclude that there is some impact of broken homes on delinquency though it appears to be moderately weak, especially for serious crime. Bumphus and Anderson (1999) conclude that traditional measures of family structure relate more to criminal patterns of Caucasians than to those of African Americans.

The American family unit has changed considerably in the last fifty years. Large and extended families, composed of various relatives living close together, at one time provided mutual aid, comfort, and protection. Today, the family is smaller and has relinquished many of its socialization functions to specialized organizations and agencies that exert a great amount of influence in the education, training, care, guidance, and protection of children. This often results in normative conflict for youths who find their attitudes differing from the views and standards of their parents. These changes have brought more economic wealth to the family, but they may have made it more difficult for parents to give constructive guidance and protection to their children.

Over the years there has been considerable interest in children with working parents who have come to be known as "latchkey" children. This term generally describes school-age children who return home from school to an empty house. Estimates indicate that there

Single-parent families have become increasingly common place.
Photo Disc

may be as many as ten million children left unsupervised after school (Willwerth 1993). These youth are often left to fend for themselves before going to school in the morning, after school in the afternoon, and on school holidays when parents are working or otherwise occupied. This has resulted in older (but still rather young) children being required to care for younger siblings during these periods and is also a factor in the increasing number of youth found in video arcades, shopping malls, and other areas without adult supervision at a relatively young age. While the vast majority of latchkey children appear to survive relatively unscathed, some become involved in illegal or marginally legal activity without their parents' knowledge (Coohey 1998; Flannery, Williams, and Vazsonyi 1999).

There is little doubt that family structure is related to delinquency in a variety of ways. However, relying upon official statistics to assess the extent of that relationship may be misleading. It may be that the police, probation officers, and judges are more likely to deal officially with youth from broken homes than they are to deal officially with youth from more "ideal" family backgrounds. Several authorities, including Fenwick (1982) and Simonsen (1991) have concluded that the decision to drop charges against juveniles depends first upon the seriousness of the offense and the juvenile's prior record, and second upon the youth's family ties. "Youths are likely to be released if they are affiliated with a conventional domestic network" (Fenwick 1982, p. 450). "When parents can be easily contacted by the police and show an active interest in their children and an apparent willingness to cooperate with the police, the likelihood is much greater (especially in the case of minor offenses) that a juvenile will be warned and released to parental custody" (Bynum & Thompson 1999, p. 364).

It often appears that the difference between placing juveniles in institutions and allowing them to remain in the family setting depends more upon whether the family is intact than upon the quality of life within the family. Concentrating on the broken family as the major or only cause of delinquency fails to take into account the vast number of juveniles from broken homes who do not become delinquent as well as the vast number of juveniles from intact families who do become delinquent.

Education

Schools, education, and families are very much interdependent and play a major role in shaping the future of youth.

In our society, education is recognized as one of the most important paths to success. The educational system occupies an important position and has taken over many functions formerly performed by the family. The total social well-being of youth, including health, recreation, morality, and academic advancement, is a concern of educators. Some of the lofty objectives espoused by various educational commissions were summarized by W. E. Schafer and Kenneth Polk (1967) more than a quarter century ago.

> All children and youth must be given those skills, attitudes, and values that will enable them to perform adult activities and meet adult obligations. Public education must ensure the maximum development of general knowledge, intellectual competence, psychological stability, social skills, and social awareness so that each new generation will be enlightened, individually strong, yet socially and civically responsible. (224)

The child is expected by his or her parents and by society to succeed in life, but the child from a poor family, where values and opportunities differ from those of white, middle-class America, encounters many difficulties early in school. Studies indicate that students from middle-class family backgrounds are more likely to have internalized the values of competitiveness, politeness, and deferred gratification which are likely to lead to success in the public schools (Braun 1976). Braun also found that teachers' expectations were influenced by physical attractiveness, socioeconomic status, race, gender, name, and older siblings. Lower expectations existed for children from lower socioeconomic backgrounds, who belonged to minority groups, and who had elder siblings who had been unsuccessful in school. Alwin and Thornton (1984) found that the socioeconomic status of the family was related to academic success both in early childhood and in adolescence. Blair, Blair, and Madamba (1999) found that social class-based characteristics were the best predictors of educational performance among minority students.

In Practice 3.2

One factor usually not mentioned in studies of education problems is the crucial role families play in children's school achievement. A child born to a teenage, unmarried dropout obviously does not start life as propitiously as a youngster with a well-educated mother and father committed to parenting well.

A mother who uses illegal drugs or drinks more than a minimal amount of alcohol during pregnancy may condemn her youngster to acquiring learning problems or worse.

Growing up without a father—as do 15 million American youngsters—handicaps children in many ways, an accumulation of studies shows. They are more likely to be poor, of course. But the absence of a father makes youngsters more likely to have problems in school, to drop out before graduation, to get involved with drugs and violence, to score lower on IQ tests and to have behavior difficulties.

Schools cannot be expected to compensate completely for all of the problems and handicaps students bring with them from home. (*Chicago Tribune,* 1990, sec. 5, p. 12)

Numerous studies show that although some difficulties may be partially attributable to early experience in the family and neighborhood, others are created by the educational system itself. The label of *low achiever* or *slow learner* or *learning disabled* may be attached shortly after, and sometimes even before, entering the first grade, based on the performance of other family members who preceded the child in school. Teachers may expect little academic success as a result. Identification as a slow learner often sets into motion a series of reactions by the student, his or her peers, and the school itself, which may lead to negative attitudes, frustrations, and eventually to a climate where school becomes a highly unsatisfactory and bitter experience. Kelley (1977) found that early labeling in the school setting had a lasting impact on the child's educational career and that such labeling occurred with respect to children both with very great and very limited academic potential.

Kvaraceus (1945) believed that while school may not directly cause delinquency, it may present conditions that will foster delinquent behavior. When aspirations for success in the educational system are blocked, the student's self-assessment, the value of education, and of the school's role in his or her life may progressively deteriorate. Hawkins and Listiner (1987) indicate that low cognitive ability, poor early academic performance, low attachment to school, low commitment to academic pursuits, and association with delinquent peers appear to contribute to delinquency. Unless the youth is old enough to drop out of this highly frustrating experience, the only recourse may be to seek others within the school who find themselves in the same circumstances.

Thornberry et al. (1985) noted that dropping out of school was positively related to delinquency and later crime over both the long and short terms. Although the presence of others who share the frustrating experience of the educational system may be a satisfactory alternative to dropping out of school, the collective alienation may lead to delinquent behavior. Rodney and Mupier (1999) found that being suspended from school, being expelled from school, and being held back in school increased the likelihood of being in juvenile detention among adolescent African American males. Lotz and Lee (1999) found that negative school experiences are significant predictors of delinquent behavior among white teenagers. Jarjoura (1996) found that dropping out of school is more likely to be associated with greater involvement in delinquency for middle than for lower socioeconomic class youth.

Most theorists agree that negative experiences in school act as powerful forces that help project youth into delinquency. Achievement and self-esteem will be satisfied in the peer group or gang. In many ways the school contributes to delinquency by failing to provide a meaningful curriculum to the lower class youth in terms of future employment opportunities. There is a growing recognition by many youths of the fact that satisfying educational requirements is no guarantee of occupational success (Monk-Turner 1990). Some twenty years ago, Kenneth Polk and Walter Schafer (1972) noted that the role of the school was rarely acknowledged as producing these unfavorable conditions. Instead of recognizing and attacking deficiencies in the learning structure of the schools, educational authorities place the blame on "delinquent youth" and thus further alienate them from school. In summarizing, Schafer and Polk listed the following as unfavorable experiences:

(1) Lower socioeconomic-class children enter the formal educational process with a competitive disadvantage due to their social backgrounds; (2) The physical condition and educational climate of a school located in working class areas may not be conducive for the learning process; (3) Youths may be labeled early and placed in ability groups where expectations have been reduced; and (4) Curriculum and recognition of achievement revolve around the "college bound youth" and not the youth who intends to culminate his educational pursuit by graduating from high school (189).

Yablonsky and Haskell (1988), Battistich and Hom (1997), Yogan (2000), and Kowaleski-Jones (2000) have all discussed how school experiences may be related to delinquency. First, if a child experiences failure at school every day, that child not only learns little, but becomes frustrated and unhappy. Curricula that do not promise a reasonable opportunity for every child to experience success in some area may therefore contribute to delinquency. Second, teaching without relating the subject matter to the needs and aspirations of the student leaves him or her with serious questions regarding the subject matter's relevancy. Third, for many lower socioeconomic class children, school is a prison or a "baby-sitting" operation where they pass time. They find little or no activity designed to give pleasure or indicate an interest in their abilities. Fourth, the impersonal school atmosphere, devoid of close relationships, may contribute toward the youth seeking relationships in peer groups or gangs outside the educational setting (179–191). In a similar vein, Polk (1984) contends that the number of marginal youth is growing, and agrees that this is so not only because less successful students have unpleasant school experiences, but also because their future occupational aspirations are severely limited.

In 1981, Zimmerman et al. investigated the relationship between learning disabilities and delinquency. They concluded, "proportionately more adjudicated delinquent children than public school children were learning disabled," although self-report data indicated no significant differences in the incidence of delinquent activity. They hypothesized that "the greater proportion of learning-disabled youth among adjudicated juvenile delinquents may be accounted for by differences in the way such children are treated within the juvenile justice system, rather than by differences in their delinquent behavior" (1).

In another study, Smykla and Willis (1981, p. 225) found that 62 percent of the youth under the jurisdiction of the juvenile court they studied were either learning disabled or mentally retarded. They concluded: "The findings of this study are in agreement with previous incidence studies that have demonstrated a correlation between juvenile delinquency and mental retardation. These results also forcefully demonstrate the need for special education strategies to be included in any program of delinquency prevention and control."

Others, including Brownfield (1990) also conclude that poor school performance and delinquency are related. Browning and Loeber (1999) found that low IQ was related to delinquency independently of socioeconomic status, ethnicity, neighborhood, and impulsivity.

The emptiness that some students feel toward school and education demands our attention. Rebellion, retreatism, and delinquency may be a response to the false promises of education or simply a response to being "turned off" again in an environment where this has too frequently occurred. Without question, curriculum and caliber of instruction need to be relevant for all youth. Social and academic skill remediation may be one means of preventing learning disabled youth from becoming involved in delinquency (Winters 1997). Beyond these primary educational concerns, the school may currently be the only institution where humanism and concern for the individual are expressed in an otherwise bleak environment. Even this onetime sanctuary is under attack by gang members involved with drugs and guns. In some cases the question is not whether or not a child can learn in school, but whether or not he or she can get to school and back home alive. Armed security guards, barred windows, and metal detectors have given many schools the appearance of being the prisons that some youth have always found them to be. The Office of Juvenile Justice and Delinquency Prevention stated in a 2001 report that although student fears of being attacked at school have declined, statistics vary among racial groups. As Figure 3.1 shows, larger percentages of African American and Hispanic students feared attacks than did white students. This may be a direct result of the geographic area in which these schools are located, an impersonal school atmosphere, and/or a lack of support or understanding that African American and Hispanic students feel in the school environment.

In another survey of American schoolchildren (*School Safety: Annual Report, 1998,* 1999) it was found that 5 percent were injured by an attacker using a weapon in or around their schools during the twelve months prior to the survey and 12 percent had been injured on purpose by an attacker without a weapon. Additionally, 6 percent said they had carried a weapon to school on at least one day during the past twelve months.

Social Class

In the 1950s and 1960s, a number of studies emerged focusing upon the relationship between social class and delinquency (Merton 1955; Cloward and Ohlin 1960; Cohen 1955; Miller 1958). These studies indicated that socioeconomic status was a major contributing factor in delinquency. According to further research, the actual relationship between social class and delinquency may be that social class is important in determining if a particular

School performance and deliquency appear to be related in many ways.
Photo Disc

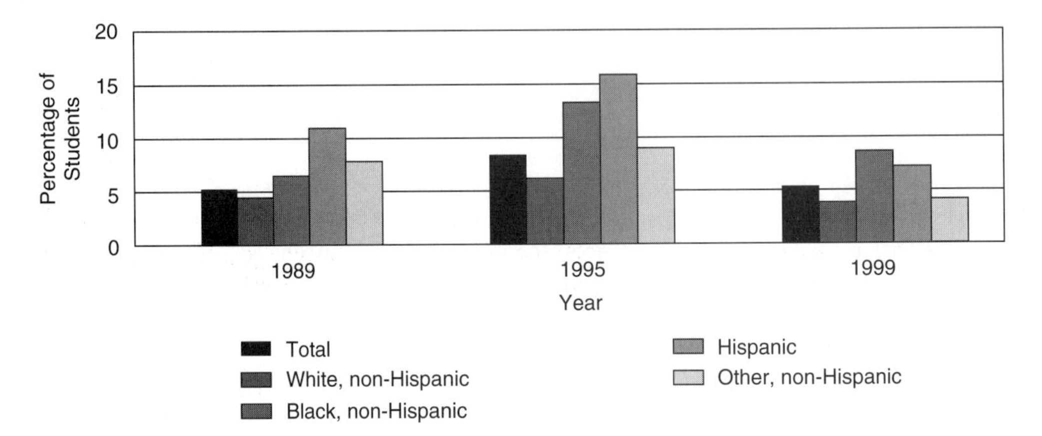

Figure 3.1 Students Ages 12 through 18 Who Said They Feared Being Attacked or Harmed at School

Note: Includes students who reported that they sometimes or most of the time feared being victimized in this way. "At school" means in the school building, on school grounds, or on a school bus.

Source: U.S. Department of Justice, Bureau of Justice Statistics, School Crime Supplement to the National Crime Victimization Survey, 1989, 1995, and 1999. In Small, M., & Dressler Tetrick, K. (2001). *School Violence: An overview.* Washington D.C.: office of Juvenile Justice and Delinquency Prevention, p. 10.

juvenile becomes part of the official statistics, not in determining if a juvenile will actually commit a delinquent act (Short and Nye 1958; Dentler and Monroe 1961; Tittle, Villemez, and Smith 1978). Most studies of self-reported delinquency have shown little or no difference by social class in the actual commission of delinquent acts. Morash and Chesney-Lind (1991), however, did find evidence that lower social class youth report more delinquency and Elliott and Ageton (1980) found that lower-class juveniles may be more likely to commit serious offenses. Ackerman (1998) also concluded that crime is a function of poverty, at least in smaller communities.

Research indicates that middle-class youths are involved in delinquency to a far greater extent than previously suspected. Joseph Scott and Edmund Vaz (1963), for example, found that the middle-class delinquent adheres to specific patterns of activities, standards of conduct, and values different from his parents. Young people a generation ago had more in common with their parents, such as attitudes and outlook on life. However, today's middle-class youth are securely entrenched in a youth culture that is often apart from, or in conflict with, the dominant adult culture. Within the youth culture, juveniles are open to the influence of their peers and generally conform to whatever behavior patterns prevail. Scott and Vaz identified partying, joy riding, drinking, gambling, and various types of sexual behavior as dominant forms of conduct within the middle-class youth culture. By participating in and conforming to the youth culture, status and social success are achieved through peer approval. Scott and Vaz argued that the bulk of middle-class delinquency occurs in the course of customary nondelinquent activities but moves to the realm of delinquency as the result of a need to "be different" or to "start something new." Wooden and Blazak (2001, pp. 4–5) note that these trends continue at the present time. "In the 1990s research began revealing what those who had survived the 1980s already knew: The safe cocoon of middle-class youth was eroding. . . ." In *Youth Crisis: Growing Up in a High-Risk Society,* Nanette J. Davis (1999) points out that adolescence is a period of transition from childhood to adulthood. Each of the institutions of this transition (the family, education, employment, and so on) is in a state of turmoil, causing youth to be in a state of crisis.

Accessibility to social objects for participating in the youth culture is an important part of delinquent behavior. Social objects, such as cars, latest styles, alcoholic beverages, and drugs, are frequently part of middle-class delinquency. Peer recognition for male middle-class youths may be a reason for senseless acts of destruction of property. Acts of vandalism in which one's bravery can be displayed for peer approval are somewhat different from the violent behavior often seen in lower-class youths, who may demonstrate their bravery by gang fights/shootings, muggings, robbery, and other crimes against people. Wooden and Blazak (2001, p. 19) indicate that suburban youth are often told to act like adults but are not given the privileges of adulthood, forcing them into a subculture characterized by delinquency-producing focal concerns. Some end up in trouble-oriented male groups and they sometimes get involved in violent crime in order to conform to group norms. More typically, those in middle-class coed groups get involved in petty theft and drug use.

While most evidence indicates that youths from all social classes may become delinquent, the subculture theorists maintain that many delinquents grow up in lower social class slum areas. According to Richard Cloward and Lloyd Ohlin (1960), the type of delinquency exhibited depends in part on the type of slum in which juveniles grow up. The

Middle-class juveniles of both genders may be involved in delinquency to a greater extent than indicated by official statistics.
Tom & Dee Ann McCarthy/corbisstockmarket

slum that produces professional criminals is characterized by the close-knit lives and activities of the people in the community. Constant exposure to delinquent and criminal processes coupled with an admiration of criminals provides the model and impetus for future delinquency and criminality. Cloward and Ohlin describe this subculture as a "criminal subculture" in which youth are encouraged and supported by well-established conventional and criminal institutions. Going one step further, Walter B. Miller (1958) in his study of lower-class and middle-class norms, values, and behavioral expectations, concludes that a delinquent subculture is inherent in lower socioeconomic class standards and goals. The desirability of the achievement of status through toughness and smartness, as well as the concepts of trouble, excitement, fate, and autonomy, are interpreted differently depending on one's socioeconomic status. Miller concludes that by adhering to lower socioeconomic class norms, pressure toward delinquency is inevitable and is rewarded and respected in the lower socioeconomic class value system. Lawbreaking is not in and of itself a deliberate rejection of middle-class values, but it automatically violates certain moral and legal standards of the middle class. Miller believes that lower socioeconomic class youth, who become delinquent, are primarily conforming to traditions and values held by their families, peers, and neighbors. As indicated above, Wooden and Blazak (2001) use this same approach to describe middle-class delinquency in the twenty-first century.

In summarizing the findings with respect to the relationship between social class and delinquency, Johnson (1980) concluded that some conceptualizations of social class may have been inappropriate, and that a more appropriate distinction is that between the "underclass" and the "earning class." His results suggest, however, that even given this distinction, there is no reason to expect that social class will emerge as a "major correlate of delinquent behavior, no matter how it is measured" (86). Current evidence presented by Wooden and Blazak (2001) seems to indicate that this may well be the case, as does the paucity of current research in this area.

Still, the concept of underclass (that extremely poor population that has been abandoned in the inner city as a result of the exodus of the middle class) seems to attract continuing attention (Bursik and Grasmick 1995). As the more affluent withdraw from inner-city communities, they also tend to withdraw political support for public spending designed to benefit that community. They do not want to pay taxes for schools they don't use and they are not likely to use them because they find those left behind too frightening to be around (Ehrenreich 1990). Those left behind are largely excluded, on a permanent basis, from the primary labor market and mainstream occupations. Economically motivated delinquency is one way of coping with this disenfranchisement in order to maintain a short-term cash flow. Since many youth growing up in these circumstances see no relationship between attaining an education and future employment, they tend to drop out of school prior to graduation. Some then become involved in theft as a way of meeting economic needs, often as members of gangs which may become institutionalized in underclass neighborhoods (Bursik and Grasmick 1995, p. 122).

GANGS

The influence of juvenile gangs is so important and has received so much attention in the recent past, that we have devoted a separate chapter (chapter 12) to the subject. In this section we will simply say that gangs are an important factor in the development of delinquent behavior, not only in inner-city areas, but increasingly in suburban and rural areas.

DRUGS

While drugs clearly have physical effects on those who use them, drug use is also a social act. We will have more to say about drug use later, but for now a brief discussion of the topic is in order.

Our society is characterized by high rates of drug use and abuse, and it should not be surprising to find such use and abuse among juveniles. The manufacture, distribution, and use of illicit drugs seems to be on the rise, and one new drug in particular, methamphetamine ("meth," "ice," "crystal," "glass," or "speed") has experienced a tremendous resurgence in popularity in the past few years (Scaramella 2000). In a study reported by the National Center for Education Statistics (1997), 30 percent of sixth- through twelfth-graders surveyed reported that alcohol and marihuana were available in their schools, and 20 percent said other drugs were available. One-third said they had seen other students under the influence of alcohol at school and 27 percent said they had seen students under the influence of other drugs. Another study found that as many as 51 percent of high school seniors reported using illicit

Both males and females are involved in gang activities and associated violence.
A. Ramey/Photo Edit

drugs at some time (Cohn 1999). Keep in mind that these figures apply to students still in school and do not include data from youth who have dropped out of school. A 1985 study by Fagan and Pabon (1990) found that 54 percent of dropouts reported using illicit drugs in the past year compared with 30 percent of students. Addiction to alcohol, tobacco, prescription drugs, and illicit drugs frequently occurs in early adolescence, and there is evidence that the age at first illicit drug use has been dropping (Inciardi 1993).

There has, of course, been a good deal written about the relationship between illegal drug use and crime. This has been particularly true since the mid-1980s when crack cocaine appeared. As Inciardi, Horowitz, and Pottieger (1993, p. 48) note: ". . . cocaine is the drug of primary concern in examining drug/crime relationships among adolescents today. It is a powerful drug widely available at a cheap price per dose, but its extreme addictiveness can rapidly increase the need for more money." Today, this concern has been replaced in many areas by a concern with methamphetamines. "Methamphetamine and cocaine have similar behavioral and psychological effects on users. . . . Both psychostimulants spark a rapid accumulation in the brain of the neurotransmitter dopamine, which causes a feeling of euphoria. . . . Tests have found that . . . meth damages the neurons that produce dopamine and seratonin, another neurotransmitter. . . . Cocaine is not neurotoxic. . . . A high from smoking crack cocaine lasts about 20–30 minutes. A meth high can last more than 12 hours. . . . Heavy use can also lead to psychotic behavior such as paranoia and hallucinations. Some evidence suggests that chronic meth users tend to be more violent than heavy cocaine users" (Parsons 1998, p. 4).

There is also considerable interest in the relationship between illegal drugs and gangs. For example, gang members accounted for 86 percent of serious delinquent acts, 69 percent of violent delinquent acts, and 70 percent of drug sales in Rochester, New York (Cohn 1999). Possession, sale, manufacture, and distribution of any of a number of illegal drugs are, in themselves, crimes. Purchase and consumption of some legal drugs, such as alcohol or tobacco, by juveniles are also illegal. Juveniles who violate statutes relating to these offenses may be labeled delinquent or status offenders. Equally important, however, are other illegal acts often engaged in by drug users in order to support their drug habits. Such offenses are known to include theft, burglary, robbery, and prostitution, among others. It also is possible that use of certain drugs, such as cocaine and its derivatives and amphetamines, is related to the commission of violent crimes, though the exact nature of the relationship between drug abuse and crime is controversial. Some maintain that delinquents are more likely to use drugs than nondelinquents—that is, drug use follows rather than precedes delinquency—while others argue the opposite (Thornton, Voight, and Doerner 1987; Dawkins 1997; Williams, Ayers, and Abbott 1999). Whatever the nature of the relationship between drug abuse and delinquency, the two are intimately intertwined for some delinquents, while for others drug abuse is not a factor. Why some youths become drug abusers while others in similar environments avoid such involvement is the subject of a great deal of research. The single most important determinant of drug abuse appears to be the interpersonal relationships in which the juvenile is involved, particularly interpersonal relationships with peers. Drug abuse is a social phenomenon that occurs in social networks accepting, tolerating, and/or encouraging such behavior. Though the available evidence suggests that peer influence is most important, there is also evidence to indicate that juveniles whose parents are involved in drug abuse are more likely to abuse drugs than juveniles whose parents are uninvolved. Further, behavior of parents and peers appears to be more important in drug abuse than the values and beliefs espoused (Schinke and Gilchrist 1984; Williams, Ayers, and Abbott 1999).

There is no way of knowing how many juveniles suffering from school, parent, or peer-related depression and/or the general ambiguity surrounding adolescence turn to drugs as a means of escape, but the prevalence of teen suicide, combined with information obtained from self-reports of juveniles, indicate that the numbers are large. While juvenile involvement with drugs in general appeared to have declined in the 1980s, it now appears that the trend has been reversed. There is little doubt that such involvement remains a major problem, particularly in light of gang-related drug operations. When gangs invade and take over a community, drugs are sold openly in junior and senior high schools, on street corners, and in shopping centers. The same is true of methamphetamines that are manufactured easily and sold inexpensively (Bartollas 1993, p. 341; Scaramella 2000).

PHYSICAL FACTORS

In addition to social factors, a number of physical factors are often employed to characterize juvenile delinquents. The physical factors most commonly discussed are age, gender, and race (all of the data presented in this section are from the FBI's *Crime in the United States, 1999,* 2000).

Age

For purposes of discussing official statistics concerning persons under the age of eighteen, we should note that little official action is taken with respect to delinquency under the age of ten. Rather than considering the entire range from birth to age eighteen, we are basically reviewing statistics covering an age range from ten to eighteen years. Keep in mind also our earlier observations concerning the problems inherent in the use of official statistics (chapter 2) as we review the data provided by the FBI.

As Table 3.1 indicates, in 1999, 19 percent of all arrests for Index crimes (murder/non-negligent manslaughter, forcible rape, robbery, aggravated assault, burglary, larceny/theft, motor vehicle theft, and arson) involved persons under eighteen years of age (the maximum age for delinquency in a number of states). The first four Index crimes are crimes of violence, and about 12 percent of all offenders arrested in 1999 for committing such crimes were under eighteen years of age. The last four Index crimes are crimes against property, and about 22 percent of those arrested for these crimes were under eighteen.

Table 3.1 also includes statistics on less-serious offenses. These offenses, however, are very important for our purposes because, as we have noted previously, much juvenile misconduct falls into this category. Note, for example, that 42 percent of those arrested for vandalism in 1999 were under eighteen years of age, 24 percent of those arrested for liquor law violations were in this age group, and 24 percent of those apprehended for buying, receiving, or possessing stolen property were in the same age category.

As illustrated in Table 3.2, the total number of persons under the age of eighteen arrested for all crimes decreased 9 percent and the number of persons in this category arrested for Index crimes decreased 24 percent between 1995 and 1999. The number arrested for violent crimes decreased 23 percent. Comparable figures for those age eighteen and over decreased 2, 16, and 12 percent, respectively. Looking at specific violent crimes, we find that murder, robbery, and aggravated assault all decreased significantly among the under-eighteen age group for the period in question, while all violent crimes in the eighteen-and-over age group decreased by smaller amounts. Among offenses other than Index crimes, carrying/possessing weapons (27 percent decrease), offenses against family and children (16 percent increase), gambling (49 percent decrease), driving under the influence (36 percent increase), and liquor law violations (31 percent increase) showed significant change among those under eighteen.

Juveniles under the age of eighteen accounted for an estimated 26 percent of the 1999 U.S. population. Persons in this age group accounted for 16 percent of violent crime clearances and 32 percent of property crime clearances. Murder (9 percent) and aggravated assault (14 percent) show the lowest percentage of juvenile involvement in violent crime, and robbery shows the highest (25 percent). With respect to other Index crimes, juveniles appear to be overrepresented in burglaries (34 percent), larceny-theft (31 percent), motor vehicle theft (35 percent), and arson (54 percent), especially when we consider the fact that we are for all practical purposes only dealing with youth between the ages of ten and eighteen (approximately 17 percent of the nation's population).

It is sometimes interesting to compare short-term trends, like those in table 3.2, with trends over the longer term. Table 3.2a shows trends in juvenile offenses over a ten-year period. As you can see, between 1990 and 1999, the total number of arrests of persons under age eighteen increased 11 percent. This is in sharp contrast to the 9 percent decline reported in table 3.2 for the past five years and indicates that juveniles arrested increased

TABLE 3.1 Arrests of Persons under 15, 18, 21, and 25 Years of Age, 1999 [8,546 agencies; 1999 estimated population 171,831,000]

Offense charged	Total all ages	Number of persons arrested				Percent of total all ages			
		Under 15	Under 18	Under 21	Under 25	Under 15	Under 18	Under 21	Under 25
TOTAL	9,141,201	506,817	1,588,839	2,920,051	4,150,925	5.5	17.4	31.9	45.4
Murder and nonnegligent manslaughter	9,727	114	919	3,016	4,979	1.2	9.4	31.0	51.2
Forcible rape	18,759	1,221	3,182	5,733	8,323	6.5	17.0	30.6	44.4
Robbery	73,619	4,888	18,735	34,763	45,676	6.6	25.4	47.2	62.0
Aggravated assault	318,051	16,139	45,080	82,359	126,748	5.1	14.2	25.9	39.9
Burglary	192,570	24,561	64,481	100,753	122,244	12.8	33.5	52.3	63.5
Larceny-theft	794,201	100,635	249,100	366,424	445,932	12.7	31.4	46.1	56.1
Motor vehicle theft	94,335	8,508	33,255	51,390	62,806	9.0	35.3	54.5	66.6
Arson	10,811	3,874	5,791	6,823	7,578	35.8	53.6	63.1	70.1
Violent crime[1]	420,156	22,362	67,916	125,871	185,726	5.3	16.2	30.0	44.2
Property crime[2]	1,091,917	137,578	352,627	525,390	638,560	12.6	32.3	48.1	58.5
Crime Index total[3]	1,512,073	159,940	420,543	651,261	824,286	10.6	27.8	43.1	54.5
Other assaults	844,728	64,980	151,645	237,723	346,865	7.7	18.0	28.1	41.1
Forgery and counterfeiting	69,853	565	4,481	15,412	26,795	.8	6.4	22.1	38.4
Fraud	225,934	1,730	7,940	32,632	68,652	.8	3.5	14.4	30.4
Embezzlement	11,208	68	1,101	3,240	5,150	.6	9.8	28.9	45.9
Stolen property; buying, receiving, possessing	80,426	5,044	18,865	35,266	46,713	6.3	23.5	43.8	58.1
Vandalism	182,043	33,736	76,319	105,427	125,590	18.5	41.9	57.9	69.0
Weapons; carrying, possessing, etc.	113,880	8,945	27,596	49,493	67,356	7.9	24.2	43.5	59.1
Prostitution and commercialized vice	63,927	126	877	5,381	12,463	.2	1.4	8.4	19.5
Sex offenses (except forcible rape and prostitution)	60,120	5,384	10,641	16,620	22,752	9.0	17.7	27.6	37.8
Drug abuse violations	1,007,002	20,428	128,286	315,374	472,621	2.0	12.7	31.3	46.9
Gambling	7,023	95	835	2,029	3,071	1.4	11.9	28.9	43.7
Offenses against the family and children	92,849	2,137	6,093	13,251	24,461	2.3	6.6	14.3	26.3
Driving under the influence	931,235	391	13,803	93,905	236,129	[4]	1.5	10.1	25.4
Liquor laws	427,873	10,748	103,734	296,017	327,795	2.5	24.2	69.2	76.6
Drunkenness	437,153	1,861	14,082	52,197	109,501	.4	3.2	11.9	25.0
Disorderly conduct	421,662	42,467	113,303	176,378	238,248	10.1	26.9	41.8	56.5
Vagrancy	20,213	326	1,597	4,121	6,217	1.6	7.9	20.4	30.8
All other offenses (except traffic)	2,416,544	78,007	275,397	601,815	973,022	3.2	11.4	24.9	40.3
Suspicion	4,907	330	1,153	1,961	2,690	6.7	23.5	40.0	54.8
Curfew and loitering law violations	114,220	31,513	114,220	114,220	114,220	27.6	100.0	100.0	100.0
Runaways	96,328	37,996	96,328	96,328	96,328	39.4	100.0	100.0	100.0

[1]Violent crimes are offenses of murder, forcible rape, robbery, and aggravated assault.

[2]Property crimes are offenses of burglary, larceny-theft, motor vehicle theft, and arson.

[3]Includes arson.

[4]Less than one-tenth of 1 percent.

Source: Federal Bureau of Investigation. (2000). *Crime in the United States—1999.* Washington, D.C.: U.S. Government Printing Office, p. 228.

TABLE 3.2 Five-Year Arrest Trends, Totals 1995–1999 [6,622 agencies; 1999 estimated population 146,328,000; 1995 estimated population 140,281,000]

Offense charged	Number of persons arrested								
	Total all ages			Under 18 years of age			18 years of age and over		
	1995	1999	Percent change	1995	1999	Percent change	1995	1999	Percent change
TOTAL[1]	8,064,651	7,823,028	–3.0	1,489,461	1,348,731	–9.4	6,575,190	6,474,297	–1.5
Murder and nonnegligent manslaughter	10,900	7,611	–30.2	1,777	783	–55.9	9,123	6,828	–25.2
Forcible rape	17,754	15,307	–13.8	2,936	2,605	–11.3	14,818	12,702	–14.3
Robbery	85,681	64,285	–25.0	27,070	16,626	–38.6	58,611	47,659	–18.7
Aggravated assault	311,094	278,684	–10.4	45,419	39,467	–13.1	265,675	239,217	–10.0
Burglary	208,551	166,200	–20.3	72,791	55,751	–23.4	135,760	110,449	–18.6
Larceny-theft	841,285	677,997	–19.4	272,248	210,949	–22.5	569,037	467,048	–17.9
Motor vehicle theft	111,202	84,197	–24.3	45,177	29,497	–34.7	66,025	54,700	–17.2
Arson	10,991	8,814	–19.8	5,857	4,760	–18.7	5,134	4,054	–21.0
Violent crime[2]	425,429	365,887	–14.0	77,202	59,481	–23.0	348,227	306,406	–12.0
Property crime[3]	1,172,029	937,208	–20.0	396,073	300,957	–24.0	775,956	636,251	–18.0
Crime Index total[4]	1,597,458	1,303,095	–18.4	473,275	360,438	–23.8	1,124,183	942,657	–16.1
Other assaults	738,712	715,990	–3.1	126,596	128,528	+1.5	612,116	587,462	–4.0
Forgery and counterfeiting	64,288	58,413	–9.1	4,572	3,848	–15.8	59,716	54,565	–8.6
Fraud	195,727	182,950	–6.5	5,852	6,779	+15.8	189,875	176,171	–7.2
Embezzlement	7,872	9,639	+22.4	636	936	+47.2	7,236	8,703	+20.3
Stolen property; buying, receiving, possessing	92,262	63,396	–31.3	24,791	15,442	–37.7	67,471	47,954	–28.9
Vandalism	184,351	155,594	–15.6	82,369	65,628	–20.3	101,982	89,966	–11.8
Weapons; carrying, possessing, etc.	138,303	98,724	–28.6	33,433	24,397	–27.0	104,870	74,327	–29.1
Prostitution and commercialized vice	62,074	57,005	–8.2	824	745	–9.6	61,250	56,260	–8.1
Sex offenses (except forcible rape and prostitution)	52,693	53,192	+.9	8,452	9,224	+9.1	44,241	43,968	–.6
Drug abuse violations	820,506	880,657	+7.3	110,617	112,010	+1.3	709,889	768,647	+8.3
Gambling	7,881	6,325	–19.7	1,445	740	–48.8	6,436	5,585	–13.2
Offenses against the family and children	78,456	73,231	–6.7	3,589	4,177	+16.4	74,867	69,054	–7.8
Driving under the influence	794,149	788,709	–.7	8,328	11,291	+35.6	785,821	777,418	–1.1
Liquor laws	274,591	353,852	+28.9	64,966	85,182	+31.1	209,625	268,670	+28.2
Drunkenness	426,102	378,344	–11.2	12,878	12,284	–4.6	413,224	366,060	–11.4
Disorderly conduct	396,934	348,091	–12.3	95,480	92,768	–2.8	301,454	255,323	–15.3
Vagrancy	17,014	16,494	–3.1	1,988	1,291	–35.1	15,026	15,203	+1.2
All other offenses (except traffic)	1,913,572	2,101,505	+9.8	227,664	235,201	+3.3	1,685,908	1,866,304	+10.7
Suspicion	3,000	2,819	–6.0	969	790	–18.5	2,031	2,029	–.1
Curfew and loitering law violations	88,373	96,586	+9.3	88,373	96,586	+9.3	—	—	—
Runaways	113,333	81,236	–28.3	113,333	81,236	–28.3	—	—	—

[1]Does not include suspicion.

[2]Violent crimes are offenses of murder, forcible rape, robbery, and aggravated assault.

[3]Property crimes are offenses of burglary, larceny-theft, motor vehicle theft, and arson.

[4]Includes arson.

Source: Federal Bureau of Investigation. (2000). *Crime in the United States—1999.* Washington, D.C.: U.S. Government Printing Office, p. 218.

TABLE 3.2A Ten-Year Arrest Trends, Totals 1990–1999 [6,364 agencies; 1999 estimated population 140,836,000; 1990 estimated population 128,207,000]

Offense charged	Total all ages 1990	Total all ages 1999	Total all ages Percent change	Under 18 years of age 1990	Under 18 years of age 1999	Under 18 years of age Percent change	18 years of age and over 1990	18 years of age and over 1999	18 years of age and over Percent change
TOTAL[1]	7,475,108	7,417,589	–.8	1,166,660	1,294,513	+11.0	6,308,448	6,123,076	–2.9
Murder and nonnegligent manslaughter	10,870	6,599	–39.3	1,478	665	–55.0	9,392	5,934	–36.8
Forcible rape	19,988	14,704	–26.4	2,871	2,498	–13.0	17,117	12,206	–28.7
Robbery	79,763	59,588	–25.3	18,096	15,138	–16.3	61,667	44,450	–27.9
Aggravated assault	263,310	258,576	–1.8	34,735	36,095	+3.9	228,575	222,481	–2.7
Burglary	238,946	158,751	–33.6	79,068	53,847	–31.9	159,878	104,904	–34.4
Larceny-theft	849,035	660,069	–22.3	250,129	211,621	–15.4	598,906	448,448	–25.1
Motor vehicle theft	114,702	71,294	–37.8	49,193	25,142	–48.9	65,509	46,152	–29.5
Arson	10,205	8,827	–13.5	4,476	4,896	+9.4	5,729	3,931	–31.4
Violent crime[2]	373,931	339,467	–9.2	57,180	54,396	–4.9	316,751	285,071	–10.0
Property crime[3]	1,212,888	898,941	–25.9	382,866	295,506	–22.8	830,022	603,435	–27.3
Crime Index total[4]	1,586,819	1,238,408	–22.0	440,046	349,902	–20.5	1,146,773	888,506	–22.5
Other assaults	546,772	670,746	+22.7	80,764	119,692	+48.2	466,008	551,054	+18.2
Forgery and counterfeiting	50,403	56,813	+12.7	4,084	3,811	–6.7	46,319	53,002	–14.4
Fraud	182,752	166,413	–8.9	4,517	4,983	+10.3	178,235	161,430	–9.4
Embezzlement	7,708	9,692	+25.7	563	918	+63.1	7,145	8,774	+22.8
Stolen property; buying, receiving, possessing	89,109	62,170	–30.2	24,679	15,479	–37.3	64,430	46,691	–27.5
Vandalism	173,451	149,953	–13.5	70,683	64,081	–9.3	102,768	85,872	–16.4
Weapons; carrying, possessing, etc.	115,972	87,327	–24.7	22,193	21,291	–4.1	93,779	66,036	–29.6
Prostitution and commercialized vice	59,304	49,576	–16.4	909	685	–24.6	58,395	48,891	–16.3
Sex offenses (except forcible rape and prostitution)	59,354	50,828	–14.4	8,861	8,863	[5]	50,493	41,965	–16.9
Drug abuse violations	589,944	805,024	+36.5	43,213	100,352	+132.2	546,731	704,672	+28.9
Gambling	8,713	4,719	–45.8	411	422	+2.7	8,302	4,297	–48.2
Offenses against the family and children	47,697	75,900	+59.1	1,924	4,679	+143.2	45,773	71,221	+55.6
Driving under the influence	1,021,753	749,454	–26.7	11,031	11,024	–.1	1,010,722	738,430	–26.9
Liquor laws	350,108	355,761	+1.6	80,634	87,996	+9.1	269,474	267,765	–.6
Drunkenness	554,867	378,234	–31.8	14,944	11,893	–20.4	539,923	366,341	–32.1
Disorderly conduct	358,146	317,946	–11.2	59,742	87,428	+46.3	298,404	230,518	–22.7
Vagrancy	25,026	16,856	–32.6	2,316	1,300	–43.9	22,710	15,556	–31.5
All other offenses (except traffic)	1,506,209	1,991,610	+32.2	154,145	219,555	+42.4	1,352,064	1,772,055	+31.1
Suspicion	10,742	4,000	–62.8	2,690	1,024	–61.9	8,052	2,976	–63.0
Curfew and loitering law violations	46,619	99,383	+113.2	46,619	99,383	+113.2	—	—	—
Runaways	94,382	80,776	–14.4	94,382	80,776	–14.4	—	—	—

[1]Does not include suspicion.

[2]Violent crimes are offenses of murder, forcible rape, robbery, and aggravated assault.

[3]Property crimes are offenses of burglary, larceny-theft, motor vehicle theft, and arson.

[4]Includes arson.

[5]Less than one-tenth of 1 percent.

Source: Federal Bureau of Investigation. (2000). *Crime in the United States—1999.* Washington, D.C.: U.S. Government Printing Office, p. 216.

dramatically during the first part of the decade. You can compare the figures from the two charts to determine which crimes (e.g., robbery, burglary) account for this difference. By comparing these figures, it is apparent that we have seen a major decrease in arrests for violent crimes among juveniles in the past five years, while the decrease in property crimes arrests seems to have been fairly consistent over the decade. Compare for yourself the differences in reported arrests for such offenses as drug abuse violations, offenses against the family and children, and curfew and loitering law violations. Some of these differences may reflect changes in actual behavior, but some may also reflect changes in laws and/or changes in reporting.

Gender

Historically, we have observed three to four arrests of juvenile males for every arrest of a juvenile female. In the period from 1995 to 1999, this ratio remained relatively constant (see Table 3.3). The total number of arrests of males under age eighteen decreased 12 percent while the total number of arrests of females under age eighteen increased by 1 percent. Considering the Index crimes, we note that among those under age eighteen, arrests for violent crimes decreased 26 percent for males, but decreased only 6 percent for females. Total arrests for Index crimes decreased 27 percent for males and decreased about 15 percent for females.

Considering all crimes, we note an increase in the number of females arrested for aggravated assault (4 percent), other assaults (13 percent), embezzlement (75 percent), driving under the influence (48 percent), offenses against family and children (42 percent), and sex offenses (35 percent). Significant decreases in arrests occurred for murder (42 percent), robbery (40 percent), motor vehicle theft (30 percent), arson (27 percent), buying and receiving stolen property (33 percent), and runaways (27 percent).

Increases among males in the under-eighteen age category occurred with respect to fraud and embezzlement (27 percent each), driving under the influence (33 percent), and other liquor law violations (27 percent). Significant decreases occurred with respect to murder (57 percent), robbery (38 percent), motor vehicle theft (36 percent), buying and receiving stolen property (38 percent), gambling (50 percent), and runaways (30 percent).

A study by Steffensmeier and Steffensmeier (1980) concluded that female delinquency had remained generally stable over the decade between 1970 and 1980 and that patterns of female delinquency, especially as revealed in nonofficial sources, had changed little in that period. However, major changes have clearly occurred in the 1990s for members of both sexes. Initially, delinquency rates increased dramatically, but in the last half of the decade significant decreases in reported delinquency occurred (compare the data in Table 3.3a with data from table 3.3). Johnson (1998) found that female juveniles are increasingly becoming involved in the juvenile justice network requiring new intervention strategies.

According to Chesney-Lind (1999), females have been largely overlooked by those interested in juvenile justice and, indeed, many of their survival mechanisms (such as running away when confronted with abusers) have been criminalized. It appears that the juvenile justice network doesn't always act in the best interests of female juveniles because it often ignores their unique problems (Holsinger 2000). Still, the number of girls engaging in problematic behavior is increasing, and it may well be that we need to

TABLE 3.3 Five-Year Arrest Trends by Sex, Totals 1995–1999 [6,662 agencies; 1999 estimated population 146,328,000; 1995 estimated population 140,281,000]

Offense charged	Males						Females					
	Total			Under 18			Total			Under 18		
	1995	1999	Percent change	1995	1999	Percent change	1995	1999	Percent change	1995	1999	Percent change
TOTAL[1]	6,423,465	6,120,671	–4.7	1,121,363	984,523	–12.2	1,641,186	1,702,357	+3.7	368,098	364,208	–1.1
Murder and nonnegligent manslaughter	9,956	6,796	–31.7	1,683	728	–56.7	944	815	–13.7	94	55	–41.5
Forcible rape	17,530	15,133	–13.7	2,866	2,555	–10.9	224	174	–22.3	70	50	–28.6
Robbery	77,723	57,833	–25.6	24,622	15,166	–38.4	7,958	6,452	–18.9	2,448	1,460	–40.4
Aggravated assault	259,734	224,221	–13.7	36,984	30,666	–17.1	51,360	54,463	+6.0	8,435	8,801	+4.3
Burglary	183,963	144,158	–21.6	65,412	49,296	–24.6	24,588	22,042	–10.4	7,379	6,455	–12.5
Larceny-theft	561,949	437,735	–22.1	184,122	135,814	–26.2	279,336	240,262	–14.0	88,126	75,135	–14.7
Motor vehicle theft	95,932	71,043	–25.9	38,368	24,716	–35.6	15,270	13,154	–13.9	6,809	4,781	–29.8
Arson	9,294	7,582	–18.4	5,136	4,232	–17.6	1,697	1,232	–27.4	721	528	–26.8
Violent crime[2]	364,943	303,983	–16.7	66,155	49,115	–25.8	60,486	61,904	+2.3	11,047	10,366	–6.2
Property crime[3]	851,138	660,518	–22.4	293,038	214,058	–27.0	320,891	276,690	–13.8	103,035	86,899	–15.7
Crime Index total[4]	1,216,081	964,501	–20.7	359,193	263,173	–26.7	381,377	338,594	–11.2	114,062	97,265	–14.7
Other assaults	594,781	554,824	–6.7	92,067	89,458	–2.8	143,931	161,166	+12.0	34,529	39,070	+13.2
Forgery and counterfeiting	40,141	36,129	–10.0	2,914	2,438	–16.3	24,147	22,284	–7.7	1,658	1,410	–15.0
Fraud	108,438	102,928	–5.1	3,808	4,817	+26.5	87,289	80,022	–8.3	2,044	1,962	–4.0
Embezzlement	4,425	4,825	+9.0	368	468	+27.2	3,447	4,814	+39.7	268	468	+74.6
Stolen property; buying, receiving, possessing	78,869	53,536	–32.1	21,803	13,448	–38.3	13,393	9,860	–26.4	2,988	1,994	–33.3
Vandalism	159,562	132,061	–17.2	73,685	57,889	–21.4	24,789	23,533	–5.1	8,684	7,739	–10.9
Weapons; carrying, possessing, etc.	127,816	91,042	–28.8	30,840	22,113	–28.3	10,487	7,682	–26.7	2,593	2,284	–11.9
Prostitution and commercialized vice	23,425	21,382	–8.7	431	319	–26.0	38,649	35,623	–7.8	393	426	+8.4
Sex offenses (except forcible rape and prostitution)	48,586	49,387	+1.6	7,933	8,525	+7.5	4,107	3,805	–7.4	519	699	+34.7
Drug abuse violations	680,218	724,312	+6.5	96,221	95,845	–.4	140,288	156,345	+11.4	14,396	16,165	+12.3
Gambling	7,230	5,543	–23.3	1,412	712	+49.6	651	782	+20.1	33	28	–15.2
Offenses against the family and children	64,000	57,640	–9.9	2,267	2,636	+16.3	14,456	15,591	+7.9	1,322	1,541	+16.6
Driving under the influence	681,905	663,830	–2.7	7,066	9,422	+33.3	112,244	124,879	–11.3	1,262	1,869	+48.1
Liquor laws	220,449	275,660	+25.0	46,460	58,847	+26.7	54,142	78,192	+44.4	18,506	26,335	+42.3
Drunkenness	376,614	331,033	–12.1	10,860	9,971	–8.2	49,488	47,311	–4.4	2,018	2,313	+14.6
Disorderly conduct	314,894	268,439	–14.8	73,215	66,710	+8.9	82,040	79,652	–2.9	22,265	26,058	+17.0
Vagrancy	13,417	13,304	–.8	1,763	1,052	–40.3	3,597	3,190	–11.3	225	239	+6.2
All other offenses (except traffic)	1,552,502	1,670,251	+7.6	178,945	176,636	–1.3	361,070	431,254	+19.4	48,719	58,565	+20.2
Suspicion	2,499	2,224	–11.0	782	627	–19.8	501	595	+18.8	187	163	–12.8
Curfew and loitering law violations	62,366	67,031	+7.5	62,366	67,031	+7.5	26,007	29,555	+13.6	26,007	29,555	+13.6
Runaways	47,746	33,013	–30.9	47,746	33,013	–30.9	65,587	48,223	–26.5	65,587	48,223	–26.5

[1]Does not include suspicion.

[2]Violent crimes are offenses of murder, forcible rape, robbery, and aggravated assault.

[3]Property crimes are offenses of burglary, larceny-theft, motor vehicle theft, and arson.

[4]Includes arson.

Source: Federal Bureau of Investigation. (2000). *Crime in the United States—1999.* Washington, D.C.: U.S. Government Printing Office, p. 219.

TABLE 3.3A Ten-Year Arrest Trends by Sex, 1990–1999 [6,364 agencies; 1999 estimated population 140,836,000; 1990 estimated population 128,207,000]

Offense charged	Males						Females					
	Total			Under 18			Total			Under 18		
	1990	1999	Percent change	1990	1999	Percent change	1990	1999	Percent change	1990	1999	Percent change
TOTAL[1]	6,092,905	5,788,285	-5.0	897,082	939,176	+4.7	1,382,203	1,629,304	+17.9	269,578	355,337	+31.8
Murder and nonnegligent manslaughter	9,741	5,880	-39.6	1,397	616	-55.9	1,129	719	-36.3	81	49	-39.5
Forcible rape	19,774	14,535	-26.5	2,814	2,450	-12.9	214	169	-21.0	57	48	-15.8
Robbery	72,993	53,465	-26.8	16,580	13,784	-16.9	6,770	6,123	-9.6	1,516	1,354	-10.7
Aggravated assault	229,471	208,264	-9.2	29,667	28,147	-5.1	33,839	50,312	+48.7	5,068	7,948	+56.8
Burglary	215,967	137,505	-36.3	72,290	47,618	-34.1	22,979	21,246	-7.5	6,778	6,229	-8.1
Larceny-theft	575,614	425,314	-26.1	178,745	135,989	-23.9	273,421	234,755	-14.1	71,384	75,632	+6.0
Motor vehicle theft	102,851	60,118	-41.5	43,600	20,908	-52.0	11,851	11,176	-5.7	5,593	4,234	-24.3
Arson	8,938	7,603	-14.9	4,070	4,341	+6.7	1,267	1,224	-3.4	406	555	+36.7
Violent crime[2]	331,979	282,144	-15.0	50,458	44,997	-10.8	41,952	57,323	+36.6	6,722	9,399	+39.8
Property crime[3]	903,370	630,540	-30.2	298,705	208,856	-30.1	309,518	268,401	-13.3	84,161	86,650	+3.0
Crime Index total[4]	1,235,349	912,684	-26.1	349,163	253,853	-27.3	351,470	325,724	-7.3	90,883	96,049	+5.7
Other assaults	457,158	517,385	+13.2	61,770	83,116	+34.6	89,614	153,361	+71.1	18,994	36,576	+92.6
Forgery and counterfeiting	32,473	34,994	+7.8	2,683	2,401	-10.5	17,930	21,819	+21.7	1,401	1,410	+.6
Fraud	98,579	90,558	-8.1	2,993	3,298	+10.2	84,173	75,855	-9.9	1,524	1,685	+10.6
Embezzlement	4,450	4,911	+10.4	353	478	+35.4	3,258	4,781	+46.7	210	440	+109.5
Stolen property; buying, receiving, possessing	78,345	52,472	-33.0	22,266	13,467	-39.5	10,764	9,698	-9.9	2,413	2,012	-16.6
Vandalism	154,711	127,384	-17.7	64,701	56,400	-12.8	18,740	22,569	+20.4	5,982	7,681	+28.4
Weapons; carrying, possessing, etc.	107,563	80,497	-25.2	20,850	19,356	-7.2	8,409	6,830	-18.8	1,343	1,935	+44.1
Prostitution and commercialized vice	23,158	19,655	-15.1	427	309	-27.6	36,146	29,921	-17.2	482	376	-22.0
Sex offenses (except forcible rape and prostitution)	54,862	47,307	-13.8	8,367	8,210	-1.9	4,492	3,521	-21.6	494	653	+32.2
Drug abuse violations	488,454	660,104	+35.1	38,005	85,226	+124.2	101,490	144,920	+42.8	5,208	15,126	+190.4
Gambling	7,537	4,069	-46.0	383	397	+3.7	1,176	650	-44.7	28	25	-10.7
Offenses against the family and children	40,193	59,130	+47.1	1,287	2,992	+132.5	7,504	16,770	+123.5	637	1,687	+164.8
Driving under the influence	893,756	629,889	-29.5	9,478	9,158	-3.4	127,997	119,565	-6.6	1,553	1,866	+20.2
Liquor laws	286,026	277,294	-3.1	58,613	60,692	+3.5	64,082	78,467	+22.4	22,021	27,304	+24.0
Drunkenness	500,375	330,902	-33.9	12,692	9,628	-24.1	54,492	47,332	-13.1	2,252	2,265	+.6
Disorderly conduct	290,239	242,822	-16.3	47,475	62,755	+32.2	67,907	75,124	+10.6	12,267	24,673	+101.1
Vagrancy	21,426	13,520	-36.9	1,949	1,053	-46.0	3,600	3,336	-7.3	367	247	-32.7
All other offenses (except traffic)	1,244,366	1,580,872	+27.0	119,742	164,551	+37.4	261,843	410,738	+56.9	34,403	55,004	+59.9
Suspicion	9,150	3,144	-65.6	2,175	794	-63.5	1,592	856	-46.2	515	230	-55.3
Curfew and loitering law violations	33,890	68,927	+103.4	33,890	68,927	+103.4	12,729	30,456	+139.3	12,729	30,456	+139.3
Runaways	39,995	32,909	-17.7	39,995	32,909	-17.7	54,387	47,867	-12.0	54,387	47,867	-12.0

[1]Does not include suspicion.

[2]Violent crimes are offenses of murder, forcible rape, robbery, and aggravated assault.

[3]Property crimes are offenses of burglary, larceny-theft, motor vehicle theft, and arson.

[4]Includes arson.

Source: Federal Bureau of Investigation. (2000). *Crime in the United States—1999.* Washington, D.C.: U.S. Government Printing Office, p. 217.

develop treatment methods that address their specific problems. For example, a study conducted by Ellis, O'Hara, and Sowers (1999) found that troubled female adolescents have a profile distinctly different from that of males. The female group was characterized as abused, self-harmful, and social while the male group was seen as aggressive, destructive, and asocial. The authors conclude that different treatment modalities (more supportive and more comprehensive in nature) may have to be developed to treat troubled female adolescents. Johnson (1998) believes that the increasing number of delinquent females can only be addressed by a multiagency approach based on nationwide and systemwide cooperation. Peters and Peters' findings (1998) seem to provide support for Johnson's proposal. They conclude that violent offending by females is the result of a complex web of victimization, substance abuse, economic conditions, and dysfunctional families, and this would seem to suggest the need for a multiagency response. It is fairly common, for example, for girls fleeing from an abusive parent to be labeled *runaways.* If they are simply dealt with by being placed on probation, the underlying causes of the problems they confront are unlikely to be addressed. To deal with these causes, counseling may be needed for all parties involved, school authorities may need to be informed if truancy is involved, and further action in adult court may be necessary. If, as often happens, the girl's family moves from place-to-place, the process may begin all over because there is no transfer of information or records from one agency or place to another.

Race

Official statistics on race are subject to a number of errors, as pointed out in chapter 2. Any index of nonwhite arrests may be inflated as a result of discriminatory practices among criminal justice personnel. For example, the presence of a black under "suspicious circumstances" may result in an official arrest even though the police officer knows the charges will be dismissed (see In Practice 3.3). Frazier, Bishop, and Henretta (1992) found that black youth receive harsher dispositions from the justice system when they live in areas with high proportions of whites (that is, where they are true numerical minority group members). Kempf (1992) found that juvenile justice outcomes were influenced by race at every stage except adjudication. Feiler and Sheley (1999), collecting data via phone interviews in the New Orleans metropolitan area, found that both black and white citizens were more likely to express a preference for transfer of youth to adult court when the juvenile offender in question was black. Sutpen, Kurtz, and Giddings (1993), using vignettes with police officers, found that blacks were charged with more offenses more often than whites and whites received no charges more often than blacks. Leiber and Stairs (1999) found partial support for their hypothesis that African Americans charged with drug offenses would be treated more harshly in jurisdictions characterized by economic and racial inequality and adherence to beliefs in racial differences than in jurisdictions without such characteristics. Taylor (1994) points out that young black males are more likely to be labeled *slow learners* or *educable mentally retarded,* to have learning difficulties in school, to lag behind their peers in basic educational competencies or skills, and to drop out of school at an early age. Black boys are also more likely to be institutionalized or placed in foster care.

Many minority group members live in lower social class neighborhoods in large urban centers in which the greatest concentration of law enforcement officers exists.

In Practice 3.3

On the streets late at night, the average young black man is suspicious of others he encounters, and he is particularly wary of the police. If he is dressed in the uniform of the "gangster," such as a black leather jacket, sneakers, and a "gangster cap," if he is carrying a radio or a suspicious bag (which may be confiscated), or if he is moving too fast or too slow, the police may stop him. As a part of the routine, they search him and make him sit in the police car while they run a check to see whether there is a "detainer" on him. If there is nothing, he is allowed to go on his way. After this ordeal the youth is often left afraid, sometimes shaking, and uncertain about the area he had previously taken for granted. He is upset in part because he is painfully aware of how close he has gotten to being in "big trouble." He knows of other youths who have gotten into a "world of trouble" simply by being on the streets at the wrong time or when the police were pursuing a criminal. (Anderson 1990, p. 190)

Since arrest statistics are more complete for large cities, we must take into account the sizable proportion of blacks found in these cities rather than the 12 percent statistic derived from calculating the proportion of blacks in our society. It is these same arrest statistics which lead many to believe that any overrepresentation of black youth in these statistics reflects racial inequities in the juvenile and criminal justice networks (see In Practice 3.4 above).

Analysis of official arrest statistics of persons under the age of eighteen has traditionally shown a disproportionate number of blacks. Data presented in Table 3.4 show that blacks accounted for 25 percent of all arrests in 1999. Blacks accounted for about 40 percent of reported arrests for violent crime in the under-eighteen age category, 29 percent of the arrests for Index crimes, and about one-fourth (27 percent) of the arrests for property crimes.

With respect to specific crimes, blacks under the age of 18 accounted for more than half of the arrests for robbery (54 percent), almost half of the arrests for murder (49 percent), and 41 percent of arrests for fraud. They also accounted for over three-fourths of all arrests for gambling. Based on population parameters, blacks under the age of 18 accounted for lower than expected arrest rates for driving under the influence (5 percent), other liquor law violations (5 percent), and drunkenness (8 percent). Other minority group arrests account for less than 3 percent of total arrests for Index crimes.

As previously indicated, social-environmental factors have an important impact on delinquency rates and perhaps especially on official delinquency rates (Leiber and Stairs 1999). A disproportionate number of blacks are found in the lower socioeconomic class with all of the correlates conducive to high delinquency. Unless these conditions are changed, each generation caught in this environment not only inherits the same conditions that created high crime and delinquency rates for its parents, but also transmits them to the next generation. It is interesting to note that, according to research, when ethnic or racial groups leave high crime and delinquency areas, they tend to take on the crime rate

In Practice 3.4

Racial Inequities in America's Criminal Justice System Start Early

Tom Teepen

Here's another study that tells us what we already know. Do you suppose we'll pay attention this time? Not a chance. We'd have to change some bad habits and give up some prejudices that, if not exactly comforting, at least enjoy the cache of familiarity.

"And Justice for Some," a study commissioned by the Youth Law Center and conducted by the National Council on Crime and Delinquency, has found that at every step in the juvenile justice system, minority kids are treated more harshly than white kids.

If you are wondering where that grotesque disproportion of African-American men in state and federal prisons comes from, here's the starting point. From their first arrests as children, the inequities visited on Latino and, especially, black kids begin compounding.

And Congress and President Clinton, grandstanding in this election year, seem more or less literally hellbent on making matters worse.

Just look at some of these numbers and how they pile up:

Black kids are 15 percent of the under-18 population, but between 1990 and '98—the latest data—black youths were 26 percent of juvenile arrests, 44 percent of youth detainees, 46 percent of young people tried as adults and 58 percent of youths sent to adult prisons.

In 1993, 373 of every 100,000 black youths with no record were incarcerated for their offense—but only 59 of every 100,000 white youth offenders were. Black youths are charged with 40 percent of drug crimes, but 63 percent of all youths tried as adults for drug crimes were black.

Note: When white and black kids are charged for the same offenses, blacks with no prior record are six times more likely than whites to be incarcerated. (Latinos, three times.) White kids are sent home with a warning for transgressions that land minority kids in jail.

Even granting that black youths proportionally commit more crimes than white youths—itself questionable, but that's another story—the outcomes for minority kids at every step of the criminal justice process are on average grossly more Draconian than for white kids.

The consequences are devastating black community life and undermining job opportunities, economic accumulation and even family formation. (Ex-cons are not top-notch husband prospects.) And the disturbances from those pathologies ripple through all American life.

Pandering to a perceived national hysteria about juvenile crime—which in fact has been steadily falling for years—Congress, with the president's encouragement, is pushing juvenile justice "reforms" that in fact would have the effect of trying more youths as adults and of easing the legal hesitations to sending more to adult prisons.

The Senate bill would even scrap the current, mild injunction to states to work at reducing disproportionate minority confinement.

It is a screwy politics that, faced with challenges like these, assiduously goes about fashioning legislative products that will deepen them.

Teepen, T. (2000, April 29). Racial inequities in America's criminal justice system start early. *Star Tribune,* p. 22A.

TABLE 3.4 Arrests by Race, 1999 [8,545 agencies; 1999 estimated population 171,823,000]

Offense charged	Arrests under 18					Percent distribution				
	Total	White	Black	American Indian or Alaskan Native	Asian or Pacific Islander	Total	White	Black	American Indian or Alaskan Native	Asian or Pacific Islander
TOTAL	1,584,718	1,140,123	398,010	20,295	26,290	100.0	71.9	25.1	1.3	1.7
Murder and nonnegligent manslaughter	923	434	452	16	21	100.0	47.0	49.0	1.7	2.3
Forcible rape	3,176	2,001	1,096	35	44	100.0	63.0	34.5	1.1	1.4
Robbery	18,709	8,101	10,184	133	291	100.0	43.3	54.4	.7	1.6
Aggravated assault	45,003	27,993	15,819	486	705	100.0	62.2	35.2	1.1	1.6
Burglary	64,360	46,736	15,749	773	1,102	100.0	72.6	24.5	1.2	1.7
Larceny-theft	248,523	173,430	65,645	3,787	5,661	100.0	69.8	26.4	1.5	2.3
Motor vehicle theft	33,202	18,998	12,901	441	862	100.0	57.2	38.9	1.3	2.6
Arson	5,759	4,595	1,049	56	59	100.0	79.8	18.2	1.0	1.0
Violent crime	67,811	38,529	27,551	670	1,061	100.0	56.8	40.6	1.0	1.6
Property crime	351,844	243,759	95,344	5,057	7,684	100.0	69.3	27.1	1.4	2.2
Crime Index total	419,655	282,288	122,895	5,727	8,745	100.0	67.3	29.3	1.4	2.1
Other assaults	151,413	98,452	49,132	1,826	2,003	100.0	65.0	32.4	1.2	1.3
Forgery and counterfeiting	4,471	3,473	881	34	13	100.0	77.7	19.7	.8	1.9
Fraud	7,926	4,533	3,223	48	122	100.0	57.2	40.7	.6	1.5
Embezzlement	1,099	695	377	2	25	100.0	63.2	34.3	.2	2.3
Stolen property; buying, receiving, possessing	18,817	11,099	7,173	201	344	100.0	59.0	38.1	1.1	1.8
Vandalism	76,175	62,330	11,838	1,035	972	100.0	81.8	15.5	1.4	1.3
Weapons; carrying, possessing, etc.	27,548	18,658	8,148	263	479	100.0	67.7	29.6	1.0	1.7
Prostitution and commercialized vice	877	506	347	9	15	100.0	57.7	39.6	1.0	1.7
Sex offenses (except forcible rape and prostitution)	10,621	7,722	2,720	81	98	100.0	72.7	25.6	.8	.9
Drug abuse violations	128,055	88,564	37,079	1,113	1,299	100.0	69.2	29.0	.9	1.0
Gambling	835	135	680	1	19	100.0	16.2	81.4	.1	2.3
Offenses against the family and children	5,586	4,239	1,162	42	143	100.0	75.9	20.8	.8	2.6
Driving under the influence	13,641	12,531	708	242	160	100.0	91.9	5.2	1.8	1.2
Liquor laws	103,311	94,639	4,707	3,012	953	100.0	91.6	4.6	2.9	.9
Drunkenness	14,055	12,781	1,091	95	88	100.0	90.9	7.8	.7	.6
Disorderly conduct	113,171	75,600	35,380	1,269	922	100.0	66.8	31.3	1.1	.8
Vagrancy	1,592	1,191	361	26	14	100.0	74.8	22.7	1.6	.9
All other offenses (except traffic)	274,478	202,858	63,870	2,990	4,760	100.0	73.9	23.3	1.1	1.7
Suspicion	1,151	831	308	1	11	100.0	72.2	26.8	.1	1.0
Curfew and loitering law violations	114,027	82,617	28,753	1,244	1,413	100.0	72.5	25.2	1.1	1.2
Runaways	96,214	74,381	17,177	1,034	3,622	100.0	77.3	17.9	1.1	3.8

Source: Federal Bureau of Investigation. (2000). *Crime in the United States—1999.* Washington, D.C.: U.S. Government Printing Office, p. 231.

of the specific part of the community to which they move. It should also be noted that there are differential crime and delinquency rates among black neighborhoods, which gives further credibility to the influence of the social-environmental approach to explaining high crime and delinquency rates. It is unlikely that any single factor can be used to explain the disproportionate number of black juveniles involved in some type of delinquency. The most plausible explanations currently center on environmental and socioeconomic factors characteristic of ghetto areas. Violence and a belief that planning and thrift are not realistic possibilities may be transmitted across generations. This transmission is cultural, not genetic, and may account in part for high rates of violent crime and gambling (luck as an alternative to planning).

Whatever the reasons, it is quite clear that black youth are overrepresented in delinquency statistics, especially with respect to violent offenses, and that inner-city black neighborhoods are among the most dangerous places in America to live. Since most black offenders commit their offenses in black neighborhoods against black victims, these neighborhoods are characterized by violence, and children living in them grow up as observers and/or victims of violence. Such violence undoubtedly takes a toll on children's ability to do well in school, to develop a sense of trust and respect for others, and to develop and adopt nonviolent alternatives. The same concerns exist for members of other racial and ethnic groups growing up under similar conditions.

Career Opportunity—Criminalist

Job Description: Includes positions of laboratory technicians who examine evidence such as fingerprints and documents. Use chemistry, biology, forensic science techniques to examine and classify/identify blood, body fluid, DNA, fiber, fingerprint evidence which may be of value in solving criminal cases. Often on-call, work in dangerous locations and in proximity to dead bodies, chemical and biological hazards. Sometimes testify in court as to evidentiary matters.

Employment Requirements: At least a four-year degree in chemistry, biology, physics, or forensic sciences. In some agencies applicant must be a sworn police officer and must complete entry-level requirements for that position before moving to forensics. In other jurisdictions, civilians are hired as criminalists.

Beginning Salaries: Between $25,000 and $35,000. Benefits vary widely depending upon jurisdiction and whether or not the position requires a sworn officer.

Summary

Official profiles of juvenile offenders reflect only the characteristics of those who have been apprehended and officially processed. While they tell little or nothing about the characteristics of all juveniles who actually commit delinquent acts, they are useful in dealing with juveniles who have been officially processed. These official statistics currently lead us to some discomforting conclusions about the nature of delinquency in America as it relates to social and physical factors.

It may not be the broken home itself that leads to delinquency, but the quality of life within the family in terms of consistency of discipline, level of tension, and ease of communication. Therefore, in some instances, it may be better to remove a child from an intact family that does not provide a suitable environment than to maintain the integrity of the family. In addition, it may not be necessary to automatically place juveniles from broken homes in institutions, foster homes, and so forth, provided the quality of life within the broken home is acceptable.

We perhaps need to rethink our position on the "ideal" family consisting of two biological parents and their children. This family no longer exists for most American children. For many youth, the family of reality consists of a single mother who is head of the household or a biological and stepparent. While many such one-parent families experience varying degrees of delinquency and abuse/neglect, children in many others are valued, protected, and raised in circumstances designed to give them a chance at success in life.

Since education is an important determinant of occupational success in our society and since occupational success is an important determinant of life satisfaction, it is important that we attempt to minimize the number of juveniles who are "pushed out" of the educational system. Both juvenile justice practitioners and school officials need to pursue programs that minimize the number of juveniles who drop out. It may be that we are currently asking too much of educators when we require them to provide not only academic and vocational information, but also to promote psychological and social well-being, moral development, and a sense of direction for juveniles (formerly provided basically by the family). At the present time, however, if educators fail to provide for these concerns, the juvenile often has nowhere else to turn except his or her peers, who may be experiencing similar problems. One result of this alienation from both the family and the educational system is the development of delinquent behavior patterns. Another may be direct attacks on school personnel or fellow students.

We have concentrated our interest and research activities on delinquency and abuse/neglect of the lower social class and have generally ignored the existence of these problems in the middle and upper classes. The importance of lower socioeconomic class delinquency cannot be ignored, but we must also realize that the problem may be equally widespread, though perhaps in different forms, in the middle and upper classes. We can no longer afford the luxury of viewing delinquency as only a problem of the lower social class neighborhoods in urban areas. The problem of delinquency is increasing at a rapid rate in what were commonly considered to be "quiet middle-class suburban areas." Since motivations and types of offenses committed by middle-class delinquents may differ from those of their lower socioeconomic-class counterparts, new techniques and approaches for dealing with these problems may be required.

If those working with children can develop more effective ways of promoting good relationships between juveniles and their families and making the importance of a relevant education clear to juveniles, concern with gang activities may be lessened. At the present time, however, understanding the importance of peer group pressure and the demands of the gang on the individual juvenile are extremely important in understanding drug abuse and related activities. If gangs could be used to promote legitimate rather than illegitimate concerns, one of the major sources of support for certain types of delinquent activities (for example, vandalism and drug abuse) could be weakened considerably. Reasonable alternatives to current gang activities need to be developed and promoted.

Finally, there is no denying that black youth are disproportionately involved in official delinquency. While there are still those who argue racial connections to such delinquency, the evidence that such behavior is a result of family, school, and neighborhood conditions rather than genetics is overwhelming. Whatever the reasons for the high rates of delinquency, and especially violent offenses, in black neighborhoods, it behooves us all to address this issue with as many resources as possible in the interests both of those living in high crime areas and the larger society.

None of the factors discussed in this chapter can be considered a direct cause of delinquency. It is important to remember that official statistics reflect only a small proportion of all delinquent activities. Profiles based on the characteristics discussed in this chapter are valuable to the extent that they alert us to a number of problem areas that must be addressed if we are to make progress in the battle against delinquency.

Attempts to improve the quality of family life and the relevancy of education, and attempts to change discriminatory practices in terms of social class, race, and gender are needed badly. Improvements in these areas will go a long way toward reducing the frequency of certain types of delinquent activity.

Internet Exercises

There are many social and physical factors that may influence delinquency. The juvenile court must address each of these factors every day when diverting children from court, adjudicating children in court, sentencing children in court, and treating or rehabilitating children who have fallen under the jurisdiction of the juvenile court. In order to better understand how these social and physical factors may influence delinquency, visit the website of the Office of Juvenile Justice and Delinquency Prevention (OJJDP) at *http://ojjdp.ncjrs.org/*. This organization provides information to juvenile courts nationwide on issues in juvenile justice.

1. From the OJJDP homepage, click on JJ Facts and Figures. From the menu, click on Publications. Choose General (publications) and then click on the National Report found under Juvenile Offenders and Victims Series.
2. In Chapter One of the national report, juvenile population characteristics are discussed. After reading this chapter, explain how the information regarding the social characteristics influencing delinquency impact the juvenile court system.
3. Go to Chapter Three of the report and read the information on official and unofficial statistics of juvenile crime. Discuss whether or not these statistics support or contradict the information provided in chapter 3 of your textbook.
4. Next, click on Chapter Six of the national report. After reading the information provided in chapter six, explain whether race, age, and gender affected the types of delinquency committed and the numbers of delinquent acts committed by the children in the report. Also, did race, age, and gender factor into the detainment of the delinquent child? If so, in what type of offenses? Did race, age, and gender determine whether or not a case was handled formally or informally by the juvenile justice system? Why or why not?
5. From the information provided in the national report, did any other social or physical characteristics influence delinquency or the response of the juvenile court system to the delinquency?
6. In Chapter Seven of the national report, read and then discuss whether or not differences in race, age, and gender were apparent among children held in detention centers. Using the information provided, explain whether or not race, age, and gender shaped when and if the child was detained. Were there differences in the types of crimes committed by females and males and the types of crimes resulting in detainment of females and males? What about racial differences and age differences? Did social factors influence whether a child was detained? If so, what social factors were the most influential? Why?

USEFUL WEBSITES

Juvenile Justice Experts Should Focus on Girls' Unique Needs—*http://www.psych.org/pnews/00-01/girls.html*

Juvenile Justice Research Publications—*http://www.wsipp.wa.gov/crime/JuvJustice.html*

Juvenile Offenders and Victims: 1997 Update on Violence—*http://ojjdp.ncjrs.org/pubs/juvoff/hom_off.html*

Coalition for Juvenile Justice—*http://www.nassemby.org/html/mem_cjj.html*

Racial Differences in Juvenile Delinquency—*http://preview.biblioalerts.com/info/com.biblioalerts_biblioalerts_SOC000095.html?se=ink*

Keep Schools Safe—*http://www.keepschoolssafe.org*

National Center for Education Statistics—*http://www.nces.ed.gov/*

CRITICAL THINKING QUESTIONS

1. What is the relationship between profiles of delinquents based on official statistics and the actual extent of delinquency?
2. Discuss the relationships among the family, the educational system, drugs, and delinquency.
3. Discuss some of the reasons for the overrepresentation of black juveniles in official delinquency statistics. What could be done to decrease the proportion of young blacks involved in delinquency? How do area of the city, race, and social class combine to affect delinquency? Is delinquency basically a lower social class phenomenon? If so, why should those in the middle and upper classes be concerned about it?
4. Discuss the methamphetamine "crisis." How does it differ from other drug-related crises we have faced in the past? What do you think can be done to deal with this crisis?

SUGGESTED READINGS

Anderson, E. (1990). *Streetwise.* Chicago: University of Chicago Press.

Battistich, V., & Hom, A. (1997, December). The relationship between students' sense of their school as a community and their involvement in problem behaviors. *American Journal of Public Health, 87,* 1997–2001.

Bumphus, V. W., & Anderson, J. F. (1999). Family structure and race in a sample of criminal offenders. *Journal of Criminal Justice, 27* (4), 309–320.

Campbell, A. (1997). Self definition by rejection: The case of gang girls. In G. L. Mays (ed.), *Gangs and gang behavior* (pp. 129–149). Chicago: Nelson-Hall.

Ellis, R. A., O'Hara, M., & Sowers, K. (1999). Treatment profiles of troubled female adolescents: Implications for judicial disposition. *Juvenile and Family Court Journal, 50* (3), 25–40.

Holzman, H. R. (1996). Criminological research on public housing: Toward a better understanding of people, places, and spaces. *Crime & Delinquency, 42,* 361–378.

Mays, G. L. (1997). *Gangs and gang behavior.* Chicago: Nelson-Hall.

Nadelman, E. A. (1998). Commonsense drug policy. *Foreign Affairs, 77* (1), 111–126.

Smith, C. A., & Stern, S. B. (1997). Delinquency and antisocial behavior: A review of family processes and intervention research. *Social Service Review, 71,* 382–420.

Sutpen, R., Kurtz, D., and Giddings, M. (1993). The influence of juveniles' race on police decision-making: An exploratory study. *Juvenile and Family Court Journal, 44* (2), 69–76.

Teepen, T. (2000, April 29). Racial inequities in America's criminal justice system start early. *Star Tribune,* p. 22A.

CHAPTER

4 THEORIES OF CAUSATION

CHAPTER LEARNING OBJECTIVES

Upon completion of this chapter, students should be able to:

Recognize the requirements for a good theory
Understand and discuss the strengths and limitations of various theories
Recognize and discuss the importance of the relationship between theory and practice
Evaluate research relating to theories of causation

KEY TERMS

scientific theory
conceptual schemes
demonology
trephining
classical theory
free-will approach
neoclassical approach
postclassical theory
rational choice theory
routine activities theory
positivist school of criminology
biological theory
atavist
anomalies
phrenology
somatotypes
XYY chromosomes
psychological theory
psychoanalytic approach
id, ego, superego
personality inventories
psychopath
learning theory
behaviorists
conditioning
sociological theory
anomie
strain
illegitimate opportunity structure
ecological approach
concentric zone theory
theory of differential association
theory of differential-anticipation
labeling theory
conflict theory
radical theory
critical theory
Marxist theory
feminism
control theory

Let us now examine some of the theories which have been developed in an attempt to explain offenses by and against juveniles. It is important to note from the outset that numerous studies over the past fifty years have suggested links between delinquency and child abuse/neglect. For example, Scudder et al. (1993, p. 321) note that the results of their research "suggest that children who break the law, especially through acts of violence, often have a history of maltreatment as children." The results of their research indicate further that "a child abused at a young age is at higher risk for subsequent delinquent behaviors than a nonabused child." While

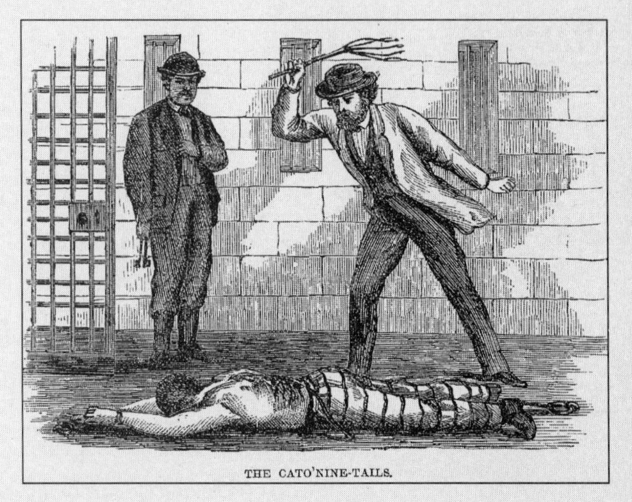

Torture is one way of driving out evil spirits that cause crime.
The Granger Collection

dozens of conceptual schemes have been proposed in attempts to specify the causes of such offenses, only a few of the more prominent attempts will be discussed here.

SCIENTIFIC THEORY

A **scientific theory** may be defined as a set of deductively interrelated propositions, at least some of which are empirically testable, which describe and explain some phenomenon (Fitzgerald and Cox 1994; Akers 1994, pp. 1–2). Although this definition may sound complex, it is really quite simple if we look at it one part at a time. A proposition is simply a statement of a relationship between two or more variables. Propositions that are deductively interrelated are simply related in a logical manner so that some propositions can be derived (deduced) from others. For example:

Proposition 1—All delinquents are from broken homes.

Proposition 2—Harry is a delinquent.

Proposition 3—Harry is from a broken home.

In this case, Proposition 3 is derived from Propositions 1 and 2; that is, Proposition 3 is said to be explained by Propositions 1 and 2 and is logically correct. Our definition of a theory, however, requires that at least some of the propositions be empirically testable. To be acceptable, then, a theory must be logically correct *and* must accurately describe events in the real world. Suppose Harry is not, in fact, from a broken home. Clearly our explanation of delinquency is erroneous and our theory must be revised or rejected.

While **conceptual schemes** which suggest relationship between variables but do not meet our requirements for theory may be useful stepping stones in describing delinquency or abuse, only a logically correct and empirically accurate theory will enable us to explain these phenomena. As we discuss some theories, you may find it useful to assess the extent to which they meet the requirements of our definition and the extent to which they are useful in helping us to understand offenses by and against juveniles. As Klofas and Stojkovic (1995, p. 37) indicate, "Our ideas about crime—what it means and why it happens—have varied considerably over the past several hundred years. We have changed from (1) viewing crime as the work of the devil to (2) describing it as the rational choice of free-willed economic calculators to (3) explaining it as the involuntary causal effects of biological, mental, and environmental conditions, and then back to (2)." Our intent in this chapter is simply to familiarize you with some of the numerous conceptual schemes and to note some of the strengths and weaknesses of these schemes. For those who desire more detailed information about specific theories, the Suggested Readings list at the end of the chapter should prove useful.

SOME EARLY THEORIES

Demonology

Early attempts to explain various forms of deviant behavior (crime, delinquency, mental illness) focused on demon or spirit possession. Individuals who violated societal norms were thought to be possessed by some evil spirit, which forced them to commit evil deeds through the exercise of mysterious supernatural power. Deviant behavior, then, was viewed not as a product of free will, but as determined by forces beyond the control of the individual (thus the demonological theory of deviance is referred to as a *deterministic approach*). In order to cure or control deviant behavior, a variety of techniques were employed to drive the evil spirits from the mind and/or body of the perceived deviant.

One process that was employed was **trephining,** which consisted of drilling holes in the skulls of those perceived as deviants to allow the evil spirits to escape. Various rites of exorcism, including beating and burning, were practiced to make the body of the perceived deviant such an uncomfortable place to reside that the evil spirits would leave, or to make the deviant confess his or her association with evil spirits. As might be expected, such torture of the body often resulted in death or permanent disability to the individual who was allegedly possessed. In addition, either confession or failure to confess could be taken as evidence of possession. Tortured sufficiently, many individuals undoubtedly confessed simply to prevent further torture. Those who persisted in claiming innocence were often thought to be so completely under the control of evil spirits that they could not tell the truth. Needless to say, the consequences for both categories of accused were frequently very unpleasant.

Many observers feel that belief in spirit possession as a cause of deviance is rare today, but our analysis of news articles over the past few years has turned up numerous articles on ritual abuse of children by persons or groups claiming to have been instructed by deities, typically God or Satan, to commit the acts in question (Stearns and Garcia 2001; Charton 2001; Omaha-World Herald 2001). As Klofas and Stojkovic (1995, p. 39) note, supernatural bases for crime have not been totally rejected, although they have been largely supplanted by more scientific explanations.

Perhaps demonology as a explanation of deviance persists because, in some respects, attempts to deal with deviance thought to be caused by spirits are logical if the basic premise is accepted as true: that is, if one believes that spirit possession causes deviance, it makes sense to drive the spirits away if possible. As is the case with all theories of deviance, this one implies a method of cure or control. While such an explanation of deviance seems simplistic to criminologists today, it cannot be scientifically disproved and it is still clearly accepted as valid by significant numbers of people in a substantial number of countries. Precisely because it cannot be scientifically tested, however, this attempt to explain deviant behavior is of little value from our theoretical perspective.

Classical Theory

In the last half of the eighteenth century, the classical school of criminology (often referred to as a **free-will approach**) emerged in Italy and England in the works of Cesare Beccaria and Jeremy Bentham, respectively. This approach to explaining and controlling crime was based upon the belief that human beings exercise free will and that human behavior results from rationally calculating rewards and costs in terms of pleasure and pain. In other words, before an individual commits a specific act, he or she determines whether the consequences of the act will be pleasurable or painful. Presumably, acts that have painful consequences will be avoided. To control crime, then, society simply had to make the punishment for violators outweigh the benefits of their illegal actions. Thus, penalties became increasingly more severe as offenses became increasingly more serious. Under

classical theory, threat of punishment is considered to be a deterrent to criminals who rationally calculate the consequences of their illegal actions.

By the early 1800s, Beccaria's approach had been modified in recognition of the fact that not all individuals were capable of rationally calculating rewards and costs. The modified approach (generally referred to as the **neoclassical approach**) called for the mitigation of punishment for the insane and juveniles (Conklin 1998, p. 41). By definition, the insane were not capable of rational calculation and youth, up to a certain age, at least, were thought to be less responsible than adults.

It is important to understand the classical approach, since its propositions (punishment deters crime, the punishment should fit the crime, and juveniles and the insane should be treated differently than sane adults) are basic to our current criminal and juvenile justice system.

Rational Choice Theory

The **postclassical** or **rational choice theory** of the twentieth century also involves the notion that before people commit crimes, they rationally consider the risks and rewards. A burglar noting no lights on and no police presence at an expensive mansion over several nights might rationally conclude that the risk is relatively low and the potential rewards worth pursuing and therefore commit the crime. According to the rationale choice model, focusing on the development of rational thought and the application of scientific laws, and using empirical research, might help the state develop policies that better control crime and deviance and thereby improve quality of life (Lanier and Henry 1998, p. 72; Bohm 2000, p. 15).

This view, that delinquents exercise free will and rationally calculate the consequences of their behavior, fits well with the conservative ideology and the "get tough" approach to delinquency. If delinquency is a product of free will and not predetermined by social conditions, the delinquent may best be deterred by the threat of punishment rather than the promise of treatment. Gang members who go into the drug business with the clear intent of making a profit by outwitting both their competitors and law enforcement officials may be described as using rational choice theory.

Routine Activities Theory

Routine activities theory is yet another extension of the belief that rational thought and sanctions largely determine criminal behavior. According to this approach, crime is simply a function of peoples' everyday behavior. One's presence in certain types of places, frequented by motivated offenders, makes him/her a suitable target, and, in the absence of capable guardians, is likely to lead to crime (Lanier and Henry 1998, p. 82; Conklin 1998, p. 319). Indeed there is research that supports the existence of "hot spots," or areas in which crimes occur repeatedly over time (Sherman and Weisburd 1995; Buerger, Cohn, and Petrosino 2000). In other cases, however, victims' absence may be critical to the crime in question (burglary is easier if no one is home).

Unfortunately, the classical approach to controlling crime has never been very successful. While there seems to be some logic to the approach, the premise that the threat of punishment deters crime, at least as currently employed, is inaccurate. There are a variety of possible sources of error in this premise. First, it may be that man does not always rationally calculate rewards and costs. An individual committing what we commonly refer to as a "crime of passion" (as in the case of the murder of a spouse caught in an adulterous act, or excessive corporal punishment of a child in a moment of anger) may not stop to think about the consequences. If this individual does not stop to make such calculations, then the threat of punishment (no matter how severe) will not affect that person's behavior. Second, an individual may calculate rewards and costs in a way that appears rational to him or her (but perhaps not to society) and may decide that certain illegal acts are worth whatever punishment he or she will receive if apprehended (as in the case of a starving person stealing food). Finally, the individual may rationally calculate rewards and costs, but have no fear of punishment because he or she feels the chances of apprehension are slight (as in the case of many juveniles involved with alcohol and minor vandalism). If the individual believes that he or she will not be apprehended for his or her illegal acts, the threat of punishment has little meaning. Additionally, the individual may believe that even if he or she is caught, punishment will not be administered (as in the case of many juveniles who are aware that most juvenile cases never go to court, and parents who abuse their children in the name of discipline).

For whatever reasons, the classical approach to explaining and controlling crime has not proved successful. It would appear that whatever possibility of success this approach has rests with delivering punishment relatively immediately and with a great deal of certainty. Since our society largely continues to rely upon the classical approach and since neither immediacy of punishment nor certainty of apprehension exists, it is not surprising that we are unsuccessful in our attempts to control crime and delinquency.

In spite of the fact that severe punishment does not appear to lead to desirable behavior, many child abusers obviously believe that such punishment will lead to improved behavior on behalf of their children. Thus, when children fail to meet the expectation of abusive parents, whether in the area of toilet training, eating habits, schoolwork, or showing proper deference to the parents, emotional and/or physical abuse results. This often leads to lowered self-esteem on behalf of the child whose performance then suffers even more, leading to more severe punishment on the part of the parent, and so on. This "cycle of violence," once begun, is difficult to break, and there is at least some evidence that the abused child may later abuse his or her own children in the same ways (Knudsen 1992, pp. 61–63).

The Positivist School

The **positivist school of criminology** (also known as the Italian school) emerged in the second half of the nineteenth century. Cesare Lombroso is recognized as the founder of the positivist school and also as the "father" of modern criminology. Lombroso, with other positivists such as Garofalo and Ferri, believed that criminals should be studied scientifically and emphasized determinism as opposed to free will (classical school) as the basis of criminal behavior. While a number of positivists believed that heredity is the determining factor in criminality, others believed the environment determined in large measure whether or not an individual became a criminal.

The positivists emphasized the need for empirical research in criminology and some stressed the importance of environment as a causal factor in crime. While their methodology was unsophisticated by modern standards, their contributions to the development of modern criminology are undeniable. Lombroso may also be considered, earlier in his career at least, as one of the founders of the biological school of criminology.

BIOLOGICAL THEORIES

The **biological theory** of delinquency was initially based on the assumption that delinquency (criminality) is inherited. Over the past century, the approach has tended to emphasize more the belief that offenders differ from nonoffenders in some physiological way (Conklin 1998, p. 146). This approach has offered a number of different explanations of delinquency, ranging from glandular malfunctions to learning disabilities to racial heritage to nutrition. As we examine some of these explanations, keep in mind our definition of an acceptable theory.

Lombroso

Lombroso became known for the theory of the "born criminal." As a result of his research, he became convinced at one point in his career that criminals were **atavists,** or throwbacks to more primitive beings. According to Lombroso, these born criminals could be recognized by a series of external features, such as receding foreheads, enormous development of the jaw, and large or handle-shaped ears. These external traits were thought to be related to personality types characterized by laziness, moral insensitiveness, and absence of guilt feelings.

Individuals with a number of these criminal features or **anomalies** were thought to be incapable of resisting the impulse to commit crimes except under very favorable circumstances. Many of Lombroso's assumptions can be traced to the influence of Darwinism (which provided a means of ranking animals as more or less primitive) at the end of the nineteenth century, and to the influence of **phrenology** (the study of the shape of the skull) and physiognomy (the study of facial features) as they related to deviance (Conklin 1998, pp. 146–47).

Later in his career, Lombroso modified his approach by recognizing the importance of social factors, but his emphasis on biological causes encouraged many other researchers to seek such causes. Lombroso remains important today largely because of his attempts to explain crime scientifically, rather than as a result of his particular theories.

Other Biological Theories

Following Lombroso, there have been a number of attempts over the years to find biological or genetic causes for crime and delinquency. Identical twin studies were conducted based on the belief that if genetics determine criminality, when one twin is criminal, the other will also be. In general, these studies provide evidence that genetic structure is not the sole cause of crime, since none of them indicate that 100 percent of the twins studied were identical with respect to criminal behavior. Research on the relationship between genetics and crime in twins continues nonetheless. The results of twin studies conducted over the past 75 years do seem to indicate that there may be a genetic factor in delinquency/crime, but the exact nature of the relationship remains undetermined (Fishbein 1990).

Cesare Lombroso
Bettman/CORBIS

The next logical step in studying the relationship between heredity and crime involved studies of children adopted at an early age who had little or no contact with biological parents. Would the offense rates and types of the children more closely resemble those of the adoptive or biological parents? Evidence suggest a hereditary link, but it is very difficult to separate the effects of heredity and environment (Bohm 2001, pp. 36–41).

Dugdale made the Jukes family a famous test case in the late 1800s when he demonstrated that over generations this family had been characterized by criminality. Dugdale felt that crime and heredity were related, but his own admission that over the years the family had established a reputation for deviant behavior points to the possibility that other factors (learning and labeling, for instance) might be of equal or greater importance in explaining his observations (Dugdale 1888).

Other researchers, including Ernst Kretschmer (1925), William H. Sheldon (1949), and Sheldon and Eleanor Glueck (1950), turned to studies of the relationship between **somatotypes** (body types) and delinquency/criminality. Causes of delinquency and body type were thought by Sheldon, for example, to be biologically determined and selective breeding was suggested as a solution to delinquency. The Gluecks continued the body type tradition of explaining delinquency, but have included in their analysis a variety of other factors as well. The basic conclusion of the Gluecks' work with respect to body type and crime is that a majority of delinquents are muscular as opposed to thin or obese. One possible explanation for this conclusion, which does not require any assumptions about biological determination, is that youth who are not particularly physically fit recognize this fact and therefore consciously tend to avoid at least those delinquent activities which might require strength and fitness. Additionally, measurements of body type are rather subjective and the data presented by the body typists do not account for different individuals with the same body type being delinquent on the one hand and nondelinquent on the other.

In the past several years, emphasis in the biological school has shifted somewhat. Studies examining the relationships among learning disabilities, chromosomes, chemical imbalances, and delinquency have emerged. We have already discussed some of the literature on the relationship between learning disabilities and delinquency in chapter 3. Here we will simply state that, as typically conceived, many learning disabilities are clearly psychosocial (as opposed to biological) in nature. Others are more clearly organic in nature, and there is some evidence that brain dysfunctions and neurological defects are more common among violent individuals than among the general population. Such individuals seem to have defects in the frontal and temporal lobes of the brain and these may lead to loss of self-control. Other dysfunctions include dyslexia (the failure to attain language skills appropriate to intellectual level), aphasia (problems with verbal communication and understanding), and attention deficit disorder (manifested in hyperactivity and inattentiveness). Satterfield (1987) found that children who are hyperactive are several times more likely to be arrested during adolescence than children without the disorder. None of these disorders, at this point in time, have been shown to be directly causally related to delinquency. In fact, Satterfield found that arrest rates for hyperactive children were affected by social class, with those from the lower social class more likely to be arrested. In addition, many learning disabled youth adapt and find ways to overcome the handicap. Perlmutter (1987) has suggested there is little middle ground and indicates that those who are not able to overcome the disability appear to be at risk of developing emotional and behavioral difficulties as adolescents.

In the 1960s, a number of researchers explored the relationship between the presence of an extra Y chromosome in some males and subsequent criminal behavior. Mednick and Christiansen (1977) found that about 42 percent of the **XYY chromosome** cases identified in Denmark had criminal histories compared to only 9 percent of the XY population. Research is still being conducted on the possible relationship between chromosomes and criminality, though little if any work has been done specifically on the relationship between delinquency and chromosomes.

At present, it is safe to say that a direct relationship between chromosome structure and criminality has not been scientifically established and that many of the studies conducted to date are characterized by serious methodological problems.

Jeffery (1978; 1996), Booth and Osgood (1993), and Denno (1994) view behavior as the product of interaction between a physical environment and a physical organism and believe that contemporary criminology should represent a merger of biology, psychology, and sociology. The basis for this argument is that most contemporary criminologists believe that criminal/delinquent behavior is learned, but neglect the fact that learning involves physical (biochemical) changes in the brain. These researchers contend that while criminality is not inherited, the biochemical preparedness for such behavior is present in the brain, and will, given a particular type of environment, produce criminal behavior (Turkheimer 1998).

There are numerous other attempts to explain both delinquency and crime in terms of biology, genetics, and biochemistry. As early as 1939, Ernest Hooton wrote of the consequences of biological causes of crime for rehabilitation and control of offenders. According to Hooton, if criminality is inherited, the solutions to crime lie in isolation and/or sterilization of offenders to prevent them from remaining active in the genetic pool of a society. A third alternative, which Hooton opposed, is extermination, and a fourth is the practice of eugenics. At various times, European societies have isolated (Devil's Island, the Colonies), sterilized and exterminated offenders. Experiments with eugenics have also been conducted on numerous occasions, but raise serious ethical and moral issues. So serious are these concerns that a conference on genetics and crime which was scheduled to be held in 1992 lost National Institutes of Health funding and had to be cancelled (Conklin 1998, p. 158). While the conference was eventually held in revamped form, the focus was more on the affect of biological research than on the content of such research (Jeffery 1996). The extent to which genetic engineering becomes acceptable as a means of dealing with a wide variety of social problems will likely determine its use in controlling criminality if genetic deficiencies or abnormalities are shown to be causes of crime and delinquency. Recent developments which have made it possible to create human genetic blueprints, hailed as one of the greatest scientific contributions of the twenty-first century, make it likely that if there is a genetic link to crime it will be discovered (Friend 2000).

Psychological Theories

The human mind has long been considered a source of abnormal behavior and therefore crime (Lanier and Henry 1998, p. 113). Early varieties of **psychological theories** of delinquency and crime focused on lack of intelligence and/or personality disturbances as major causal factors. Several of the early pioneers in the psychological school were convinced that biological factors played a major role in determining intelligence, and they could therefore be considered proponents of both schools of thought. Goddard's (1914) studies of the Kallikak family and the intellectual abilities of reformatory inmates, for instance, led him to conclude that feeblemindedness, which he believed to be inherited, was an important contributing factor in criminality. He suggested that "eliminating" a large proportion of mental defectives would reduce the number of criminals and other deviants in society. Similarly, Charles Goring (1913) focused on defective intelligence and psychological characteristics as basic causes of crime in his attempt to refute Lombroso and the other positivists. As we have indicated previously, research concerning the relationship between defective intelligence, IQ, or learning disabilities and delinquency continues. Problems concerning the reliability and validity of IQ tests and personality inventories, as well as other methodological shortcomings, continue to plague such research and the psychological school as a whole has taken other directions. Still, many believe that those who commit heinous crimes must be emotionally disturbed—in some identifiable way different from the rest of us (see In Practice 4.1).

Sigmund Freud's Psychoanalytic Approach

Sigmund Freud, born in 1856, spent most of his life in Vienna, Austria. He is regarded as the founder of psychoanalysis, a **psychoanalytic approach** to explaining behavior which relies heavily upon the techniques of introspection (looking inside one's self) and retrospection (reviewing past events). Freud's theories were introduced in the United States in the early 1900s. He divided personality into three separate components, the id, the ego, and the superego. The function of the **id,** according to Freud, is to provide for the discharge of energy which permits the individual to seek pleasure and reduce tension. The id is also said to be the seat of instincts in human beings and not thought to be governed by reason. The **ego** is said to be the part of the personality that controls and governs the id and the superego by making rational adjustments to real-life situations. For example, the ego might prevent the id from causing the individual to seek immediate gratification of his or her desires by deferring gratification to a later time. The development of the ego is said to be a product of interaction between the individual's personality and the environment and is thought to be affected by heredity as well. The **superego** is viewed as the moral branch of the personality and may be roughly equated with the concept of conscience. Both the ego and the superego are thought to develop out of the individual's interactions with his or her environment, while the id is said to be a product of evolution.

In general, deviance is viewed as the product of an uncontrollable id, a faulty ego, an underdeveloped superego, or some combination of the three. Therefore, those who commit a criminal or delinquent act do so as the result of a personality disturbance. In order to correct or control this behavior, the causes of the personality disturbance are located primarily through introspection and retrospection, with a particular emphasis upon childhood experiences, and then eliminated through therapy.

Freud is one of the most important figures (if not the most important figure) in the history of psychology. There are, no doubt, many cases where psychoanalytic techniques prove effective in therapeutic treatment. As a system for explaining the causes of deviance, however, Freudian psychology has several shortcomings. First, the existence of the id, ego, and superego cannot be empirically demonstrated. Second, instincts, which Freud viewed as the driving forces in the id, are thought by many behavioral scientists to be extremely rare or nonexistent in humans. Third, there seems to be faulty logic among practitioners using Freud's system. They accept the premise that those who commit deviant acts must be experiencing personality disturbances; that is, they employ circular reasoning rather than logical deduction (Akers 1994, p. 85; Lanier and Henry 1998, p. 117). In response to the question, How do you know X has a disturbed personality? they often answer: Since he committed a deviant act, he must have been experiencing a personality disturbance. Such a response is more a statement of faith than a matter of fact. At present, it is safe to say that the psychoanalytic approach is of very little value in explaining crime and delinquency (or any other form of deviance, for that matter). Nonetheless, the Freudian approach has remained popular in

In Practice 4.1

MAN FREED IN ILLINOIS MURDER RETRIAL ARRESTED IN CALIFORNIA RACIAL ATTACK

Rodney Woidtke, the mentally ill drifter released from prison after being acquitted in a retrial in March in the murder case of a St. Louis area newspaper intern, has been arrested in California.

Woidtke, 40, was accused of an alleged racial attack Aug. 4 outside a Roseville, Calif., supermarket. He is being held in the Placer County Jail near Sacramento.

Woidtke, who, according to Illinois court documents is a schizophrenic in need of daily medication, was charged with felony assault with a deadly weapon and a misdemeanor count of violation of a person's civil rights through force or threat. Bond was set at $40,000 but has been reduced to $5,000. Lt. Steve Uribe of the Roseville Police Department, said Woidtke, who is white, assaulted 20-year-old Brandon Jones of Roseville while Jones was using a pay telephone at the Bel Air Market. Uribe said Woidtke swung a heavy bicycle cable and attached lock at Jones while shouting, "I'm going to kick your ass because you're black."

Jones was not seriously injured.

Uribe said that before the attack, Woidtke was riding a bicycle and hanging around the front of the store.

"He was talking about some blacks who shot a white guy in Sacramento. He wasn't making much sense," said Uribe.

Cliff Gessner, supervising deputy district attorney for Placer County, said his office will drop the misdemeanor count and file paperwork to enhance the assault charge. Gessner said the enhanced charge will be filed at the next scheduled court appearance Thursday because Woidtke allegedly displayed racial bias in the attack.

Gessner said if a judge allows it, the enhanced count could get Woidtke seven years in state prison.

much of the Western world, and Freud has had many disciples who have applied his techniques directly to delinquency.

Among those emphasizing the psychoanalytic perspective were Healy and Bronner (1936), who believed that the delinquent was a product of a personality disturbance resulting from thwarted desires and deprivations which led to frustration and a weak superego. Healy and Bronner interviewed numerous juvenile offenders and came to the conclusion that 90 percent of them were emotionally disturbed. Adler (1931), Halleck (1971), and Fox and Levin (1994) conclude that those who are frustrated, believe the world is against them, and feel inferior may turn to crime as a compensatory means of expressing their autonomy.

Others, using a variety of **personality inventories** (including the Minnesota Multiphasic Personality Inventory [MMPI] and the California Personality Inventory [CPI]), have concluded that such inventories do appear to discriminate between delinquents and non-

California prosecutors had initially been operating under the assumption that Woidtke had been convicted of murdering Belleville (Ill.) News-Democrat intern Audrey Cardenas. California law doubles the prison time for those previously convicted of serious offenses.

But Gessner said his office learned Monday that Woidtke was acquitted of the murder in a retrial.

The body of Cardenas, 24, of College Station, Texas, was found in a dry creek bed June 26, 1988.

Illinois prosecutors contended Woidtke killed Cardenas, beating her with a pipe, after she spurned his sexual advances during a chance meeting. Woidtke, a diagnosed schizophrenic, had been living in the woods and sleeping in the trees for several months around Belleville before he was arrested.

Woidtke confessed to the crime three times, but recanted those confessions. Also, some of his claims were contradicted by physical evidence. In fact, there was no physical evidence linking Woidtke to the killing. Experts have testified that DNA, blood and hair tests were all inconclusive.

Woidtke was convicted by a judge in his first trial in 1989 and sentenced to 45 years in prison. In April 2000, an appeals court ordered that he be given a new trial after finding that his first attorney had a conflict of interest because he also represented another suspect in the killing.

Woidtke's second trial was barely under way in January when the judge declared a mistrial out of concern over testimony from a prosecution witness.

In his third trial, Woidtke was acquitted March 30 by a St. Clair County, Ill., jury after only three hours of deliberation.

Woidtke has been living with his younger brother, Rick, and Rick's wife, Marjorie, since he returned with them to the Sacramento area in early April.

Rodney Woidtke is a diagnosed paranoid schizophrenic who was forcibly medicated for most of his time in prison. When off his medication, he reports hallucinations and says he hears voices.

Woidtke has reportedly refused to take any medication since his release from prison.

Associated Press. *(2001, August 28). Man freed in Illinois murder retrial arrested in California racial attack.*

delinquents, but the reasons for such discrimination are not at all clear-cut and neither are the numerous definitions of "abnormal" personality employed (Bohm 2001, pp. 56–57). Akers (1994, p. 88) concludes: "The research using personality inventories and other methods of measuring personality characteristics has not been able to produce findings to support personality variables as major causes of criminal and delinquent behavior."

Psychopathology

One of the terms most commonly employed to describe certain types of criminals and delinquents is **psychopath.** Typically, the term is used to describe aggressive criminals who act impulsively with no apparent reason. Sutherland and Cressey (1978) indicated that some fifty-five descriptive terms are consistently linked with the concept of psychopathy (sociopathy or antisocial personality). Bohm (2001, p. 54) lists sixteen characteristics ranging from "unreliability" to "fantastic and uninviting behavior" to "failure to follow any life plan." Attempts have been made to clarify the concept of psychopathology, but such attempts have helped little in understanding the relationship between psychopathology and criminality since criminality is typically included in the symptomatic basis for psychopathology. In other words, the two conditions are often perceived as being one and the same.

While the concept of psychopathology is generally considered to be too vague and ambiguous to distinguish psychopaths from nonpsychopaths, there have been attempts to operationalize the concept in more meaningful fashion. Gough (1948; 1960) conceptualized psychopathy as the inability to take the role of the other (the inability to identify with others). The scales he developed to measure role-taking ability generally result in lower scores for offenders than nonoffenders. Whether or not such differences could have been detected before the offenders committed offenses is another matter.

Research in this area continues. Martens (1999) reports a case in which psychopathy appears to have been cured as a result of therapeutic psychosocial influences and life events. In this case, the individual began a career in delinquency at age fifteen and went on to commit offenses, including fraud, theft, rape, and assaults, until age twenty-six. Following life-changing events and therapy, the individual has remained crime free for more than twenty years and appears to be leading a "normal" life.

Poythrees, Edens, and Lilienfeld (1998) administered the Psychopathic Personality Inventory (PPI), a self-report measure of psychopathic personality features, and the Psychopathy Checklist Revised (PCL-R) to youthful offender prison inmates. They found that PPI could be used to accurately predict PCL-R classifications of psychopath and nonpsychopath, raising the possibility that the PPI could be used for clinical purposes to detect psychopathic personalities.

Lynam (1998) hypothesized that there is a developmental relationship between adult psychopathy and children with symptoms of hyperactivity, impulsivity, attention problems, and conduct problems (HIA-CP). Using a large sample of adolescent boys, Lynam found that boys who were hyperactive and impulsive, with attention disorders and conduct problems, scored high on a measure of psychopathic personality. These boys were the most antisocial, most disinhibited, and tended to be the most neuropsychologically impaired of the groups studied. Further support for the relationship between adolescent behavior patterns of this type and adult psychopathy comes from Gresham, MacMillan, and Bocian (1998) who found marked differences between HIA-CP third and fourth grade children and others on peer measures of rejection and friendship and teachers' ratings of social skills. The notion of the "fledgling psychopath" appears to emerge from these recent studies. Still, as Akers (1994, p. 87) concluded, based upon the research currently available, the term *psychopath* appears to be so broad that it could be applied to anyone who violates the law.

After reviewing attempts to relate psychopathy to child abuse, Knudsen (1992) concludes that there is little evidence of such a relationship. Wolfe (1985) also found no relationship between underlying personality attributes and child abuse beyond general descriptions of stress-related complaints and displeasure in the parenting role. Steinmetz (1986) indicated that less than 10 percent of child abuse can be directly attributed to psychopathological offenders.

Further research on the relationship between psychopathology and delinquency and abuse is clearly needed. On the one hand, it may turn out that behavior patterns involving

In Practice 4.2

Behavior modification or behavior therapy tries to shape conduct by rewarding desirable actions (for example, with money) and punishing undesirable ones (for example, by withdrawing institutional privileges). This form of treatment does not regard criminal behavior as a symptom of underlying personality flaws that must be corrected, but sees it instead as a problem that has to be dealt with directly.

A major question about behavior modification is whether changes produced in inmates will persist after they are released. A review of twenty-four treatment programs of this sort concluded that virtually all of them succeeded in modifying the behavior of the institutionalized offenders, most of whom were juveniles. Only four programs followed offenders after release. And only one found a lasting and significant effect of the program. Thus, there is little reason to believe that behavior modification programs within institutions can significantly change how offenders will act after they are released. (Conklin 1998, p. 516)

hyperactivity, impulsivity, and inattention, combined with conduct problems, are forerunners of psychopathology. On the other hand, most youth exhibit one or more of these behaviors periodically, but do not turn out to be psychopaths.

Behaviorism and Learning Theory

In the later nineteenth century, a number of psychologists became increasingly concerned about weaknesses in the theory and techniques developed by Freud and his followers and those of the biological school emphasizing heredity. Tarde, by contrast, thought crime was learned by normal people in the process of interacting in specific environments (Bohm 2000, p. 82). He and others called for a change in focus from genetics and the internal workings of the mind to observable behavior. While the major work on this **learning theory** model as it relates to delinquency has been done by sociologists and will be discussed under that topic, the psychological underpinnings will be discussed here.

As we indicated above, **behaviorists** called for a change of techniques from the subjective, speculative approach based on introspection and retrospection to a more empirical, objective approach based on observing and measuring behavior. Perhaps the most important individual in the behaviorist tradition was B. F. Skinner (1953), who directed his attention toward the relationship between a particular stimulus and a given response and to the learning processes involved in connecting the two. Human social behavior, then, is viewed as a set of learned responses to specific stimuli. Criminal and delinquent behavior are viewed as varieties of human social behavior, learned in the same way as other social behaviors. Through the process of **conditioning** (rewarding for appropriate behavior and/or punishing for inappropriate behavior), any type of social behavior can be taught (see In Practice 4.2). Therefore, when an individual behaves in a delinquent manner (exhibits an inappropriate response in a given situation), his or her behavior can be modified using conditioning. To control and rehabilitate delinquents, then, the therapist

B. F. Skinner
AP/Wide World

employs behavior modification techniques to extinguish inappropriate behavior and/or to replace it with appropriate behavior.

While behaviorists do not seek to explain the ultimate causes of social behavior except in the sense that they are learned, their approach holds considerably more promise for understanding and controlling delinquent behavior than the psychoanalytic approach. The behaviorist approach forces us to focus on the specific problem behavior and to recognize that it is learned, so it can—hypothetically at least—be unlearned. With this focus, we are dealing with observable behavior that can be measured, counted, and perhaps modified. Success in modifying behavior in the laboratory has been noted (Krasner and Ullman 1965; Martin and Peas 1978; Paul, Marx, and Orsillo 1999; Echeburua, Fernandez-Montalvo, and Baez 2000). The extent to which this success can be transferred to the world outside the laboratory remains an empirical question (Ross and McKay, 1978; Shelton, Barkley, and Crosswait 2000; Florsheim, Shotorbani, and Guest-Warnick 2000). Think about the difficulties of transferring desirable behavior from the laboratory to the street in the following hypothetical case.

For example, Joe Foul Up, a juvenile, is repeatedly apprehended for fighting. Finally, he is turned over to a therapist who, over a period of several weeks, eliminates the undesirable behavior by punishing (with electric shock, for example) Joe when he begins to exhibit the undesirable behavior and by rewarding him when he exhibits appropriate alternative behavior. After therapy ends, Joe's behavior has been modified and he returns home to his old neighborhood and his old street gang. When Joe refuses to fight, the gang thinks it is appropriate they punish him by calling him a coward and excluding him from gang activities. When he does fight, they reward him by treating him like a hero. What are the chances that the behavior modification that occurred in the laboratory will continue to exist?

We will have more to say about the learning theory or behaviorist approach in the following section.

SOCIOLOGICAL THEORIES

There have been a number of different **sociological theories** of delinquency causation, some dealing with social class and/or family differences (Cohen 1955; Miller 1958; Cloward and Ohlin 1960; Quinney 1975), some with blocked educational and occupational goals (Merton 1938), some with neighborhood and peers (Thrasher 1927; Shaw and McKay 1942; Miller 1958), and some with the effects of official labeling (Becker 1963). Most of these theories share the notion that delinquent behavior is the product of social interaction rather than the result of heredity or personality disturbance. For sociologists, delinquency must be understood in social context. Thus, for example, we must consider time, place, audience, and nature of the behavior involved when studying delinquency.

Anomie and Strain Theory

Beginning in the 1930s in the United States, a number of theorists focused on a systems model to explain crime and delinquency. Adapting Durkheim's theory of **anomie** (a breakdown of social norms or the dissociation of the individual from a general sense of morality of the times), Merton (1938) focused on the discrepancy between societal goals and the legitimate means of attaining those goals. He argued that **strain** is placed upon those who wish to pursue societal goals but lack the legitimate means of doing so. According to Merton, people adapt to this strain in different ways: some attempt to play the game, some retreat (and may become addicts and outcasts), some develop innovative responses (including the illegitimate responses of crime and delinquency), and some rebel (another potential source of crime).

In the 1950s, Cohen (1955) adapted Merton's theory in an attempt to explain juvenile gangs. He argued that the lower class feel the strain of being unsuccessful in middle-class terms, especially in the school setting. Since many lower-class youth find success in school difficult to achieve, they reject middle-class values and seek to gain status by engaging in behaviors contrary to middle-class standards. Thus, they establish their own anti–middle-class value system and, through mutual recruitment, form delinquent gangs. Miller (1958) disagreed with Cohen's theory that lower-class youth acted in terms of inverted middle-class values, and focused on what he called the "focal concerns" (toughness, trouble, smartness, fate, autonomy, and excitement) of the lower social class as the sources of delinquent behavior.

Cloward and Ohlin (1960) extended anomie or strain theory by focusing on the differential opportunities that exist among youth. If an **illegitimate opportunity structure** is readily available, they argue, youth who are experiencing strain or anomie are attracted to that structure and are likely to become involved in delinquent activities.

In 1985, Agnew again revised strain theory by suggesting that rather than pursuing specific goals, many people are simply interested in being treated justly based upon their own efforts and resources. People who do not perceive themselves to be treated fairly experience strain, according to Agnew. Reactions to this perception of unfair treatment may lead to crime and delinquency.

There are numerous criticisms of strain/anomie theory. It tends to focus almost exclusively on lower-class delinquency. It also ignores the effects of labeling and fails to explain why many youth who undoubtedly experience strain do not turn to delinquency as a means of attaining their goals.

The Ecological Approach

The **ecological approach** to explaining crime and delinquency was developed in the 1930s and 1940s and is one of the oldest interest areas of American criminologists. The ecological approach focuses on the geographic distribution of delinquency. Clifford Shaw and Henry McKay (1942), and later others, found that crime and delinquency rates were not distributed equally within cities. They mapped the areas marked by high crime and delinquency rates along with the socioeconomic problems of those areas. Using Ernest Burgess's **concentric zone theory** of city growth (1952), the ecological studies generally found that zones of transition between residential and industrial neighborhoods consistently had the highest rates of crime and delinquency. These zones are characterized by physical deterioration and are located adjacent to the business district of the central city. The neighborhoods in this zone are marked by deteriorating buildings and substandard housing, with accompanying overcrowdedness, lack of sanitation, and generally poor health and safety features. In addition, the area is marked by a transient population, high unemployment rates, poverty, broken homes, and a high adult crime rate. In short, the area is characterized by a general lack of social stability and cohesion.

Judith Wilks (1967) best summarized early ecological studies and their findings on the distribution of delinquency. Her conclusions were:

1. Rates of delinquency and crime vary widely in different neighborhoods and within a city or town.
2. The highest crime and delinquency rates generally occur in the low-rent areas located near the center of the city and the rates decrease with increasing distance from the city center.

Ecological studies examining the distribution of delinquency within cities or towns have found that areas adjacent to the business district of the central city have the greatest incidence of crime and delinquency.

3. High delinquency rate areas tend to maintain their rates over time, although the population composition of the area may change radically within the same time period.
4. Areas which have high rates of truancy also have high rates of juvenile court cases and high rates of male delinquency, and usually have high rates of female delinquency. The differences in area rates reflect differences in community background. High rate areas are characterized by such things as physical deterioration and declining population.
5. The delinquency rates for particular nationality and ethnic groups show the same general tendency as the entire population; namely, they are high in the central area of the city and low as the groups move toward the outskirts of the city.
6. Delinquents living in areas of high delinquency rates are the most likely to become recidivists and are likely to appear in court several times more often than those from areas with low delinquency rates.
7. In summary, delinquency and crime follow the pattern of social and physical structure of the city with concentration occurring in disorganized, deteriorated areas.

According to Wilks, in order to predict delinquency using the ecological approach it is necessary to be aware of the existing social structure, social processes, and the population composition as well as the area's position within the large urban societal complex, since these variables all affect the distribution of delinquency. In general, the ecological approach found that family and neighborhood stability were lacking and that the street environment was the prevailing determinant of behavior. If delinquent behavior is learned behavior, this learning would be maximized in environments such as those in transitional zones. In transitional zones, those agencies or institutions that traditionally produce stability, cohesion, and organization have often been replaced by the street environment of adult criminals and delinquent gangs.

The ecological approach to explaining delinquency has been challenged on the grounds that using only one variable to explain delinquency is not likely to lead to success. In Lander's study (1970) of Baltimore, for example, he found anomie, or normlessness, to be a more appropriate explanation of delinquency rates than socioeconomic area. Nonetheless, follow-up studies by Shaw and McKay (1969) in other American cities (Boston, Philadelphia, Cleveland) support their contention that official delinquency rates decrease from the central city out to the suburbs. Similarly, Lyerly and Skipper (1981) found that significantly less delinquent activity was reported by rural youths than by urban youths in their study of youths in detention. Stark (1987) concluded that certain geographic areas (those characterized by high population density, poverty, transience, dilapidation, etc.) attract deviant people who drive out those who are not so deviant, and these places then become "deviant places" with high crime rates and weak social control. Whatever the cause, the fact remains that high official delinquency rates are found in certain areas or types of areas where serious and repetitive misconduct is not only common, but appears to have become traditional and more or less acceptable. There is a real danger here, however, of drawing false conclusions based upon what has been called the "ecological fallacy." This term refers to false conclusions drawn from analyzing data at one level (the group level, let us say) and applying those conclusions at another level (the individual level). In short, group crime rates tell us nothing about whether a particular individual is likely to become involved in crime (Bohm 2000, p. 71).

Sutherland-Differential Association Theory

Edwin Sutherland (1939) developed what is known as the **theory of differential association.** Sutherland's approach combines some of the principles of behaviorism (or learning theory) with the notion that learning takes place in interaction within social groups. For Sutherland, the primary group (family or gang) is the focal point of learning social behavior, including deviant behavior. In this context, individuals learn how to define different situations as appropriate for law-abiding or law-violating behavior. Therefore, seeing an unattended newsstand might be defined as a situation appropriate to the theft of a newspaper by some passersby, but not by others. The way that a given individual defines a particular situation depends upon that individual's prior life experiences. An individual who has a balance of definitions favorable to law-violating behavior in a given situation is likely to commit a law-violating act. The impact of learned definitions on the individual depends upon how early in life the definitions were learned (priority), how frequently the definitions are reinforced (frequency), the period of time over which such definitions are reinforced (duration), and the importance of the definition to the individual (intensity). (Sutherland, Cressey, and Luckenbill 1992, pp. 88–90).

Sutherland's approach has the advantage of discussing both deviant and normal social behavior as learned phenomena. The approach also indicates that the primary group is crucial in the learning process. In addition, Sutherland suggests some important variables to be considered in determining whether behavior will be criminal or noncriminal in given situations. Finally, Sutherland suggests that it is not differential association with criminal and noncriminal types that determines the individual's behavior, but differential association with, or exposure to, definitions favorable or unfavorable to law-violating behavior.

The learning theory and differential association approaches have been used to try to explain child abuse and neglect as well as delinquency. According to this approach, abusive parents learned abusive behavior when they were abused as children. Thus, child abuse is said to be an intergenerational phenomenon. Kaufman and Zigler (1987: 190), after reviewing self-report data, concluded that the rate of abuse by individuals with a history of abuse is six times higher than in the general population. This finding supports the belief that abusive behavior is learned in primary groups which define it as acceptable behavior (as Sutherland suggests is the case with other forms of deviance). However, other researchers have criticized Kaufman and Zigler and have failed to find a relationship between being abused and abusing. Thus, Knudsen (1992, p. 63) concludes that the cycle of violence appears to be a minor factor in explaining child abuse.

There are a number of criticisms of Sutherland's approach. It is clearly difficult to operationalize the terms *favorable to* and *unfavorable to.* There are serious problems with trying to measure the variable *intensity.* How many exposures to definitions favorable to law violation are required before definitions unfavorable to law violation are outweighed and the individual commits the illegal act? These and other weaknesses have been pointed out over the years by critics of differential association. Nonetheless, there is a certain logic to Sutherland's approach. Some of the propositions are empirically testable, and the description of the learning process seems to be relatively accurate. Sutherland's approach has sensitized us to an approach to understanding crime and delinquency that has been built upon by other theorists and researchers (Glaser 1960; Burgess and Akers 1968; Curran and Renzetti 1994; Akers 1998).

One attempt to improve upon Sutherland's theory has been made by Daniel Glaser (1978). Glaser refers to his theory as the **theory of differential-anticipation** which, in his view, combines differential association and control theory and is compatible with biological and personality theories. Differential-anticipation theory assumes that a person will try to commit a crime wherever and whenever the expectations of gratification from it—as a result of social bonds, differential learning, and perceptions of opportunity—exceed the unfavorable anticipations from these sources (126–27). In short, expectations determine conduct and expectations are determined by social bonds, differential learning, and perceived opportunities. Burgess and Akers (1968) have also expanded upon the learning theory approach developing differential association–differential reinforcement theory. Akers (1985; 1992) later refers to his theoretical approach as social learning theory. This theory holds that social sanctions of engaging in (deviant) behavior may be perceived differently by different individuals. However, as long as these sanctions are perceived as more rewarding than alternative behavior, the deviant behavior will be repeated under similar circumstances. Progression into sustained deviant behavior is promoted to the extent that reinforcement, exposure to deviant models, and definitions are not offset by negative sanctions and definitions. These theories are eclectic in the sense that they extend Sutherland while being compatible with most of the approaches we have discussed above and with labeling theory, to which we now turn our attention.

Labeling Theory

A number of social scientists have contributed to what might be called the "labeling school" of crime/delinquency causation. Howard S. Becker (1963) has discussed the process of labeling deviants as *outsiders.* Kai Erikson (1962) has pointed out the importance of what he calls the labeling "ceremony" for deviants. These authors and others have shifted the focus of attention from the individual deviant (delinquent, criminal, mentally ill, and so forth) to the reaction of the audience observing and labeling the behavior as deviant. As we have indicated repeatedly, it is clear that many individuals commit deviant acts, but only some are dealt with officially. The time at which the act occurs, the place in which it occurs, and the people who observe the act are all important in determining whether or not official action will be taken. Thus, the juvenile using heroin in the privacy of his gang's hangout in front of other gang members is not subject to official action. If, however, he used heroin in a public place in the presence of a police officer who was observing his behavior, official action would be most likely.

From the labeling theorist's point of view, then, society's reaction to deviant behavior is crucially important in understanding who becomes labeled *deviant.* Erikson (1962) discusses the ceremony that deviants typically go through once the decision to take official action has been made. First, the alleged deviant is apprehended (arrested or taken into custody). Second, the individual is confronted, generally at a trial or hearing. Third, the individual is judged (a verdict, disposition, or decision is rendered). Finally, he or she is placed (imprisoned, committed to an institution, or put back in society on probation). The end result is that the individual is officially labeled *deviant.*

One of the consequences of labeling in our society is that, once labeled, the individual may never be able to redeem himself or herself in the eyes of society. Therefore, *John Q. Convict* does not become *John Q. Citizen* upon release from prison. Instead, he becomes *John Q. Ex-Convict.* Having been labeled may make it extremely difficult for the rehabilitated deviant to find employment and establish successful family ties. The more difficult it becomes for the rehabilitated deviant to succeed in the larger society, the greater the chances that he or she will return to old associates and old ways. Of course, these are often the very associates and ways that led the individual to become officially labeled in the first place. Thus, the individual may be more or less forced to continue his or her career in deviance, partially as a result of the labeling itself.

Research by Blankenship and Singh (1976) indicated that a juvenile's prior career of delinquent behavior (the extent to which he or she has been previously officially labeled) is indeed an important determinant of official action. They, and Covington (1984), point out that labeling comes in different forms (legalistic versus peer group, for example) and has different consequences for different types of offenders (whites versus blacks, for instance). If we could assume that society *never* makes a mistake in attaching the label *deviant* and that rehabilitation programs *never* succeed, we might regard the consequences of labeling as somewhat less alarming. As we have already seen in chapters 2 and 3, the assumption that society never makes a mistake is unwarranted. We shall see later that there is at least some hope that rehabilitation programs do succeed. If the end result of official labeling forces the labeled individual back into a deviant career, then, in the case of juveniles at least, we are accomplishing exactly the opposite of what we intended when we created a separate juvenile justice system designed to protect, educate, and treat juveniles rather than to punish them. One of the consequences of negative societal reaction to the label of *delinquent* may be the changing of the delinquent's self-concept, so the individual, like society, begins to think about himself or herself in negative terms. Possibilities for rehabilitation may be lessened as a result.

An interesting contribution to labeling theory has been made by Braithwaite (1989). He discusses what he refers to as "disintegrative shaming" (negative stigmatization) and notes that it is destructive of social identities because it morally condemns and isolates people, but involves no attempt to reintegrate the shamed person at some later time. He contrasts this harmful approach to stigmatization with "reintegrative shaming" in which there is an attempt to reconnect the stigmatized person to the larger society.

The labeling approach accurately describes how individuals become labeled, why some maintain deviant careers, and some of the possible consequences of labeling. It does not deal with the issue of why some individuals initially commit acts that lead them to be labeled, but only with what is referred to as *secondary deviance.* In addition, those who support the approach often lose sight of the fact that the individual is in some way responsible for the actions which are viewed as unacceptable; that is, social audiences do not appear to attach negative labels haphazardly. They are responding to some stimulus presented by the individual committing a crime for which he or she must accept some responsibility (unless we return to a completely deterministic concept of deviance).

Despite some weaknesses, the labeling approach contributes significantly to our understanding of deviance. Through this approach deviance is viewed as a product of social interaction, in which the actions of both the deviant and his or her audience must be considered.

CONFLICT AND RADICAL/CRITICAL/MARXIST THEORIES

Chambliss (1984) describes **conflict theories** of crime as focusing on whole political and economic systems and on class relations in those systems. Conflict theorists argue that conflict is inherent in all societies, not just capitalist societies, and focus on conflict resulting from gender, race, ethnicity, power, and other relationships. Conflict results from competition for power among many groups. Those who are successful in this competition define criminality at any given time. Thus criminal behavior is not viewed as universal or inherent, but as situational and definitional. This view does not account for individual acts of criminality occurring outside the group context, but serves basically to alert us to the social factors that may be related to criminality. Why, for example, do we pass laws with severe sanctions for use of marihuana, but deal with tobacco use among teens much less harshly? Is it because the tobacco lobby is powerful and able to convince legislators that tobacco use among juveniles should, at most, be regulated but not outlawed?

The **Marxist theory** of criminology and delinquency finds the causes of such phenomena in the repression of the lower social classes by the "ruling class." In short, laws are passed and enforced by those who monopolize power against those who are powerless (the poor and minorities, for example). The causal roots of crime are assumed, by many proponents of this approach, to be inherent in the social structure of capitalistic societies. Crime control policies are developed and implemented by those who have power (own the means of production, have wealth, and so on), and these policies serve to criminalize those who threaten the status quo (Vold 1958; Turk 1969; Quinney 1974; 1970; Chambliss and Mandoff 1976; Platt 1977; Beirne and Quinney 1982). Labeling the discontented as criminals and delinquents allows the ruling class to call upon law enforcement officials to deal with such individuals without having to grant legitimacy to their discontent. While there are a number of variations on the theme as discussed here, these are the essential components of most radical or critical explanations of delinquency and crime.

Radical criminology became relatively popular in the United States in the 1960s and 1970s, but its popularity has declined over the past few years and some of its most important spokespersons have abandoned, in part at least, this approach as an explanation of crime and delinquency. Little empirical research has been done which supports the radical/critical approach.

As we have indicated earlier, delinquency appears to be rather uniformly distributed across social classes, contrary to the teachings of the Marxist approach. In addition, as we have indicated earlier, this approach fails to recognize that the legal order serves the purpose of maintaining the system in all known types of societies, including those which claim to be Marxist/communist/socialist (Cox 1975). As Klockars (1979) notes, "The leading figures of American Marxist criminology have not raised the details of Gulag or Cuban solutions to the problems of crime in America, nor have they seriously examined such solutions in states which legitimate them" (p. 477). "Today, it probably makes little sense to speak of capitalist and socialist societies anyway, because no pure societies of either type exist (They probably never did.)" (Bohm 2000, p. 119).

Feminism

Feminism as an approach to studying crime and delinquency focuses on women's experiences, typically in the areas of victimization, gender differences in crime, and differential treatment of women by the justice network. Some feminists focus on equal rights and equal participation for women, some on the ills of capitalist society, and others on the issue of patriarchal oppression (in the form of male control over sex, money, power), which has resulted in second-class citizenship for women in our society. Traditional criminology has certainly largely ignored female crime, raising the issue of whether any of the theories of crime apply directly to women. Further, there are clearly differences in the extent and nature of crime by gender, and there is a question as to whether or not current theories can explain these differences (Daly and Chesney-Lind 1988). Still, the focus on gender as a major determinant of criminal behavior has been seriously questioned since there appears to be limited empirical support for the approach (Akers 1994, p. 177; Bohm 2000, p. 122).

CONTROL THEORIES

Control theories assume that all of us must be held in check or "controlled" if we are to resist the temptation to commit criminal or delinquent acts. The types of systems used to control or check delinquent behavior fall into two categories: personal (internal) and social (external). The containment theory of Walter Reckless (1961; 1967), for instance, emphasizes the importance of both inner controls and external pressures on self-concept. A poor self-concept is thought to increase the chances that a youth will turn to delinquency; a positive self-concept is seen as insulating youth from delinquent activities. Negative self-concepts and low self-esteem have also been frequently noted as characteristics of those who abuse or neglect children (Rosenburg and Repucci 1983; Shorkey and Armendariz 1985).

Hirschi's control theory (1969) places more emphasis on social factors (bonds and attachments) than on inner controls. For example, the term *attachment* is used to refer to the feelings one has toward other persons or groups. The stronger one's attachment to nondelinquent others, the less likely one is to engage in delinquency. The same type of argument is applied to commitment (profits associated with conformity versus losses associated with nonconformity), involvement (in conforming versus nonconforming activities), and beliefs (in the conventional value system versus some less conventional value system). Although these four components of control theory may vary independently, Hirschi believes that in general they vary together. Strong positive ties in each of these four areas minimizes the possibility of delinquency, while strong negative ties maximizes the likelihood of delinquency.

While there is some empirical evidence to support portions of the control-theory approach, this approach leaves unanswered a number of important questions. What is the exact nature of the relationship between self-concept and labeling? How is it that some youth who appear to be well insulated from negative attachments and bonds commit delinquent acts? Do such bonds and attachments themselves actually inhibit delinquent behavior, or are the bonds and attachments perceived by law enforcement and criminal justice personnel simply used to determine whether or not to take official action? Are there longitudinal data which support the approach? Attempts to answer some of these questions are ongoing. In a reanalysis on Hirschi's original data, Costello and Vowell (1999) found support for Hirschi's theory. May (1999) found that social control theory had a significant association with juvenile firearms possession in school. But, Greenberg's reanalysis (1999) of Hirschi's data found that social control theory has only limited explanatory power.

CAREER OPPORTUNITY—CRIMINAL JUSTICE PROFESSOR

Job Description: Teaches courses in the field of criminal justice, criminology, juvenile justice with respect to causes, consequences, extent and nature of crime/delinquency, justice system responses, and problems. Conducts research related to these issues.

Employment Requirements: At least a master's degree and preferably a Ph.D. in criminology, criminal justice, sociology, psychology, law, or a related field.

Beginning Salaries: Between $30,000 and $50,000. Benefits include tenure (job security) for those who are successful as teachers, researchers, and in publishing the results of their research. Other benefits include health and life insurance for the faculty member and his or her family and solid retirement plans.

SUMMARY

We have provided a brief overview of some of the attempts to explain delinquency. It should be clear at this point that, using our definition of theory, few, if any, of these attempts have resulted in explanations that are scientifically sound. Many have been more or less discarded over time, while others continue to provide leads that need to be pursued. Bridging the gap between theory and practice is crucial to control delinquency and to improve the juvenile justice network. The input of practitioners is extremely useful in testing our theoretical statements. The benefits to be reaped, if and when a sound theoretical base is established, are considerable. We can no longer afford to ignore the importance of theory, nor can we continue to rely on commonsense notions of causation, which are, as we have seen, very often inaccurate.

Unlike demonology, which has been largely discounted as an explanation of delinquency today, the classical school of criminology remains important as a basis of our current criminal and juvenile justice networks. Public opinion continues to indicate a belief that severe punishment will deter crime/delinquency and legislatures around the country continue to pass "get tough" measures in the hopes of meeting public expectations. As a result, there is pressure for more arrests, more convictions, and more severe punishment, none of which seem to have accomplished the desired goal, perhaps because of the lack of certainty and swiftness of punishment. Even capital punishment, which certainly deters the subject, has been shown to have little effect on others, and the procedures currently employed are fraught with difficulties leading to moratoria in some states.

Biological theories of causation raise some important issues. While biological factors do not appear to be a direct cause of delinquency, we must remain constantly alert to the possibility that physiological malfunctions or abnormalities may be important in assessing juveniles' behaviors. For example, a juvenile who has become increasingly aggressive, irrational, and uncooperative with others could conceivably be suffering from brain damage (tumor or lesion, for instance) which causes these symptoms. In cases where physical ailments might be related to delinquency, it is obviously best to provide for appropriate medical intervention.

There is always, of course, the possibility that some emotional or psychological difficulty may be present in a specific delinquent. The evidence in support of personality disturbances as causes of delinquency is ambiguous at best, in part due to measurement and definitional difficulties. Nevertheless, the psychological approach to explaining delinquency remains important because psychotherapy of some type—individual or group therapy or counseling—is often prescribed as treatment within correctional facilities. Whether or not such treatment is likely to help remains an empirical question, but some successes are reported.

The sociological school views delinquency as a result of social interaction, learned in much the same way as nondelinquent behavior. According to this approach, much of the juvenile justice network makes sense, but some doesn't. For example, if labeling is an important factor in delinquency, attempts to keep juvenile proceedings confidential makes sense. However, it does not make sense, within this theoretical context, to house minor or first-time delinquents in large institutions with more serious delinquents from whom they are likely to learn additional delinquent behaviors. This may account for our failure to rehabilitate many delinquents in such settings. Additionally, the sociological approach looks for causes of delinquency in society as well as in the individual. It may be that the only way to significantly reduce delinquency rates is to change some social policies, such as those leading to educational and racial discrimination and unemployment. Finally, the sociological approach suggests methods of control and rehabilitation that do not require the death penalty, the practice of eugenics, or complete restructuring of the individual's personality. This approach suggests that positive reinforcement, administered in surroundings in which the juvenile lives, and by those with whom the juvenile regularly interacts, may provide more positive results than many techniques currently employed. While the sociological approach is not a panacea, it does provide a number of leads for future research and treatment that may prove beneficial, provided public and agency cooperation can be obtained.

INTERNET EXERCISES

In chapter 4 the theories of delinquency are discussed. As mentioned in the chapter, there is no one reason why individuals commit crime. There is also no one theory to explain it. Because we cannot identify one single cause of delinquency, programs designed to treat delinquency rely upon a number of theories in their treatment of children. These programs vary from state to state and from child to child. It is the juvenile court's responsibility to determine which program is in the best interests of the child by looking at the aspects of the program and determining if the theory being practiced within the program is what needs to be addressed in the child's life. For example, if a specific treatment program is sponsoring a behavior-modification curriculum that focuses on learned drug behaviors, the juvenile court should only sentence children to that program who demonstrate a need to learn how to relinquish the drug lifestyle they learned from their families, friends, or community.

In order to better understand how programs apply theories of delinquency to treatment and rehabilitation, you must become familiar with a variety of different programs practiced in the United States. In order to familiarize yourself with delinquency programs, visit the Florida Department of Juvenile Justice at *http://www.djj.state.fl.us/delinquency.html.*

1. At the homepage click on Programs and Facilities in the menu section. Choose District 2 from the Florida map provided. Choose Featured Programs from the menu listing.
2. Using the information provided on the featured programs, determine which theories of delinquency are being applied in these treatment programs. What factors or characteristics of the programs led you to this decision? Choose another program listed and determine which theory of delinquency is being applied in that program. What are the major strengths and weaknesses of the program based upon your knowledge of the theory being applied and the program's use of the theory?
3. Next, choose District 14 from the Florida map and click on Featured Programs from the menu listing.
4. After reading about the programs provided, discuss whether or not District 14 relies more heavily on psychological, sociological, or classical theories to treat and explain criminal behaviors. Based upon your knowledge of both districts what is the most popular type of theory being used to treat delinquency?

USEFUL WEBSITES

Causal Theories of Juvenile Delinquency—*http://www.skidmore.edu/academics/english/courses/en205d/student7/gilmooreproj2.html*

Poverty and Juvenile Delinquency—*http://www.chat.carleton.ca/~mrushton/Juveniledelinquency.html*

Murray Research Center—*http://www.radcliffe.edu/murray/data/ds/ds0896.htm*

Strain and Subcultural Theories—*http://www.indiana.edu/~theory/Kip/Strain.htm*

CRITICAL THINKING QUESTIONS

1. What is a scientific theory, and why is the development of such theories crucial to our understanding and control of delinquency?
2. What are the strengths and weaknesses of our current juvenile justice network in terms of the learning theory and labeling theory approaches? Discuss some of the reasons why the classical approach to the control of delinquency has been and continues to be ineffective. Why do you think the approach has remained popular in spite of its ineffectiveness? What contemporary theories are extensions of the classical approach?
3. What are the major strengths and weaknesses of the psychological approach to understanding and controlling delinquency? What has been Freud's impact on the treatment of delinquency?
4. Is there evidence in support of the biological school of delinquency causation? Discuss some of the attempts to demonstrate a relationship between biology and delinquent behavior.
5. What is your overall assessment of the sociological approach to understanding and controlling delinquency? Which of the various attempts in this school do you think do the best job of explaining delinquency? The worst job?

SUGGESTED READINGS

Braithwaite, J. (1989). *Crime, shame and reintegration.* Cambridge: Cambridge University Press.

Cornish, D., & Clarke, R. (1986). *The reasoning criminal: Rational choice perspectives on offending.* New York: Springer-Verlag.

Cullen, F. T., & Agnew, R. (1999). *Criminological theory: Past to present.* Los Angeles: Roxbury.

Genetics and crime (Symposium—March 1996; University of Maryland Conference). *Politics & Life Sciences, 15,* 83–109.

Greenberg, D. F. (1999). The weak strength of social control theory. *Crime and Delinquency, 45* (1), 66–81.

Leshner, A. I. (1998). Addiction is a brain disease—and it matters. *National Institute of Justice Journal,* (237), 2–6.

Lynam, D. R. (1998). Early identification of the fledgling psychopath: Locating the psychopathic child in the current nomenclature. *Journal of Abnormal Psychology, 107,* (4), 566–575.

Paul, R. H., Marx, B. P., & Orsillo, S. M. (1999). Acceptance-based psychotherapy in the treatment of an adjudicated exhibitionist: A case example. *Behavior Therapy, 30* (1), 149–162.

Turkheimer, E. (1998). Heritability and biological explanations. *Psychological Review, 105* (4), 782–791.

CHAPTER

5

PURPOSE AND SCOPE OF JUVENILE COURT ACTS

CHAPTER LEARNING OBJECTIVES

Upon completion of this chapter, students should be able to:

Discuss the purpose and scope of juvenile court acts
Compare and contrast adult and juvenile justice systems
Understand the concepts of stigmatization, jurisdiction, waiver, and double jeopardy
Discuss the constitutional rights of juveniles in court proceedings
List and discuss the various categories of youth covered by juvenile court acts

KEY TERMS

purpose statement of juvenile court acts
scope of juvenile court acts
delinquency cases
neglect cases
abuse cases
dependency cases
adjudicatory hearing
dispositional hearing
petition
Uniform Juvenile Court Act
due process beyond reasonable doubt standard
unruly children/in need of supervision
status offenses
preponderance of evidence standard
exclusive jurisdiction
concurrent jurisdiction
automatic waiver
discretionary waiver
double jeopardy

Since the inception of the juvenile court in 1899, some critics have argued that the court ought to be abandoned. Some feel the court is now far removed from the original concepts upon which it was based or too limited in scope to be viable today. Others feel it is currently incapable of meeting the purposes for which it was created. In this chapter, we will review the purpose and scope of a variety of juvenile court acts in terms of both constitutional requirements and legislative differences among several states.

Every juvenile court act contains sections that discuss purpose and scope. The **purpose statement of a juvenile court act** spells out the

Juvenile court in session.
AP/Wide World

intent or basic philosophy of the act. The **scope of the act** is indicated by sections dealing with definitions, age, jurisdiction, and waiver. In this chapter, we will discuss and refer to the Uniform Juvenile Court Act (1968) which was developed in an attempt to encourage uniformity of purpose, scope, and procedures in the juvenile justice network (a copy of the act is included in appendix A). For purposes of comparison, sections of various state juvenile codes will be presented and analyzed. Revisions of most states' juvenile court acts are now in accord with the recommendations of the Uniform Juvenile Court Act.

Please note that many of the examples we provide are taken from the Illinois Juvenile Court Act. This is true for two reasons. First, the Illinois Juvenile Court Act (the first in the nation) has long been regarded as one of the more progressive in the nation. Second, it is virtually impossible for us (or anyone else for that matter) to keep current on all the changes occurring in all the juvenile court acts around the country. We have chosen to illustrate our points using the law with which we are most familiar. Those using the text in other states are encouraged to provide comparable examples from their juvenile court acts.

PURPOSE

As indicated previously, the first juvenile court act in the United States was passed in Illinois in 1899. By 1945 all states had a juvenile court act within their statutory enactments or constitutions (Tappan 1949). Juvenile court acts typically authorize the creation of a juvenile court with the legal power to hear designated kinds of cases, such as **delinquency, neglect, abuse, dependency,** and other special cases numerated in the acts.

Typically, juvenile court acts establish both procedural and substantive law relative to youths within the court's jurisdiction. Historically, the law was administered in a general atmosphere of rehabilitation and parental concern rather than with punitive overtones. However, recent trends at the federal and state levels appear to have somewhat deemphasized traditional rehabilitative philosophy in favor of a more punitive approach. This change is largely in response to more serious and often violent youth crime and a desire to hold those committing such acts accountable for their actions.

Juvenile court proceedings were conceptualized originally as civil, not criminal, proceedings (Davis 2001: sec. 1.3). As a result of reformers' interests in divorcing the juvenile court from the criminal court in 1899, a separate nomenclature was developed, based upon the philosophy underlying juvenile courts as opposed to criminal courts. This nomenclature is still followed today in spite of the "get tough" approach that has been suggested for serious delinquents.

Comparison of Adult Criminal Justice and Juvenile Justice Systems

As figure 5.1 indicates, we find "a petition alleging that the respondent may have committed a delinquent act," instead of "a complaint charging a defendant with a crime." We find **"adjudicatory"** and **"dispositional" hearings,** instead of a "criminal trial" and "sentencing hearing." The entire proceeding is initiated by a **"petition"** in the "interests of" the juvenile rather than by a "complaint against" the minor. The juvenile, therefore, may not be found "guilty" in juvenile court, but may be "adjudicated delinquent." Juve-

Figure 5.1 Comparison of Adult Criminal Justice and Juvenile Justice Systems

Adult	Juvenile
Arrest	Taking into Custody
Preliminary Hearing	Preliminary Conference/Detention Hearing (both optional)
Grand Jury/Information/Indictment	Petition
Arraignment	—
Criminal Trial	Adjudicatory Hearing
Sentencing Hearing	Dispositional Hearing
Sentence—Probation, Incarceration, etc.	Disposition—Probation, Incarceration, etc.
Appeal	Appeal

nile court acts are predicated on the basic assumption that all personnel involved in the juvenile justice system act in the best interests of the juvenile. There are, however, differences of opinion concerning how to best ensure the interests of the juvenile. In August 1968, in the hope of bringing some uniformity to legal definitions of delinquency and delinquency proceedings, the National Conference of Commissioners on Uniform State Laws drafted and recommended for enactment in all the states a **Uniform Juvenile Court Act.** This act was approved by the American Bar Association at its annual meeting during the same year. Since that time, the Uniform Juvenile Court Act has served as a model for states to follow in developing their own acts.

In essence, section 1 of the Uniform Juvenile Court Act reaffirms the basic philosophy of all juvenile court acts by specifically stating that the major purpose of the act is "to provide for the care, protection, and wholesome moral, mental, and physical development of children coming within its provisions" (*Uniform Juvenile Court Act* 1968: sec. 1). This basic philosophy was first stated in the Cook County Juvenile Court Act of 1899 and has been stated in each state's juvenile court act adopted or revised since then. The philosophy has been controversial because of the questionable ability of the juvenile justice network to provide the specified benefits to juveniles. Considerable documentation exists on the deficiencies of the state's ability to provide for the welfare of juveniles. A week seldom passes where a column in a newspaper or an article in a journal or magazine does not relate an instance of neglect by the state in its parental role (see In Practice 5.1). Although the philosophy of providing "care, guidance, and protection" is well entrenched in the juvenile justice network, it would appear that a reevaluation of the state's effectiveness in adhering to that philosophy is in order.

Other basic themes expressed in the Uniform Juvenile Court Act include protecting juveniles who commit delinquent acts from the taint of criminality and punishment and substituting treatment, training, and rehabilitation; keeping the juvenile within the family whenever possible and separating the juvenile from his or her parents only when necessary for his or her welfare or in the interest of public safety; and providing a simple judicial procedure to execute and enforce the act, yet, one which ensures a fair hearing with constitutional and other legal rights recognized and enforced. We will now discuss each of these philosophical themes.

In Practice 5.1

OBSERVERS DECRY APPROACH TO DELINQUENT GIRLS

Curtis Krueger

The number of girls in the juvenile justice system is rising, and officials say intervention efforts must grow, too.

With a father in prison and a mother who wasn't around, Sherri started running with the wrong friends, dabbling in drugs, feeling suicidal. Eventually her troubles snowballed: She was sent to juvenile court and locked up in a program for delinquents.

Sherri, 16, came to a gathering of child advocates Thursday who say Florida's juvenile justice system is sending girls like her down the wrong path—into detention centers and locked institutions, instead of programs that could keep them out of trouble in the first place.

"I know there are better alternatives out there to being locked up," said Sherri, now an excellent student at the PACE Center for Girls, a school for teenagers who have faced similar troubles. She spoke to the group on the condition her full name not be used.

Luanne Panacek agrees. She's executive director of the Hillsborough Children's Board, which sponsored Thursday's meeting. The event was designed to show that Florida should be increasing prevention efforts, in contrast to the Juvenile Justice department's current plan to reduce their budget.

It's a serious problem in Florida, where one in four juvenile offenders are now girls, according to state figures.

In Thursday's meeting, Leslie Acoca, of the San Francisco–based National Council on Crime and Delinquency, said statewide figures show juvenile charges against girls increased 30 percent between 1993 and 1998, and just 5 percent for boys in Florida.

Protecting the Juvenile from Stigmatization

For a long time, some states allowed a wide variety of activities to be labeled *delinquent.* However, a majority of states have revised their juvenile codes and changed their legal definitions of acts considered delinquent. At issue is the difference between unthinking, mischievous misbehavior of a nonserious nature and vicious, intentional conduct that endangers life and property. It is difficult to ascertain exactly when mischievous behavior ends and vicious conduct begins. As a result, we sometimes encounter cases where the hard-core delinquent has benefited from the treatment/rehabilitation philosophy of the juvenile court to the point where any concept of justice or accountability has been eliminated. The same is true for those who abuse or neglect their children to an extent that raises concern, but where it is difficult to determine whether the legal standards required for abuse/neglect have been satisfied. Similarly, we sometimes note that mischievous youth are treated as

Interviews and a review of 1,000 girls' case files in Duval County showed that girls who were truant were five times as likely as other girls to get into trouble. They were three times as likely if they had family members who had been incarcerated, and two times as likely if they had poor grades or had been pregnant.

Overall, data show that "school failure is more linked to entry into the juvenile justice system for girls than it is for boys," she said.

All that points to education over incarceration, or deciding "whether or not we're going to go toward handcuffs or classrooms for girls," Acoca said. She recommended that the state halt any plans to expand a prison-like program for delinquent girls in Palm Beach County and put more effort on reaching academically struggling middle school girls.

Vicki Adelson, a Clearwater-based consultant, recently completed a Hillsborough County study that says it's not uncommon for a girl to be locked up in moderate- or maximum-risk programs—"for her own sake"—when caseworkers think her family can't support her.

Speakers on Thursday echoed critics who recently have charged that the Department of Juvenile Justice is backing away from prevention efforts by cutting $16-million—or more, if necessary—from programs aimed at preventing delinquency, truancy, and other problems.

But department spokeswoman Diane Hirth said "we're on the same wavelength" with many of the speaker's recommendations. She said the department strongly believes "we need to target early intervention and services to girls and also to their families in a very strong and positive manner."

One prevention initiative cited by Juvenile Justice Secretary William Bankhead in a recent interview is called intensive delinquency diversion, which provides close supervision and family support to first-time offenders who are considered highly likely to become habitual juvenile offenders. The program works with girls and boys.

"That's the kind of female juvenile offender we're going to be helping intensively that we did not before," Hirth said Thursday.

Bankhead said his department has been forced to adjust to a difficult budget year and belt-tightening directives.

Krueger, C. (2000, December 15). Observers decry approach to delinquent girls. *St. Petersburg Times*, p. 3B.

hard-core delinquents. Clearly, rehabilitation and treatment might be helpful to both mischievous offenders and hard-core delinquents, as well as for children who are abused or neglected. For the mischievous offender, a variety of rehabilitative/treatment programs have been developed as alternatives to punishment and are more or less effective in community-based agencies. For delinquents who commit serious offenses, rehabilitative/treatment programs have been typically located in institutions. Some serious juvenile offenders learn how to "play the game" and are able to shift all responsibility for their actions to others or to society and therefore escape accountability under the rehabilitative/treatment philosophy. Such offenders and/or their attorneys are able to convince juvenile court judges, prosecutors, and the police to "give them a break." Others, less skilled at "playing the game," or unable to retain private counsel, may be unable to escape more serious consequences for acts that may be less serious. The dilemma facing reformers of the juvenile court revolves around the obvious—avoid labeling juveniles who don't deserve the label *delinquent* and at the same time prevent the juvenile court from becoming so informal that those who are a threat to the community remain at large.

Maintaining the Family Unit

The concept that a child should remain in the family unit whenever possible is another basic element of the Uniform Juvenile Court Act. The child and family are not to be separated unless there is a serious threat to the welfare of the child or society. However, once there is an established necessity for removing the child, the juvenile court must have the power to move swiftly in that direction. Determining exactly when it is necessary to remove the youth is not, of course, an easy task. Careful investigation of the total family environment and its effect on the juvenile is typically required in cases of suspected abuse, neglect, and delinquency. Removal may be permanent or it may include an option to return the child if circumstances improve. Careful consideration is given to the family's attitudes toward the child and the past record of relationships among other family members.

While most of us would agree that it is generally desirable to maintain the family unit, there are certainly circumstances when removal is in the best interests of both the minor and society. The welfare of the child is clearly jeopardized by keeping him or her in a family where gross neglect, abuse, or acts of criminality occur. The emphasis placed upon maintaining the integrity of the family unit seems at times to be taken so seriously by juvenile court judges and other juvenile justice practitioners that they maintain family ties even when removal is clearly the better alternative (see In Practice 5.2).

Preserving Constitutional Rights in Juvenile Court Proceedings

The Uniform Juvenile Court Act provides judicial procedures so all parties are assured fairness and recognition of legal rights. The early philosophy of informal hearings void of legal procedures and evidentiary standards has a limited place in the modern juvenile justice network. The application of due process standards has not deterred the court from its rehabilitative pursuits. If the issue is delinquency and the act for which the child has been accused is theft, then the procedural rules of evidence should support the allegation and the result would be an adjudication of delinquency. If the evidence does not support the allegation, no adjudication of delinquency should occur. In an informal hearing where there is an absence of established guilt and where an adjudication of delinquency is based upon the attitude of the child, the types of peers with whom that child associates, or his or her family's condition, the rights of the juvenile and perhaps other parties have been violated. The philosophy of a fair hearing, where constitutional rights are recognized and enforced and where a high standard of proof to establish delinquency is strictly enforced, has been generally established in juvenile court acts since 1967, when the United States Supreme Court decided in the *Gault* case (*In re Gault,* 387 U.S. 1, 78–81 [1967]) that **due process** (observing constitutional guarantees and rules of exclusion) was generally required in juvenile court adjudicatory proceedings. Informality is generally accepted in postadjudicatory hearings on disposition of the juvenile and is often permitted in prehearing stages. The adjudicatory hearing for delinquency must, however, be based on establishing **beyond a reasonable doubt** (with as little doubt as possible) that the allegations are supported by the admissible evidence.

The general purpose of juvenile court acts, then, is to ensure the welfare of juveniles while protecting their constitutional rights in such a way that removal from the family

In Practice 5.2

STATE'S HUMAN RESOURCES DIRECTOR RESIGNS

Charles Yoo

The head of Georgia's Department of Human Resources has resigned after an 18-month tenure in which she tried to reshape the troubled agency.

Commissioner Audrey Horne inherited the state's largest department just before revelations that a high number of children in Georgia had died after their families were reported for mistreatment to the agency's Division of Family and Children Services. Horne has said her department would need more than $27 million in enhancements next year to help improve the badly flawed child protection system.

She will leave the office Dec. 31 to work at Georgia State University's Andrew Young School of Policy Studies as a consultant on health issues, according to Joselyn Butler, a spokeswoman for Gov. Roy Barnes. Horne was unavailable for comment Monday night.

"Her determination and commitment have allowed us to make significant strides in the level of service the department provides for all Georgians," Barnes said in a statement.

Barnes named Gary Redding, director of the Division of Medical Assistance for the Department of the Community Health, interim DHR commissioner.

The 1998 death of 5-year-old Terrell Peterson, who weighed only 29 pounds after months of abuse, shed a light on the inadequacies of DFCS.

"I'm so sorry to see her go," said Sen. Nadine Thomas (D-Ellenwood), vice chairwoman of the Health and Human Services Committee. "I thought she was doing a good job considering the situation she went into. She was thrown in and had a lot of cleaning up to do."

DHR's new leader must tackle problems such as the department's low morale and the need for speedier database computerization, said Mary Margaret Oliver, a former state senator who focused on children's issues. "Anybody who is the commissioner of HR will have a very hard job," she said.

Yoo, C. (2000, December 19). State's human resources director resigns. *The Atlanta Journal and Constitution*, p. 1A.

unit is accomplished only for a reasonable cause and in the best interests of the juvenile and society. A review of your state's juvenile court act should reflect these basic goals.

SCOPE

In addition to the basic themes previously discussed, all juvenile court acts define the ages and subject matter (conduct) within the scope of the court.

Age

Section 2 of the Uniform Juvenile Court Act defines a *child* as a person who is under the age of eighteen years; or under the age of twenty-one years, but who committed an act of delinquency before reaching the age of eighteen years; or under twenty-one years who committed an act of delinquency after becoming eighteen years and is transferred to the juvenile court by another court having jurisdiction over him or her (*Uniform Juvenile Court Act* 1968: sec. 2).

As stated in chapter 2, both upper and lower age limits vary among the states (see your state's code). The Uniform Juvenile Court Act establishes the age of eighteen as the legal age where actions of an illegal nature will be considered criminal and the wrongdoer will be considered accountable and responsible as an adult. Prior to the eighteenth birthday, illegal activities will be considered acts of delinquency with the wrongdoer processed by the juvenile court in a way that removes the taint of criminality and punishment and substitutes treatment, training, and rehabilitation in its place. The Uniform Juvenile Court Act allows two exceptions regarding the legal jurisdictional age of eighteen. Section 2 (1, iii) states that a person under the age of twenty-one, who commits an act of delinquency after becoming eighteen, can be transferred to the juvenile court by another court having jurisdiction and therefore would be accorded all of the protection and procedural guidelines of the juvenile court. Section 34 allows for a transfer to other courts of a child under eighteen, if serious acts of delinquency are alleged and the child was sixteen or older at the time of the alleged conduct (*Uniform Juvenile Court Act* 1968: sec. 34). There are stringent guidelines to follow before a waiver to adult court jurisdiction may be permitted. Waivers of juvenile jurisdiction are occurring more and more frequently and will be discussed later in this chapter.

In establishing the age of eighteen as the legal breakpoint between childhood and adulthood, two thirds of the states are consistent with the Uniform Juvenile Court Act. As we have indicated elsewhere, there is no clearly established minimum age set by juvenile courts with respect to their jurisdiction. Thus children may be found to be neglected at or before birth (by reason of drug addiction of the mother, for example). Some states adhere to the common law presumption that children under the age of seven cannot be presumed to be able to form intent and therefore cannot commit a crime (delinquent act).

Delinquent Acts

The Uniform Juvenile Court Act clearly limits the definition of delinquency by stating in essence that a delinquent act is an act designated as a crime by local ordinance, state law, or federal law. Excluded from acts constituting delinquency are vague activities, such as incorrigibility, ungovernability, habitually disobedient, and other status offenses, which are legal offenses only applicable to children and not to adults. At the time the Uniform Juvenile Court Act was drafted in 1968, many states legally defined delinquency as encompassing a broad spectrum of behavior. The proposal by the drafters of the Uniform Juvenile Court Act excluded the broader definition of activities labeled as *delinquent* and focused only on violations of laws that are applicable to both adults and minors. This narrow interpretation was consistent with the legalistic trend occurring in the latter 1960s. By narrowing the legal definition of delinquency, the Uniform Juvenile Court Act did not ignore other types of activities that fall within the court's jurisdiction, but placed these activities outside the realm of delinquent acts. A minor who is "beyond the control of his parents," "habitually truant from school," or "habitually disobedient, uncontrolled, wayward, incorrigible, indecent, or deports himself or herself as to injure or endanger the morals or health of themself or others" was at one time considered to be delinquent in some states

(*Ind. Code Ann.* 31-37-1-1 to 31-37-2-6: 1997). The number of states with such a broad definition of delinquency is decreasing. A major difficulty with including these vague activities within the delinquent behavior category concerns the issue of who defines what is incorrigible, indecent, or habitual misconduct and the nature of the standard used to determine this behavior. These statutory expressions and a number of others like them have invited challenge on the grounds that they are unconstitutionally vague. There are no standardized definitions for *habitual, wayward, incorrigible,* and so on. As a result, such charges in conjunction with delinquency will inevitably be challenged in the courts.

It is interesting to note that prior to the development of the Uniform Juvenile Court Act in 1968, several states had already started restricting the definition of *delinquency* to include only those activities that would be punishable as crimes if committed by adults. For example, in New York under the pre-1962 Children's Court Act, the term *juvenile delinquency* included ungovernability and incorrigibility. However, in 1962, the Joint Legislative Committee on Court Reorganization, which drafted the Family Court Act (*New York Sessions Laws,* vol. 2, 3428, 3434, McKinney: 1962), developed the concept of a "person in need of supervision" to cover noncriminal status offenses and the term *juvenile delinquent* was narrowed to include only persons over seven and less than sixteen years who commit any act that, if committed by an adult, would constitute a crime. With a more specific definition of delinquency, it was inevitable that due process procedures, rules of evidence, and constitutional rights would emerge as important issues in Supreme Court decisions involving the rights of juveniles in delinquency proceedings. As the states moved toward a more specific definition of delinquency, additional appellate decisions were rendered regarding "due process and fair treatment." The effect of this narrow interpretation of delinquency has been the advent of an adjudicatory process that is more formalized and that ensures and protects the juvenile's procedural and constitutional rights. This trend is clearly consistent with the spirit behind the creation of the Uniform Juvenile Court Act. Some states even list all forms of conduct subject to juvenile court jurisdiction in one general category (*Mich. Comp. Laws Ann.* 712A.2 Supp.: 1999; *Neb. Rev. Stat. 43–247: 1998; Utah Code Ann.* 78-3a-104 (1) Supp.: 1999).

Section 2(3) of the Uniform Juvenile Court Act indicates that an adjudicated delinquent is in need of "treatment or rehabilitation." The development of narrower definitions of delinquency and more formalized "due process models" is not intended to cause the juvenile court to abandon rehabilitation and treatment. This philosophy was stated as early as 1909, when it was pointed out that "the goal of the juvenile court is not so much to crush but to develop, not to make the juvenile a criminal but a worthy citizen" (*Consolidated Laws of New York Ann.* bk. 29A, art. 7, McKinney: 1975). This initial concept of rehabilitation and treatment has been affirmed in many decisions and is briefly summarized by the Supreme Court case, in re *Gault,* where the Court reaffirms the original juvenile court philosophy that "the child is to be 'treated' and 'rehabilitated' and the procedures, from apprehension through institutionalization, are to be 'clinical' rather than 'punitive' " (Faust and Brantingham 1974: 369–370). It is important to remember that although it operates under the "treatment and rehabilitation" concept, the juvenile court is also charged with protecting the community against unlawful and violent conduct. To fulfill this obligation the court may resort to incarceration or imprisonment. This clash between the rehabilitative ideal and the clear, present necessity to protect the community in certain situations has been described as the "schizophrenic nature" of the juvenile court process (*Consolidated Laws of New York*

Ann. bk. 29A, art. 7, McKinney: 1975). In North Carolina, for example, if a minor is thirteen years of age and commits what would be a class A felony, waiver to adult court is automatic (*N.C. Gen. Stat.* 7B-2200: 1999). Other states have followed suit, mostly with respect to violent crimes, and some have given the prosecutors discretion as to which court to use (*Ariz. Rev. Stat. Ann.* 13-501 (A) West Supp.: 1999; *Conn. Gen. Stat. Ann.* 466-127 (a) West Supp.: 1999; *Wyo. Stat. Ann.* 14-6-203 (c)–(f), 14-6-211, Michie: 1999; *La. Children's' Code Ann.* art. 305 (B) West Supp.: 1999).

It is clear that a majority of the states have moved toward a narrower definition of delinquency. Inherent in this trend is the movement toward formalizing the legal procedures and processes accorded the accused delinquent. The importance of this trend is twofold. First, legal definitions of delinquency have become more standardized and by law require a violation or attempted violation of the criminal code. Second, the process of proving the allegation of delinquency may include only the same types of evidentiary materials that would be admitted if the same charges were leveled against an adult. This is a considerable change from past practices in many juvenile courts where much of the evidentiary material that was introduced to prove an act of delinquency was basically irrelevant material concerning the juvenile's family, peers, school behavior, and other information about his or her environment. The establishment of reasonable proof that the juvenile did violate the law was lost in the process. The case was often weighed and decided on factors other than establishing, beyond reasonable doubt, that the juvenile committed the act for which he or she had been accused. The juvenile court is a court of law. The juvenile adjudicatory process and the juvenile court must be totally dedicated to working within a legal framework that is conducive to reaching the truth and serving the ends of justice. To do otherwise would result in what is best described in an often-quoted passage of the Kent decision, where the Supreme Court stated:

> There is evidence . . . that the child receives the worse of both worlds; that he gets neither the protections accorded to adults nor the solicitous care and regenerative treatment postulated for children. (Justice Fortas in *Kent v. United States,* 383 U.S. 541, 546 1966)

Without a doubt, there is a place in the juvenile justice network for consideration of the adjudicated delinquent's family and his or her environment. However, such consideration should be given only after an adjudication of delinquency rather than used as the basis for adjudication. For instance, suppose as an adult you have been accused of "breaking and entering" and throughout the pretrial process and during the course of the trial almost all of the evidence and information introduced centers around your family, your associations, your attitude, and your overall environment. Furthermore, only a minimum amount of court time and effort is devoted toward establishing beyond a doubt that you did in fact violate the law by breaking and entering and even then most of this evidence is hearsay, not subjected to cross-examination, and based on belief rather than proof. Yet, you are convicted. Such cases were fairly common in the juvenile justice system until the *Gault* decision in 1967. The focus on due process to protect the accused juvenile's constitutional rights is as important as determining whether the act was committed by the accused. The legal issue of delinquency must be determined not on the basis of a social investigation describing the minor's environment, but on the basis of whether the evidence supports or denies the allegation of delinquent acts.

Unruly Children

Section 2(4) of the Uniform Juvenile Court Act defines an unruly child as a child who

> (i) while subject to compulsory school attendance is habitually and without justification truant from school;
> (ii) is habitually disobedient of the reasonable and lawful commands of his parent, guardian, or other custodian and is ungovernable; or
> (iii) has committed an offense applicable only to a child; and
> (iv) in any of the foregoing is in need of treatment or rehabilitation.

At one time, a majority of states included these activities in the category of delinquent behavior and that often resulted in the official label of *delinquent* and led to the possibility of being incarcerated in a juvenile correctional institution for treatment and rehabilitation. The Uniform Juvenile Court Act recognizes that such activities may require the aid and services provided by the juvenile court but also recognizes that these minors should not be included in the category *delinquent.* According to section 32 of the Uniform Juvenile Court Act, the unruly child cannot be placed in a correctional institution unless the court finds after a further hearing that the child is not amenable to treatment or rehabilitation under a previous noncorrectional disposition.

The **unruly child** is generally characterized by activities that are noncriminal or minor violations of law. Types of offenses, such as curfew violations or running away from home, are referred to as **status offenses** or acts that are offenses only because of the age of the offender. If the same act were committed by an adult, it would not be a violation of law. A substantial number of states have separated the types of activities described as unruly by the Uniform Juvenile Court Act from delinquency and have placed them in the nondelinquent category of **in need of supervision** (*District of Columbia Code* 16–2301(8): 1997; *New York Family Court Act* 712(a) McKinney: 1999; *S.D. Cod. Laws Ann.* 26-8B-02: 1999).

Regardless of the title, the importance of the development of this category lies in separating the delinquent from the nonserious violator and in realizing that the behavioral activities included in the categories *unruly child* or *child in need of supervision/ assistance* are often symptomatic of problems in the juvenile's home life and environment and may not indicate criminal tendencies. The *unruly child* category allows the juvenile court to be involved with the minor who needs supervision and allows the court flexibility and options short of the label *delinquent.* Still, the labels *unruly child* or *in need of supervision* may become terms of disrepute and produce a stigmatizing effect on the juvenile similar to the label *delinquent.* As a result, one of the major benefits of the distinction is lost.

To further distinguish the differences between the delinquent and the unruly child, most states have developed different procedural requirements. These requirements allow the civil **standard of preponderance of evidence** in the adjudicatory hearing for the latter, where the bulk of the evidence, but not necessarily all of it, must support the charges. They also provide for different dispositional options and for different upper ages for the category of *unruly* or *in need of supervision.* Again, reviewing your state's juvenile code will provide information on how these issues are addressed in your jurisdiction.

In distinguishing between juveniles whose misconduct is criminal and those whose misconduct is not, it is assumed that the unruly child's behavior may be of a predelinquent nature and that early remedial treatment might prevent the incipient delinquency. However, it may be that the unruly child has more intense emotional and behavioral problems than some delinquents who commit a single criminal act or a series of minor criminal acts.

The *unruly* or *in need of supervision* categories are generally written without specificity since it is difficult to define and describe all of the noncriminal (delinquent) conduct that could ultimately fall within these categories. The term *habitually* is frequently used to distinguish between isolated incidents and a recurring pattern of incorrigibility, ungovernability, or disobedience. The flagrant, repetitive nature of these behaviors often serves as the basis for filing a petition.

It was noted earlier that in some instances the behavior engaged in by the juvenile and alleged in a petition (often filed by the parents) may actually reflect neglect rather than an unruly child. A lack of parental supervision, whether due to unwillingness or inability of the parents, may have created a situation within the family that resulted in the juvenile's behavior. This behavior, although alleged to be "unruly" in the petition, may have been precipitated by a family crisis resulting in the minor rebelling against the family.

Deprived, Neglected, or Dependent Children

In section 2(5) of the Uniform Juvenile Court Act, a "deprived" child is defined as a child under the age of eighteen who

> (i) is without proper parental care or control, subsistence, education as required by law, or other care or control necessary for his physical, mental, or emotional health, or morals, and the deprivation is not due primarily to the lack of financial means of his parents, guardian, or other custodian;
> (ii) has been placed for care or adoption in violation of law; {or}
> (iii) has been abandoned by his parents, guardian, or other custodian: {or}
> (iv) is without a parent, guardian, or legal custodian.

A number of jurisdictions use a single classification to describe a child who is without a parent or who has been abandoned, abused, or is without adequate parental care or supervision. Such a child is variously referred to as a "dependent child" (*Alabama Code* 12-15-1(10): 1995; *ILCS* Ch. 705, art. 2, sec. 405/2–4: 1999), a "deprived child" (*Georgia Code Ann.* 15-11-2(8): 1999; *N.D. Cent. Code* 27-20-02(5): 1999), or a "neglected child" (*District of Columbia Code* 16-2301(9): 1997; *Wyo. Stat. Ann.* 14-3-402 (a) (xii) Michie: 1999: 1991).

Some states separate deprived children into several categories with specific labels. For example, the category *neglected minor* includes any minor who is neglected as to proper or necessary support, education as required by law, or as to medical or other remedial care recognized under state law or other care necessary for his/her well-being, including food, clothing, and shelter, or who is abandoned by his/her parents, guardian, or custodian or whose environment is injurious to his or her welfare; or a newborn infant whose blood or urine contains any amount of a controlled substance not as a result of medical treatment (*ILCS* ch. 705, art. 2, sec. 405/2-3-1: 1999).

Within the neglect language of some codes is a special section on abused youth who are minors under a given age whose parent or immediate family member, custodian, or any person living in the same family or household, or a paramour of the minor's parent: (1) inflicts, causes to be inflicted, or allows to be inflicted physical injury which causes death, disfigurement, impairment of physical or emotional health, or loss or impairment of any bodily function; or (2) creates a substantial risk of physical injury, or (3) commits or allows to be committed any sex offense; or (4) commits or allows to be committed acts of torture; or (5) inflicts excessive corporal punishment (*ILCS* ch. 705, art. 2, sec. 405/2-(i)-(v): 1999).

Frequently, juvenile court acts have a special "dependent child" provision for children under a specified age who have no living parent, who have been abandoned, or who lack adequate parental care or supervision (*Ala. Code* 12-15-1 (10): 1995; *Ga. Code* 15-11-2 (8) Supp.: 1999; *N.D. Cent. Code* 27-20-02 (8) Supp.: 1999; *District of Columbia Code* 16–2301: 1997; *Wyo. Stat. Ann.* 14-3-402 (a) (xii) Michie: 1999). Illinois, for example, has a separate category for "dependent minors" which generally includes youth below a given age who are: (1) without a parent, guardian or legal custodian; or (2) without proper care because of the physical or mental disability of his or her parent, guardian, or custodian; or (3) without proper medical or remedial care or other care necessary for his or her well-being through no fault, neglect, or lack of concern by his or her parents, guardian, or custodian; or (4) who have a parent, guardian, or legal custodian who with good cause, wishes to be relieved of all residual parental rights and responsibilities, guardianship, or custody, and who desires the appointment of a guardian of the person with power to consent to the adoption of the minor (*ILCS* ch. 705, art. 2, sec. 405/2–4: 1999).

Even though the Uniform Juvenile Court Act specifically disallows "a lack of financial means" as a basis for alleging that a minor is a "deprived child," some states, under circumstances where the deprivation is so extreme that it seriously endangers the well-being of the child, provide for handling these cases under the "neglected child" portion of the juvenile court act. Deprivation may be considered "gross neglect," if the amount of parental income is sufficient, but the income is misappropriated and jeopardizes the well-being of the children within the family. Appropriate juvenile court remedies are generally available for this type of deprivation. According to Sanford Fox (1984, p. 58), "where a statutory distinction is made between a neglected child and one who is dependent, the difference generally is a matter of the presence of some parental fault in the former case and its absence in the latter." The Illinois distinction between the neglected child and dependent child clearly illustrates the difference between the "parental fault concept" for the "neglected" child and the "no fault concept" for the "dependent" child. Regardless of the statutory definitions of *deprived, neglected, abused,* or *dependent child,* it is quite clear that the situations described in these statutes exist basically through no fault of the child.

Jurisdiction

The jurisdiction of a court concerns persons, behavior, and relationships over which the court may exercise authority. The word *jurisdiction* also may be used to describe geographical areas or to describe the process through which the juvenile court acquires authority to make orders concerning particular individuals. As Regoli and Hewitt (1994) point out, the question of jurisdiction is of basic importance to the juvenile court judge; without jurisdiction over the subject matter and the subject, that judge's court has no power to act. The term *jurisdiction* means, "the legal power, right, or authority to hear and determine a cause or causes" (Regoli and Hewitt 1994: 390). Jurisdiction is created and defined in juvenile court acts.

There is a distinction between the juvenile court's inherent jurisdictional powers and its discretion to exercise jurisdiction over a case. For example, the statutory law creating the juvenile court in a state may give that court exclusive jurisdiction in any proceeding involving cases of delinquency, unruly children, dependency, or neglect, provided the respondent is within the age range and geographical area specified by the court. However, unless a petition is duly filed and the respondent receives a copy or summary of the petition as well as adequate notification of when and where the allegations against him or her will be presented and heard, the court has not exercised proper jurisdiction over the case.

In some states the juvenile court act has been repealed and a broader family court act has been created allowing for broader jurisdictional powers over virtually all problems directly involving families (*N.Y. Fam. Ct. Act* 301.2 (1) McKinney: 1999; *Tex. Fam. Code Ann. 51.02 West: 1996*). Adoptions, divorces, proceedings concerning mentally retarded or mentally ill children, custody and support of children, paternity suits, and certain criminal offenses committed by one family member against another are all within the jurisdiction of some family court acts. It is important to note, however, that for the most part, those adults who abuse or neglect their children are subject to prosecution not in juvenile courts, but in criminal courts. The children who are abused or neglected may nonetheless be removed from their homes and placed in shelter care or other living arrangements by the juvenile court judge and/or the state department of children and family services.

Age is obviously an important factor in determining jurisdiction in all states. As previously stated, age limits for delinquency vary among the states. The majority of juvenile court acts are silent on the lower age limits; however, in some states the common-law age of seven has been established by statute as the lower age limit for delinquency. Statutes in sixteen states define the minimum age for delinquency (North Carolina specifies six years of age, Maryland, Massachussettes, New York specify seven years of age, Arizona specifies eight, and a number of states specify ten) (Bilchik 1999, p. 9). In the remaining states, it is technically possible that a child could be adjudicated delinquent from birth. Such adjudication is unlikely since the juvenile court requires a reasonable degree of capacity, such as the ability to understand the act and to know or appreciate its consequences (*In re William A.,* 313 Md. 690, 548 A.2d 130 (1998); *In re Register,* 84 N.C. App. 336, 352 S.E.2d 889 (1987) [dictum]).

The unruly child or child in need of supervision has been generally subjected to the same upper age limit for jurisdictional purposes as the delinquent. Since common law does not deal directly with this category; the common-law age of seven has not been traditionally recognized as the minimum age for the unruly child.

Determining the upper or lower age limits in delinquency raises difficult questions about the factor of responsibility and accountability in law. For example, a child of six, who is fully aware of the wrongfulness of a criminal act and its consequences and still commits the act, will be immune from prosecution if the jurisdictional age of seven is part of the state's juvenile court act. Another child, who is less mature at seven years, may commit the same act while unaware of its consequences and may have to face juvenile court.

States differ about whether a juvenile who commits a delinquent act while within the age jurisdiction of the juvenile court, but who is not apprehended until he or she has passed the maximum age of jurisdiction, can be handled as a juvenile. Some states have determined through court decisions or previous statutory enactments that it is the age at the time of the offense that determines jurisdiction and not the age at the time of apprehension. The Uniform Juvenile Court Act in section 2(1, iii) allows a person under twenty-one who commits an act of delinquency before reaching the age of eighteen to be considered a child and within the juvenile court's jurisdiction for delinquency proceedings.

States differentiate between the upper ages for delinquency and other categories; they believe that a minor may still need the care and protection of the family even though he or she is beyond the age for an adjudication of delinquency. Similarly, the "deprived," "neglected," "abused," or "dependent child" is generally not subject to a lower age limit, since a younger child may have a greater need for the protection of the juvenile court than an older counterpart. Currently, some states have set one age for all categories included in the juvenile court act, while others have different ages for each category. For example, Texas defines a child as a person ten years or older, but under seventeen, or over seventeen, but under eighteen years of age, respectively, for wardship petition or delinquency petition (*Tex. Fam. Code Ann.* 15.02 (2) West: 1996). Illinois continues to follow different ages for delinquency–up to the seventeenth birthday and for a "minor requiring authoritative intervention," "dependency," "abused," and "neglect"–up to the eighteenth birthday (*ILCS* ch. 705, sec. 405/2-3; 405/2-4; 405/3-3; and 405/5-105 (3): 1999). The Uniform Juvenile Court Act recommends in section 2 the establishment of an upper age of eighteen for all categories.

Concurrent or Exclusive Jurisdiction

The issue of concurrent or exclusive jurisdiction of the juvenile court is generally determined by the legislature and specifically stated in the juvenile court act. The Uniform Juvenile Court Act in section 3 provides the juvenile court with exclusive jurisdiction of certain proceedings listed in that section. In effect, **exclusive jurisdiction** means that the juvenile court will be the only tribunal legally empowered to proceed and that all other courts are deprived of jurisdiction. In some juvenile court acts, **concurrent jurisdiction** may be present when certain specified situations exist. For example, certain criminal acts may be concurrently under the jurisdiction of the juvenile court and the criminal court (*Ark. Code Ann.* 9-27-318 © Michie Supp.: 1999; *Colo. Rev. Stat.* 19-2-517 (1): 1999; *Fla. Stat. Ann.* 985.225 West Supp.: 1999; *Mich. Comp. Laws Ann.* 712 A2d West Supp.: 1999). The court that acts first may exercise jurisdiction over a case, not because the court has exclusive jurisdiction but simply because it exercises its jurisdiction before the other court acts. In some states, juvenile court acts may allow exclusive jurisdiction over adults who play a role in encouraging a minor to violate a law. In other states, this jurisdiction may be concurrent with the criminal court. In still other states, the juvenile court may have no jurisdiction over such adults, so exclusive jurisdiction rests with the criminal courts. In order to determine if the juvenile court has exclusive or concurrent jurisdiction over the subject matter and the subject, it is necessary to refer to the juvenile court act of the state in question. Concurrent jurisdiction is at times awkward (*Md. Cts. & Jud. Proc. Code Ann.* 3-804 (e) (1), (4): 1998; *Iowa Code Ann.* 232.8 (1) (c) West Supp.: 1999; *Miss. Code Ann.* 43-21-105 (j), 43-21-159 (4) Supp.: 1999). Every state has a statutory scheme for waiving jurisdiction in the best interests of the minor and/or in the best interests of the community.

In section 4 of the Uniform Juvenile Court Act, provision is made for the juvenile court to have concurrent jurisdiction with another court where the proceedings are to treat or commit a mentally retarded or mentally ill child.

Waiver

As previously stated, statutory provisions in juvenile court acts have given juvenile courts original and exclusive jurisdiction over certain cases if the subject is within the defined jurisdiction. However, juvenile court acts contain provisions for the waiver of the juvenile court's jurisdiction over certain offenses committed by minors of certain ages. Policies regarding waiver of juveniles to the criminal justice system differ from state to state. In some states the juvenile judge is the decision maker. In others, the prosecutor has been given the discretion to file certain types of cases in criminal court.

The waiver should not be confused with concurrent jurisdiction where two courts have simultaneous jurisdiction over the subject matter and the subject. *Waiver,* in this case, refers to the process by which a juvenile over whom the juvenile court has original jurisdiction is transferred to adult criminal court. Most authorities agree that the waiver represents a critical stage of the juvenile justice process. At this point, the juvenile may lose the *parens patriae* protection of the juvenile court, including its emphasis on treatment and rehabilitation as opposed to punishment. Once transferred (waived) to the criminal justice network, the juvenile is subjected to contact with adult offenders, may obtain a criminal record, and finds himself or herself in a generally vulnerable position. In some states an **automatic waiver** of the exclusive jurisdiction of the juvenile court occurs when specific offenses are allegedly committed by a juvenile. For example, in Illinois, "any minor alleged to have committed a traffic, boating or fish and game violation or an offense punishable by fine only, may be prosecuted therefore and if found guilty punished under any statute or ordinance relating thereto without reference to the procedures set out in the Juvenile Court Act of this state" (*ILCS* ch. 705, art. v, sec. 405/5-125: 1999).

Among jurisdictions that permit waivers, the provisions setting forth the circumstances under which such waivers may be granted are quite varied. Most jurisdictions require that the child be over a certain age and that he/she be charged with a particularly serious offense before jurisdiction may be waived (*Colo. Rev. Statutes* 19-2-518 (1): 1999; *La. Children's' Code Ann.* art. 857 West Supp.: 1999; *Conn. Gen. Stat. Ann.* 46b-127 West Supp.: 1999; *Mich Comp Laws Ann.* 712A 4 (1) West Supp.: 1999; *N.J. Stat. Ann.* 2A:4A-27 West Supp.: 1999).

For the most part, automatic waivers are restricted to the more serious offenses and to lesser offenses, such as traffic violations. Even in the most serious offenses, an automatic waiver may occur only if the youth involved is over a certain age. For example, in Indiana, the youth must be over the age of ten before a waiver is possible for murder (*Ind. Code Ann.* 31-30-3-2-0-6 Michie: 1997). In Illinois, a waiver may occur if the minor is thirteen or older and the alleged act constitutes a crime under the laws of the state (*ILCS* ch. 705, sec. 405/5-805 (1)-(3): 1999). Other states authorize waivers similarly (see figure 5.2), if the jurisdictional age is established and met and the specific offense is within the statutory allowance for such a waiver. In some states with statutory exclusion provisions, certain types of juvenile cases originate in criminal rather than juvenile court.

Another type of waiver is the **discretionary waiver.** A number of states permit waivers of jurisdiction over children above a certain age without regard to the nature of

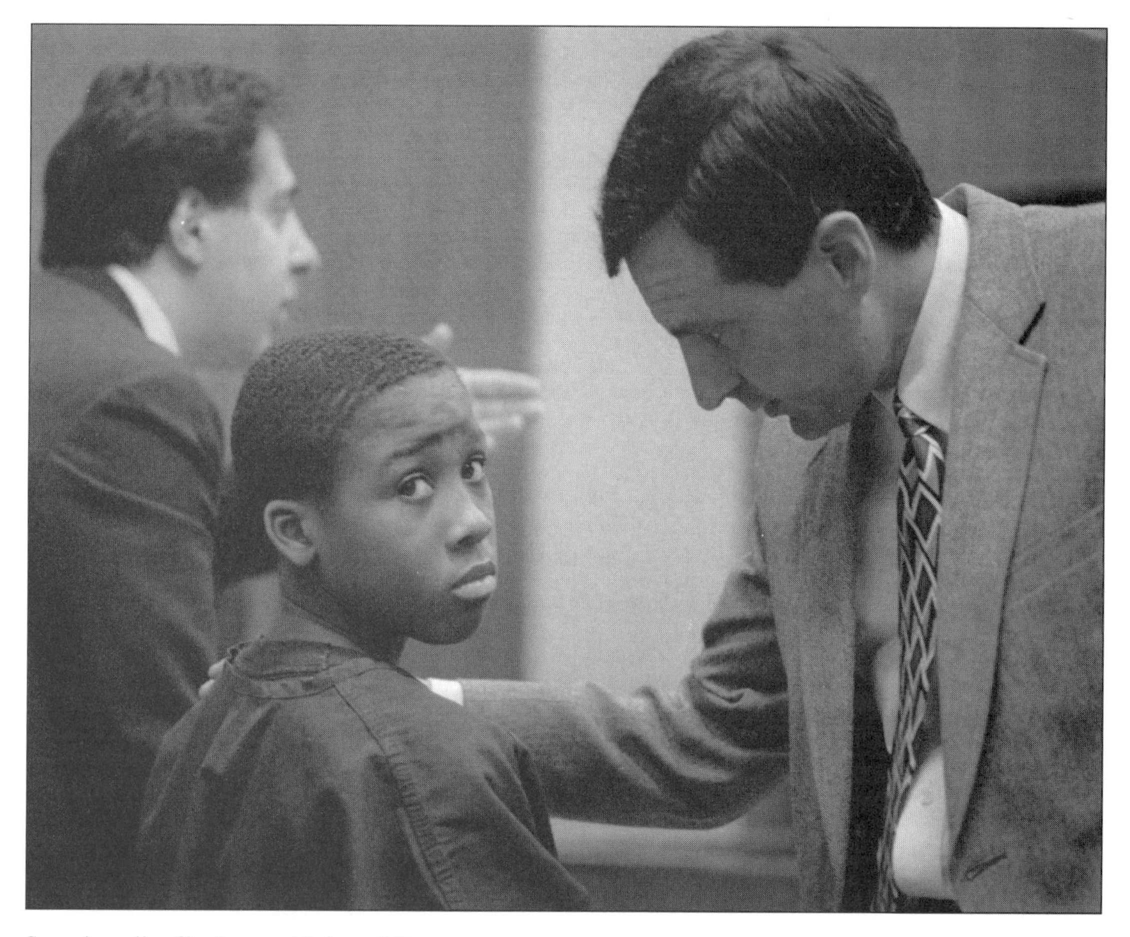

Some juvenile offenders are tried as adults.
Richard Sheinwald/AP/Wide World

the offense involved. Where the juvenile court finds that the minor is not a fit and proper subject to be dealt with under the juvenile court act and the seriousness of the offense demands that the best interests of society be considered, the juvenile court judge may order criminal proceedings to be instituted against the minor (Bilchik 1999, p. 16).

Discretionary determination of waivers may be left to juvenile court judges to decide after a petition for a waiver has been filed and a hearing has been conducted on the advisability of granting the waiver. In general, the criteria used by juvenile court judges to determine the granting or denial of waivers of juveniles to criminal courts are rather vague and, for the most part, quite subjective. As previously stated, "if the minor is not a fit and proper subject to be dealt with under the Juvenile Court," an order instituting criminal proceedings may be rendered by the juvenile court. Factors typically cited by the courts as weighing heavily in the decision to waive jurisdiction include the seriousness of the offense, the age of the juvenile, and the past history of the juvenile. However, some jurisdictions confer upon the prosecutor the authority to decide which court (juvenile or criminal) should hear the case. Wyoming empowers the prosecutor to make this decision when a juvenile is

Figure 5.2 State Transfer Provision

Summary of Transfer Provisions, 1997

State	Judicial Waiver			Direct File	Statutory Exclusion	Reverse Waiver	Once an Adult/ Always an Adult
	Discretionary	Mandatory	Presumptive				
Total States:	46	14	15	15	28	23	31
Alabama	■				■		■
Alaska	■		■		■		
Arizona	■		■*	■	■	■	■
Arkansas	■			■		■	
California	■		■				■
Colorado	■		■	■		■	
Connecticut		■				■	
Delaware	■	■			■	■	■
Dist. of Columbia	■		■	■			■
Florida	■			■	■		■
Georgia	■	■		■	■	■	
Hawaii	■				(r-97)		■
Idaho	■				■		■
Illinois	■	■	■		■		
Indiana	■	■			■		■
Iowa	■				■	■	■
Kansas	■		■		(r-96)		■
Kentucky	■	■				■	
Louisiana	■	■		■	■		
Maine	■						■
Maryland	■				■	■	
Massachusetts	(r-96)			■	■		
Michigan	■			■			■
Minnesota	■		■		■		■
Mississippi	■				■	■	■
Missouri	■						■
Montana	■			■	■		
Nebraska				■		■	
Nevada	■		■		■	■	■
New Hampshire	■		■				■
New Jersey	■		■				
New Mexico					■		
New York					■	■	
North Carolina	■	■					
North Dakota	■	■	■				■
Ohio	■	■					■
Oklahoma	■			■	■	■	■
Oregon	■				■	■	■
Pennsylvania	■		■		■	■	■

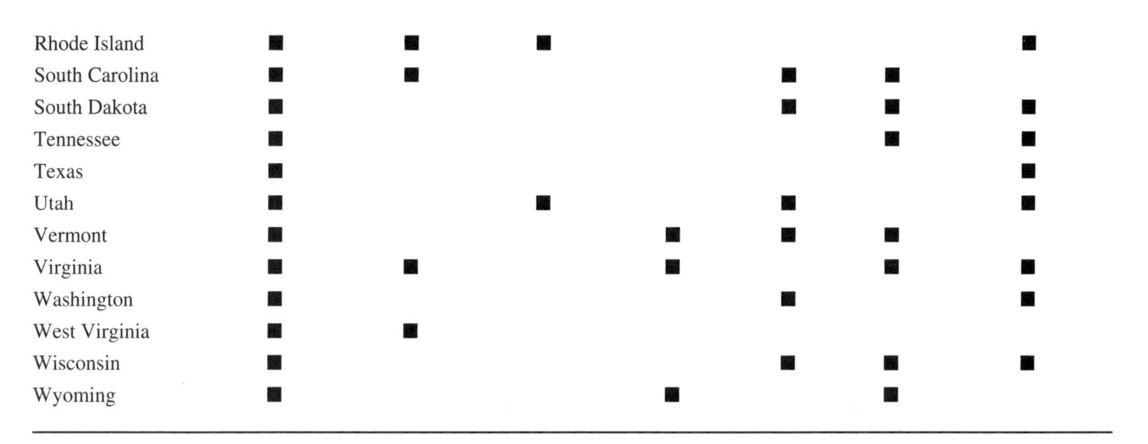

Rhode Island	■	■	■				■
South Carolina	■	■			■	■	
South Dakota	■				■	■	■
Tennessee	■					■	■
Texas	■						■
Utah	■		■		■		■
Vermont	■			■	■	■	
Virginia	■	■		■		■	■
Washington	■				■		■
West Virginia	■	■					
Wisconsin	■				■	■	■
Wyoming	■			■		■	

Legend: ■ indicates the provision(s) allowed by each State as of the end of the 1997 legislative session; "r" indicates repealed; * indicates by court rule.

Discretionary waiver- at the discretion of the juvenile court judge.

Mandatory waiver- law mandates waiver.

Presumptive waiver- there is a presumption that a waiver will be granted.

Direct file- the prosecutor determines whether to file a case in juvenile or adult court.

Statutory exclusion- grant criminal courts jurisdiction over a whole class of cases involving juveniles.

Reverse waiver- case moved from criminal to juvenile court.

Adapted from: Office of Juvenile Justice and Delinquency Prevention. (1998, December). *Trying juveniles as adults in criminal court: An analysis of state transfer provisions.* Washington, D.C.: U.S. Government Printing Office.

charged with a misdemeanor, or if the juvenile is seventeen or older and charged with a felony, or is fourteen or older and is charged with a violent felony, or is charged with a felony and has been adjudicated delinquent twice previously for felonies (*Wyo. Statutes Ann.* 14-6-203 (c)–(f), 14-6-211): 1999. Likewise, in Arizona the prosecutor has discretion to file charges in criminal court against any child fourteen or older alleged to have committed a Class 1 or 2 felony or certain offenses of Class 3, 4, 5, and 6 felonies (Ariz. Rev. Statutes Ann. 13-501 (B): 1999). In Louisiana, the prosecutor has discretion in cases involving youth fifteen or older charged with attempted first- or second-degree murder, manslaughter, armed robbery, aggravated burglary, and numerous other offenses including some drug-related offenses (Lo. Children's Code Ann. Art. 305 (B): 2000). Similar prosecutorial discretion can be seen in numerous other states and the District of Columbia.

With respect to waivers, in the case of *Kent v. U.S.* (1966), the Supreme Court ruled that in order to protect the constitutional rights of the juvenile, the juvenile is entitled to

1. a full hearing on the issue of a waiver,
2. the assistance of legal counsel at the hearing,
3. full access to the social records, used to determine whether such transfer should be made,
4. statement of the reasons why the juvenile judge decided to waive the juvenile to (adult) criminal court. (*Kent v. United States,* 383 U.S. 541, [1966])

In *Kent,* the Supreme Court held that a waiver of jurisdiction is a critically important stage in the juvenile process that must be considered in terms of due process and fair treatment as required by the fourteenth Amendment. Although the *Kent* decision applied only to the District of Columbia, most states that allow waivers have incorporated the waiver procedures of *Kent* into their juvenile court acts. A clear majority of states statutorily guarantee a waiver hearing.

Some states have attempted to establish at least some criteria that would aid the juvenile court judge in making a determination on a motion to waive the juvenile court's jurisdiction. For example, in Illinois, the court must consider the following:

1. the seriousness of the alleged offense;
2. whether there is evidence that the alleged offense was committed in an aggressive and premeditated manner;
3. the age of the minor;
4. the previous delinquency history of the minor;
5. the culpability of the minor;
6. whether there are facilities particularly available to the juvenile court for the treatment and rehabilitation of the minor;
7. whether the best interest of the minor and the security of the public may require that the minor continue in custody or under supervision for a period extending beyond his minority; and
8. whether the minor possessed a deadly weapon when committing the alleged offense (*ILCS* ch. 705, art. v, sec. 405/5-805 (3) (b): 1999).

The juvenile court judge, as well as the prosecuting officials, must weigh the consequences of a waiver for the future of the juvenile. The question, concerning a waiver of a juvenile to the adult criminal court for prosecution of offenses that might result in a felony record, is extremely important due to the lasting effects that a felony record might have. To justify a waiver for criminal prosecution, the juvenile court must agree to accept the more punitive, retributive, and punishment-oriented approach of the adult court. In such cases, not only must the juvenile court judge act "in the best interest of the minor," but also in the best interest of the community by protecting the community against further unlawful and perhaps violent conduct by the juvenile offender. Juvenile court judges, realizing the full effect of a felony record (in terms of future employment, for example), generally permit a waiver for criminal prosecution only when the offense is so serious that relegating the offense to the realm of delinquency would be unconscionable and would result in a mockery of justice and when the offense is not an isolated act but a series of acts showing a trend toward becoming more serious.

Double Jeopardy

The Fifth Amendment states that no person shall be subject to being tried twice for the same offense. Courts in the United States at one time held that the **double jeopardy** clause did not prohibit a juvenile adjudicated delinquent from subsequently being tried for the same offense in criminal court. In *Breed v. Jones* (421 U.S. 519 [1975]), the Supreme Court unanimously ruled that the Fifth Amendment's prohibition against double jeopardy precludes criminal prosecution of a juvenile subsequent to proceedings in juvenile court involving the same act.

After dealing with scope and purpose, most juvenile court acts go on to describe in detail the procedures to be employed by various components of the juvenile justice system in handling the juvenile. We will discuss these procedural requirements in the following chapter.

CAREER OPPORTUNITY—COURT ADMINISTRATOR

Job Description: Assists the chief judge in scheduling the court calendar; ensures correct assignment of cases; sees that appropriate transfer of cases occurs; coordinates judges schedules; may help plan court security.

Employment Requirements: Must have a four-year degree; prior administrative experience may be required.

Beginning Salaries: Between $20,000 and $40,000 depending upon jurisdiction. Benefits vary widely, but are typically included.

SUMMARY

A thorough understanding of both the purpose and scope of juvenile court acts is crucial since, without this understanding, the intent of the juvenile court acts cannot be carried out.

The primary purpose of juvenile court acts is to ensure the welfare of the juvenile within a legal framework while maintaining the family unit and protecting the public. Most of us would agree that this is an admirable goal. At the same time, however, we should be aware of the inherent difficulties of achieving this goal. Consider, for example, the police officer who has apprehended a particular juvenile a number of times for increasingly serious offenses. Repeated attempts at enlisting the aid of the youth's family in correcting the undesirable behavior have failed. If the officer decides that protection of the public is now of primary importance, the officer may feel compelled to arrest the juvenile, even though this action may result in the juvenile being sent to a detention facility. As a result, the family unit is broken up and the welfare of the juvenile has been, to some extent, sacrificed by placing him or her in detention.

Also consider the dilemma of the juvenile court judge who must make the final decision concerning what is in the best interests of both the juvenile and the public. If he or she adheres to the philosophy of the juvenile court, the judge may be tempted to leave the juvenile with his or her family, even though the public may suffer. In addition, the judge and prosecutor are faced with the difficult task of making distinctions between *unruly* and *delinquent* juveniles. These distinctions are crucial, since different types of treatment, correctional, and rehabilitation programs are available depending upon the label attached.

A thorough understanding of the scope of juvenile court acts is equally important. The police officer on the street must be aware of both the age limits and the different categories into which juveniles are separated, if the requirements of the juvenile court act are to be met. Prosecutors and judges must be certain that jurisdictional requirements have been met and must understand the consequences of requesting or granting waivers. In short, the purposes of juvenile court acts cannot be achieved without thorough knowledge of the subjects and behaviors dealt with in the scope of such acts.

The purposes of juvenile court acts are, in general, to create courts with the authority to hear designated kinds of cases, to discuss the procedural rules to be used in such cases, and to provide for the best interests of juveniles while at the same time protecting the interests of the family and society. Unfortunately, it is not always possible to achieve all of these purposes in any one case. For example, it might be in the best interests of society to send a particular juvenile to a correctional facility, but this action is not likely to be in the best interests of the juvenile.

Sections in juvenile court acts dealing with scope generally include information on age requirements, geographical requirements, types of behaviors covered by the act, and waivers.

The Uniform Juvenile Court Act requires legal accountability, narrows the definition of delinquency (excludes status offenses), and attempts to ensure the best interests of juveniles while maintaining the family unit and protecting the public.

In 1967, the President's Commission on Law Enforcement and Administration of Justice recommended that serious thought be given to completely eliminating from juvenile court jurisdiction youth who commit noncriminal acts, or status offenses. Consistent with this recommendation, two national commissions (the American Bar Association Standards Project in 1977 and the Twentieth Century Task Force on Sentencing Policy Toward Youthful Offenders, 1978) proposed the elimination of juvenile court jurisdiction over status offenders, and most states have followed this recommendation.

INTERNET EXERCISES

Chapter 5 discusses the purpose and scope of the juvenile court as stated in the Uniform Juvenile Court Act of 1968. All states have juvenile court acts that state the purpose and scope of their respective juvenile courts. Because the federal Uniform Juvenile Court Act is not mandated to the states, each state's juvenile court act may differ in magnitude from the Uniform Juvenile Court Act depending upon the individual state's delinquency and at-risk needs. View Missouri Compiled Statutes regarding juvenile court by visiting *http://www.moga.state.mo.us/STATUTES/C211.HTM.*

1. First, read Section 211.011, "Purpose of Law—How Construed," for similarities and differences from the purpose of juvenile court provided by the Uniform Juvenile Court Act of 1968. Discuss the similarities and differences you find between the two juvenile court acts.
2. Click on Section 211.031, "Juvenile Court to Have Exclusive Jurisdiction, When—Exceptions." After reading the information provided, provide an example of when the Missouri juvenile court would not have jurisdiction of a child and an example of when the Missouri juvenile court would have jurisdiction of a status offender. Explain when the Missouri juvenile court has and does not have exclusive jurisdiction of juveniles.
3. By looking at the Missouri Compiled Statutes juvenile chapter, identify which types of children the Missouri juvenile court has jurisdiction over. What types of dispositions does the Missouri juvenile court have available to it with regard to each type of juvenile?
4. Using Section 211.071, "Certification of Juvenile for Trial as Adult—Procedure—Mandatory Hearing, Certain Offenses—Misrepresentation of Age, Effect" discuss whether or not the Missouri juvenile court provides for the *parens patriae* doctrine to those children who are waived to adult court. Does the Missouri juvenile court provide for the requirements of the *Kent vs. U.S.* (1966) decision in their certification

procedures? Discuss how these requirements are met. If the Missouri juvenile court does not meet the *Kent* requirements, explain what is missing from the court's proceedings.

USEFUL WEBSITES

The 'lectric Law Library—*http://www.lectlaw.com*

Virtual Law Library—*http://www.law.indiana.edu/law/v-lib/lawindex.html*

Legal Information Institute—*http://www.law.cornell.edu/topics/juvenile.html*

Legal Online—*http://www.legalonline.com*

CRITICAL THINKING QUESTIONS

1. In addition to protecting the community from youthful offenders, what are the three major purposes or goals of juvenile court acts?
2. How and why did the Uniform Juvenile Court Act (see appendix A) come into existence? Has this act had much impact on the various state juvenile court acts? Give some examples to support your answer.
3. What are some of the considerations of jurisdiction that fall within the scope of juvenile court acts? Why are these considerations important?
4. Suppose a juvenile, age fifteen, is taken before juvenile court in the county in which he resides for allegedly repeatedly refusing to obey his parents' orders to be home before ten o'clock at night. Would such behavior fall within the scope of most juvenile court acts? Would the youth be dealt with as a delinquent under Uniform Juvenile Court Act recommendations? If not, why?

SUGGESTED READINGS

Anderson, D. C. (1998). When should kids go to jail? *American Prospect,* (38), 72–78.

Bilchik, S. (1999). Juvenile justice: A century of change. *1999 National Report Series—Juvenile Justice Bulletin.* Washington, D.C.: U. S. Department of Justice.

Davis, S. M. (2001). *Rights of juveniles: The juvenile justice system.* 3rd ed. New York: Clark Boardman and Callaghan.

Gondles, J. A., Jr. (1997). Kids are kids, not adults. *Corrections Today, 59,* 6.

Howell, S. (1996). Juvenile transfers to the criminal justice system: State of the art. *Law & Policy, 18* (1 & 2), 17–60.

Palmer, E. A. (2000). Weary of juvenile justice logjam, members move provisions separately (Aimee's law). *CQ Weekly, 58* (29), 1727–1728.

Redding, R. E. (1999). Examining legal issues: Juvenile offenders in criminal court and adult prison. *Corrections Today, 61* (2), 92–95.

Schwartz, I. M., Weiner, N. A., & Enosh, G. (1999). Myopic justice? The juvenile court and child welfare systems. *Annals of the American Academy of Political & Social Science, 564,* 126–141.

Snyder, H., & Sickmund, M. (2000). *Juvenile transfers to criminal court in the 1990's: Lessons learned from four studies: Report.* Washington, D.C.: U.S. Department of Justice, Office of Juvenile Justice and Delinquency Prevention.

Van Vleet, R. K. (1999). The attack on juvenile justice. *Annals of the American Academy of Political & Social Science, 564,* 203–214.

Winner, L., Lanza-Kaduce, L., Bishop, D., & Frazier, C. (1997). The transfer of juveniles to criminal court: Re-examining recidivism over the long term. *Rime & Delinquency, 43,* 548–563.

CHAPTER

6 Juvenile Justice Procedures

Chapter Learning Objectives

Upon completion of this chapter, students should be able to:

Understand and discuss juvenile court procedures
Discuss the rights of juveniles at various stages, from taking into custody through appeals
Understand requirements for bail, notification, and filing of petitions
Discuss procedures involved in detaining juveniles

Key Terms

petition
stationhouse adjustment
preliminary conference
totality of circumstances
guardian ad litem
Fourth Amendment
bail
taking into custody
interrogation
detention hearing
shelter care
notification
adjudicatory hearing
Sixth Amendment
beyond a reasonable doubt
clear and convincing evidence
continuance under supervision
social background investigation
dispositional hearing
unruly child
appeals

Juvenile court acts not only discuss the purposes and scope of the juvenile justice system, but also discuss the procedure the juvenile courts are to follow. Proceedings concerning juveniles officially begin with the filing of a **petition** alleging that a juvenile is delinquent, dependent, neglected, abused, in need of supervision, or requiring authoritative intervention. Most juvenile court acts, however, also discuss the unofficial or diversionary activities available as remedies prior to the filing of a petition such as **stationhouse adjustments** or **preliminary conferences.** Stationhouse adjustments occur when a police officer negotiates a settlement with the juvenile and, often, his/her parents, without taking further official action. A

Judge addresses a juvenile and his lawyer.
Billy E. Barnes/Photo Edit

preliminary conference is a voluntary meeting arranged by a juvenile probation officer with the victim, the juvenile, and typically the juvenile's parents or guardian in an attempt to negotiate a settlement without taking further official action. Juvenile court acts clearly indicate those persons who are eligible to file a petition. For example, in Illinois,

> any adult person (over the age of 21), agency or association by its representative may file a petition, or the court on its own motion may direct the filing through the State's Attorney of a petition in respect to a minor under the Act. (*ILCS.* ch. 705, art. 1, sec. 405/1-3: 1999)

While it is true that a petition may be filed by any eligible person by going directly to the prosecutor (state's attorney, district attorney), a large proportion of petitions are filed following police action or by social service agencies dealing with minors. In order to understand the step-by-step procedures involved in processing juveniles, we will discuss the typical sequence of events occurring after the police take a juvenile into custody. We will rely heavily upon the procedures given in the Uniform Juvenile Court Act and the Illinois Juvenile Court Act, which closely resemble similar acts in many states. While a general discussion of juvenile justice procedures will be given, some states differ with respect to specific requirements. You should consult the juvenile court act or code relevant to your state for exact procedural requirements.

Rights of Juveniles

Regardless of the particular jurisdiction, juveniles in the United States have been (since the 1967 *Gault* decision) guaranteed a number of basic rights at the adjudicatory stage. Thus, a juvenile who is alleged to be delinquent has the following rights:

1. the right to notice of the charges and time to prepare for the case;
2. the right to counsel;
3. the right to confront and cross-examine witnesses; and
4. the right to remain silent in court. (*In re Gault,* 387 U.S. 1 [1967])

As a direct result of the *Gault* decision, the constitutional guarantees of the Fifth and Sixth Amendments are applicable to states through the Fourteenth Amendment and apply not only to delinquency matters, but have been extended to some cases involving the need for supervision or intervention. The question remaining after the *Gault* decision concerned the extent to which its mandate logically extended to other stages of the juvenile justice process, particularly the police investigatory process. *Gault* and the *Kent* decision (*Kent v. U.S.,* 385 U.S. 541 [1966]) have been interpreted to require the application of the Fourth Amendment and the exclusionary rule to the juvenile justice process. The most difficult issue has revolved around the juvenile's competency to waive his/her rights under *Miranda.* Generally, the courts have relied upon a **totality of circumstances** approach in determining the validity of the waiver. Circumstances considered include the age, competency, and educational level of the juvenile, his/her ability to understand the nature of the charges, and the methods used in and length of the interrogation (Davis 2000: sec. 3.13, pp. 3-86–3-90).

The Uniform Juvenile Court Act (1968: sec. 26) provides that all parties to juvenile court proceedings are entitled to representation by counsel. Many jurisdictions currently provide for representation by counsel in neglect, abuse, and dependency proceedings, which extends the *Gault* decision to such cases (*Ga. Code Ann.* 15-11-31(b): 1999; *Mont.*

Code Ann. 41-5-331 (1): 1999; *N.M. Stat. Ann.* 32-A-Z-14 (c) Michie: 1995). In neglect and abuse cases, legal counsel for the minor may be the state's attorney, who represents the state that has a duty to protect the child. In addition, the court may also appoint a **guardian ad litem** for a juvenile, if the juvenile has no parent or guardian appearing on his or her behalf or if the parents' or guardians' interests conflict with the juvenile's.

The protection afforded by the **Fourth Amendment** against illegal search and seizure extends to juveniles. All courts that have specifically considered the issue of the applicability of the Fourth Amendment to the juvenile justice process have found it applicable, or more correctly, none have found it inapplicable (Davis 2000: 3–17). The Uniform Juvenile Court Act (1968: sec. 27(b)) states that evidence seized illegally will not be admitted over objection. Similarly, a valid confession made by a juvenile out of court is, in the words of the Uniform Juvenile Court Act, "insufficient to support an adjudication of delinquency unless it is corroborated in whole or in part by other evidence." This extends some protection to juveniles not normally accorded to adults. In addition, the Uniform Juvenile Court Act (sec. 27(a)) recommends that a party be entitled to introduce evidence and otherwise be heard in his or her own behalf and to cross-examine adverse witnesses. Furthermore, a juvenile accused of a delinquent act need not be a witness against or otherwise incriminate himself or herself. A majority of juvenile court acts do not spell out a detailed code of evidence. However, most do specify whether the rules permit only competent, material, and relevant evidence and whether the rules of evidence that apply in criminal or civil cases are applicable in juvenile cases. A number of states provide that the rules of evidence applicable in criminal cases apply in delinquency proceedings and the rules of evidence applicable in civil cases apply in other proceedings (i.e., neglect, dependency, and in-need-of-supervision cases).

The Children's Bureau of the Department of Health and Human Services recommended many years ago that, unless the child is advised by counsel, the statements of a child made while in the custody of the police or probation officers, including statements made during a preliminary inquiry, predisposition study, or consent decree, not be used against the child prior to the determination of the petition's allegations in delinquency, in-need-of-supervision/intervention cases, or in a criminal proceeding prior to conviction (Children's Bureau 1969: sec. 26). In abuse and neglect cases, however, the courts have eased restrictions on the admission of spontaneous utterances, statements made in the totality of circumstances and so on (see chapter 11).

It should be noted that some rights guaranteed adults are not guaranteed juveniles in most jurisdictions. As a result of the ***McKeiver* decision** (*McKeiver v. Pa.,* 403 U.S. 528 [1971]), juveniles are not generally guaranteed the right to a trial by jury or a public trial. The Supreme Court, in deciding *McKeiver,* indicated that a jury was not necessary for fact-finding purposes and left the issue of trial by jury up to the individual states. While the majority of jurisdictions provide for hearings without juries, some provide for jury trials by statute or judicial decision (*Col. Rev. Stat. Ann.* 19-2-107: 1999; *Mont. Code. Ann.* 41-5-1502 (1): 1999; *W. Va. Code* 49-5-6: 1999; *Mass. Gen. Laws Ann.* ch. 119, sec. 55A, West Supp: 1999; *Mich. Comp. Laws Ann.* 712A.17 (2) West Supp: 1993). In addition, the *McKeiver* decision leaves open the question of whether juvenile court proceedings are necessarily adversary in nature, and left upon the states the burden of establishing that a separate justice system for juveniles represents a useful alternative to criminal processing. There is a clear-cut trend toward treating all juvenile court procedures as adversarial.

BAIL

The issue of **bail** (release from custody pending trial after payment of a court-ordered sum) for juveniles is also controversial at present. Some jurisdictions permit bail, whereas others do not on the grounds that the juvenile has not been charged with a crime and is, therefore, not entitled to bail. Because of special release provisions for juveniles (to the custody of parents or guardians), bail has not been a question of paramount concern in terms of litigation. A number of states forbid the use of bail with respect to juveniles (*Hawaii Rev. Stat.* 571-32 (h): 1993; *Oregon Rev. Stat.* 419C. 179: 1995; *Conn. Gen. Stat. Ann.* 466-133b, West: 1991), several states authorize release on bail at the discretion of a judge (*Minn. Stat. Ann.* 260.171(1) West: 1998; *Neb. Rev. Stat.* 43-253: 1998; *Tenn. Code Ann.* 37-1-117(e): 1996; *Vt. Stat. Ann.* tit. 33. sec. 5513(c): 1991), and some states allow the same right to bail enjoyed by adults (*Colo. Rev. Stat.* 19-2-509: 1999; *Ga. Code Ann.* 15-11-19 (d): 1999; *Ok. Stat. Ann.* tit. 10, sec. 7301-4.3 (c) West Supp: 1998.

Finally, most jurisdictions require that official records kept on juveniles be maintained in separate and confidential files. These may be opened only by court order or following stringent guidelines established by state statutes.

TAKING INTO CUSTODY

The Uniform Juvenile Court Act (sec. 13) states:

> A child may be taken into custody pursuant to an order of the court under that Act, or pursuant to the laws of arrest; or, by a law enforcement officer if there are reasonable grounds to believe that the child is suffering from illness or injury or is in immediate danger from his surroundings and that his removal is necessary; or, by a law enforcement officer if there are reasonable grounds to believe that the child has run away from his parents or guardian.

The broad jurisdictional scope of the juvenile courts generally provides that any juvenile can be **taken into custody** (detained) without a warrant if the law enforcement officer reasonably believes the juvenile to be delinquent, in need of supervision, dependent, abused, or neglected as defined within that state's juvenile court act. However, some states have recognized that removing a juvenile from home before there has been any trial is a power to be used on a limited basis. For truancy, disobedience, and even neglect, the legal process should begin with a summons unless there is "imminent danger" involved and unless waiting for the court's permission would result in unnecessary and dangerous delay. In Illinois, a law enforcement officer may, without a warrant, take into temporary custody a minor whom the officer, with reasonable cause, believes to be a delinquent minor requiring authoritative intervention, dependent, abused, or neglected child as defined within that state's juvenile court act (*ILCS.* ch. 705, sec. 405/2-5, 3-4, 4-4, 5-401: 1999). In addition, the officer may take into custody any juvenile who has been adjudged a ward of the court and has escaped from any commitment ordered by the court. The officer may also take into custody any juvenile who is found in any street or public place suffering from any sickness or injury requiring care, medical treatment, or hospitalization. The taking into temporary custody under the Uniform Juvenile Court Act does not constitute an official arrest. Although statutes in various states provide that taking into custody is not deemed an arrest, this is somewhat a legal fiction since the juvenile is often held in involuntary cus-

Delinquent being taken into custody.
AP/Wide World

tody. In light of recent court decisions, when delinquency is the alleged reason for taking into custody, law enforcement officers must adhere to appropriate constitutional guidelines. For categories other than delinquency, the *parens patriae* concern for protecting minors from dangerous surroundings will suffice constitutionally as reasonable grounds for taking minors into custody when it is not abused by law enforcement officers.

Interrogation

While in custody, the juvenile has rights similar to those of an adult with respect to **interrogation.** To determine whether a confession or statement was given freely and voluntarily, the totality of circumstances surrounding the giving of the statement is to be considered. Even prior to *Gault,* the Supreme Court in *Haley v. Ohio* (332 U.S. 596 [1948]) and *Gallegos v. Colorado* (370 U.S. 49 [1969]) used the voluntariness test to determine the admissibility of statements made by juveniles to the police. Should the police desire to question the juvenile concerning a delinquent act, the juvenile should be given the Miranda warning and should be clearly told that a decision to remain silent will not be taken as an indication of guilt (see In Practice 6.1). Many police administrators, prosecutors,

In Practice 6.1

Defense Asks Judge to Exclude Juvenile's Statements to Police

Tom Sheehan

Although she was argumentative and evasive at first with investigators who questioned her about Jason Bell's disappearance, Stacey DiGian later told Delaware police that she thought two acquaintances were just going to steal his car.

After she was arrested March 17 in connection with Bell's abduction, DiGian, 14, told investigators she didn't think Scott A. Spriggs and T. William Ellis would harm Bell, whose body was found that same day in a Columbus motel.

"I didn't know any of this was going to happen," she said in a videotaped police interview played in Delaware County Juvenile Court yesterday. "They told me they were going to take his car."

DiGian, who was not in court yesterday during the hearing on whether statements she made to police should be suppressed, is charged with various delinquency counts of conspiracy, kidnapping and aggravated robbery.

She remains in custody.

Spriggs, 18, of 2496 Rt. 257 in Ostrander in western Delaware County and Ellis, 19, formerly of Worthington both pleaded guilty last month in Delaware County Common Pleas Court to kidnapping, robbing and killing the 20-year-old Bell as part of a plot to steal his car.

By pleading guilty to those charges Aug. 30, both avoided aggravated murder trials that could have sent them to Death Row if convicted.

Ellis immediately was sentenced by Judge Everett H. Krueger to life in prison with no chance of parole for 35 years. Spriggs is to be sentenced in November by Judge Henry E. Shaw Jr.

Yesterday, Police Officer William Deckling and Detective Sgt. Russ Martin told Judge Thomas Louden that police decided to interview DiGian the morning of March 16 because of statements she had made to other investigators.

DiGian told a Delaware police officer who had questioned her the night before

and juvenile court judges feel that it is best not to question the juvenile unless his or her parents or counselor are present. In Colorado, for example, "no statement or admission of a child made as a result of interrogation by law enforcement officials . . . shall be admissible . . . unless a parent, guardian, or custodian was present . . . and the child was advised of his right to counsel and to remain silent" (*Col. Rev. Stat. Ann.* 19–2–511 (1): 1999). Any confession obtained without these safeguards might be considered invalid on grounds that the juvenile did not understand his or her rights or was frightened. Other state statutes and the Uniform Juvenile Court Act (see sec. 27 (b)) contain similar provi-

that she might have known who had been with Bell.

Authorities have said she was an acquaintance of Bell, who was last seen March 14. Deckling took a missing person's report on Bell on March 15.

Martin said DiGian was interviewed twice March 16 and again about 4 a.m. March 17 after her arrest.

She was not read her Miranda rights during the first two interviews because she was not a suspect in Bell's disappearance, he said.

After her arrest early March 17, she was read her rights before the third interview.

"It was simply me asking her questions if she knew where Jason was and who he might be with," Martin said of the first two interviews.

He characterized her actions during the interviews as "periodically argumentative, evasive and sometimes combative."

During the interview after her arrest, DiGian clashed with her mother while being questioned about going to a Wal-Mart store in Delaware. Both Spriggs and Ellis testified last month that duct tape used to bind Bell was purchased at the store.

"I'm sitting in jail," she said in the taped interview. "What the hell you trying to do? Get me in trouble?"

Her mother, Tamara DiGian, testified yesterday that Stacey can be very dramatic and that it's difficult to get her to stop talking once she gets going.

She said her daughter takes medication for a bipolar personality.

Mrs. DiGian testified that neither she nor her daughter understood the Miranda rights.

"It just all kind of took me by surprise," Mrs. DiGian said. "I've never been in a situation like that before. . . . I just wanted her to tell the truth, if there was something she needed to say."

Defense attorney Keith Boger told Louden that police compromised Stacey DiGian's rights during the interviews.

Assistant County Prosecutor Marianne Hemmeter disagreed. She pointed to the comment the girl made to her mother about being at the Wal-Mart store.

"She understood what was going on," Hemmeter said.

Louden said he will rule later on the motion to suppress the statements.

The girl's trial is to begin Dec. 4.

Sheehan, T. (2000, Sept. 12). Defense asks judge to exclude juvenile's statements to the police. *The Columbus Dispatch*, p. 3D.

sions (*Cal. Welf. & Inst. Code,* 625, 627.5, West: 1998; *Conn. Gen. Stat. Ann.* 46 (b)-137 (a) West: 199; *N.C. Gen. Stat.* 7B-2101: 1999).

Youths taken into custody may be either detained or released to the custody of their parents or guardian. Most model juvenile court acts and the Uniform Juvenile Court Act (sec. 15) dictate that the police make an "immediate" and "reasonable" attempt to notify the juvenile's parents or guardian of his or her custody. The maximum length of time considered to be immediate is usually established by statute. The definition of reasonable usually includes attempts to phone and/or visit the residence of the juvenile's parents, place of employment, and any other known "haunts."

THE DETENTION HEARING

If the juvenile is not released to his or her parents soon after being taken into custody, most states require that a **detention hearing** (a court hearing to determine whether detention is required) be held within a specified time period. Sufficient notification must, of course, be given to all parties concerned before the proceeding. Section 17 of the Uniform Juvenile Court Act indicates that, if a juvenile is brought before the court or delivered to a detention or **shelter care** facility, the intake or other authorized officer of the court will immediately make an investigation and release the juvenile unless it appears that further detention or shelter care is warranted or required. If the juvenile is not released within seventy-two hours after being placed in detention, an informal detention hearing shall be held to determine whether further detention is warranted or required.

Reasonable notice of the hearing must be given to the juvenile and to the parents or guardians. In addition, notification of the right to counsel and of the juvenile's right to remain silent regarding any allegations of delinquency or unruly conduct must also be given by the court to the respondents. States vary with respect to the criteria used to determine the need for further detention, but they usually focus on the need to ensure the protection of society and the juvenile and the possibility of fleeing the jurisdiction (see In Practice 6.2). For example, in Illinois, after a minor has been delivered to the place designated by the court,

> the in-take personnel shall immediately investigate the circumstances of the minor and the facts surrounding his being taken into custody. The minor shall be immediately released to the custody of his parents unless the in-take officer finds that further detention is a matter of immediate and urgent necessity for the protection of the minor, or of the person or property of another or that he is likely to flee the jurisdiction of the court. (*ILCS.* ch. 705. sec. 5-501 (2): 1999)

Detention can be authorized by the in-take officer (generally a designated juvenile police officer or the juvenile probation officer) for up to thirty-six hours, at which time the minor is either released to his or her parents or brought before the court for a detention hearing. Failure to file a petition or to bring the juvenile before the court within forty hours will result in a release from detention (*ILCS.* ch. 705, sec. 405/5-415: 1999). In Illinois, the detention hearing focuses first on whether there is probable cause to believe that the minor is within the category of delinquency, in need of intervention, abused/neglected, or dependent. The court then decides, using the same criteria as the in-take officer, whether further detention is a matter of immediate and urgent necessity (*ILCS.* ch. 705, sec. 405/5-501 (2): 1999; see figure 6.1 for a sample temporary custody order).

Substantial numbers of juvenile cases are "unofficially adjusted" by law enforcement personnel at the initial encounter as well as at the station house. Among those juveniles who are turned over to the court's in-take personnel, a substantial number are disposed of at the in-take stage and at the detention hearings. In many instances the in-take personnel, the minor and his or her family, and the injured party are able to informally adjust the differences or problems that caused the minor to be taken into custody. Only the most serious cases of delinquency, unruly behavior, and cases involving serious abuse or neglect result in processing through the entire juvenile justice system. There are both legal and ethical questions about unofficial dispositions at the in-take stage and the assumption of

In Practice 6.2

BOY CHARGED WITH ARSON LOCKED UP

A judge orders the detention of a 10-year-old accused with three other juveniles in several fires

Deborah Alexander and Tara Deering

A 10-year-old boy accused of setting a four-alarm fire at the Chicago Lumber Co. was ordered into detention Thursday by a Douglas County juvenile court judge. The judge said the boy is a danger to himself, the community and property.

The 10-year-old is one of four boys, ages 10 and 11, who are facing juvenile charges of second-degree arson in connection with six fires, including the Chicago Lumber Co. fire, which caused an estimated $2 million in damage.

The 10-year-old and an 11-year-old are suspected of setting the July 13 blaze that destroyed three Chicago Lumber Co. warehouses, north of Pierce Street near 14th Street, and threatened nearby homes.

Fire investigators said Thursday afternoon that they suspect the boys set six of 17 to 20 fires that were reported earlier this year in the boys' neighborhood, an area bounded by 13th, Vinton, 24th and Pierce Streets, Official still are trying to determine who was responsible for the other fires.

Three of the boys were arrested last week. The fourth was arrested Wednesday.

Fire officials said the boys all knew each other and referred to themselves as a gang.

Deputy Douglas County Attorney Melissa Stanosheck said in court Thursday that the boys called their group "KOB"—Killing Off Bitches.

Stanosheck said when the 10-year-old accused in the Chicago Lumber fire was interviewed, he told investigators he had smoked marijuana before setting the fire.

The boys, who are in the fourth, fifth and sixth grades, sometimes would tell their parents or guardians that they were going to stay the night with their friends, said Omaha Fire Capt. Joe Gibilisco, the lead fire investigator in the case. Other times, he said, they would meet up after sneaking out of their homes at night.

"Most of these fires were done under the cover of darkness in the early-morning hours," said Battalion Chief Dave Adolf, another fire investigator.

Fire officials wouldn't give details about how the boys started the fires. They said only that accelerants sometimes were used.

At Thursday's juvenile-court hearing for the 10-year-old accused in the Chicago Lumber fire, Judge Douglas Johnson expressed concern about whether the boy understood the seriousness of the allegations.

Before the hearing, the boy, dressed in a dark navy jumpsuit, played with a swivel chair, spinning it around.

"The court is concerned about public safety," Johnson said. "It's fortunate that no one was hurt. It does strike the court that he is very young."

Stanosheck said the boy was charged with three felony arson counts. The three charges are in connection with the Chicago Lumber fire and two other fires, on June 10 and Aug. 3, that caused $10,000 in damage at a vacant single-family home at 2015

—Continued on page 130

—*Continued from page 129*

Dupont St. An 11-year-old also is accused in the Dupont Street fires.

Stanosheck said the 10-year-old said in a signed statement that he knew who lived at the Dupont Street address and that he hated the person. Stanosheck added that the boy said one of the fires was set at the Dupont Street address because the group was bored.

Public Defender Katie Conrad said the boy would not fight the detention order. However, Jeffrey Wagner, the court-appointed guardian for the boy, said his client was at serious risk at the facility because of his size.

A woman identified as the boy's grandmother said the child needed to be in a more structured environment.

At the end of the hearing, the boy kissed his grandmother before being escorted from the courtroom.

The lumber-company blaze the boy was accused of setting was by far the worst of the six fires in which the group is accused. Crews responding to the inferno along the west side of 14th Street between Pierce and Pacific Streets contended with extreme heat, exploding propane tanks and downed electrical wires. It took firefighters three hours to contain the fire, which was reported at 1:18 a.m.

Chicago Lumber plans to rebuild at the site of the fire.

Fire officials said the boys also are suspects in the following arsons, which caused a total of $56,000 in damage:

A July 30 fire reported at 8:07 a.m. in a portable classroom at Castelar Elementary School, 2316 S. 18th St., that caused an estimated $6,000 in damage. A 10-year-old and an 11-year-old are accused of setting it.

A July 1 fire reported at 2:39 a.m. in a detached garage at 2111 Martha St. that caused an estimated $10,000 in damage. An 11-year-old is accused of starting the fire.

A May 25 fire reported at 12:41 a.m. in a home being remodeled at 2713 S. 17th St. Damage was estimated at $40,000. An 11-year-old is accused of setting the fire.

Each of the boys has been charged with second-degree arson for each fire he has been accused of starting.

Fire investigators said a man, whose name they wouldn't release, called last week and tipped them off to the group. The man told fire officials that some children had threatened to set fire to his house because he stopped allowing his child to play with them.

"He was the key that led us in a little direction of where to go with this," Gibilisco said.

Fire officials said the boys were arrested in their homes, at school or at Central Police Headquarters. They were taken to the Douglas County Youth Detention Center, then released to their parents or guardians.

At first, Gibilisco said, the juveniles showed no remorse. He said it seemed like it never occurred to them that they would be caught.

"Only when they found out that they had to go to the detention center did they show any remorse," he said. "They cried when they realized they were going to get taken out of their homes and away from their families."

Gibilisco said investigators had not indicated whether the group had a leader. "They kind of like to point fingers at each other, but all of them stated their involvement," he said.

Adolf said he wasn't surprised that children are suspected because many children have a fascination with fire.

"When you recognize more than 50 percent of arson fires are committed by juveniles," he said, "it wasn't that surprising."

But Adolf said the case is unusual because of the number of fires and amount of damage.

Alexander, D. and Deering, T. (2000, October 27). Boy charged with arson locked up: A judge orders the detention of a 10-year-old accused with three other juveniles in several fires. *Omaha World-Herald*, p. 1.

Figure 6.1 Temporary Custody Hearing Order

❑4100

SS:

IN THE COURT OF THE 9th JUDICIAL CIRCUIT
McDONOUGH COUNTY, ILLINOIS

NO.

IN THE INTEREST OF:

Ex Parte ❑
Without Prejudice ❑

____
Minor(s)

TEMPORARY CUSTODY HEARING ORDER
(705) ILCS 405/2-10)

THIS CAUSE coming to be heard upon the motion of ___________________for___________________.
The Court having jurisdiction over the matter and parties, and being fully advised in the premises.

THE COURT FINDS:

1. The minor's

Mother received	❑ notice	❑ no notice and was	❑ present	❑ not present
Father received	❑ notice	❑ no notice and was	❑ present	❑ not present
Guardian/custodian/relative received	❑ notice	❑ no notice and was	❑ present	❑ not present

2. Probable cause
   ❑ A. does not exist that the minor is (abused/neglected/dependent); or
   ❑ B. does exist that the minor is (abused/neglected/dependent)
   The basis of the finding is:____
   ____
   ____
   ____

3. Immediate and urgent necessity
   ❑ A. does not exist to support removal of the minor from the home; or
   ❑ B. does exist to support the removal of the minor from the home and remaining in the home is contrary to the child's welfare, safety, or best interest.
   The basis of the finding is:____
   ____
   ____

4. Reasonable efforts
   ❑ A. have been made but have not eliminated the immediate and urgent necessity to remove the child(children) from the home; or
   ❑ B. cannot, reasonably be made at this time, for good cause, prevent or eliminate the necessity of removal of the minor(s) from the home; or
   ❑ C. have been made and have eliminated the immediate and urgent necessity to remove the child(children) from the home.
   ❑ D. have not been made.
   The basis of the finding is:____
   ____
   ____
   ____

—Continued on page 132

—*Continued from page 131*

5. Consistent with the health, safety and best interest of the minor
   ❑ A. the minor shall be released to the parent; or
   ❑ B. the minor shall be placed in shelter care.

Case #____________________

IT IS ORDERED:

❑ A. The petition is dismissed
❑ B. Consistent with the health, safety and best interests of the minor, the minor shall (be returned to/remain) in the custody of the (mother/father/parents/guardian/custodian/responsible relative).
❑ C. Consistent with the health, safety and best interests of the minor, the minor shall be removed from the home; and

1. Temporary custody of the minor is granted to
   - ❑ a. private custodian/guardian ____________________whose relationship to the minor is ____________________.
   - ❑ b. DCFS Guardianship Administrator with the right to place the minor.
2. The temporary custodian is authorized to consent to:
   - ❑ a. ordinary and routine medical care *AND* major medical care* on behalf of the minor (temporary custody with the right to consent to major medical care).
   - ❑ b. only ordinary and routine medical care on behalf of the minor (temporary custody without the right to consent to major medical care.

***Major medical care is defined as those medical procedures which are not administered or performed on a routine basis and which involve hospitalization, surgery, or use of anesthesia (e.g. appendectomies, blood transfusion, psychiatric hospitalization).**

- ❑ c. ____
  ____
  ____
- ❑ d. A 405/2-25 or 405/2-20 Order of Protection entered this date is incorporated herein against ____.
- ❑ e. DCFS shall investigate the need for services in the following areas:
  ____
  ____
  ____
  ____
- f. If there is a finding of no reasonable efforts under paragraph 4 above, DCFS shall make all reasonable efforts to ameliorate the causes contributing to the finding of probable cause or the immediate and urgent necessity which led to the removal of this child from the home. These efforts shall include
  ____
  ____
  ____
- ❑ g. DCFS shall prepare and file with the court on or before __________, 20 __, a 45 day Case Plan pursuant to 705 ILCS 405/2-10.1
- h. The Order on Visiting entered this date or on subsequent dates is incorporated herein by reference.
- ❑ i. A Social Investigation shall be filed by _____________, 20 __.
- j. The next hearing is set on __________________, 20__, at _______am/pm for
  - ❑ presentation of an affidavit of diligent efforts to notify ❑ progress report
  - ❑ status ❑ adjudication hearing ❑ court family conference
  - ❑ before the judge ❑ before the hearing officer
  - ❑ The first permanency hearing date is ________________, 20__.

DATED:________________ **ENTERED:** ____

JUDGE **Judge's No.**

Figure 6.2 **Petition for Adjudication of Wardship**

In the Circuit Court for the Ninth Judicial Circuit
McDonough County, Illinois

IN THE INTEREST OF:)
)

PETITION FOR ADJUDICATION OF WARDSHIP

I, , State's Attorney, on oath state on information and belief:

1. That is a male minor, born on , who resides or may be found at , McDonough County, Illinois.

2. The names and residence addresses of the minor's parents are:

The minor and the persons named in this paragraph are designated respondents.

3. That the minor is delinquent by reason of the following:

4. The minor is/is not in detention custody;

5. It is in the best interests of the minor and the public that the minor be adjudged a ward of the Court. I ask that the minor be adjudged a ward of the Court, and for other relief under the Juvenile Court Act.

____
Assistant State's Attorney

I have read the aforesaid Petition for Adjudication of Wardship, and do hereby swear that the facts contained herein are true and correct to the best of my knowledge and belief.

____
Assistant State's Attorney

Subscribed and sworn to before me
this _____ day of ________, 2000.

____
Notary Public

Assistant State's Attorney
McDonough County
McDonough County Courthouse
Macomb, Illinois 61455

---

guilt that often leads to some prescribed treatment program. While most practitioners make it clear that participation in informal dispositions is voluntary and that following advice or referrals is not mandatory, there may still be some official pressure perceived by the juvenile or the juvenile's parents that violates the presumption of innocence. (See figure 6.2 for a sample diversion program agreement.)

DETENTION/SHELTER CARE

Under the Uniform Juvenile Court Act,

> a child taken into custody shall not be detained or placed in shelter care prior to the hearing on the petition unless such detention is required to protect the person or property of others or of the child or because the child may abscond (flee) or be removed from the jurisdiction of the court or because he has no parent or guardian who is able to provide supervision and to return him to the court when required or an order for detention or shelter care has been made by the court pursuant to this Act. (*Uniform Juvenile Court Act,* sec. 14)

Absence of any of these conditions must result in the child's release to his or her parents or guardian with their promise to bring the child before the court as requested (sec. 15(1)). Failure to bring the child before the court will result in the issuance of a warrant directing that the child be taken into custody and brought before the court (sec. 15(b)).

The Uniform Juvenile Court Act requires that the "person taking a child into custody, with all reasonable speed and without first taking the child elsewhere, shall release the child to his parents or guardian . . . unless detention or shelter care is warranted or required (sec. 15(a, 1)). This section of the Uniform Juvenile Court Act is designed to reduce the number of children in detention by specifying criteria that would "require and warrant" further detention.

If reasonable cause for detention cannot be established, the juvenile should be released to his or her parents. In practice, and according to most juvenile court acts, the juvenile is taken to a police or juvenile facility at which time the parents are contacted. However, the Uniform Juvenile Court Act implies that the juvenile should be taken immediately to his or her parents unless detention appears to be warranted. This policy spares the juvenile the experience of being held in the most depressing and intimidating of all custodial facilities, the jail or police lockup.

In some states, if the juvenile is not released to his or her parents, the juvenile must be taken without unnecessary delay to the court or to a place designated by the court to receive juveniles (*ILCS.* ch. 705, sec. 405/5-405: 1999). The Uniform Juvenile Court Act does allow detention in a local jail if, and only if, a detention home or center for delinquent children is unavailable (sec. 16 (a, 4). If confined in a jail, detention must be in a room separate and removed from those for adults. This required separation from confined adults is commonly found in statutes and extends to cell, room, or yard and sometimes from any sight or sound. In all categories other than delinquency, the child is normally taken to a designated shelter care facility, which according to the Uniform Juvenile Court Act (sec. 2(6)) means a "physically unrestricted facility." The procedures for contacting the parents and the criteria that are used to maintain custody in such a facility are the same as for the delinquent child. Shelter care facilities are generally licensed by the state and designated by the juvenile court to receive children who do not require the physically restrictive surroundings of a jail or juvenile detention center.

Maximum time limits for detention are set forth in the various juvenile court acts, so a juvenile will not be detained for lengthy periods without a review by the courts. In some cases the issue of bail may arise (see discussion earlier in this chapter).

Once the juvenile has been taken into custody and either released to his or her parents or, with just cause, placed in a detention facility, an officer of the court may attempt to settle the case without a court hearing by arranging for a preliminary conference.

THE PRELIMINARY CONFERENCE

The Uniform Juvenile Court Act (sec. 10) includes a provision that allows a probation officer or other officer designated by the court to hold a preliminary conference in order to give counsel or advice with a view toward an informal adjustment without filing a petition. This preliminary conference is in order only if the admitted facts bring the case within the jurisdiction of the court and if such an informal adjustment, without an adjudication, is in the best interests of the public and the child. The conference is to be held only with the consent of the juvenile's parents or guardian. However, such a conference is not obligatory (sec. 10(a)). A similar provision is found in the Illinois Juvenile Court Act, which states that "the court may authorize the probation officer to confer in a preliminary conference with any person seeking to file a petition . . . concerning the advisability of filing the petition, with a view to adjusting suitable cases without the filing of a petition" (*ILCS*. ch. 705, sec. 405/5-305: 1999). If agreement between the parties can be reached at the preliminary conference, no further official action may be necessary. If judicial action seems necessary, then the probation officer may recommend the filing of a petition. However, should the injured party demand that a petition be filed, that demand must be satisfied. Although the preliminary conference or informal adjustment may be of value in diverting cases that could be settled better outside of juvenile court, it has been subject to criticism as a method of engaging in legal coercion without trial (Tappan 1949: 310-311). Generally, information or evidence presented at the preliminary conference is not admissible at any later stage in the juvenile court proceedings.

THE PETITION

As indicated earlier, juvenile court proceedings begin with the filing of a petition naming the juvenile in question and alleging that this juvenile is delinquent, dependent, abused, neglected, or a minor in need of intervention/supervision. A copy of a sample petition is found in figure 6.2. Although states vary about who is eligible to file a petition, similarities do exist concerning the content of petitions and the initiation of follow-through activities as a result of the petition. In some states, a preliminary inquiry may be conducted by juvenile court personnel to determine whether the best interests of the child or the public will require a petition to be filed. In other states, this inquiry is accomplished after the petition has been filed and may result in the petition being dismissed by the court if the alleged facts are not supported. Regardless of whether the inquiry is conducted before or after the filing of a petition, a stipulation that is commonly found is one in which a court authorizes a person to endorse the petition as being in the best interest of the public and the child. The Uniform Juvenile Court Act (sec. 20) specifies that "a petition may be made by any person who has knowledge of the facts alleged or is informed and believes that they are true." The act also states that "the petition shall not be filed unless the court or designated person has determined and endorsed upon the petition that the filing is in the best interest of the child and the public" (sec. 21(1)). It should be noted that the signing of a petition and the authority to file the petition may be separate and distinct acts. This has led to some confusion. Some states require designated court personnel to sign the petition in order to establish some sufficiency of the allegations at the outset.

The contents of the petition are governed by statutory requirements in each juvenile court act. The petition may be filed on "information and belief" rather than on verified facts necessary for an adjudicatory hearing. The petition is generally prefaced with the words "in the interests of." The petition continues by giving the name and age of the child and frequently the names and addresses of the parents. It also typically indicates whether the minor is currently in detention. Also included in the petition is the statement of facts that bring the child within the jurisdiction of the juvenile court. This particular requirement has been a troublesome area since questions are often raised about whether sufficient facts have been stated and about the specificity of the charges. According to the Uniform Juvenile Court Act (sec. 21(1)), the petition must also contain allegations that relate to the child's need of treatment or rehabilitation, if delinquency or unruly conduct is alleged. Once the petition has been filled out, it is filed with the prosecutor who then decides whether or not to prosecute. If the prosecutor decides to go ahead with the case, proper notice must be given to all concerned parties.

NOTIFICATION

In establishing a **notification** (requirement, that all interested parties be given official notice of time, places, and changes), the court in *Gault* set forth two conditions that must be met: timeliness and adequacy. While petitions may not have to meet all the legal requirements of an indictment, they do have to describe the alleged misconduct with some particularity so that all parties involved are clear as to the nature of the charges involved. Delinquency petitions, for example, must contain sufficient factual details to inform the juvenile of the nature of the offense leading to allegation of delinquency and must be sufficient to enable the accused to prepare a defense to the charges.

Once a petition has been filed, the court will issue a summons to all concerned adult parties informing them of the time, date, and place of the adjudicatory hearing and of the right of all parties to counsel. In addition, many states direct a separate summons to the child who is above a certain age and is within a designated category such as *delinquent* or *unruly child.* A copy of the petition will accompany the summons, unless the summons is served "by publication" (that is, printed in a newspaper of reasonable circulation). States vary about the length of time required between the serving of the summons and the actual proceedings. However, in accordance with the *Gault* decision, a reasonable amount of time should be allowed in order to provide the parties with sufficient time to prepare. Unnecessary and long delays should be avoided particularly in those cases where a child is held in detention or shelter care. For example, Illinois allows at least three days before appearance when the summons is personally served to the parties, five days if notification is by certified mail, and ten days if notification is by publication. If it becomes necessary to change dates, notice of the new dates must be given, by certified mail or other reasonable means, to each respondent served with a summons (*ILCS.* ch. 705, sec. 405/5-525: 1999). Illinois law and the Uniform Juvenile Court Act (sec. 23 (a,b)) provisions on service of summons are similar. The Uniform Juvenile Court Act allows at least twenty-four hours before the hearing when the summons is personally served and five days if certified mail or publication is used.

Service of the summons may be made by any person authorized by the court, usually a county sheriff, coroner, or juvenile probation officer. If the information received by the court indicates that the juvenile needs to be placed in detention or shelter care, the court may endorse upon the summons an order that the child should be taken into immediate custody and taken to the place of detention or shelter care designated by the court.

Following the filing of the petition and proper notification, the adjudicatory hearing is held. In delinquency cases, this is the juvenile court's equivalent of an adult criminal trial.

THE ADJUDICATORY HEARING

The **adjudicatory hearing** is a fact-finding hearing to determine whether the allegations in the petition are valid. In delinquency cases, it is the rough equivalent of a criminal trial. In cases of dependency, neglect, or authoritative intervention, the adjudicatory hearing more closely resembles a civil trial. Although the Supreme Court has extended the legalistic principle of due process to the juvenile justice system, not all rights accorded under the Constitution and its Amendments have been incorporated into the juvenile system. For example, in 1971 the Supreme Court held (*McKeiver,* 403 U.S. 528 [1971]) that juveniles had no constitutional right to a jury trial since the "juvenile proceeding had not yet been held to be a 'criminal prosecution' within the meaning and reach of the **Sixth Amendment**. . . ." The Court reiterated that the due process standard of "fundamental fairness" should be applied to juvenile court proceedings. However, the Court further stated that it was unwilling to "remake the juvenile proceeding into a full adversary process." As previously indicated, some states do currently allow trial by juries. However, most cases are tried by a juvenile judge. The Uniform Juvenile Court Act (sec. 24 (a)) recommends that hearings shall be conducted by the court without a jury. The Supreme Court was clear in its holding that when the state undertakes to prove a child delinquent for committing a criminal act, it must do so **"beyond a reasonable doubt."** (*In re Winship,* 397 U.S. 358, 90 S.Ct. 1068: [1970]). The Uniform Juvenile Court Act not only advocates this standard of proof for the delinquency issue, but also extends this standard to the *unruly* category (sec. 29 (b)). Some states have adopted this recommended standard (*Georgia Code Ann.* 15-11-33 (c): 1999; *N.Y. Fam. Ct. Act.* 342.2 (2), 744 (b) McKinney: 1999; *Texas Fam. Code Ann.* 54. 03 (f), West: 1996; *N.D. Cent. Code.* 27-20-29 (2): 1991). The standard applicable to such categories as *deprived, abuse/neglected,* or *dependent* is usually the civil standard of "preponderance of evidence" or "clear and convincing evidence." For example, the Uniform Juvenile Court Act (sec. 29(c)) requires "beyond a reasonable doubt" to determine delinquency, but allows the civil standard of "**clear and convincing evidence**" to determine if the adjudicated delinquent is in need of treatment or rehabilitation. Generally, of course, it is more difficult to establish guilt beyond a reasonable doubt (no reasonable doubt in the mind of the judge) than it is to determine guilt based on a preponderance of evidence, that is, even though there may be some doubt remaining as to guilt.

The adjudicatory hearing is generally closed to the public. If the juvenile court judge agrees, certain persons, agencies, or associations who have a direct interest in the case may be admitted. Although the Sixth Amendment declares that "in all criminal prosecutions, the accused shall enjoy the right to a speedy and public trial," juvenile court acts prohibit these public hearings on the grounds that opening such hearings would be detrimental to the child. Although the application of the "public trial" concept of the Sixth

Amendment has not been adopted in most juvenile court acts, other due process provisions of the Amendment have been incorporated into juvenile court acts as a result of the *Gault* decision. The Uniform Juvenile Court Act (sec. 24(d)) states that the general public shall be excluded except parties, counsel, witnesses, and other persons requested by a party and approved by the court as having an interest in the case or in the work of the court. Those persons having an interest in the work of the court include members of the bar and press who may be admitted on the condition that they will refrain from divulging any information that could identify the child or family involved.

As previously discussed, the due process concept of "speedy trial" contained in the Sixth Amendment has been incorporated into juvenile court acts. Specific time frames are contained in most acts designating the length of time between custody, detention, adjudicatory, and disposition hearings. Requests for delays are entertained by the juvenile court whenever reasonable and justifiable motions are submitted. Unfortunately, it has been common in some jurisdictions for the juvenile court judge to ignore the time limits established by the statute so a "speedy trial" may not result. Some judges appear to ignore the statutory requirement of an adjudicatory hearing within thirty days of the time the petition is filed (without detention), even when there is no motion for a continuance by defense counsel (Butts 1997; Schwartz, Weiner, and Enosh 1999). In cases such as these, the juvenile might not be brought before the court for an adjudicatory hearing for as long as six months, a clear violation of the statutory requirement. It is possible, of course, for defense counsel to move for dismissal or to appeal, but very seldom are such actions taken. When motions to dismiss based upon procedural irregularities are made, they are almost routinely overruled. Once again, the gap between theory and practice comes to light.

According to section 29 of the Uniform Juvenile Court Act, after hearing the evidence on the petition the court shall make and file its findings about whether the child is deprived, delinquent, abused, neglected, or unruly as alleged in the petition. If the evidence does not support the allegation, the petition shall be dismissed and the child discharged. If the court finds that the allegation is supported by evidence using the appropriate standard of proof for that hearing, the court may proceed immediately or hold an additional hearing to hear evidence and decide whether the child is in need of treatment or rehabilitation. In the absence of evidence to the contrary, the finding of delinquency where felonious acts were committed is sufficient to sustain a finding that the child is in need of treatment or rehabilitation. However, even though the court may find that the child is within the alleged criteria of the petition, the court may not find that the child is in need of treatment or rehabilitation. The court may then dismiss the proceeding and discharge the child from any detention or other restrictions (sec. 29 a and b).

It should also be noted that juvenile court judges in many states may decide prior to, or in the early stages of, the adjudicatory hearing to "continue the case under supervision." An example of an order for "**continuance under supervision**" is shown in figure 6.3. This usually means that the judge postpones adjudication and specifies a time period during which the judge (through court officers) will observe the juvenile. If the juvenile has no further difficulties during the specified time period, the petition will be dismissed. If the juvenile does get into trouble again, the judge will proceed with the original adjudicatory hearing.

Continuance under supervision may benefit the juvenile by allowing him or her to escape adjudication as delinquent. It is generally used by juvenile court judges for precisely this purpose. However, if the juvenile did not commit the alleged delinquent act, he

Figure 6.3 **Continuance Under Supervision Form**

IN THE CIRCUIT COURT FOR THE NINTH JUDICIAL CIRCUIT
McDONOUGH COUNTY, ILLINOIS

IN THE INTEREST OF:)
)
a MINOR.)

CONTINUANCE UNDER SUPERVISION
(Before Adjudication)

This cause coming before the Court on the Motion of the Petitioner for an Order of Continuance Under Supervision (Before Adjudication) pursuant to Chapter 705, Act 405, Section 5-19 of the Illinois Compiled Statutes.

And the Court having been fully advised in the premises and there being no objection made in Open Court by the minor, his counsel, parents, guardian or responsible relative; the Court finds that the Petition has been proved by stipulation of the parties in the manner and form as alleged in the Petition for Adjudication of Wardship signed and sworn on , 2000.

NOW THEREFORE IT IS ORDERED that this matter is continued until ____________________, at _______ p.m. The minor shall be subject to the following conditions during the period of said continuance:

1. That the minor shall not violate any criminal statute or city ordinance of any jurisdiction;

2. That the minor shall not possess a firearm or any other dangerous weapon;

3. That the minor shall not leave the State of Illinois without written permission of the State's Attorney's Office and the Probation Officer;

4. That the minor shall attend school while it is in session without any absences unless excused by the school; shall abide by all school rules; and shall cooperate with school officials;

5. That the minor shall report to the Juvenile Probation Officer as directed by the officer and shall permit the officer to visit him at any time or place, with or without prior notice, and he shall at all times abide by the directives of the Probation Officer;

6. That the minor shall notify the Probation Officer within twenty-four (24) hours of a change of address, or of any arrest or traffic ticket;

7. That the minor shall follow his parents rules of supervision;

8. That the minor shall write a letter of apology to apologizing for his actions;

9. That the minor shall pay probation fees in the amount of $ _________;

10. That the minor shall consent to having his photograph taken by the Probation Officer to be placed in the Probation file.

11. That the minor shall participate in and successfully complete the LIFT Program if accepted into said program;

12. That the minor shall obtain a mental health evaluation at the Fulton/McDonough County Community Mental Health Center and shall successfully complete all recommendations of said evaluation;

DATED: ________________

____
JUDGE

or she may be unjustly subjected to court surveillance. If the juvenile's parents or counselor object to the procedure and request the judge to proceed with the adjudicatory hearing, the judge must, in most jurisdictions, comply with their wishes.

In the adjudicatory hearing, the Uniform Juvenile Court Act as well as the juvenile court acts of many states separate the issues of establishing whether the child is within the defined category and whether the state should exercise wardship or further custody. The determination of further custody or wardship is usually made on the basis of what type of treatment or rehabilitation the court feels is necessary.

The term *ward of the court* means simply that the court as an agency of the state has found it necessary to exercise its role of *in loco parentis.* The decisions that are normally made by the parents are now made by a representative of the court, usually the juvenile probation officer in consultation with the juvenile court judge. As indicated in the Uniform Juvenile Court Act (sec. 29(c and d)), the determination for continued custody for treatment or rehabilitation purposes may be made as part of the adjudicatory hearing or in a separate hearing. The court in determining wardship will receive both oral and written evidence and will use this evidence to the extent of its probative value even though such evidence may not have been admissible in the adjudicatory hearing. The standard of clear and convincing evidence is recommended by the Uniform Juvenile Court Act (sec. 29 (c)) in determining wardship. The Uniform Juvenile Court Act (sec. 29 (e)) also permits a continuance of hearings for a reasonable period in order to receive reports and other evidence bearing on the disposition or the need of treatment or rehabilitation. The child may be continued in detention or released from detention and placed under the supervision of the court during the period of continuance. Priority in wardship or dispositional hearings shall always be given to those children who are in detention or have been removed from their homes pending a final dispositional order.

In order to avoid giving a child a record, it has become a common practice in some jurisdictions for juvenile courts to place a child under probation supervision without reaching any formal finding. This practice may be engaged in without filing any formal petition. Placing children under probation supervision should not be confused with continuances granted by the court in order to complete investigations for wardship or disposition proceedings. "Unofficial probation or supervision," while it may help divert less serious cases from adjudication and thus avoid stigmatizing the child involved, has been subject to much criticism as the result of disregarding due process requirements.

THE SOCIAL BACKGROUND INVESTIGATION

After a determination in the adjudicatory hearing that the allegations in the petition have been established and that wardship is necessary, a dispositional hearing is set to determine final disposition of the case. There are differences among the states about whether the dispositional hearing must be separated from the adjudicatory hearing (*Cal. Welf. & Inst. Code.* 701, 702, West: 1998; *Ga. Code Ann.* 15-11-33 (b), (c): 1999; *ILCS.* 705, sec. 405/2-22 (1): 1999). In some states the two hearings are separate since different procedures and rights are involved. For example, in some states in an adjudicatory hearing on delinquency the standard of proof and the rules of evidence in the nature of criminal proceedings are applicable; however, the civil rules of evidence and standard of proof are applicable to adjudicatory hearings on neglect, dependent, abuse, and minor-requiring-authoritative-intervention (in-need-of-supervision) cases (*Cal. Welf. & Inst. Code.* 405/2-18 (1) West: 1998; *ILCS.* ch. 705, sec. 405/2-18(1): 1999; *Iowa Code Ann.* 232.47 (5) West: 1994). Yet, in the Illinois dispositional hearing for all categories, all evidence helpful in determining the disposition, including oral and written reports, may be admitted and relied upon to the extent of its probative value, even though it may not be competent for the purposes of the adjudicatory hearing (sec. 405/5-22). Similar wording and evidentiary concepts are contained in the Uniform Juvenile Court Act's (sec. 29(d)) references to determination of whether the adjudicated child requires treatment and rehabilitation and to the dispositional stage of the case.

Between the adjudicatory hearing and the dispositional hearing, the court's staff (usually probation officers) is engaged in obtaining information useful in aiding the court to determine final disposition of a case. This information is obtained through social background investigations and is premised on the belief that individualized justice is a major function of the juvenile court. **Social background investigations** typically include information about the child, the child's parents, school, work, and general peer relations as well as other environmental factors. This information is gathered through interviews with relevant persons in the community and is compiled in report form to aid the judge in making a dispositional decision. The probative value of some information collected is questionable and can certainly be challenged in the dispositional hearing. Some juvenile judges delegate the court's staff to make recommendations and to justify the elimination of some options or alternatives from consideration. Unfortunately, social investigations have been used by some courts prior to the adjudicatory hearing and have resulted in an adjudication of delinquency without proving that the accused juvenile did commit the acts of delinquency alleged in the petition. As a result of the *Kent* (*Kent v. U.S.,* 383 U.S. 541 [1966]) decision, counsel for the juvenile has been extended the right to review the contents of staff social investigations used in waiver hearings, since there is no irrefutable presumption of accuracy attached to staff reports. This principle has been extended by most juvenile court acts to legal counsel representing the child in dispositional hearings.

THE DISPOSITIONAL HEARING

Whereas the adjudicatory hearing determines whether the allegations are supported by the evidence, the **dispositional hearing** is only concerned with what alternatives are available to meet the needs of the youth. In fact, some states specify by statute that the rules of evidence do not apply during dispositional proceedings (*Ga. Code Ann.* 15-11-33 (d): 1999; *ILCS.* 705 sec. 405/2-22 (1): 1999; *D. C. Code.* 16-2316 (b): 1997). Dispositional alternatives are clearly stated in each state's juvenile court act. The state may differ in the dispositional alternatives available to juveniles in the separate categories. An option available for the deprived child may not be available for the delinquent child. According to section 30 of the Uniform Juvenile Court Act, the "deprived child" may remain with his or her parents, subject to conditions imposed by the court including supervision by the court. Also according to section 30 of the Uniform Juvenile Court Act, the "deprived child" may be temporarily transferred legally to any of the following:

i) any individual . . . found by the court to be qualified to receive and care for the child;
ii) an agency or other private organization licensed or otherwise authorized by the law to receive and provide care for the child; or

iii) the Child Welfare Department of the [county] [state] [or other public agency authorized by law to receive and provide care for the child];
iv) an individual in another state with or without supervision.

For the delinquent child, the Uniform Juvenile Court Act (sec. 31) states that the court may make any disposition best suited to the juvenile's treatment, rehabilitation, and welfare including

1) any order authorized by section 30 for the disposition of a "deprived child";
2) probation under the supervision of the probation officer . . . under conditions and limitations the court prescribes;
3) placing the child in an institution, camp, or other facility for delinquent children operated under the direction of the court [or other local public authority]; or
4) committing the child to [designate the state department to which commitments of delinquent children are made or, if there is no department, the appropriate state institution for delinquent children].

We would add here, that under certain circumstances, the death penalty may also be an option for the judge. We will have more to say about the circumstances under which this extreme penalty may be applied in chapter 10.

The **unruly child** may be disposed of by the court in any authorized disposition allowable for the delinquent except commitment to the state correctional agency. However, if the "unruly child" is found not amenable to treatment under the disposition, the court, after another hearing, may make any disposition otherwise authorized for the delinquent (sec. 32).

A general trend occurring in juvenile court acts is to refrain from committing all categories, other than delinquents, to juvenile correctional institutions unless the "unruly" or "in-need-of-supervision" child warrants such action after other alternatives have failed. Commitment to an institution is generally regarded as a last resort.

Most juvenile court acts also provide for transferring a juvenile demonstrating mental retardation or mental illness to the appropriate authority within the state. A similar section is included in the Uniform Juvenile Court Act (sec. 35). With the advent of a multiplicity of community treatment programs and child guidance centers, many of the current dispositions contain conditions for attendance at these centers. Dispositions of probation or suspended sentence often require compulsory attendance at a community-based treatment or rehabilitation program. Violation of these conditions may result in revocation of probation or a suspended sentence. This is accomplished through a revocation hearing. Most states now specify the maximum amount of time for confinement of a juvenile. Extensions of the original disposition generally require another hearing with all rights accorded in the original dispositional hearing. The court may, under some circumstances, terminate its dispositional order prior to the expiration date if it appears that the purpose of the order has been accomplished. Juvenile court acts generally terminate all orders affecting the juvenile upon reaching the age of majority in that state. This termination results in discharging the juvenile from further obligation or control. If the disposition is probation, both the conditions of probation and its duration are spelled out by the court. For copies of dispositional and sentencing court orders, see figures 6.4 and 6.5.

Figure 6.4 Dispositional Order

IN THE CIRCUIT FOR THE NINTH JUDICIAL CIRCUIT
McDONOUGH COUNTY, ILLINOIS

IN THE INTEREST OF:)
)
both MINORS.)

DISPOSITIONAL ORDER

This cause coming to be heard for the purposes of a Dispositional Hearing, , Assistant State's Attorney for McDonough County present, with of the Illinois Department of Children and Family Services; Guardian-ad-Litem present for the minor(s), _______________ ; Attorney present with respondent father, _______________ ; and Attorney present with respondent mother, _______________ .

The Court, having received the evidence and heard the arguments of counsel, having jurisdiction and being fully advised in the premises FINDS:

1. That it is in the best interests of the minors that Guardianship shall be granted to the Guardianship Administrator of the Illinois Department of Children and Family Services.

IT IS HEREBY ORDERED:

1. That Guardianship of the children shall be granted to the Guardianship Administrator of the Illinois Department of Children and Family Services, with the Department having the right to consent to medical and dental care and the right to place;

2. That shall successfully complete the _____ program, individual counseling, and all other services as outlined in the client service plan;

3. That shall successfully complete counseling, participate in Victim Services programs, secure and maintain safe and appropriate housing and complete all other services as outlined in the client service plan;

4. That shall adhere to her safety plan regarding contact between _______ and the minor(s), _______________ ;

5. That shall cooperate with the Illinois Department of Children and Family Services, shall comply with the client service plan and correct the conditions which led to the Department's involvement or shall risk loss of custody and possible termination of parental rights;

6. That the Permanency Goal shall be ________;

7. That shall comply with all early childhood education services for _______________;

8. That a Status Hearing shall be held on ______________, at _____________ .m.

DATED:__________

____
JUDGE

Figure 6.5 Sentencing Order

STATE OF ILLINOIS
IN THE CIRCUIT COURT FOR THE NINTH JUDICIAL CIRCUIT
COUNTY OF McDONOUGH

CASE NO. ___ JD ___

IN THE INTEREST OF:

a MINOR.

Date of Hearing:

Parties present for hearing:

Assistant State's Attorney:

Minor:	Attorney for Minor:
Mother:	Attorney for Mother:
Father:	Attorney for Father:

SENTENCING ORDER

THIS MATTER comes before the Court for hearing on the date noted above with the parties indicated being present. The parties have been advised of the nature of the proceedings as well as their rights and the dispositional alternatives available to the Court. The minor admits the allegations of Count I __________ of the Petition filed __________. The Court makes the following FINDINGS:

___ 1. The Court has jurisdiction of the subject matter.
___ 2. The Court has jurisdiction of the parties.
___ 3. The admission by the minor is knowingly and voluntarily made.
___ 4. The minor has signed an Admission form.
___ 5. There is a factual basis for the admission by the minor.
___ 6. The parties have agreed to a sentencing recommendation with regard to this matter.

THEREFORE, it is the ORDER OF THIS Court that the request of the parties for an immediate sentencing hearing is GRANTED:

THIS MATTER then proceeds to sentencing hearing. Both parties waive the preparation of a social investigation. The agreement of the parties is heard. The Court makes the following FINDINGS:

1. The agreement of the parties is in the best interest of the minor.
2. The agreement of the parties should be affirmed and incorporated in the Sentencing Order of this Court.

THEREFORE, it is the ORDER of this Court that:

1. The minor is adjudicated to be a delinquent minor.
2. The minor is made a Ward of this Court.
3. The minor is placed on probation pursuant to 705 ILCS 405/5-23 for a period of __________.
4. This probation is conditioned upon the following terms and conditions:

___ The respondent minor shall obey his/her parents rules of supervision; and
___ The respondent minor shall attend school regularly and put forth his or her best efforts; and

___ The respondent minor shall maintain a 9:00 p.m. to 7:00 a.m. curfew unless he or she is accompanied by a parent or responsible adult. Discretion shall be left to the Juvenile Probation Officer to adjust the respondent minor's curfew; and

___ The respondent minor shall not possess any firearm or other dangerous weapon; and
___ The respondent minor and parents shall cooperate with the Juvenile Probation Officer in any and all programs deemed to be in the minor's best interest; and
___ The respondent minor shall meet with the Juvenile Probation Officer as directed; and
___ The respondent minor shall notify the Juvenile Probation Officer within twenty-four (24) hours of a change in address; and
___ The respondent minor shall reside in McDonough County unless authorized to reside elsewhere by the Probation Officer, the State's Attorney's Office and the Court; and

___ The respondent minor shall not leave the State of Illinois without the approval of the Probation Officer, the State's Attorney's Office and the Court; and
___ The respondent minor shall obey all federal, state and local laws; and
___ The respondent minor shall obtain a Drug and Alcohol evaluation and follow any and all recommendations of the evaluator; and
___ The respondent minor shall obtain a Mental Health evaluation and follow any and all recommendations of the evaluator; and
___ The respondent minor shall refrain from having in his or her body the presence of any illicit drug prohibited by the Cannabis Control Act or the Illinois Controlled Substance Act, unless prescribed by a physician. Furthermore, if the Juvenile Probation Officer receives any report of illicit drug or alcohol use by the minor, the minor shall submit to random drug screens to determine the presence of any illicit drug. The minor shall be responsible for all related costs to the drug screens; and

___ The respondent minor shall pay $ ________ in restitution to the McDonough County Circuit Clerk's Office for the benefit of the victim in this case; and
___ The respondent minor shall draft a letter of apology to __________. The letter shall be approved and sent by the Probation Officer. The minor shall continue to revise the letter until the Probation Officer is satisfied with the content of the letter; and
___ Other terms and conditions shall be:

THIS ORDER MAY BE MODIFIED BY THE COURT.

Entered this ___ day of __________, 2000.

____
JUDGE

APPEALS

Historically, **appeals** from juvenile courts have been rare due to the absence of formality in the system until recently. While a few states do not allow appeals of juvenile court decisions, most allow appeals on behalf of any aggrieved party. The Uniform Juvenile Court Act (sec. 59 (and b)) provides for such appeals. A number of courts have held that, although there is no constitutional right to appeal from juvenile court orders, all statutory appeals procedures must be applied fairly to all persons to avoid denial of equal protection to a particular class of persons (Davis 2000, sec 6.10).

CAREER OPPORTUNITY—MAGISTRATE

Job Description: Judges who determine whether probable cause exists when the police make arrests; determine whether, and ensure that, defendants have been properly advised of their rights; decide whether or not to detain defendants; supervise preliminary hearings; hold trials; and sentence offenders.

Employment Requirements: Must have a law degree and be admitted to the bar.

Beginning Salaries: Vary widely depending upon jurisdiction. Benefits also vary widely.

SUMMARY

It is essential that those involved in the juvenile justice network be completely familiar with appropriate procedures for dealing with juveniles and with the rules governing other members of the juvenile justice system. This awareness helps to ensure that the interests of juveniles will be protected within the guidelines established by society. Otherwise, juveniles' rights may be violated, practitioners may be put in a position where they cannot take appropriate action, and society may not be protected as a result of ignorance of proper procedure.

For example, a police officer may take a juvenile into custody for a serious delinquent act (robbery, for instance). The officer may, upon interrogation, obtain a confession from the juvenile. It may be impossible for the prosecutor to prosecute, if the police officer has failed to warn the juvenile of his or her rights according to *Miranda,* or if a reasonable attempt to contact the youth's parents was not made, or if the youth was frightened into confessing when his or her parents or legal representative were not present, or if the evidence in the case was obtained illegally. Of course, there will be no adjudication by the judge, and rehabilitation/corrections personnel will have no chance to rehabilitate, correct, or protect through detention. In the long run, then, neither the best interests of society nor those of the juvenile will be served.

Every state has a juvenile court act spelling out appropriate procedures for dealing with juveniles from the initial apprehension through final disposition. In looking at several juvenile court acts, we have seen that there are many uniformities in these acts as well as many points of disagreement. Uniformities are often the result of Supreme Court decisions, while differences often result from legislative efforts in the individual states. It is crucial, therefore, for all juvenile justice practitioners to become familiar with the juvenile court act under which they operate so that the best interests of juveniles, other practitioners, and society may be served to the maximum extent possible.

INTERNET EXERCISES

Juvenile court, like the adult court system, has numerous procedures that must be maintained in order for the court to operate efficiently. Chapter 7 provides an explanation of each of the stages of juvenile court. You may see a visual pictorial of juvenile court by going to the Office of Juvenile Justice and Delinquency Prevention (OJJDP) website at http://ojjdp.ncjrs.org/ and clicking on JJ Facts and Figures. Choose Case Flow Through the Juvenile Justice System.

1. Once the chart has appeared, trace the steps discussed in chapter 6 by looking at the stages provided in the chart. Using the example of a child taken into custody for misdemeanor shoplifting, explain the various experiences the child will have as he or she progresses through the juvenile justice system. Next, use the example of a child taken into custody for armed robbery. What experience will this child have in the juvenile court system? Can the experiences differ between misdemeanor and felony offenders?
2. Click on the written explanation of the case flow chart, and read the information provided. How has the deinstitutionalization of status offenders changed the experiences these offenders have within the juvenile justice system? How will the stages in the case flow chart differ for abused and neglected children?

You may also review the juvenile justice system in practice by looking at the Iowa juvenile court system at http://www.judicial.state.ia.us/.

1. At the homepage, click on Families and Children and, then, Juvenile Court.
2. After reading the information provided on the Iowa Juvenile Court, choose Delinquency Proceedings from the menu.
3. Click on the Iowa Juvenile Court flow chart and compare the practices of the state of Iowa with the flow chart provided by the National Office of Juvenile Justice and Delinquency Prevention. What similarities or differences do you see? Are there any stages missing or modified? Why would stages be missing or modified? Using the same examples from above, walk a misdemeanant, felony offender, abused and neglected child, and a status offender through the Iowa juvenile court system.

USEFUL WEBSITES

The American Bar Association's Juvenile Justice Center—*http://www.abanet.org/crimjust/juvjus/home.html*

Legal Information Institute—*http://www.law.cornell.edu/topics/juvenile.html*

Oyez—*http://oyez.nwu.edu*

Teen Court—*http://tqd.advanced.org/2640*

Law related sites—*http://www.vitinc.com/~ocjs/links.html*

CRITICAL THINKING QUESTIONS

1. What are the constitutional rights guaranteed to adults in our society, which are not always guaranteed juveniles in juvenile court proceedings? What is the rationale for depriving juveniles of these rights?
2. What are the benefits of the current trend toward a more legalistic stance in juvenile court proceedings? Are there any disadvantages for juveniles in this trend? If so, what are they?

3. What are the strengths and weaknesses of informal adjustments, unofficial probation, and continuance under supervision?
4. Assume a fifteen-year-old male has been caught shoplifting a small transistor radio at a local discount store. The security guard at the store calls the police. The police officer arriving on the scene has settled similar disputes between this particular juvenile and the management of the chain store on several previous occasions. In addition, the police officer knows that, besides shoplifting frequently, the juvenile frequently runs away from home and is gone for days at a time. The security guard and store manager are determined to prosecute the juvenile. Based on the juvenile court act in your particular state, answer the following questions:
   a. What steps *must* the police officer take after he or she has taken the juvenile into custody?
   b. What steps may the probation officer take in an attempt to settle the dispute?
   c. If further custody is a consideration, what steps must be taken in order to continue such custody?
   d. Assuming a petition has been filed, what are the juvenile court's obligations with respect to all parties to the proceedings?
   e. What are the two major findings to be determined at the adjudicatory hearing? What degree of proof is required? What are the juvenile's rights during the hearing?
   f. At the dispositional hearing, what alternatives are available to the juvenile court judge, and what information does the judge have at hand to help to arrive at the proper disposition?

SUGGESTED READINGS

Cohn, A. W. (2000). Juvenile focus. *Federal Probation,* 64 (1), 73–75.

Davis, S. M. (2001). *Rights of juveniles: The juvenile justice system.* New York: Clark Boardman.

Del Carmen, R., Parker, M., & Reddington, F. P. (1998). *Briefs of leading cases in juvenile justice.* Cincinnati: Anderson.

Dorne, C., & Gewerth, K. (1998). *American juvenile justice: Cases, legislation and comments.* San Francisco: Austin & Winfield.

Gahr, E. (2001). Judging juveniles. *American Enterprise, 12* (4), 26–28.

Mohr, W., Gelles, R. J., & Schwartz, I. M. (1999). Shackled in the land of liberty: No rights for children. *Annals of the American Academy of Political & Social Science, 564,* 37–55.

Schiraldi, V., & Drizin, S. (1999). 100 years of the children's court—giving kids a chance to make better choices. *Corrections Today, 61* (7), 24.

CHAPTER

7

JUVENILES AND THE POLICE

CHAPTER LEARNING OBJECTIVES

Upon completion of this chapter, students should be able to:

Discuss the importance of police discretion in juvenile justice
Compare and contrast unofficial and official police procedures in dealing with juveniles
Discuss the importance of training police officers to deal with juveniles
Describe police-school liaison programs
Discuss the impact of community policing on the relationships among the police, school authorities, and juveniles

KEY TERMS

police discretion
demeanor
overpolicing
street-corner/stationhouse adjustments
mandated reporters
official procedures
police/school consultant or liaison programs
D.A.R.E.
G.R.E.A.T.
Youth-Focused Community Policing
S.H.O.C.A.P.

One of the first specializations in police departments following World War II was the juvenile bureau. Juvenile bureaus grew in number in the 1940s, 50s, and 60s until virtually all police departments of any size had one by the 1970s (Mays and Winfree 2000, pp. 61–62). Historically, the police are the first representatives of the juvenile justice network to encounter delinquents, dependent, and abused or neglected children (Kratcoski and Kratcoski 1995). The importance of the police in the juvenile justice system is considerable for this very reason (see In Practice 7.1). If the police decide not to take into custody or arrest a particular juvenile, none of the rest of the official legal machinery can go into operation. In fact, although the police often decide not to take official action when dealing with juveniles, roughly 85 percent of all cases referred to juvenile court are referred by the police (Drowns and Hess 1990, p. 138).

In Practice 7.1

Brownsville Takes Family Under Wing; Community Provides a Home for Christmas

James Pinkerton

Brownsville—It started as a routine call about two kids shoplifting at the Wal-Mart store.

But instead of ending in an arrest or juvenile detention, Brownsville police mounted an emergency operation to bring Christmas and much more to a mother and three children who have spent the last seven to eight months camped out in a rickety, unheated garage.

On Tuesday morning, Elisa Hernandez, 40, and her three children woke up in a freshly painted three-bedroom apartment at the Citrus Gardens housing project. Donated curtains hung in the windows, new beds with sheets and blankets stood in each room, and the kitchen was equipped with a new toaster, plates, glassware and even a set of pots and pans.

A dinette set is on the way, and a singing plastic Christmas tree belted out Santa Claus is Coming to Town while it blinked brightly in the living room.

"I can't believe it's been so fast, all the help," said Hernandez, who marveled at the events of the past few days. "That I already have a house and have a Christmas tree, which is what my kids wanted."

And she is heartened that so many Brownsville residents have joined police and merchants in helping out.

"I didn't think I was going to get this help, because I have been living like this for some time and I thought nobody cared," said Hernandez, who is separated from her husband. "And now that I see these people calling, it feels good to know people care."

The community's benevolence came after police discovered the family's plight when Hernandez's young children were arrested for shoplifting on Sunday. Officer Joe Barrios asked 6-year-old Sergio Hernandez and his 10-year-old sister, Melissa, why they were trying to steal video games and toys.

"They said they weren't going to have a Christmas, so that's all they could do," said Lt. Orlando Rodriguez, head of the department's criminal-investigation unit.

Troubled by the poor condition of the children's clothes and their disheveled appearance, Barrios decided to take them

Police Discretion in Encounters with Juveniles

It is well established that a considerable amount of **police discretion** (individual judgment concerning the type of action to take) is exercised in handling juveniles. While the exercise of discretion is a necessary and normal part of police work, the potential for abuse exists, since there is no way to routinely review this practice. Police officers are often inconsistent in the decision-making process because, as Meehan (1992, p. 475) states: "What is most revealing about the bulk of police problems with juveniles is the

home and look around. When he and other officers arrived at the home a few blocks from the store, they were astonished.

"Home" was a drafty one-car garage Hernandez and her children had been living in for seven months since an electrical fire gutted her mother-in-law's house in front, where they had been staying. They were using a crock pot for a commode, police said.

"They were living in a one-car garage, broken down, unfurnished, one bed, no plumbing, no water, no electricity, no restroom facilities, nothing whatsoever," Rodriguez said. "Mother and three children sharing one full-size mattress.

"It was a wood-frame structure with gaps in the wood, and they were using duct tape to close them up. It was just terrible, terrible living conditions, and that's when the officer realized something had to be done."

Wal-Mart officials decided not to press charges, police said, and instead donated toys and new furnishings.

Barrios and his fellow officers wasted little time, passing the hat and quickly raising $500 to buy clothes, food and other necessities. Learning that the oldest daughter's 16th birthday was Sunday, the police officers threw her a party at a local restaurant.

Later that night, they took Hernandez and her children to a shelter. On Monday, police met with Brownsville housing officials, who already had Hernandez on a long waiting list for one of the few available apartments.

"We're going to do everything we can to help the family get back into the mainstream—make sure the kids go to school and get them in touch with social services," said Remberto Arteaga, executive director of the Brownsville Housing Authority.

At the apartment, Hernandez was working hard to make her children draw the right lessons from the experience. She told them to be happy and properly grateful for the outpouring of help from the community, while emphasizing that their conduct at the store was wrong.

"I told them that one way or another, I could have got them something (for Christmas), maybe not big, but something decent. But they shouldn't have done that," she said, turning to remind her children again.

On Tuesday, Police Chief Ben Reyna dropped by the Hernandez apartment to make sure gas service was connected so the children could take baths. He gave Hernandez his office number and told her to call if she needed help, and he pledged to get the children in touch with counselors who would talk to them about shoplifting.

"This is one of those cases," the chief said, "that the officers went above and beyond really what they are supposed to do and took care of a family where there was an immediate need."

Pinkerton, J. (2000, December 21). Brownsville takes family under wing: Community provides a home for Christmas. *The Houston Chronicle*, p. 33A.

obvious ambiguity with respect to whether any formal rule of law applies in the instances where officers are summoned by the citizen's call for service. Yet the officer is nonetheless held organizationally accountable for the reported problem."

There are a number of cues to which most police officers respond in making decisions about whether to take official action against a particular juvenile. These cues include the following:

1. the wishes of the complainant;
2. the nature of the violation;
3. the race, attitude, and gender of the offender;

Informal contacts between police and juveniles occur frequently.
Mug Shots/corbisstockmarket

4. knowledge about prior police contacts with the juvenile in question;
5. the perceived ability and willingness of the juvenile's parents to cooperate in solving the problem; and
6. the setting or location (private or public) in which the encounter occurs (Wertham and Piliavin 1967; Black and Reiss 1970; Piliavin and Briar 1964; Regoli and Hewitt 1994; Mays and Winfree 2000).

In general, the wishes of the complainant and the nature of the offense weigh heavily upon police officers' decisions. If the offense is serious (a violent robbery, for example), the officer is generally expected by his or her department and by the public to arrest, and, under most circumstances, the officer does so. There is some evidence, however, that the police may not arrest, even for serious offenses, if the complainant does not wish to pursue the matter (Davis 1975). If the offense is minor and the complainant does not desire to pursue the matter, the police will often handle the case unofficially. Again, in the case of a minor offense, the police will often intervene on behalf of the juvenile to persuade the complainant not to take official action. It should be noted, however, that in most jurisdictions the police cannot prevent a complainant from filing a petition if he or she insists. Further, research by the Office of Juvenile Justice and Delinquency Prevention (1992) found that the police are more likely to refer juveniles to the juvenile court than in the past.

Historically, research has shown that juveniles who show proper respect for the police, who have few if any known prior police contacts, and who are perceived as having cooperative parents are more likely to be dealt with unofficially than those who show little respect, who have a long history of encounters with the police, and who are perceived as having uncooperative parents (Black and Reiss 1970). Most authorities agree that those juveniles who are most likely to have a "police record of arrest are those who conform to police preconceptions about delinquent types, who are perceived as a threat to others, and who are most visible to the police" (Morash 1984). Morash indicates she found a "convincing demonstration of regular tendencies of the police to investigate and arrest males who have delinquent peers regardless of these youths' involvement in delinquency" (110). Moyer (1981), while indicating that sex and race are not critical factors in the police decision-making process with respect to adults, indicates that the nature of the offense and demeanor of the offender when confronting the police are important in determining the type of action taken by the police. Biases on behalf of the police may lead to more informal adjustments for certain types of juveniles. This is largely a matter of speculation, since records of such dispositions have not been routinely kept, although there is currently a trend to formalize such dispositions. It is clear, however, that based upon their perceptions of a number of cues, police officers make decisions as to whether official action is in order or whether a particular juvenile can be dealt with unofficially (Sutpen, Kurtz, and Giddings 1993).

Research on the relationship between the police and juveniles was sparse during the 1970s and 80s. However, recent research by Engel, Sobol, and Worden (2000) on some twenty-four police departments in three metropolitan areas indicates that in most situations, "officers do not treat hostile adults and juveniles, males and females, and blacks and whites differently." The authors found that the police are likely to take official action in cases where there are disrespectful suspects who are intoxicated by use of alcohol or other drugs and in circumstances where disrespect is demonstrated in front of other officers. The effects of **demeanor,** then, were not contingent upon suspects' personal characteristics, at least in this study. In contrast, Sealock and Simpson (1998) in analyzing data collected from a 1958 Philadelphia birth cohort found that race, gender, and socioeconomic status significantly affect the arrest decision. They also note that within gender categories, officers consider the seriousness of the offense and the number of prior police contacts in making arrest decisions.

Bazemore and Senjo (1997), looking at the relationship of police and juveniles from the community-policing viewpoint, analyzed data collected from field research and ethnographic interviews over a ten-month period. Among the community police officers they studied, they found a distinctive style of interaction with young people, different attitudes toward juveniles, and unique views of the appropriate role of officers in response to youth crime. The authors conclude that the officers' efforts to enhance prevention, creative diversion, and advocacy provide at least partial support for the belief that community policing (as discussed above) can lead to positive outcomes.

While the exact nature of the relationships among personal characteristics, demeanor, and police decisions remains unclear, it is likely that all of these factors and others continue to play a role in police juvenile encounters. On numerous occasions we have seen police officers respond differently to male and female juveniles, for example. As we point out in chapter 3, it appears that male officers seldom search ("pat down") juvenile females even in circumstances in which they are likely to be carrying drugs and/or weapons for their male companions. Wooden and Blazak (2001, pp. 32–33) discuss the emergence of the "mall rat" as a type of delinquent, noting that petty theft is the most frequent crime committed by these youth and that females are as likely to be caught as males, though the latter are more likely to be arrested.

In inner-city neighborhoods, police beat officers often arrive at a kind of "working peace" with groups of young black males hanging out on street corners (Anderson 1990). They may allow the youth to get away with certain minor violations for which they could take official action in order to keep the peace. The police face a dilemma in such neighborhoods. On the one hand, the police are accused of **overpolicing** in black

According to some authorities, race makes a difference, at all levels of the juvenile justice process.
© Martin Jones/Unicorn Stock Photos

neighborhoods; on the other hand, they are accused of failing to provide sufficient protection. Complaints concerning the former are typically voiced by young black males who are often stopped, frisked, and questioned on the streets, complaints concerning the latter often arise when the police fail to act against street-corner juveniles or upon domestic violence situations in which the police fail to make an arrest (Walker, Spohn, and DeLone 1996, p. 91).

According to Lardiero (1997), race makes a difference in all stages of the juvenile justice process, but may be most important at the initial point of contact with the police. He believes that minority representation throughout the juvenile justice network would drop if the police used arrest as a last rather than a first resort.

Unofficial Procedures

As Irving Piliavin and Scott Briar (1964) point out, police officers who encounter juveniles involved in delinquent activities have a number of alternatives available for handling such juveniles (see figure 7.1). Basically, the police officer may simply release the juvenile in question, or release the juvenile and submit a "juvenile card" briefly describing the encounter, or reprimand the juvenile and release him or her, or the officer may take the juvenile into custody in order to make a "stationhouse adjustment," or the officer may arrest the juvenile and request that the state's attorney file a petition in juvenile court. Only the last two alternatives involve official action. Each of the other alternatives may occur either on the street or in a police facility. These informal adjustments are commonly referred to as **"street-corner"** or **stationhouse adjustments.** A typical street-corner adjustment might occur when the police have been notified by a home owner that a group of juveniles have congregated on his property and have refused to leave when asked to do so. Since the offense is not serious and since the home owner is likely to be satisfied once the juveniles have left, the officer may simply tell

Figure 7.1 Considerations for Child Abuse Investigations

When You Receive the Referral

- Identify personal or professional biases with child abuse cases. Develop the ability to desensitize yourself to those issues and maintain an objective stance.
- Know department guidelines and State statutes.
- Know what resources are available in the community (therapy, victim compensation, etc.) and provide this information to the child's family.
- Introduce yourself, your role, and the focus and objective of the investigation.
- Assure that the best treatment will be provided for the protection of the child.
- Interview the child alone, focusing on corroborative evidence.
- Don't rule out the possibility of child abuse with a domestic dispute complaint; talk with the children at the scene.

Getting Information for the Preliminary Report

- Inquire about the history of the abusive situation. Dates are important to set the timeline for when abuse may have occurred.
- Cover the elements of crime necessary for the report. Inquire about the instrument of abuse or other items on the scene.
- Don't discount children's statements about who is abusing them, where and how the abuse is occurring, or what types of acts occurred.
- Save opinions for the end of the report, and provide supportive facts. Highlight the atmosphere of disclosure and the mood and demeanor of participants in the complaint.

Preserving the Crime Scene

- Treat the scene as a crime scene (even if abuse has occurred in the past) and not as the site of a social problem.
- Secure the instrument of abuse or other corroborative evidence that the child identifies at the scene.
- Photograph the scene and, when appropriate, include any injuries to the child. Rephotograph injuries as needed to capture any changes in appearance.

Followup Investigation

- Be supportive and optimistic to the child and the family.
- Arrange for a medical examination and transportation to the hospital. Collect items for a change of clothes if needed.
- Make use of appropriate investigative techniques.
- Be sure the child and family have been linked to support services or therapy.
- Be sure the family know how to reach a detective to disclose further information.

During the Court Phase

- Visit the court with the child to familiarize him or her with the courtroom setting and atmosphere before the first hearing. This role may be assumed by the prosecutor or, in some jurisdiction, by victim/witness services.
- Prepare courtroom exhibits (pictures, displays, sketches) to support the child's testimony.
- File all evidence in accordance with State and court policy.
- Unless they are suspects, update the family about the status and progress of the investigation and stay in touch with them throughout the court process. Depending on the case, officers should be cautious about the type and amount of information provided to the family, since they may share the information with others.
- Provide court results and case closure information to the child and the family.
- Follow up with the probation department for preparation of the presentence report and victim impact statement(s).

Office of Justice Programs. (1997, May). *Law enforcement response to child abuse.* Washington, D.C. Office of Juvenile Justice and Delinquency Prevention.

the juveniles to leave and not return. If, for some reason, the police officer is not satisfied that the orders to move on and not return will be obeyed, the officer may take the juveniles to the police station and request that the juveniles' parents meet with him or her there. If an agreement can be reached among the juveniles and their parents that the event leading to the complaint will not recur, the officer may release the juveniles in what is commonly referred to as a stationhouse adjustment (Smith 1986; Meehan 1992; *ILCS* 1999). In either case, there is no further official action taken by others in the juvenile justice network, and often no official record of the encounter is kept. While information cards and/or computer notes kept on juveniles do not constitute official records, they are sometimes used by juvenile officers to determine the number of prior contacts between a particular juvenile and the police and therefore, may be used to determine whether official action will be taken. In some states, formal records of stationhouse adjustments are now required for certain offenses (*ILCS*. ch. 705, sec. 405/5–301: 1999).

Informal adjustments such as these usually cause little controversy as long as all parties (complainant, police, parents, and juveniles) are reasonably satisfied. In fact, some states such as Illinois have attempted to formalize the station adjustment process by spelling out exactly what the police officer's alternatives are in such adjustments (*ILCS*. ch. 705, sec. 405/5–301: 1999). For example, in Illinois a police officer may, with the consent of the minor and his/her guardian, require the minor to perform public or community service or make restitution for damages. Although police officers often see solutions of this type as being better for the juvenile than official processing, some serious objections have been raised by parents, the courts, and sometimes the juveniles involved.

Suppose a juvenile was allegedly involved in vandalism in which the juvenile spray-painted some derogatory comments on the front of a school building. Also suppose that, as a condition of not taking official action, a police officer instructs the youth to spend every night after school cleaning the paint off the school building with paint remover and brushes that are provided at the expense of the juvenile or his or her parents. Finally, suppose the juvenile persists in maintaining his or her innocence. The implications of this type of "treatment without trial" should be relatively clear. First, it has not been demonstrated that the juvenile did commit the delinquent act in question; that is, the juvenile has not been adjudicated delinquent in a court of law. Second, since it has not been demonstrated that he or she committed the vandalism, there is no legal basis for punishment. Third, even if the juvenile did in fact commit the offense, the police generally have no legal authority to impose punishment on alleged offenders, unless of course such offenders voluntarily agree to the punishment. But how voluntary is such agreement?

While many police officers who employ informal adjustments realize that their actions may not be strictly legal, they justify the use of informal adjustments on the basis that the juvenile or parent (guardian) entered into it voluntarily. These officers reason that since the treatment or punishment is not mandatory and is in the juvenile's best interests, there does not need to be prior adjudication of delinquency or finding of guilt. Many of these officers fail to recognize that the extent to which their "suggested" treatment or punishment programs are voluntary is highly questionable. The threat of taking official action, if unofficial suggestions are not acceptable to the offenders involved, largely removes any element of voluntarism and is coercive. In cases of this type (which are not atypical), the juvenile may be upset at being punished for an act that he or she did not commit, the parents may be upset because their child did not receive a fair trial, and the juvenile court judge may be upset because the functions of the court have been usurped (taken over) by the police. All stationhouse adjustments, of course, are not negative. Some can be very successful in resolving minor instances of delinquency through proper referral to competent counselors by officers skilled in accurately assessing the needs of the juvenile.

With respect to abused or neglected children, police options are technically more restricted. As **mandated reporters** (those required to report suspected cases of abuse to the state), they are often required to report suspected incidents of child abuse or neglect to the state department of children and family services even though they may not have enough evidence to arrest the suspected abuser. Investigators from the children and family services unit are typically required to contact the parties involved within 48 to 72 hours from the time of notification. If the investigators are convinced neglect or abuse is occurring, or if the original investigating officer is convinced, the child may be taken into protective custody until further hearings can be held. It is the responsibility of the local law enforcement department to develop the procedures to handle abuse and neglect situations, to ensure that law enforcement officials are properly trained in identifying cases of abuse/neglect, to objectively investigate abuse and neglect cases, and to interview victims and perpetrators of abuse and neglect (see figure 7.1).

The major concerns of police officers when dealing with abused or neglected children are, of course, the safety and well-being of the minors involved. Still, there are officers who, for a variety of reasons, prefer not to take formal action in cases which they conclude do not involve serious abuse or neglect. "Rarely are abusive and neglectful parents arrested. Exceptions exist when the injury to the child is extremely severe or obviously sadistically inflicted, when a crime has been committed, when the parents present a danger to others, or when arrest is the only way to preserve the peace" (Tower 1993, p. 275). Official action is more likely to occur today because of mandated reporting laws. Still, even though they are mandated reporters, officers sometimes hesitate to take official action. This is sometimes the case because police officers are concerned about the possibility of false allegations or of being used by one party to a hostile divorce or separation to cause trouble for the other party through implanting false allegations in the mind of the child or by falsely reporting abuse or neglect (Goldstein and Tyler 1998).

In spite of the difficulties just mentioned, estimates are that as many as 85 percent of all police-juvenile contacts are resolved informally (Black and Reiss 1970; Mays and Winfree 2000). The proportion of child abuse/neglect cases handled unofficially is unknown, but probably considerable. Police officers who use informal dispositions often see such dispositions as more desirable than official processing, which is certain to leave the offender with a record and may lead to detention for some period of time. Most police officers agree that neither juvenile records nor attempts to rehabilitate juveniles who are detained are beneficial to juveniles. The latter holds true for child abusers as well, although when the abuse is severe, officers are typically more than willing to take official action (Willis and Welles 1988). When police officers act informally, they often sincerely believe they are doing so in the best interests of the parties involved. This may be the case if we assume that all the persons apprehended did commit a delinquent or criminal act and if we assume that treatment and rehabilitation are of little or no value. However, if we recognize that sometimes the police do make mistakes, that some juveniles and some parents do need and might benefit from treatment of some type, that the police have no mandate to impose punishment or treatment, and that the juvenile court judge often has no way of knowing how many times a particular juvenile or abusive parent has been dealt with informally, the problems inherent in informal adjustments become very apparent (Portwood, Grady, and Dutton 2000).

Official Procedures

The **official procedures** to be followed when processing juveniles are clearly spelled out in juvenile court acts. It is important to note that police procedures for juvenile offenders differ in most jurisdictions from adult procedures. As a rule, these procedures are tailored specifically toward implementing the juvenile court philosophy of treatment, protection, and rehabilitation rather than punishment. As a result, in order to carry out proper procedures, specialized training is necessary. It has been our observation that many officers in most jurisdictions believe that being assigned as a juvenile officer is not particularly desirable (Mays and Winfree 2000, p. 62). We have heard juvenile officers referred to as "kiddie cops" and seen distinctions made between "real" police officers and "juvenile" officers. These traditional police attitudes have slowed the development of a professional corps of juvenile officers. Nonetheless, being an effective juvenile police officer requires more skill than being a good patrol officer. In addition to learning the basics of policing, the juvenile officer is required to learn a great deal about the special requirements of juvenile law, about the nature of adolescence, about the nature of parent-child relationships, and about the social service agencies, public and private, to which juveniles may be referred for assistance (Tower 1993, p. 275). These skills are not easy to acquire, and those who have mastered them should take pride in their accomplishments. In addition, police organizations should reward those who possess and actively employ these skills in terms of both salary and promotional opportunities.

While the development of effective juvenile officers and juvenile bureaus is highly desirable, most initial contacts between juveniles and the police involve patrol officers. It would appear logical to provide at least minimal training in the area of juvenile law for all patrol personnel in order to safeguard the rights of juveniles and to ensure proper legal processing by the police. It does little good (either for the juvenile or for the prosecutor's case) to have a competent juvenile officer if the initial encounter between the juvenile or abusive parent and the police has been mishandled.

Police officers who are involved in the official processing of juveniles need to be aware that all of the guarantees in terms of self-incrimination and searches and seizures characteristic of adult proceedings also hold for juveniles. In addition, juveniles are, in most jurisdictions, extended even further protection by law. Thus, the police are required to notify the juvenile's parents about their child's whereabouts and are required to release the juvenile to his or her parents unless good cause exists for detention. Detention in a lockup routinely used for adult offenders is often illegal and the police must, in these cases, make special arrangements to transport and detain juveniles should further detention be necessary. In Illinois, for example, juveniles may not be detained in an adult jail or lockup for more than six hours, and while they are detained must not be permitted sight or sound contact with adults in custody (*ILCS.* ch. 705, sec. 405, par. 5–401: 1999). Similarly, police records concerning juveniles must, in most jurisdictions, be kept separate from adult records and are more or less confidential (see chapter 6). While fingerprints and photographs of juvenile offenders may be taken, there are often restrictions placed upon their use; that is, they may not be transmitted to other law enforcement agencies without a court order in many jurisdictions. There is, however, a trend toward making juvenile records more readily available to interested parties in the interests of more effective law enforcement efforts (*ILCS.* ch. 705, sec. 405/1–7: 1999).

Court decisions indicate that a juvenile charged with a delinquent act has a right to counsel prior to placement in a police lineup. There is some concern that a juvenile's waiver of his or her right to remain silent during interrogation without a parent or lawyer present is of questionable value (Dorne and Gewerth 1998, p. 34). As a result, many police departments delay interrogation until either a parent and/or an attorney is present.

In many jurisdictions, police officers who have been designated juvenile officers have the task of ensuring that juveniles are properly handled. These juvenile officers are, presumably, specially trained in juvenile law and procedures.

Training and Competence of Juvenile Officers

For roughly the last seventy-five years, there have been repeated calls for professionalization of the police through increased education and training. The number of two- and four-year college programs in criminal justice and law enforcement has increased dramatically during the last two decades, as has the number of special institutes, seminars, and workshops dealing with special police problems. Since juvenile cases present special problems for the police, one might expect considerable emphasis on training for juvenile officers. Indeed, the number of police officers qualified by training to serve in juvenile bureaus has increased dramatically in recent years, especially in large metropolitan departments. In these departments promotion within the juvenile bureau is possible and both male and female officers deal with juvenile offenders and victims. The possibilities of promotion and recognition for a job well done provide incentive and rewards for those choosing to pursue a career in juvenile law enforcement.

The situation of juvenile officers in smaller cities has also improved in recent years. More jurisdictions require compliance with laws mandating special training for juvenile officers, although personnel shortages and reduced financial resources sometimes make both training and specific assignment to purely juvenile matters difficult. There are still many smaller police departments with no female officers, so male officers must deal with juveniles of both sexes. Some rural departments have no officers specifically trained to deal with juveniles and others, in order to conform to statutory requirements, simply select and designate an officer, often one who has no prior training in juvenile matters, as juvenile officer. Considering the fact that juvenile officers are frequently expected to speak to civic action groups about juvenile problems, run junior police programs, visit schools and preschools, form working relationships with personnel of other agencies, and investigate cases of abused and missing children, this lack of training is a very serious matter. Police departments with ten or less sworn officers still face difficulties in providing adequately trained officers for twenty-four-hour-a-day service. When these departments do train and appoint officers to handle juvenile offenders, they can seldom afford to relieve these officers of other duties. This, in effect, makes it impossible for the appointed officers to become specialized in juvenile matters. This also eliminates the possibility of developing a stable juvenile bureau and removes the possibility of career advancement as a juvenile officer. One result of these difficulties is that officers have little incentive to volunteer for service in juvenile bureaus. Consequently, juvenile officers are frequently appointed on the basis of a perceived affinity for "getting along" with youth. Unfortunately, this affinity is not a substitute for proper training, although it may appear to be to police administrators who regard handling juvenile offenses as something less than real police work.

It is essential that police departments train officers to handle juvenile cases. In Illinois, for example, a juvenile police officer is defined by statute as "a sworn police officer who has completed a Basic Recruit Training Course, has been assigned to the position of juvenile officer by his or her chief law enforcement officer and has completed the necessary juvenile officers training as described by the Illinois Law Enforcement Training Standards Board, or, in the case of a State police officer, juvenile officer training approved by the Director of the Department of State Police" (*ILCS.* ch. 705, sec. 405/1–3: 1999).

Police/School Consultant and Liaison Programs

Over the past four decades, police departments and schools have worked together to develop programs to help prevent delinquency and improve relationships between juveniles and the police. (See In Practice 7.2.) These programs involve more than simply providing security through police presence in the schools. Rather, the programs attempt to foster a more personal relationship between youth and the police by using police officers in counseling settings, by improving communications between the police and school officials, and by increasing student knowledge of the law and the consequences of violations.

One early **police/school consultant or liaison program** was developed in Flint, Michigan, in 1958. Police/school liaison officers are located in schools and serve as sources of information and counselors for students. They are often funded, in part at least, by school districts though they work for police agencies. A 1972 evaluation of this program concluded that the police officers assigned had difficulties in being both authority figures and counselor/confidants. Since then and more recently, similar programs in Tucson, Arizona, Montgomery, Alabama, Woodburn, Oregon, and Tampa, Florida, to mention a few, have shown similar results. More recent programs have focused on the latter role for officers assigned, who act as additional resource persons in the school setting and who generally have been evaluated positively by school officials, though not always by students. These programs have proliferated, based on these evaluations and the belief that the closer the relationship between police and juveniles in nonthreatening situations (those other than investigatory or crime intervention), the better in terms of improving the image of the police, uncovering information concerning abuse and neglect, and decreasing delinquency. **D.A.R.E.** (Drug Abuse Resistance Education) programs, in which police officers teach children how to avoid use of illicit drugs, are widespread in the United States and abroad. A number of schools and police agencies throughout the country are now involved with such programs, and they appear to be having more positive than negative effects on officers, juveniles, and school authorities, particularly when the officers involved have received special training to prepare them for their assignments (Martin, Schulze, and Valdez 1988). Even though a good deal of research shows that D.A.R.E. is ineffective at preventing drug use among those who have gone through the program (Aniskievicz and Wysong 1990; Enett, Tobler, Ringwalt, and Flewelling 1994; National Institute of Justice 1994), the program may still improve understanding and relationships

In Practice 7.2

Getting Young Lives Back on Track; Juveniles: A 10-Year-Old LAPD Program for At-Risk Youths Combines Physical Training with Classes in Anger Management and Creative Arts and Instruction in Math and English

Dalondo Moultrie and Erika Hayasaki

Fifteen-year-old Sandra Vega thought she couldn't take another step after running up three flights of stairs for the seventh time at the Los Angeles Police Department's Central Division station downtown.

But exercises on the station's rooftop weren't quite over for Vega and 14 teenagers enrolled in LAPD's Juvenile Impact Program (JIP) for at-risk youths. Dressed in soiled gray sweats and dingy white T-shirts, they still had to do 20 push-ups.

That proved too much at the moment for Vega, who lay down on the floor in exhaustion. But it was not enough to sour her on the program, which she and her parents credit with helping get her life back on track.

Vega's parents sent her to JIP after she got in trouble for skipping school, fighting and hanging out with the wrong crowd. Like many in the program, Vega believes she is becoming a better person.

"It influenced me to go to school, not to do drugs or other bad things," she said.

Youngsters, between the ages of 9 and 17, are sent to the program by a judge or are recommended by parents after truancy or such crimes as assault and drug possession. About 100 youngsters from Los Angeles County are enrolled each year, and there is a long waiting list.

The 10-year-old course has expanded beyond its original boot camp tactics and now incorporates classes in anger management and creative arts and instruction in such subjects as math and English. Parents also are required to attend classes, to improve their parental skills.

Over 16 weeks, each batch of JIP participants meets Saturdays for three hours of physical exercise and focus groups, in addition to weeknight sessions.

Funded by donations, JIP is staffed by about 20 volunteers and two paid police officers. It is offered at LAPD's Central and Harbor divisions; Southeast Division recently closed its JIP group because of a redeployment of officers.

Volunteer Dawn Hagerty, the officer who runs the program at Central, said she will admit youngsters from across Los Angeles County because the need is so great.

JIP began as punishment for adolescent graffiti writers, said founder Frank DiPaola, a retired LAPD officer. He offered youth offenders 100 hours of community service instead of serving time in juvenile detention centers.

"Little by little what started happening, many of these kids, once they finished their hundred hours, they started coming back to

—Continued on page 162

—Continued from page 161

hang out with the cops," he said. "Behavioral changes started occurring, where we took the place of the gang members."

On a recent Saturday, Philip Wilson, an ex-convict, talked to the group about his experiences in prison.

"Any weed smokers?" Wilson asked.

One by one, about half the class members raised their hands.

"Any gangbangers in here?" Wilson asked.

One teenager reluctantly raised his hand.

"Only you can stop hanging out with your homeboys," Wilson told him. "Your homeboys aren't going to be there when you get in trouble, when you get arrested. They're all gonna run then."

The fight against the gangs and gang-related crimes certainly can use a helping hand, said Lewis Yablonksy, professor emeritus at Cal State Northridge who has written several books about gangs and juvenile delinquency. He said intervention programs, such as JIP, help youths change their behavior.

"A lot of times, kids want to get out of gangs, and a program like this impact program gives them a rationale to tell their homies, 'The judge told me to do this, and I have to do this, or I'll have to go to the California Youth Authority.' " he said.

Vanessa Gutierrez admitted she was irresponsible and deceitful and had little interest in school two years ago. The then-14-year-old admitted she had been experimenting with drugs and alcohol. After she was picked up for truancy a second time in 1998, her father, Victor Gutierrez, asked a judge to send her to JIP. So far, it seems to have been the right decision, the father said.

"In missing class, her first year of school ended up a washout. I think she's realizing now there is some truth to the saying, 'Every action has a reaction,' " Victor Gutierrez said.

Vanessa Gutierrez agrees that JIP has helped her. "It was either finish this program or go to Juvenile Hall," she said. "Everything that was going on at that time, I realized I had to change."

Back on the rooftop at the Central Division police station, Ricardo Sotelo, 17, held his side after having doubled over with stomach cramps from running up and down the stairs. He said he knows he deserves what comes to him because of the poor decisions he has made in the past. It's another step in this rehabilitation, he said.

"All the pain we have equals out to all the pain you gave your parents," Sotelo said, gasping.

Moultrie, D. and Hayasaki, E. (2000, December 29). Getting young lives back on track; Juveniles: A 10-year old LAPD program for at-risk youths combines physical training with classes in anger management and creative arts and instruction in math and English. *Los Angeles Times*, p. 2B.

among youth and the police officers involved. Another program, **G.R.E.A.T.** (Gang Resistance Education and Awareness Training) is based upon similar assumptions and has been subject to similar criticisms (Palumbo and Ferguson 1995).

COMMUNITY-ORIENTED POLICING AND JUVENILES

Community-oriented policing is a trend which deserves mention here. Community-oriented policing refers to a strategy which relies upon identification of problems by police and members of the community they serve and shared ownership of law enforcement/order mainte-

D.A.R.E. and other programs bring police and juveniles into classroom contact.
James Marshall/CORBIS

nance duties (Walters 1993; Webber 1991; Glensor, Correia, and Peak 2000). There are a number of community-oriented policing programs currently in existence with many more on the drawing table. While community-oriented policing is a general police strategy, it certainly has applications in police work with juveniles since it requires joint community/police identification of, and efforts to solve, problems. Thus police officers and school, probation, civic action, neighborhood, and political groups work together to find solutions to problems rather than asking the police to handle incidents as and after they occur (review In Practice 7.1 and 7.2). One example of a program of this type, sponsored by the Department of Justice, is **Youth-Focused Community Policing** (YFCP). This program provides information-sharing activities that promote proactive partnerships among the police, youth, and community agencies cooperating to identify and address juvenile problems in a manner consistent with community policing philosophy. A number of communities have established such programs, and initial evaluations are mixed (Mays and Winfree 2000, p. 85). Figure 7.2 indicates the types of agencies community policing officers meet with to share information. Schools and youth groups are regularly included in information-sharing activities.

Yet other programs have been introduced to improve the relationship between schools and the police when concerning juvenile offenders. One example is **S.H.O.C.A.P.** (Serious Habitual Offender Comprehensive Action Program), initiated in

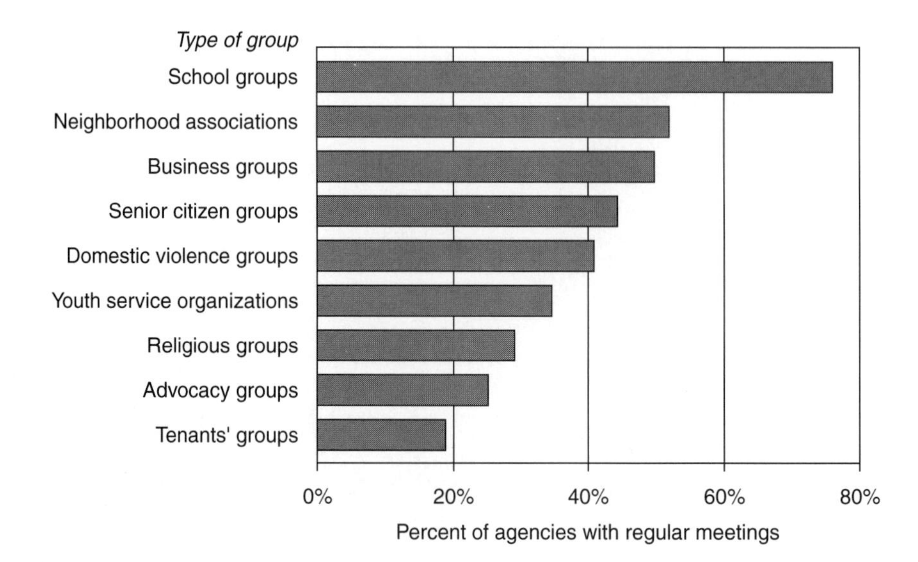

Figure 7.2 Types of groups that local police departments regularly met with to discuss crime-related problems, 1999

Source: Hickman, M. J., & Reaves, B. A. (2001). Community policing in local departments, 1997 and 1999. *Special Report.* Washington, D.C.: Bureau of Justice Statistics, p. 5.

Illinois (*ILCS,* ch. 705, sec. 405/5–145: 1999). S.H.O.C.A.P. is a multidisciplinary interagency case management and information-sharing system intended to help the agencies involved make informed decisions about juveniles who repeatedly engage in delinquent acts. Each county in Illinois (other than Cook County, which may develop several committees) is encouraged to develop a S.H.O.C.A.P. committee consisting of representatives of law enforcement, schools, the state's attorney's office, and probation. Committees are then to develop written interagency agreements which will allow for sharing of information about serious habitual offenders with other committee agencies in such a way that the information is kept confidential by the agencies involved. Hopefully, the sharing of such information on a need-to-know basis will result in better coordination of efforts to intervene and deal appropriately with repeat offenders.

Police and Juvenile Court

The police are the primary source of referral to juvenile court (Mays and Winfree 2000, p. 86), and juvenile court judges rely heavily upon the police for background information concerning juveniles who come before them. Since the police and the court may have different goals with respect to juveniles (e.g., control versus treatment), this may not always be in the best interests of juveniles. On the one hand, the juvenile court may become overly concerned with control. On the other, the police officer who feels the court is unfair to the police or too lenient with offenders may fail to report cases to the court, since, in his or her opinion, nothing will be gained by official referral (Bartollas 1993, p. 394). In some cases, the police may attempt to resolve the case at hand themselves, which, as we have pointed out earlier, may or may not be in the best interests of the youth involved. In short, whether or not a particular juvenile is referred to juvenile court depends in part upon the police officer's attitude toward the court.

CAREER OPPORTUNITY—MUNICIPAL POLICE OFFICER

Job Description: Enforcing laws and maintaining order; patrolling the community; controlling traffic; making arrests; preventing crime; investigating criminal activity; working with the public and representatives of other agencies to improve the quality of life in the community.

Employment Requirements: Must be a U.S. citizen; must have a valid driver's license; must be at least twenty years old at the time of application; must not have any felony convictions; must be able to pass physical, written, medical, polygraph, psychological, and background investigations. Must possess good communications skills. Must be a high school graduate, but preference is frequently given to those with two- or four-year degrees. Appointment contingent upon completion of basic training.

Beginning Salaries: Typically range between $20,000 and $45,000 depending upon jurisdiction; average is probably about $35,000. Additional benefits package (insurance, vacation, sick leave, pension).

Note: To become a juvenile police officer, an applicant typically needs to serve as a patrol officer first, then may be required to participate in special training to be certified as a juvenile officer.

SUMMARY

In order to implement proper juvenile procedures and benefit from theoretical notions concerning prevention, causes, and correction of delinquent behavior and child abuse/neglect, the juvenile officer must first know proper procedures and understand theories of causation. Since both types of knowledge are specialized, it is imperative that juvenile officers receive special training in these areas. This specialized training is advantageous for the police department, the juvenile, the justice network, the social service network, and the community. The police department benefits in terms of creating a more professional image and in terms of efficiency, since mistakes in processing should be reduced. The juvenile benefits in that trained personnel can better carry out the intent of juvenile court acts, which were developed to protect the best interests of the juvenile. The justice system benefits from the proper initial processing of juveniles and abusive adults who are to be processed further in that system (for example, prosecuted). Finally, the community and social service network benefit from decisions made by police officers who are properly trained. In return for these benefits, it is essential to reward juvenile officers who perform well through recognition and promotional opportunities.

The majority of police juvenile contacts result in unofficial dispositions in the form of street-corner or stationhouse adjustments. It is important that decisions concerning proper disposition of juvenile cases by police officers be based upon a thorough knowledge of procedural requirements and the problems of youth and abuse or neglectful adults. When trained, competent officers make such decisions, the imposition of punishment by the officers handling cases unofficially is reduced, and the rights of all parties are better protected. In those cases that require official disposition, further processing is facilitated by proper initial processing. In order to ensure that police officers handle juvenile cases properly, specialized training programs need to be developed and used and incentives for good performance by juvenile officers need to be provided.

INTERNET EXERCISES

Law enforcement officials spend large amounts of time working with children. The police are, in many cases, involved in juvenile matters from the time of arrest until the time of adjudication. Many law enforcement officials are also actively involved in deterrent programs with juveniles, schools, and communities. One such program is the Gang Resistance and Education Assistance Program (G.R.E.A.T.) that focuses on educating children about the hazards of gangs and providing alternatives to gangs for children in at-risk neighborhoods. To find out more about the G.R.E.A.T. program visit the Bureau of Alcohol, Tobacco, and Firearms website at *http://www.atf.treas.gov/great/index.htm.*

1. Click on Focus on Youth. Read the history of the G.R.E.A.T. program. What has happened within the last decade that brought about the proactive gang resistance education program?
2. Read the lessons provided. Why is or why isn't it important for the police to be actively involved in this program? What are the police officers involved in the program gaining from their participation? What are the children involved in the program gaining from their participation? In your opinion, why should or shouldn't the juvenile court offer this program instead of law enforcement officials? What do you believe is the most important lesson provided to youth at risk of becoming gang members?
3. Next, click on the Effectiveness section. Using your knowledge of statistics and the collection of statistics, how difficult will it be for law enforcement personnel to measure the effectiveness of the G.R.E.A.T. program? How will law enforcement officials go about gathering statistics to measure the effectiveness of the program? Will the statistics most likely be official or unofficial statistics?

USEFUL WEBSITES

The FBI's homepage—*http://www.fbi.gov*

Law Enforcement Links—*http://www.leolinks.com*

The Police Guide—*http://policeguide.com*

The International Association of Chiefs of Police—*http://www.theiacp.org*

CRITICAL THINKING QUESTIONS

1. List and discuss some of the cues frequently used by police officers in deciding whether to handle a case officially or unofficially. What are some of the dangers in relying upon these cues from the point of view of the juvenile offender? Of the victim of abuse or neglect?
2. Joe Foul Up, a thirteen-year-old white male, has just been apprehended by a police officer for stealing a bicycle. Joe admits taking the bicycle, but says he only intended

to go for a joy ride and was going to return the bicycle later in the day. Joe has no prior police contacts that the officer is aware of. The bicycle has been missing for only an hour and is unharmed. The owner of the bicycle is undecided about whether or not to proceed officially. Discuss the various options available to the police officer in handling this case. What options do you consider to be most appropriate and why?

3. Why do you think juvenile officers handle the majority of contacts with juveniles unofficially even when they could clearly proceed officially? Why are police officers often hesitant to take official action in cases involving abuse or neglect, even though they are mandated reporters? What are some of the advantages and disadvantages to both juveniles and society of unofficial dispositions?
4. Locate the website for the Department of Justice, and see what information you can obtain on the Youth-Focused Community Policing program. Is there a recent evaluation of the program? If so, what conclusions can you draw about the program based on the evaluation?

SUGGESTED READINGS

Black, D. J., & Reiss, A. J., Jr. (1970). Police control of juveniles. *American Sociological Review, 35,* 63–77.

Breen, M. D. (2001). A renewed commitment to juvenile justice. *Police Chief, 68* (3), 47–52.

Engel, R. S., Sobol, J. J., & Worden, R. E. (2000). Further exploration of the demeanor hypothesis: The interaction effects of suspects' characteristics and demeanor on police behavior. *Justice Quarterly, 17* (2), 235–258.

Hurst, Y. G., & Frank, J. (2000). How kids view cops: The nature of juvenile attitudes toward the police. *Journal of Crime and Justice, 28* (3) 189–202.

Hurst, Y. G., Frank, J., & Browning, S. L. (2000). The attitudes of juveniles toward the police: A comparison of black and white youth. *Policing: An International Journal of Police Strategies & Management, 23* (1), 37–53.

Lundman, R. L., Sykes, E. G., & Clark, J. P. (1978). Police control of juveniles: A replication. *Journal of Research in Crime and Delinquency, 15,* 74–91.

Moriarty, A., & Fitzgerald, P. (1992). A rationale for police-school collaboration. *Law and Order* (May), 47–51.

Piliavin, I., & Briar, S. (1964). Police encounters with juveniles. *American Journal of Sociology, 70,* 206–214.

Sealock, M. D., & Simpson, S. S. (1998). Unraveling bias in arrest decisions: The role of juvenile offender type-scripts. *Justice Quarterly, 15* (3), 427–457.

CHAPTER

8 KEY FIGURES IN JUVENILE COURT PROCEEDINGS

CHAPTER LEARNING OBJECTIVES

Upon completion of this chapter, students should be able to:

Explain the roles of the prosecutor, defense counsel, judge, and probation officer in juvenile court
Discuss differences between private and state-appointed defense counsel
Discuss conflicting views of the relationship between the prosecutor and defense counsel
Explain plea bargaining
Discuss the roles of child and family services and court-appointed advocates in juvenile court proceedings

KEY TERMS

prosecutor/state's attorney
unofficial probation
defense counsel
guardian ad litem
private counsel
court-appointed counsel
juvenile court judge
"parent-figure" judges
"law-giver" judges
juvenile probation officer
electronic monitoring
children and family services
court-appointed special advocates
preservice/inservice training

One of the alternatives available to the police in dealing with juvenile offenders or adults who commit offenses against children involves taking official action that can result in further processing through the juvenile (or, in the case of adult perpetrators) adult justice network. Once the decision to take official action has been made, juvenile court personnel become involved in the

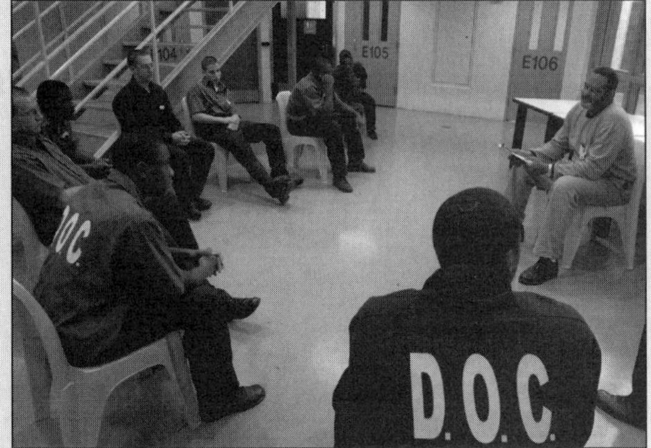

Incarceration is one possible outcome of juvenile court proceedings.
Gary Tramontina/AP/Wide World

case. We are using the term *juvenile court personnel* in a broad sense to include the prosecutor, defense counsel, the judge, the juvenile probation officer, and, in abuse and neglect cases, representatives of children and family service agencies (also known as children's protective services).

THE PROSECUTOR

The final decision about whether a juvenile will be dealt with in juvenile court rests with the prosecutor. Regardless of the source of the referral (police officer, teacher, parent), the prosecutor may decide not to take the case into court and, for all practical purposes, no further official action may be taken on the case in question. The prosecutor, then, exercises an enormous amount of discretion in the juvenile (and in the adult) justice system. While the police officer may "open the gate" to the juvenile justice system, the prosecutor may close that gate. The prosecutor may do this without accounting for his or her reasons to anyone else in the system (except, of course, to the voters who elect the prosecutor to office, which often occurs long after the case in question has been dismissed).

Clearly, there are some circumstances under which the prosecutor would be foolish to proceed with court action. For example, lack of evidence, lack of probable cause, or lack of due process may make it virtually impossible to prosecute a case successfully. There are, however, a number of somewhat less legitimate reasons for failure to prosecute. There have been instances where prosecutors have failed to take cases to court for political or personal reasons (as when the youth in question is the son or daughter of a powerful and influential citizen) or because the case load of the prosecutor includes an important or serious case in which successful prosecution will result in favorable publicity. As a result, the prosecutor may screen out or dismiss a number of "less serious" cases, such as burglary and assault (Atkins and Pogrebin 1978). In short, the prosecutor is the key figure in the justice system and is recognized as such by both defendants and defense counsel (Laub and MacMurray 1987; Mays and Winfree 2000; Ellis and Sowers 2001, p. 40).

In recent years, however, the prosecutor has lost some discretion historically afforded to him or her because of discretionary controls enacted within state legislation. These controls have been designed to decrease the amount of discretion a prosecutor has in determining whether or not a case remains in the jurisdiction of the juvenile court or is waived to adult court. In Illinois, for example, it is mandated that the prosecutor request to transfer a juvenile to adult court if the child is fifteen years or older and commits an act that is a forcible felony and has previously been adjudicated delinquent or committed the act in conjunction with a gang-based activity (*ILCS.* ch. 705, sec. 405/5-805: 1998). There are also presumptive transfers that deal with violence involving firearms and other clearly stated legislative policies on when prosecutors may use their discretion to transfer juveniles to adult criminal court. The discretionary controls have not been designed to take away from the prosecutor's role in court or to undermine the duties placed upon the prosecutor, but are in place in order to ensure that prosecutors are not abusing the position and the power given to them by the court system. The discretionary controls are also a political response to the public's recent outcries against juvenile violence. Despite the discretionary controls, prosecutors are still key figures in the juvenile court system.

The prosecutor's key role in the American juvenile justice system has emerged slowly over time. Initially, the **prosecutor (state's attorney)** was seen as both unnecessary and harmful in juvenile court proceedings which were supposedly nonadversary proceedings "on behalf of the juvenile" (*Prosecution in the Juvenile Courts: Guidelines for the Future* 1973). The *Gault* decision, along with the decisions in *Kent* and *Winship,* brought about a number of changes in juvenile court proceedings. Among these changes was a growing recognition of the need for legally trained individuals to represent both the state and the juvenile (and, in some instances, the juvenile's parents) in all stages of juvenile justice proceedings. The need resulted from increased emphasis upon procedural requirements and the adversary nature of the proceedings.

Today, the prosecutor is a key figure in juvenile justice because he or she determines whether or not a case will go to court, most waiver decisions, the nature of the petition and, to a large extent, the disposition of the case after adjudication (the judge seldom imposes more severe punishment than that recommended by the prosecutor). In addition, there is a tendency on the part of some prosecutors to impose **unofficial probation.** The prosecutor indicates that he or she has a prosecutable case, but also indicates that prosecution will be withheld if the suspect in question agrees to behave according to certain guidelines. These are often the same guidelines handed down by probation officers subsequent to an adjudication of delinquent, abused, or neglected. This amounts to a form of continuance under supervision without proving the charges in court and may result from an admission of the facts by the minor or lack of objection by the minor, his or her parents, and legal counsel to this procedure. In essence, this procedure provides an alternative to official adjudication as a delinquent and is regarded beneficial in that sense. However, while the use of unofficial probation is clearly beneficial to the prosecutor since it eliminates the need to prepare a case for court and may be beneficial for the juvenile court by reducing the number of official cases, unofficial probation has the same potential disadvantages as informal adjustments by the police. In short, unofficial probation imposed by the prosecutor amounts to punishment without trial, and the voluntary nature of this probation is highly questionable. Informal agreements may also work to the disadvantage of youth who are suspected of being abused or neglected and who are allowed to remain in the home as a result of such agreements.

In addition to enforcing the law and representing the state, the prosecutor has many of the following duties in juvenile justice proceedings:

- investigates possible violations of the law
- cooperates with the police, in-take officers, and probation officers regarding the facts alleged in the petition
- authorizes, reviews, and prepares petitions for the court
- plays a role in the initial detention or temporary placement process
- represents the state in all pretrial motions, probable cause hearings, and consent decrees
- represents the state at transfer and waiver hearings
- may recommend physical or mental examinations
- seeks amendments or dismissals of filed petitions if appropriate
- represents the state at the adjudication of the case
- represents the state at the disposition of the case
- enters into plea-bargaining discussions with the defense attorney

Prosecutor and defense counsel at work in juvenile court.
Spencer Grant/Photo Edit

- represents the state on appeal or in *habeas corpus* proceedings
- is involved in hearings dealing with violation of probation. (Siegal and Senna 1994, p. 551)

The attorney for the state (prosecutor), then, participates in every proceeding of every stage of every case subject to the jurisdiction of the family court in which the state has an interest.

DEFENSE COUNSEL

The American Bar Association (1977) has described the responsibility of the legal profession to the juvenile court in Standard 2.3 of "Standards Relating to Counsel for Private Parties." The ABA states that legal representation should be provided in all proceedings arising from or related to a delinquency or in-need-of-supervision action—including mental competency, transfer, postdisposition, probation revocation and classification, institutional transfer, and disciplinary or other administrative proceedings related to the treatment process—that may substantially affect the juvenile's custody, status, or course of treatment.

Juvenile court proceedings involving delinquency and abuse are adversary in nature, in spite of the intent of the early developers of juvenile court philosophy. It is for this reason that the role of **defense counsel** (the attorney representing the defendant) has become increasingly more important. Today in most jurisdictions all juveniles named in petitions are represented by counsel. In Illinois, for example, no proceeding under the Juvenile Court Act may be initiated unless the juvenile is represented by counsel (*ILCS*. ch. 705. sec. 405/1–5: 1998). In many cases the juvenile's parents also have legal representation. In some cases a *guardian ad litem* may be appointed by the court. The ***guardian ad litem*** is a person appointed by the court "to promote and protect the interests of a child involved in a judicial proceeding, and to assure representation of those interests in the courts and throughout the social services and ancillary service systems" (Davidson 1981). Generally the *guardian ad litem* is used in abuse, neglect, and dependency cases where the minor is in need of representation because of immaturity.

There are two basic categories of defense counsel. **Private counselors** are sometimes retained or appointed to represent the interests of juveniles in court. Frequently, however, juveniles are represented by **court-appointed counsel** (attorneys or public defenders). The former are typically drawn from a roster of practicing attorneys in the jurisdiction, while the latter are full-time, salaried employees. Both are paid by the county or state or both, to represent defendants who do not have the money to retain private counsel. For many young lawyers interested in criminal law, the position of public defender represents a stepping stone. In most areas the public defender is paid a relatively low salary, but the position guarantees a minimal income, which can be supplemented by private practice. For example, the most recent information available on defense systems for the indigent found that the average cost per case to state and local government for indigent defense was $5.37 per capita, ranging from a low of $0.11 per case in West Virginia to a high of $11.23 in Alaska (Barlow 2000, p. 374).

As a rule, public defender caseloads are heavy, investigative resources are limited, and many clients are, by their own admission, guilty or delinquent (Barlow 2000). The public defender, therefore, spends a great deal of time negotiating pleas and often very little time with clients. In fact, sometimes public defenders in juvenile court indicate to the judge that they are ready to proceed and then ask someone in the courtroom which of the several juveniles present is (are) their client(s). As a result, public defenders often enjoy a less-than-favorable image among their clients (Barlow 2000, pp. 377–379).

Some public defenders seem to have little interest in using every possible strategy to defend their clients (*Economist* 1998). On occasion, legal errors are made by prosecutors and juvenile court judges to which the public defender raises no objection (see In Practice 8.1). Appeals initiated by public defenders in cases tried in juvenile court are relatively rare even when chances of successful appeal seem to be good. There are also public defenders that pursue their clients' interests with all possible vigor; but on the whole, it appears that juveniles who have private counsel often fare better in juvenile court than those who are represented by public defenders. There is little doubt that the office of public defender is frequently underfunded, and that such underfunding is a major factor in most of the criticisms leveled at the office.

Whether defense counsel is private or public, his or her duties remain essentially the same. These duties are to see that the client is properly represented at all stages of the system, that the client's rights are not violated, and that the client's case is presented in

In Practice 8.1

CHILD ABUSE, DELINQUENCY PROMINENT IN JUDGE'S WORLD

Juvenile court paid little notice but covers widest possible range of human experience

Pam Adams

Peoria—Most people know more about McDonald's Happy Meals than juvenile court.

Most attorneys ignore it. The Peoria County Board ignores it. And the media ignores it until a tragic child-abuse case or an equally tragic case of a youth accused of serious crime.

"I don't think it's a high priority with anybody except the people who are in it," Thomas Ebel says.

Abused, neglected, dependent children—the bulk of the caseload—are ignored more than delinquents, he says.

Ebel, the associate judge who presides over Peoria County Juvenile Court, would sound more self-serving if he didn't admit he ignored juvenile court until he was assigned there, first for a few months in 1982 and again three years ago.

"I just never thought about it," he says, though he worked as an assistant state's attorney in Peoria and Tazewell counties before his judgeship.

Children's court has been a high priority for Associate Judge Brett Bode for most of the 12 years he has been a judge. Now assigned to Tazewell County's small claims court, Bode agrees with Ebel's assessment, with one addition: It irks him that the state's attorney's office uses juvenile court as a training ground for entry-level assistants.

"So you have the least-experienced attorneys handling cases that are absolutely critical to that child," Bode says.

Tucked away on the fourth floor of Peoria County Courthouse, juvenile court is closed to the public for the sake of children's confidentiality.

It is a world unto itself, peopled mostly by a small clique of attorneys, social-service workers and juvenile probation and police officers.

"It is a diverse court, that covers the widest range of the human experience," says Mark Cosimini, chief assistant state's attorney for juvenile court.

It does seem like nobody cares, says Susan Lucas, an assistant public defender who has tried juvenile cases for about nine years. "But nobody cares because nobody knows."

- A man is found murdered after his two children tell neighbors that Daddy won't wake up. The next day, the children are in juvenile court for a custody hearing.
- The girl is a chronic truant. Her mother doesn't know what to do. Ebel orders the girl to go to school or face contempt of court charges.
- The children were taken from their parents and placed in foster care almost two years ago. Their parents were involved in satanic rituals, requiring physical and sexual abuse of children, and possibly child sacrifice. They come to juvenile court every six months for a review of their foster placement.

—Continued on page 174

—Continued from page 173

- The young parents want custody back, or at least visitation rights, to their three children. The baby girl plays and swings on a courtroom gate as Ebel tells her parents they will have to wait until both parents complete chemical-dependency treatment, parenting classes and psychological evaluations.
- The boy was suspended from school for nine days in November. As punishment, according to court testimony, his uncle made him sit in a closet for nine days during school hours. The boy denies an earlier allegation that the uncle had once tied a rope around his wrists and hung him from a ceiling beam in the garage.

  His elderly grandmother has had custody since his mother died; but the uncle has taken responsibility since the grandmother's stroke. The boy and his grandmother desperately want to be with each other, but they can't be in the same house with the uncle. Ebel orders a Department of Children and Family Services worker to try to find a suitable relative to live with the boy and his grandmother. Until the next hearing, the boy returns to foster care.
- Last January, the 16-year-old was placed on one year's probation for possession of cocaine. In October, Ebel sentenced him to a juvenile prison facility on weapons charges. Attempted murder charges were dropped in exchange for a guilty plea.
- A 15-year-old girl brutally beat an employee of the juvenile detention center. Ebel had seen her in court for years, first on abuse and neglect days, then for her own delinquency hearings.

Day in and day out in juvenile court.

Monday is delinquency day; Tuesday is for abuse and neglect cases. On Wednesday, Ebel hears mental-fitness cases at Zeller Mental Health Center. Thursday is a mix of abuse, neglect and delinquency, though he tries to save it for cases involving cocaine babies. And on Friday, more abuse and neglect.

Nothing is sacred about the schedule. Anything may happen on any day, including an adoption. "Those are the happy times," he says.

Despite its informal atmosphere, juvenile court is a high-volume, emotionally intense court.

"The abuse and neglect cases bother you a lot more than the crime," he says. "There are just things you can't believe a parent would do to a child."

"The tragedy is, you get used to it."

Despite all the complaints about delinquency, in many cases, he'll put a juvenile on probation and never see him or her again.

Several hundred juveniles on probation are considered wards of the court, so they

the most favorable light possible, regardless of the client's involvement in delinquent or criminal activity (Pollock 1994, pp. 145–152). In order to accomplish these goals, the defense counsel is expected to battle, at least in theory, the prosecutor in adversary proceedings. However, the quality of representation afforded is not guaranteed. The public defender's office is frequently understaffed, and private counsel is often too expensive to be considered an option. As Siegal and Senna (1994, p. 557) note, "Representation should be upgraded in all areas of the juvenile court system."

—Continued from page 174

fall under his jurisdiction, along with those in Peoria County's Juvenile Detention Center and those he has ordered placed in residential facilities.

He comments regularly that he'd like to see the County Board allot more money for placement in residential facilities.

He recalls when the juvenile court judge was almost a part-time position.

The most common order he makes requires unfit parents to complete drug treatment if they want to regain custody of their children.

He mentions that he is not infallible. The day may come when he makes a "mistake" and returns an abused child to parents who take the child's life.

"That's an awesome decision," he says. "But the most awesome decision is terminating parental rights. This is actually a death sentence for that parent-child relationship, it doesn't exist anymore."

Angela Madison, a public defender who usually represents abused and neglected children, says another courtroom could be filled with the backlog of petitions for termination of parental rights alone.

Without the black robe, Thomas Ebel seems the perfect choice to play a wry, mischief-making Santa's elf in the all-school play. He is a funny guy with a dry wit.

When he goes to Northwoods Mall, many of the kids say, "Hiya, Judge."

"That only happens when I'm in this court—they know who's assigned to juvenile court," he says.

Growing up in Will County, he wanted to be a state trooper. But at 5-foot-6, he was 4 inches away from the old height requirement. So he joined the U.S. Air Force.

The stint in the military made him want to go to college. He graduated from Illinois Benedictine College in Lisle and Notre Dame Law School. The old desire to be a state trooper influenced his decision to enter criminal law as a prosecutor.

While in law school, he spent the summer of 1969 in the Peoria County State's Attorney Office, codifying Peoria County Board ordinances back to the 1800s, which meshed with his natural organizing tendency. Before Ebel, the only record of county ordinances were in the minutes of each meeting.

After graduation, he came back to work as an assistant state's attorney in Peoria County, then as legal adviser for the Peoria Police Department in 1972–73.

From there, he was hired as an assistant state's attorney in Tazewell County. He stayed there until he was appointed a judge in 1981 at age 39.

Though juvenile court focuses on rehabilitation and corrective behavior, Ebel doesn't believe a judge should be a social worker, a buddy or a preacher.

But he remembers the seminar, where a judge reminded other judges, "Remember, you're all these kids have to protect them."

Adams, P. (1994, March 13). Child abuse, deliquency prominent in judge's world. © *Peoria (Ill.) Journal Star,* 1A.

The Relationship between the Prosecutor and Defense Counsel—Adversary or Cooperative?

In theory, adversary proceedings result when the "champion" of the defendant (defense counsel) and the "champion" of the state (prosecutor) do "battle" in open court where the "truth" is determined and "justice" is the result. In practice the situation is quite often different due to considerations of time and money on behalf of both the state and the defendant.

The ideal of adversary proceedings is perhaps most closely realized when a well-known private defense attorney does battle with the prosecutor. The O. J. Simpson case of the 1990s is an excellent example. Prominent defense attorneys often have competent investigative staffs and considerable resources in terms of time and money to devote to a case. Thus, the balance of power between the state and the defendant may be almost even. This is generally not the case when defense counsel is a public defender who is often paid less than the prosecutor, often has less experience than the prosecutor, and generally has more limited access to an investigative staff than the prosecutor. For a variety of reasons then, both defense counsel and the prosecutor may find it easier to negotiate a particular case rather than to fight it out in court, since court cases are costly in terms of both time and money. The vast majority of adult criminal cases in the United States are settled by plea bargaining. A substantial proportion of delinquency and abuse/neglect cases is disposed of in this way, as well. In fact, it has been suggested that justice in the United States is not the result of the adversary system, but is the result of a cooperative network of routine interactions between defense counsel, the prosecutor, the defendant, and, in many instances, the judge (Blumberg 1967; Sudnow 1965; Barlow 2000, p. 349).

In plea bargaining, both prosecutor and defense counsel hope to gain through compromise. The prosecutor wants the defendant to plead guilty—if not to the original charges then to some less serious offense. Defense counsel seeks to get the best deal possible for his or her client, which may range from an outright dismissal to a plea of guilty to some offense less serious than the original charge. The nature of the compromise depends upon conditions such as the strength of the prosecutor's case and the seriousness of the offense. Most often, the two counselors arrive at what both consider a "just" compromise, which is then presented to the defendant to accept or reject. As a rule, the punishment to be recommended by the prosecutor is also negotiated. Thus, the nature of the charges, the plea, and the punishment are negotiated and agreed upon before the defendant actually enters the courtroom. The adversary system, in its ideal form at least, has been circumvented. Perhaps a hypothetical example will help to clarify the nature and consequences of plea bargaining.

Suppose our friend, Joe Foul Up, is once again in trouble. This time, Joe is seen breaking into a house. The break-in is reported to the police who apprehend Joe in the house with a watch and some expensive jewelry belonging to the home owner. This time, the police decide to take official action. Since Joe is over thirteen and since the offense is fairly serious, the prosecutor threatens to prosecute Joe as an adult in adult court. She also indicates that she intends to seek a prison sentence for Joe. Joe's attorney, realizing that the prosecutor has a strong case, knows that he cannot get Joe's case dismissed. He argues with the prosecutor that this is Joe's first appearance before the juvenile court and he is, after all, a juvenile. After some discussion, the prosecutor agrees to prosecute Joe in juvenile court, provided the allegation of delinquency is not contested. Joe's attorney agrees, provided the prosecutor recommends only a short stay in a private detention facility in the community. Joe's attorney then presents the deal to Joe and perhaps to Joe's parents, indicating that it is the best he can do and recommending that Joe accept, since he could be found guilty and sentenced to prison if he is tried in adult court. Joe accepts and the bargain is concluded. The case has been settled in the attorney's offices. All that remains is to make it official during the formal court appearance. Most judges will concur with the negotiated plea.

The benefits of plea bargaining to the prosecutor, defense counsel, and the juvenile court are clear. The prosecutor is successful in prosecuting a case (she obtains an adjudication of delinquency), defense counsel has reduced the charges and penalty against his client, and all parties have saved time and money by not contesting the case in court. The juvenile may benefit as well, since he might have been convicted of burglary in adult court (if the judge had accepted the prosecutor's motion to change jurisdiction) and might have ended up in prison with a felony record. The dangers in plea bargaining, however, should not be overlooked. First, there is always the possibility that the motion to change jurisdiction might have been denied. Second, Joe might have been found not guilty even if he had been tried in adult court or might have been found not delinquent if his case had been heard in juvenile court. Third, since negotiations occur most often in secret, there is a danger that the constitutional rights of the defendant may not be stringently upheld. For example, Joe did not have the chance to confront and cross-examine his accusers. Finally, the **juvenile court judge** is little more than a figurehead, left only to sanction the bargain, in cases settled by plea bargaining. The juvenile court judge has the responsibility to see that the hearings are conducted in the best interests of both the juvenile and society and has the responsibility to ensure due process. Neither of these can be guaranteed in cases involving plea bargaining. A final concern in all plea bargaining processes, whether adult or juvenile, is the victim who seldom feels good about the bargain.

THE JUVENILE COURT JUDGE

Theoretically, the juvenile court judge is the most powerful and central figure in the juvenile justice system, although he or she does not always exercise this power. The juvenile court judge decides whether a youth will be adjudicated delinquent, abused, in need of intervention, dependent, or neglected. Since there is no jury in most instances, the decision of the judge is final unless an appeal overturns the judge's decision. In addition, the judge makes the final determination about the disposition of the juvenile. Therefore, the juvenile court judge decides matters of law, matters of fact, and the immediate future of those who come before the bench.

In many states, hearing officers known as *referees* or *commissioners* are appointed to assist juvenile court judges. These hearing officers typically submit recommendations which must be certified by a judge before they have the effect of law (Roberts 1989, p. 114). Some of the difficulties in using such officers are pointed out in In Practice 8.2.

Within the confines of legislative mandates, juvenile judges rule on pretrial motions involving issues such as arrest, search and seizure, interrogation, and lineup identification. They make decisions about the continued detention of children prior to hearings, and they make decisions about plea bargaining agreements and informal adjustments. They hold bench hearings, rule on appropriateness of conduct, and settle

In Practice 8.2

REFEREES IN JUVENILE COURT

It is possible, however, for much of the work [of the juvenile court] to be done under the supervision of the judge by individuals who have not had legal training. Many cases are now settled by in-take officers who are not lawyers. In more than twenty-five states, the law gives juvenile court judges the authority to appoint referees, who make tentative disposals of the cases petitioned for hearing, subject to the judge's approval. This power to appoint referees makes it possible to extend the court to rural districts, far from the sites where court sessions are regularly held. If no such arrangement is made, juvenile offenses may be passed over, handled by a justice of the peace, or dealt with by some other unsatisfactory method because of the inconvenience of attending juvenile court sessions. (Sutherland, Cressey, and Luckenbill 1992, p. 4438)

questions concerning evidence and procedure. They guide the questioning of witnesses. They decide on treatment for youth. They preside over waiver hearings, and they handle appeals where allowed by statute (Siegal and Senna 1994).

While judges in some jurisdictions are assigned to juvenile court on a full-time basis, there are also many juvenile court judges who serve on a part-time basis. The latter are circuit judges who perform judicial functions in civil, criminal, probate, and other divisions of the court and are assigned occasionally to juvenile court. It is difficult for such judges to become specialists in juvenile court proceedings, though many perform well, and some are not as well versed in juvenile law as they might be.

Juvenile court judges may be placed along a continuum ranging from those who see themselves largely as parent figures to those who are mainly concerned about the juvenile court as a legal institution. The **"parent-figure" judge** is often genuinely concerned about the total well-being of juveniles who appear before the court. He or she is likely to overlook some of the formalities of due process in an attempt to serve as a parent figure who both supports and disciplines juveniles. This judge's primary concern is serving what he or she perceives as the best interests of the juveniles who appear in court, based on the assumption that they must have problems even though they may not have committed the specific acts that led to the filing of a petition or been victims of abuse or neglect in the specific instance in question. Often these judges talk to the juveniles and/or the parents involved in an attempt to obtain expressions of remorse or regret. Once these expressions are given, the acts involved can often be "forgiven," and attention centers on how to best help the youth to avoid future trouble or victimization. If these expressions of remorse or regret are not given, the judge frequently resorts to a role as disciplinarian, sometimes overlooking the facts in the case.

There is a tendency among parent-figure judges to continue juvenile cases under supervision for various lengths of time. These judges apparently assume that an adju-

In Practice 8.3

REVOLVING DOORS AND JUVENILE JUSTICE

To overcome the shortage of placement possibilities and services, many court judges opt for an easy solution and simply commit the child to a juvenile institution. Others, who hesitate to do this, grasp at the barest of straws to keep the youth in the community. The result is a revolving door policy. Children are released to the community no better prepared to survive than before they were brought before the bench. Within no time, the same child appears before the court dozens of times. Institutionalization, even to the most sympathetic judge, becomes the inevitable solution. (Simonsen 1991, p. 235)

dication of delinquency, abuse, neglect, or minor-requiring-authoritative-intervention is less desirable than using the threat of adjudication in an attempt to induce acceptable behavior. While most juvenile court acts provide for judicial continuance, this action can be carried to the extreme in situations where the case against the youth or parent or guardian is weak and the continuance period long. These continuances amount to punishment without trial in much the same way as do informal adjustments and unofficial probation.

At the other end of the continuum is the **"law-giver" judge** who is primarily concerned that all procedural requirements are fulfilled. This type of judge has less interest in the total personality of the juvenile than in the evidence of the case at hand. He or she dismisses cases that the prosecutor cannot prove beyond a reasonable doubt (or, in abuse and neglect cases, cannot demonstrate a preponderance of evidence for) and does not feel that it is his or her duty to prescribe treatment for juveniles who have not committed the offense for which they have been accused or who cannot be shown to have been victims of abuse or neglect. The dispositions of the law-giver judge are based upon statutory requirements more than upon the personal characteristics of the parties involved.

Most juvenile court judges fall somewhere between the two extremes, reflecting the lack of consensus about the proper role of the juvenile court discussed in chapter 1. Most judges make a sincere effort to maximize legal safeguards for juveniles while attempting to act in the best interests of both the juveniles and society. They ensure that legal counsel is available, they try to arrive at an objective decision during the adjudicatory hearing, and they try to ensure that the disposition of each case takes into account the needs of the juvenile involved. Tower (1993, p. 293) describes the efforts of the juvenile court judge in abuse and neglect cases as follows: "Deprived of the support of a jury (in most cases), the judge must base the final decision on the report of the investigator, on what has been heard in the courtroom, on the judge's own experience, and often on the assumption of what will be best for all concerned."

Simonsen (1991, p. 235) points out some of the dilemmas encountered by juvenile court judges (In Practice 8.3).

Tower (1993, p. 293) concludes: "Since people's motivations are never predictable, the juvenile court judge realizes there is no assurance that a child will be safe when returned home or happy in placement. Using only best judgment and the hope that it is correct, the judge renders the decision." In a study of serious child maltreatment cases brought before the Boston Juvenile Court in 1994, the authors conclude that despite some improvements in the past decade, "the system still fails to promptly find permanent placements for seriously maltreated children." (Bishop, Murphy, and Hicks 2000). In attempting to arrive at an acceptable disposition, the juvenile court judge frequently relies heavily upon the recommendations of the juvenile probation officer (MacDonald and Baroody-Hard 1999), and, in abuse and neglect cases, of the representative of children and family services.

The Juvenile Probation Officer

Probation is the oldest and most widely used disposition with over 18,000 juvenile probation officers in the United States (Torbet 1996). Probation is a disposition by the juvenile court in which the minor is placed and maintained in the community under the supervision of a duly authorized officer of the court, the **juvenile probation officer.** "Probation may be used at the 'front-end' of the juvenile justice system for the first-time, low risk offenders or at the 'back-end' as an alternative to institutional confinement for more serious offenders." (Torbet 1996, p. 1) Either way, it allows the minor to remain with the family or a foster family under conditions prescribed by the court to ensure acceptable behavior in a community setting.

The juvenile probation officer is a key figure at all levels of the juvenile justice system. He or she may arrange a preliminary conference among interested parties, which may result in an out-of-court settlement between an alleged delinquent and the injured party or between parties in cases of abuse or neglect. After an adjudicatory hearing, the juvenile probation officer is often charged with conducting a social background investigation. This investigation will be used to help the judge make a dispositional decision. Probation officers are also charged with supervising those juveniles who are placed on probation and released in the community and parents who have been deemed to have committed neglect or abuse. Probation officers have the power to request a revocation of probation if violations of the conditions of probation occur.

The duties of chief probation officers generally include assignment of cases and supervision of subordinates. They may or may not handle cases themselves, depending upon available staff. In addition, they normally serve as a liaison with judges and other department heads. The better the rapport they are able to establish with the juvenile court judge and the more effective they are in transmitting information to subordinates, other juvenile justice practitioners, and the judge, the better the opportunity to serve the interests of juveniles and the community.

The role of juvenile probation officers is an ambiguous one. They are officers of the court who must act as authority figures and disciplinarians on occasion. At the same time, they are charged with helping juveniles in trouble by attempting to keep the juveniles out of court, by recommending the most beneficial disposition, by protecting juveniles from abusive parents while counseling these parents, and by being available to help probationers solve problems encountered during their probationary period. If they are to be effective in their role as helping professionals, they must encourage open interaction and trust among the juveniles and parents or guardians they encounter (Parker-Jimenez 1997). If they seem too authoritarian, they may receive little cooperation. If they become too friendly, they may find it difficult to take disciplinary steps when necessary.

As a result of the ambiguous role requirements, several different types of juvenile probation officers exist. Some think of themselves largely as law enforcement officers whose basic function is to detect violations of probation. Others see themselves as juvenile advocates whose basic function is to ensure that the rights of juveniles are not violated by the police or potential petitioners. Still others view themselves as basically social workers whose function is to facilitate treatment and rehabilitation. The most effective juvenile probation officers exercise all of these options at different times under differing circumstances. Perhaps the most difficult task for most juvenile probation officers is the supervision of probationers. Many have excessive caseloads and have little actual contact with their clients other than short weekly or monthly meetings. Obviously, not a great deal of counseling or supervision can occur under these circumstances. When field contacts are made with probationers, probation officers are often considerably concerned about further stigmatizing their clients. Parents who have problems with their children sometimes try to use the juvenile probation officer's official position to frighten the youth into compliance with their demands. As a result of these difficulties, most juvenile probation officers in discussing probation conditions with their clients make it clear that they are available to discuss whatever problems probationers feel are significant. Some juvenile probation officers using this technique allow clients to choose the time and place for conferences in order to minimize stigmatization.

Juvenile probation officers must also work daily to overcome several issues including job safety, rising caseloads, a lack of resources, and feelings of failure. In a recent study by the Office of Juvenile Justice and Delinquency Prevention in 1996 it was reported that over one-third of juvenile probation officers had been assaulted on the job and 42 percent stated that they were usually or always concerned about their personal safety while working (Torbet 1996). In response to these concerns, some jurisdictions have implemented intensive supervision and school-based programs into local schools. Along with safety concerns, rising caseloads have also become a problem for juvenile probation officers. Respondents to the 1996 survey from the Office of Juvenile Justice and Delinquency Prevention stated that their caseloads ranged between two and more than two hundred, with the typical caseload at around forty-one probationers. It was also reported that probation caseloads are containing more violent youth than in previous years. However, the number of resources available to juvenile probation officers has not increased with the number of probationers. Juvenile probation officers are still limited in the types of placements available to probationers and in the amount of funding they can receive from the jurisdiction for treatment for juveniles on their caseloads. This often means that juvenile probation officers must be creative in their approach to their probationers' treatments and rehabilitative efforts. From the same 1996 survey by the Office of Juvenile Justice and Delinquency Prevention it was reported that "although [juvenile probation officers] chose this line of work 'to help kids,' their greatest sources of frustration are an inability to impact the lives of youth, the attitudes of probationers and their families, and difficulties in identifying successes" (p. 1).

Technological innovations such as **electronic monitoring** are of some help to probation officers in supervising their clients. Recently, the Florida Department of Corrections began a pilot project using the Global Positioning Satellite (GPS) system to track the movements and location of probationers, warn prior victims if necessary, and determine whether probationers are in "off-limits" locations (Mercer, Brooks, and Bryant 2000).

CHILDREN AND FAMILY SERVICES PERSONNEL

Although personnel from departments of **children and family services** (child protective services) do not actually work for the juvenile courts, they play major roles in investigation, presentation of evidence, and dispositional recommendations in abuse and neglect cases. Typically when law enforcement officers believe they have discovered a case of abuse or neglect, they are required to report the case to children and family services. Departments of children and family services usually maintain a central register of abuse and neglect cases. Upon receiving a report of suspected or confirmed abuse or neglect, personnel from the child protective agency begin an investigation of the allegation. In emergency cases, such investigations are to be conducted immediately, in theory at least. In other cases, investigators are normally required to conduct an investigation within a specified time period (typically 24 to 48 hours). Such investigation normally involves interviews with the alleged victim and offender and an evaluation of risk factors in the child's environment. Where appropriate, the child may be removed from the home to safeguard his or her welfare.

If the allegations of abuse or neglect are found to be true, caseworkers from children and family services are involved in assisting the youth involved in court proceedings and in formulating plans to provide services or treatment to both the youth and the families involved. In cases in which abuse or neglect occurs in institutional settings, the institutions involved, if allowed to remain open, are monitored by children and family services.

COURT-APPOINTED SPECIAL ADVOCATES

Court-appointed special advocates or CASA volunteers work closely with the departments of children and family services on abuse and neglect cases. CASA volunteers are trained citizen volunteers who are appointed by the court to give advice on the best interests of children who are victims of abuse and neglect. The volunteers are ordinary people, usually without legal expertise, who care about what happens to children who have been victimized by abusive or neglectful parents. The juvenile court rarely appoints CASAs in delinquency cases (this may happen only if the delinquent child has an extensive history of abuse and neglect that may be influencing his or her delinquent behavior).

In jurisdictions with CASA programs, CASA volunteers are assigned to one case at a time by the juvenile court judge. They are responsible for researching the background of the case, reviewing court documents, and interviewing everyone involved in the case, including the child. CASA volunteers also prepare a report for the court discussing what they believe is in the best interests of the child based upon the evidence they have reviewed. The judge may use this report when deciding upon a disposition for the child. Once the judge has decided upon the case, the CASA continues monitoring the case to ensure that the child or the family receives the services ordered by the court.

TRAINING AND COMPETENCE OF JUVENILE COURT PERSONNEL

If the goals of the juvenile justice system are to be achieved, the system needs to be staffed by well-trained, competent practitioners. Unfortunately, a number of circumstances have prevented total success in this area.

Prosecutors and defense attorneys who handle juvenile court cases generally have little to gain by large investments of time and money. Few defense attorneys have gained national renown as the result of their efforts in juvenile court. Few prosecutors can count on being reelected on the basis of successful prosecutions in juvenile court. In addition, in many locales the juvenile court is regarded as something less than a real court of law where technical proficiency in law is necessary. Prosecutors often assign inexperienced assistants to handle juvenile court cases and few defense attorneys specialize in the practice of juvenile law. As a result, many cases presented in juvenile court are poorly prepared by both sides. Some prosecutors are not thoroughly familiar with the juvenile code governing their jurisdiction. Similarly, defense attorneys will at times accept hearsay evidence, fail to present witnesses for the defense, and fail to object to procedural violations which might result in the dismissal of the petition concerning their client. In short, although the frequency of legal representation for both the state and defense has increased considerably in the last decade, the quality of such representation often leaves something to be desired.

Many judges handle juvenile cases as a part-time assignment. While many clearly have the best interest of juveniles at heart, far too many show the same unfamiliarity with juvenile codes that characterizes many attorneys appearing before them. In fact, as we have observed some appear to disregard juvenile codes altogether and rule their jurisdictions as dictators whose decisions on the bench are law.

A particularly disturbing example of judicial lack of familiarity with juvenile law was a case in which a part-time juvenile court judge sentenced a fourteen-year-old truant (MRAI) to the department of corrections. This clearly violates the juvenile code prohibiting status offenders from being transferred to that department. Intervention by the prosecutor and probation officer prevented this illegal act, which otherwise might have gone unchallenged until the department of corrections refused to accept the juvenile.

It should not be too much to ask that attorneys and judges practicing in juvenile court read and become familiar with applicable juvenile codes. If they do not, none of the constitutional guarantees or court decisions regarding due process in juvenile cases will have any impact. Treating juvenile court cases as if they did not involve the real practice of law has made practice before the juvenile court unattractive to many lawyers and judges and will continue to do so in the future. Fortunately, there is some evidence that a corps of better-informed, sincere lawyers and judges is beginning to emerge. In order to encourage the growth of such a corps, proper recognition and rewards must be forthcoming.

Many jurisdictions require a bachelor's degree for employment in probation and social service positions, and a number of practitioners in these positions have master's degrees. The typical juvenile probation officer, for example, is a college-educated white male earning between $20,000 and $39,000 annually, with a caseload of forty-one juveniles (Torbet 1996, p. 1). The Office of Juvenile Justice and Delinquency Prevention (1996) reported that over three-quarters of all probation officers responding to their survey earned less that $40,000 a year, and 30 percent of these do not receive yearly pay increases. In some states, probation officers' salaries, typically paid by the county, are subsidized by state funds in an attempt to alleviate this problem (Torbet 1996, p. 2).

In *Standards for the Administration of Juvenile Justice* (1980), published by the Institute of Justice Administration and the American Bar Association, various sections address the issue of training for juvenile court personnel. For example, one recommendation (sec. 1.4220) states that "family court judges should be provided with **preservice training** on the law and procedures governing subject matter by the family (juvenile) court, the causes of delinquency and family conflict, a thorough understanding of agencies responsible for intake and protective services. In addition, inservice education programs should be provided to judges to assure they are aware of changes in law, policy, and programs." Other recommendations (secs. 1.423, 1.424, and 1.425) address similar issues of preservice and inservice training in juvenile matters with prosecutors, public defenders, and other court personnel and their staffs. Today there is a good deal of **in-service training** available to juvenile justice court personnel. The National Council of Juvenile and Family Court Judges, for examples, sponsors training programs for court personnel on a continuing basis and publishes the *Juvenile and Family Court Journal* to keep practitioners informed of the latest happenings in juvenile justice.

Career Opportunity—Youth Service Coordinator

Job Description: Responsible for coordinating the treatment and rehabilitation services of juvenile offenders; provide for the assessment, classification, procurement, coordination, and evaluation of services for juvenile offenders incarcerated in state correctional and residential facilities; required to work with families, governmental agencies, local courts, schools, and service agencies to create and provide comprehensive treatment programs for troubled youth; may provide counseling to the youth.

Employment Requirements: Usually required to have one year of professional experience in the juvenile justice field; required to have knowledge, experience, and an understanding of group and individual counseling, interactional strategies, and child development and behavior. College education in the areas of criminal justice, psychology, sociology, social work, education, and other closely related fields needed; must complete an oral interview process before being hired.

Salary and Benefits: Benefits provided by the state, including health and life insurance, paid vacations and holidays, and retirement plans. Vary depending upon the geographical location of the position, but can range from $26,000 to $38,000.

Summary

Key figures in juvenile court proceedings include attorneys for the state and for the defendant, the judge, representatives of the department of children and family services, and the probation officer. While the frequency of legal representation in juvenile court is increasing, the quality of this representation needs to be improved. The practice of juvenile law must be taken more seriously if we do not wish to deal with juveniles who repeat their offenses and eventually come before adult courts.

Competent lawyers and judges need to be rewarded for their performances in juvenile court proceedings. Whenever possible, juvenile court judges should be assigned exclusively to juvenile court for whatever period of time. Judges who combine the best elements of the parent-figure and law-giver roles are a definite asset to the juvenile justice system. Probation officers and personnel from the department of children and family services are crucial if juvenile justice philosophy is to be implemented. Their services to the court and to juveniles with problems complement the roles of the other juvenile court personnel.

While the overall quality of juvenile court personnel is improving, there is still considerable variance. Continued emphasis on training and competence at all levels is essential.

INTERNET EXERCISES

The Office of the Family and Children's Ombudsman in Washington provides a 1999 report on *guardian ad litems* on their website at http://www.governor.wa.gov/ofco/gal/galtoc.htm. As indicated in this report, the role of *guardian ad litems* in juvenile court should not be minimized. The *guardian ad litem* is extremely important in monitoring cases involving juvenile victims of abuse and neglect. *Guardian ad litems* are also involved, many times, in cases involving juvenile offenders who are suspected of having an abusive or neglectful past. Take a moment and review the information found in the Office of the Family and Children's Ombudsman's report in order to better understand the role of the *guardian ad litem* in juvenile courts.

1. Based upon the information provided in the report, discuss the three types of *guardian ad litems* and the similarities or differences each has to the defense attorneys discussed in chapter 8 of your text.
2. In your textbook we have discussed training guidelines for police officers, probation offices, and juvenile court judges. What types of training do Washington state *guardian ad litems* have to endure before being assigned juvenile cases involving abuse and neglect? Of the three types of *guardian ad litems* in Washington, do you have any reservations about their abilities to make decisions concerning juvenile cases based upon their experiences or training? Since *guardian ad litems* are not the only decision makers in juvenile court, discuss whether or not you believe the amount of training experienced by the key figures in juvenile court is adequate. What types of training or experiences are lacking for the key figures? What changes should be made in order to provide adequate training to the key figures?
3. *Guardian ad litems* do not have to be appointed in all cases involving juvenile victims of abuse and neglect. Describe an example of a case where a *guardian ad litem* would be unnecessary. Based upon your knowledge of cases involving abuse and neglect, describe a situation where a *guardian ad litem* would be necessary but may be not assigned. Lastly, describe a case where a *guardian ad litem* would be necessary and assigned to the case.
4. Summarize the conclusion of the Office of the Family and Children's Ombudsman's report on *guardian ad litems.*

USEFUL WEBSITES

National Council of Juvenile and Family Court Judges—*http://www.ncjfcj.unr.edu/*

MSN Encarta-Public Defender—*http://encarta.msn.com/find/Concise.asp?ti=058C8000*

National District Attorney's Association—*http://www.ndaa.org/ndaa.htm*

FAQ's Juvenile Probation Department—*http://www.maricopa.gov/juvenile/FAQs/Ans3.htm*

Critical Thinking Questions

1. Discuss the roles of the prosecutor and defense counsel in juvenile court. Why is the presence of legal representatives for both sides crucial in contemporary juvenile court? Discuss the relationship between defense counsel and prosecutor.
2. Why is the judge such a powerful figure in juvenile court? What are the advantages and disadvantages of the judge as law giver and parent figure? How well trained are juvenile court judges?
3. In what sense is the role of juvenile probation officer ambiguous? What are the consequences of this ambiguity? How important is the probation officer in juvenile court proceedings?
4. What role do representatives from the department of children and family services play in juvenile court proceedings? Why are court-appointed special advocates important in juvenile court proceedings?

Suggested Readings

Berlow, A. (2000). Requiem for a public defender. *American Prospect, 11* (14), 28–32.

Bishop, S. J., Murphy, M. J., & Hicks, R. (2000). What progress has been made in meeting the needs of seriously maltreated children? The course of 200 cases through the Boston Juvenile Court. *Child Abuse & Neglect, 24* (5), 599–610.

Bridges, G. S., & Steen, S. (1998). Racial disparities in official assessments of juveniles: Attributional stereotypes as mediating mechanisms. *American Sociological Review, 63* (4), 554–570.

Editorial. (1998). Too poor to be defended (the right of indigent criminal defendants to a lawyer). *Economist, 347* (8063), 21–22.

Fox, R. W., Kanitz, H. M., and Folger, W. A. (1991). Basic counseling skills training program for juvenile court workers. *Journal of Addictions and Offender Counseling, 11* (2), 34–41.

Gahr, E. (2001). Judging juveniles. *American Enterprise, 12* (4), 26–28.

Payne, J. W. (1999). Our children's destiny. *Trial, 35* (1), 83–85.

Reddington, F. P., & Kreisel, B. W. (2000). Training juvenile probation officers: National trends and patterns. *Federal Probation, 64* (2), 28–32.

Rubin, H. T. (1980). The emerging prosecutor dominance of the juvenile court intake process. *Crime and Delinquency 6,* 229–318.

Rush, J. P. (1992). Juvenile probation officer cynicism. *American Journal of Criminal Justice, 16* (2), 1–16.

Torbet, P. M. (1996). *Juvenile probation: The workhorse of the juvenile justice system.* Washington, D.C.: Office of Juvenile Justice and Delinquency Prevention, prepared under grant number 95–JN-FX-K003.

CHAPTER

9 PREVENTION AND DIVERSION PROGRAMS

CHAPTER LEARNING OBJECTIVES

Upon completion of this chapter, students should be able to:

Discuss the advantages and disadvantages of prevention and diversion programs
Describe three major types of prevention
List and discuss several specific prevention and diversion programs
Discuss the concept of restorative justice
Refer to services provided by children and family service agencies
Critique prevention and diversion programs

KEY TERMS

preadjudication intervention
postadjudication intervention
primary prevention
secondary prevention
tertiary prevention
functionally related agencies
diversion
pure diversion
secondary diversion
territorial jealousy
social promotion
D.A.R.E.
G.R.E.A.T.
wilderness programs
restorative justice
children and family service agencies
Head Start
Follow Through
JUMP
teen courts
Scared Straight
Straight, Inc.
Radical nonintervention

Our society annually spends millions of dollars attempting to apprehend, prosecute, and correct/rehabilitate delinquents and child abusers. While some of these attempts prove more or less successful with some offenders, the results are not particularly impressive on the whole. It would seem logical, therefore, to explore the possibilities of concentrating our resources on programs that might provide better returns. Many authorities have come to believe that

A variety of programs exist to attempt to divert juveniles from juvenile court.
Mary Kate Denny/Photo Edit

most of our money is spent at the wrong end of the juvenile justice process. As Mays and Winfree (2000, p. 341) indicate, "Delinquency prevention is an attractive idea—in the abstract. Preventing delinquency means stopping undesired juvenile conduct in its tracks, before it can become delinquent, and before adolescents come to the juvenile justice system's attention. If preventive efforts were perfect, there would be no need for a separate juvenile justice system, and, in all likelihood, far less adult crime." But, "Evils do not disappear because people disapprove of them, unless conditions at their root are changed" (Friedenberg 1965).

In most cases we wait until a juvenile comes into official contact with the system before an attempt is made to modify the behavior which has, by the time contact becomes official, become more or less ingrained. Our legal system generally prevents intervention by justice authorities without probable cause, and we would have it no other way. Still, this makes it more difficult for corrections personnel, or personnel in related agencies, to modify offensive behavior after the fact either by intervening prior to adjudication (**preadjudication intervention**) or by intervening after the youth has been adjudicated (**postadjudication intervention**). It would seem more logical to bring as many resources as possible to bear to prevent the offender from engaging in illegal behavior in the first place (predelinquent intervention), or, as early as possible, try to divert juveniles who do encounter the justice system (Lundman 1993).

For example, consider the difficulty of trying to rehabilitate a juvenile addicted to heroin. The juvenile has probably developed, by the time he is addicted, apprehended, and processed, problems in his family, problems in school, and delinquent habits oriented toward ensuring his supply of heroin (for example, burglary, mugging, and pushing drugs). In order to rehabilitate the juvenile, all of these problems must be dealt with. If, however, we had effective programs to detect and help to resolve problems that are likely to lead to heroin use (or child abuse), the necessity for solving all of these complicated, related problems would be eliminated. Suppose, for example, we found the juvenile in question dissatisfied with traditional education, but interested in pursuing a specific vocation. Suppose we were to provide an alternative education that enabled the juvenile to pursue his chosen vocation and heightened his interest in success within the system. We might, then, prevent the juvenile from dropping out of school, joining a heroin-abusing gang, and developing the undesirable behavior patterns mentioned above. Or suppose we found that child abuse was common among single, teenage, unwed mothers primarily because they had no conception of child rearing and all it entails. Might we not prevent a good deal of the abuse by providing parenting skills to such mothers?

PREVENTION

There are three major types of prevention programs. The first type of program, **primary prevention,** is directed toward preventing illegal acts among the juvenile population as a whole before they occur by alleviating social conditions related to the offenders. **Secondary prevention** seeks to identify juveniles who appear to be at high risk for delinquency and/or abuse and to intervene in their lives early. **Tertiary prevention** attempts to prevent further illegal acts among offenders once such acts have been committed (Office of Juvenile Justice and Delinquency Prevention, September 2000). None of these programs is a cure-all, and there are a number of difficulties in attempting to develop and operate such programs (Mays and Winfree 2000, p. 324). Nonetheless, it may well be that our resources could be more effectively employed in prevention rather than correction of offensive behavior.

In the 1930s, several projects addressed the issue of delinquency prevention. The Chicago Area Project involved churches, social clubs, and community committees which sponsored recreation programs for youth, addressed problems associated with law enforcement, health services, and education, targeted local gangs, and helped reintegrate youth who had been adjudicated delinquent. In spite of these efforts, no solid evidence that delinquency was prevented or reduced resulted from the project (Lundman 1993).

In 1967, the President's Commission on Law Enforcement and Administration of Justice recommended the establishment of alternatives to the juvenile justice system. According to the report, service agencies capable of dealing with certain categories of juveniles should have these juveniles diverted to them. The report further recommended (19–45):

1. The formal sanctioning system and pronouncement of delinquency should be used only as a last resort.
2. Instead of the formal system, dispositional alternatives to adjudication must be developed for dealing with juveniles, including agencies to provide and coordinate services and procedures to achieve necessary control without unnecessary stigma. Alternatives already available, such as those related to court intake, should be more fully exploited.
3. The range of conduct for which court intervention is authorized should be narrowed, with greater emphasis upon consensual and informal means of meeting the problems of difficult children.

In 1973, the National Advisory Commission on Criminal Justice Standards and Goals stated (34–36) that "the highest attention must be given to preventing juvenile delinquency, minimizing the involvement of young offenders in the juvenile and criminal justice system, and reintegrating them into the community." The commission further recommended minimizing the involvement of the offender in the system. This does not mean that we should coddle offenders. It recognizes that the further the offender penetrates into the system, the more difficult it becomes to divert the youth from a criminal career. Minimizing a youth's involvement with the juvenile justice system does not mean abandoning the use of confinement for certain individuals or failing to protect victims of abuse and neglect. Until more effective means of treatment are found, chronic and dangerous delinquents should be incarcerated to protect society, and abused children must be made wards of the court and removed from unsafe conditions. However, the juvenile justice system must search for beneficial programs outside institutions for juveniles who do not need confinement or sheltered care.

Both labeling and learning theories stress the desirability of prevention rather than correction. The basic premise of labeling theory is that juveniles find it difficult to escape the stigmatization of being known as delinquents or abuse victims. Once labeled, the juvenile is often forced out of normal interaction patterns and forced into association with others who have been labeled. From this perspective, the agencies of the juvenile justice system that are established to correct delinquent behavior often contribute to its occurrence even as they try to cope with it. Learning theory holds that individuals engage in delinquent behavior because they experience an overabundance of interactions, associations, and reinforcements with definitions favorable to delinquency. Therefore, if agencies cast potential or first-time delinquents into interaction with more experienced delinquents, the process of learning delinquent behavior is greatly enhanced. Alternatively, concentration on the problems of youth that tend to lead to delinquent behavior or abuse and neglect may not only result in preventing some youth from becoming involved in progressively more serious offenses, but might also allow the justice network to concentrate efforts on hard-core delinquents and abusers whose labels and stigmatization have been earned.

Since delinquency and abuse or neglect are complex problems, no singular program is likely to emerge that will be effective in preventing all such behaviors. Delinquency prevention, for example, involves many variables and no one program is likely to be foolproof. Inherent in the multifaceted problems of delinquency and abuse prevention is the fact that these behaviors have roots in the basic social conditions of our society. Increasing urbanization with accompanying problems of poverty, inferior education, poor housing, health and sanitary problems, and unemployment are but a few social conditions that seem to be related to delinquency and abuse or neglect. Therefore, we should focus our attention on these problems if preventive efforts are to have a chance of success (Yoshikawa 1994; Johnson 1998; Lane and Turner 1999; Liddle and Hogue 2000; Kowaleski-Jones 2000). While a number of programs are important for the prevention of delinquency and abuse, we would be remiss if we focused only on programs directed specifically at preventing such behaviors and ignored these underlying conditions. Large-scale social change directed at the areas discussed above, which is clearly an important preventive measure, would enable more people to achieve culturally approved goals without having to resort to illegal means.

In June 1970, a group was invited by the Youth Development and Delinquency Prevention Administration of the Department of Health, Education, and Welfare to meet in Scituate, Massachusetts, to consider the problem of youth development and delinquency prevention. The document produced at that meeting stated: "We believe that our social institutions [school, family, church, etc.] are programmed in such a way as to deny large numbers of young people socially acceptable, responsible, and personally gratifying roles. These institutions should seek ways of becoming more responsible to youth needs." The group further stated that any strategy for youth development and delinquency prevention should give priority to "programs which assist institutions to change in ways that provide young people with socially acceptable, responsible, personally gratifying roles and assist young people to assume such roles." (Youth Development and Delinquency Prevention Administration, 1970).

It follows from this premise that the development of viable strategies for the prevention and reduction of delinquency (and, by implication, abuse and neglect) rests on the identification, assessment, and alteration of those features of institutional functioning that impede development of youth, particularly those youth whose social situation makes them most prone to the development of delinquent careers or victims of abusive behavior, or to participation in collective forms of withdrawal and deviancy. This approach does not deny the occurrence of individual deviance, but it does assert that in many cases the deviance is traceable to the damaging experiences of youth in institutional encounters.

As Daniel Katkin and his associates (1976, p. 404) pointed out some time ago, "it is social institutions in the broader community—families, churches, schools, social welfare agencies, etc.—which have the primary mandate to control and care for young people who commit delinquent acts. It is only when individuals or institutions in the community fail to divert (or decide not to divert) that the formal processes of the juvenile justice system are called into action." In this respect, Yoshikawa (1994) found that comprehensive family support combined with early childhood education may well be successful in bringing about long-term prevention. Similarly, Johnson (1998) notes that the actions of parents and teachers may reduce juvenile crime more effectively than those of the police. Lane and Turner (1999) discuss the importance of interagency cooperation in preventing delinquency, and Liddle and Hogue (2000) found that family-based intervention in the form of the Multidimensional Family Prevention model can help to build resilent family ties and strong connections with prosocial agencies among adolescents. Finally, Kowaleski-Jones (2000) found that residential stability and schools perceived as high quality by mothers were factors related to preventing youth from getting into trouble.

The responsibility for dealing with juveniles who have problems has been too frequently placed solely on juvenile justice practitioners. The public has been more than willing to place the blame for failures in preventing delinquency and abuse or neglect on these practitioners and quick to criticize their efforts. These practitioners are often faced with the task of attempting to modify undesirable behavior that has become habitual and deep rooted and which a variety of other agencies have failed to modify. In addition, the time period available for rehabilitation is usually short.

There are a number of agencies in our society with which juveniles come into contact earlier, more consistently, and with less stigmatization than the juvenile justice system. Some of these agencies or institutions are functionally related to the juvenile justice system. The term **functionally related agencies** is used to describe those agencies having goals similar to those of the juvenile justice system—improving the quality of life for juveniles by preventing offensive behavior, providing opportunities for success, and correcting undesirable behavior (see "In Practice" 9.1).

DIVERSION PROGRAMS

One form of prevention is diversion, which has carried many different, and sometimes conflicting, meanings. **Diversion** is often used to describe prejuvenile justice as well as postjuvenile justice activities. Some diversion programs are designed to suspend or terminate juvenile justice processing of youth in favor of release or referral to alternate services. Likewise, some diversionary activities involve referrals to programs outside the justice system prior to the youth entering the system. The latter is often referred to as **pure diversion** and programs of this type are not as numerous as those in the former or **secondary diversion** category. In Practice 9.2 gives an example of one of the types of diversionary programs that have been initiated throughout the United States.

Diversion is not without pitfalls. It sometimes permits intervention into juveniles' lives and their families with little or no formal processes and inadequate safeguards of individual

In Practice 9.1

Lawmakers Propose Tougher Attendance Laws

Malcolm Johnson

Michigan children would have to go to school or lose their driving privileges under a proposal unveiled Tuesday.

"One of the earliest indicators of a student who is likely to get in trouble is truancy," said Sen. Gary Peters, D-Bloomfield Township, sponsor of several Senate bills on the subject.

"A child's success in school is directly linked to his or her school attendance," said Rep. Gilda Jacobs, D-Huntington Woods, sponsor of similar House proposals. "Truancy is sometimes the first sign of a troubled child who may eventually experiment with drugs, crime and gangs and wind up another juvenile crime statistic."

The pair said they hope the Legislature will take up the issue early next year. Lawmakers are scheduled to break for the holidays later this week, ending the present session.

Although both lawmakers are in the minority party, their proposal parallels efforts among many school officials to crack down on kids who skip class and parents who don't insist they go to school.

"By intervening quickly when they first start to miss school, we may be able to help these students before they fall into a pattern of delinquency," Peters said.

One proposal sure to get teens' attention is a bill to allow a judge to order a juvenile's driver's license suspended or a delay in issuing a license if the kid is truant.

"What is the most important thing to a kid? It's their driver's license," said Ingham County Prosecutor Stuart Dunning III, who endorsed the legislation and has coordinated a similar effort with the Lansing School District.

"This matters to them," he said.

The legislation also calls for increased penalties for parents who let their kids skip class—from five days in jail and a $50 fine now to up to 90 days behind bars, a fine of up to $500 and up to 50 hours of community service.

Other proposals call for increased parental notification if a child misses class, court intervention in certain cases, furnishing data on home-schooled children, and including truancy under the law's definition of child neglect.

Officials stressed the truancy issue is complex and can involve many other family problems which require the attention of educators, police and state school services.

"If we don't have kids in school, they're going to get in trouble," Jacobs said. "We're trying to create a community alliance."

"This just makes good sense."

Peters added that both kids and their parents should be more accountable for students showing up for school.

"Students who skip school must learn there are consequences," he said. "Parents need to be held responsible for their children's school attendance."

(Note: The Senate truancy bills are Senate Bills 758–61; the House bills have not been introduced and numbered.)

Johnson, M. (1999, December 7). *Lawmakers propose tougher attendance laws.* Associated Press.

In Practice 9.2

A DECADE OF DRUG EDUCATION

When it comes to drug education, nobody raises money—or support—like D.A.R.E. America.

Some facts about the Drug Abuse Resistance Education program:

- Created: In 1983 by Los Angeles police and school officials.
- Existing programs: In 50 states and several foreign countries, including Australia, Mexico, Norway and Sweden.
- Trained officers: More than 15,000.
- Curriculum: Focuses on students in fifth and sixth grades. Topics taught include personal safety, drug use and misuse, ways to say no to drugs, and media influences on drug use.
- Funding: Executive Director Glenn Levant estimates revenues nationwide at as much as $700 million a year.
- National sponsors: Include Kimberly-Clark and Kentucky Fried Chicken Corp. "It's a great program," says KFC spokesman Steve Provo. "It's amazing the influence it has on young kids."
- National ambassador: Arsenio Hall.
- Famous volunteer: Junkbond king Michael Milken, performing his community service for securities fraud at D.A.R. E.-PLUS, a new program to keep kids in school and out of gangs.

liberties. One of the major concerns with diversion programs is that they result in "net widening," or bringing to the attention of juvenile authorities youth who would otherwise not be labeled, thereby increasing rather than decreasing stigmatization.

Before discussing specific diversion programs, a major problem in coordinating such programs and the agencies sponsoring them should be pointed out. The problem is one of territorial jealousy. **Territorial jealousy** refers to a belief commonly held by agency personnel who feel that attempts to coordinate efforts are actually attempts to invade the territory they have staked out for themselves. Agency staff members have a tendency to view themselves as experts in their particular field, to resent suggestions for change made by outsiders, and to fear that they will be found to be lacking in competence. As a result, these staff members tend to keep agency operations secret and reject attempts by personnel from other agencies to provide services or to suggest improvements.

Perhaps an example will help to clarify the concept of territorial jealousy. An attempt was made by youth services agency personnel to provide services to a school district with one of the highest dropout rates in the state. The services offered included educational and vocational counseling, alternative educational programs, and some immediate employment opportunities. When contacted by the director of the youth services agency, the principal of the local high school indicated that the school system "really had no dropout problem," that school counselors handled any existing problems, and that he would initiate contact when he needed help from a social work agency.

As the example clearly indicates, the consequences of territorial jealousy can be extremely serious for both juveniles and the taxpayer. Duplication of services is a costly enterprise in a time of budgetary cutbacks and financial restraints; however, denial of available services to youth with problems can be disastrous. Lack of cooperation, understanding, and confidence among agency personnel greatly hamper attempts to provide for the welfare of youth.

SOME EXAMPLES OF PREVENTION AND DIVERSION PROGRAMS

School Programs

In chapter 3, the importance of school personnel in shaping the behavior of youth is discussed. No other institution in our society, with the possible exception of the family, has as much opportunity to observe, mold, and modify youthful behavior. Early detection of problems frequently leads to their solution before they become serious. The importance of education as a stepping stone to future opportunities for success cannot be stressed too much. The provision of meaningful educational opportunities for youth who have been labeled *delinquent* or in need of supervision is of great importance in attempts to reintegrate these youth into society.

While it was once possible for educators to deal with problem youth by pushing them out of the educational system, recent court decisions indicate that all youth have the right to an education. Therefore, youth who have been found delinquent and status offenders can no longer legally be dismissed from school without due process. School counselors who formerly concerned themselves with academic and career counseling, advising, and scheduling also face the reality of coping with behavioral and emotional problems. Hopefully, teachers who formerly passed juveniles with such problems on to their colleagues by refusing to fail "problem youth" (giving them **social promotions**) will begin to seek other, more desirable alternatives. Educational personnel play an important role in preventing and correcting delinquent behavior by providing personal counseling or appropriate referrals.

There are numerous school programs designed to prevent youth from engaging in delinquent activities or to divert them from such activities once they become involved. We previously mentioned (chapter 7) the police officer school liaison programs which have come into existence in recent years. In Houston, a School Task Force Program has been developed to help reduce truancy (Martin, Schulze, and Valdez 1988). Assistant school principals were designated as liaison personnel to work with members of the police task force in attempting to encourage youth to remain in the school environment by improving communications between youth and all agencies working with juveniles. In addition, the program attempted to reduce the opportunity for adult offenders to prey on juveniles through the sale of narcotics, sexually explicit materials, and alcohol. Survey data from 1,000 teachers and school administrators indicated that they held favorable attitudes toward the program, though they were not totally convinced that truancy was reduced by the effort.

Alternative education programs have also become more widespread. Such programs include enhanced skills training, community internship programs, and more general attempts to integrate the schools and the community in the interests of serving the needs of marginal students and those who do not anticipate attending college. Life Skills Training Programs, implemented by teachers in the classroom, are directed at sixth and seventh graders and are designed to prevent or alleviate tobacco, alcohol, and marijuana use (http://www.ncjrs.org/ojjhome.htm 2001). Improved school counseling services and programs designed to encourage student and parent participation in combating violence and vandalism in the schools are indicative of other attempts to expand and improve the role of school personnel in preventing delinquency and diverting delinquents from further inappropriate actions. The Center for the Study and Prevention of Violence has identified a number of other programs that have been shown to be effective in reducing youth violence, including:

1. The Bullying Prevention Program—implemented primarily by school staff, these programs involve school-based intervention for the reduction of bullying.
2. Big Brothers Big Sisters of America (BBBSA)—adult mentoring programs for youth. Research has shown that children with mentors are 46 percent less likely to initiate drug use, 27 percent less likely to initiate alcohol use, and 32 percent less likely to commit assault.
3. The PATHS (Promoting Alternative Thinking Strategies) Curriculum—curriculum is primarily school based, but also includes activities for parents. Aimed at promoting emotional and social competencies. (http://www.ncjrs.org/ojjhome.htm)

Another program presented in the schools by police officers is the **D.A.R.E.** (Drug Abuse Resistance Education) program. Originally developed in California in 1983, the program rapidly spread to other states. The goal of the semester-long program aimed at fifth and sixth graders is to equip juveniles with the skills to resist peer pressure to use drugs. Trained police officers present the program as a part of the regular school curriculum in an attempt to provide accurate information about drugs and alcohol, teach students decision-making skills, help them resist peer pressure, and provide alternatives to drug abuse.

Unfortunately, research has shown that participation in the D.A.R.E. program during elementary school has no effect on later alcohol use, cigarette smoking, or marijuana use in twelfth grade, but may deter a small amount of use of illegal and more deviant drugs such as inhalants, cocaine, and LSD among teenage males (Dukes, Stein, and Ullman 1997). Other research has shown that the impact of D.A.R.E. on drug-related behavior of youths who have been through the program is minimal (Cauchon 1993; Walker 1998, p. 275). Proponents argue, perhaps with some justification, that at a minimum the programs introduce police officers and children to one another as real people at an early age and that the effects of classroom interaction may have beneficial effects for both.

Yet another program involving police and school cooperation is **G.R.E.A.T.** (Gang Resistance Education Training). This program, which is a nine-week curriculum taught by uniformed police officers to middle-school children, was recently evaluated on a nationwide basis. The researchers found that students who had completed the program had more prosocial attitudes and lower rates for some types of delinquency than did students in a comparison group who had not participated in the program (Esbensen and Osgood 1999).

Perhaps the most successful school program to prevent delinquency is the High/Scope Perry Preschool Project in Ypsilanti, Michigan. This program has focused on a group of

Wilderness programs, although difficult to evaluate, may lead to somewhat lower recidivism rates.
Richard Rowan/Photo Researchers, Inc.

123 African American three- and four year-olds identified as being at risk for school failure in 1962. Fifty-eight of the youth were assigned to the preschool program and sixty-five to a control group. Data concerning these youth was collected periodically for some forty years. The results of the research showed that those youth who had participated in the preschool program for 2½ hours per day, Monday through Friday, for two years:

1. had lower rates of delinquency than the control group;
2. had lower teen pregnancy rates than the control group;
3. were less likely to be dependent on welfare than the control group;
4. were more likely to graduate from high school than the control group. (High/Scope Educational Research Foundation, 2002)

Wilderness Programs

Wilderness programs had their origins in the forestry camps of the 1930s. These programs involve small, closely supervised groups of youth who are confronted with difficult physical challenges which require teamwork and cooperation to overcome. The intent of the programs is to improve the self-esteem of the youth involved while teaching them the value of cooperative interaction. Wilderness programs which last from about one month to a year or more do not typically accept violent youth. Some provide counseling and follow-up services while others do not. Youth may be sent directly to these programs as an alternative to detention or may participate in the programs after more traditional dispositions have been imposed.

Evaluations of wilderness programs have been fraught with methodological difficulties. Much of the information concerning the success of the programs has been provided by program developers and staff and is anecdotal in nature. Most of the evidence provided under these less-than-ideal conditions shows that the programs lead to somewhat lower recidivism rates than no program at all, but the effectiveness of the programs is in question.

Restorative Justice Programs

The philosophy of **restorative justice** centers on the assertion that *crime and delinquency affect persons* instead of the traditional *crime affects the state.* In fact, restorative justice defines a "crime [as] an offense against human relationships" (The National Victims Center 1998, p. 52). Mark Carey, director of community corrections in Dakota County, Minnesota, defines restorative justice as "a philosophical framework for responding to crime and the actions needed to mend this harm. It focuses on crime as an act against another individual or community rather than the state. It is a future-focused model that emphasizes problematic problem solving instead of just deserts" (Wilkinson 1997, p. 1).

Restorative justice advocates programs such as victim-offender mediation, victims impact panels, community service, and community sentencing. Such programs, aimed at creating or enticing emotions within criminal offenders, appear to be gaining momentum in the criminal and juvenile justice networks in the United States. Minnesota, a leader in victim-offender mediation programs in the United States, has used organizations such as the Victim Offender Mediation Association (VOMA) and the Center for Restorative Justice and Mediation (CRJM) to gain funding from the Office of Victims of Crime to sponsor nationwide training for criminal justice personnel wanting to initiate victim-offender rehabilitation programs.

Restorative justice programs have been variously called community conferencing, family-group conferencing, community justice, community corrections, balanced and restorative justice, and real justice, depending upon the agency applying the concepts. Although the name may change, the definition and core concepts of restorative justice—accountability, competency, and public safety—remain the same in all applications. Crime victims, offenders, and the community are the keys to success in restorative justice.

The question is, how well does restorative justice work in practice? Walker (1998, p. 224) indicates that "evaluations of experimental programs have tended to find slightly lower recidivism rates for offenders receiving restorative justice than for those given traditional sentences of prison or probation. The differences are not always consistent, however, and many questions remain regarding the implementation and outcomes of such programs."

While it is likely that the informal sanctions imposed by family and community are more effective than threats of formal punishment, what happens when there is no sense of family or community? The sense of family and community may well be lacking in drug-ridden and economically ravaged neighborhoods. The concept of restorative justice may make sense for young middle-class offenders involved in minor first offenses, but may be totally irrelevant for those living in the most crime-ridden areas of America (Walker 1998, p. 225). In fact, the failure of these institutions is largely responsible for the development of our current criminal justice system, and there is little evidence of the rebirth or strengthening of these institutions today (Cox and Wade 1996, pp. 48–50; Walker 1998).

Children and Family Services

As noted in chapter 7, child protective services (children and family services) have goals similar to those of the juvenile justice system. These agencies provide, among other services, day care programs, foster care programs, youth advocacy programs, and advice to unwed mothers. In addition, they investigate reported cases of child abuse and neglect. **Children and family service agencies** deal with all categories of juveniles covered by most juvenile court acts, provide individual and family counseling services, and are empowered to refer suitable cases to appropriate private agencies. In addition, they can provide financial aid to youth and families in need.

Like most state agencies, children and family services are often caught up in political change. While many of these agencies require bachelor's or master's degrees for employment and emphasize the need for professionalism among staff members, skillful and competent administrative personnel are often replaced when the political party in power changes. As a result, the continuity of policies implemented by these agencies frequently leaves much to be desired. Nonetheless, state agencies concerned with providing services to children and families often have considerable power and, when administered appropriately, can provide multiple services to youth in trouble. Inappropriate practices can also lead to disaster, as In Practice 9.3 indicates.

Federal Programs

The federal government has sponsored many programs that, although not specifically designed as delinquency prevention programs, did encourage youths to accept and attain lawful objectives through institutionalized means of education and employment. Examples of some of the varied federal programs provide some insight into the value of these programs in preventing delinquency and crime, illustrate the focal points of these programs, and show how they attempt to improve the social ills that result in delinquency (Yablonsky and Haskell 1988).

There have been a number of federally funded programs aimed at improving educational and occupational opportunities for disadvantaged youth. A secondary benefit of many of these programs was believed to be a decrease in the likelihood of delinquency among the youth involved. Projects **Head Start** and **Follow Through** were designed to help culturally deprived children catch up or keep pace in their preschool and early school years. Previously, many children from culturally and/or economically deprived parents lagged behind other children in verbal and reading skills. Starting far behind in basic skills, many of these children never caught up, and school too often became an experience characterized by failure and rejection. As a result many dropped out of school as soon as possible, often during their first or second year of high school. Of those who did drop out, many went on to become delinquent. Head Start and Follow Through have shown that children who are socioeconomically disadvantaged can and do make progress when parents, teachers, and volunteers focus their efforts on these youth (Eitzen and Zinn 1992, p. 399). The High/Scope Perry Preschool Project discussed earlier in this chapter is another example of a federally funded program.

Along slightly different lines, a number of federal laws providing assistance to the hard-core unemployed were passed. For example, the Manpower Development and Training Act, the Vocational Education Act, the Economic Opportunity Act, the Rehabilitation

In Practice 9.3

DCFS Goes on Trial for Missing Abuse

Steve Warmbir

The soles of the 1-year-old's feet were beaten so badly, with the skin flayed off, she couldn't walk for a month.

Her 3½-year-old brother, allegedly abused by the same man, couldn't talk.

And their older sister, 10, who witnessed the reported torture of her brother and sister, still bears emotional scars. That was the scene sketched out before jurors in federal court Monday in Chicago as attorneys for the three children claimed a Department of Children and Family Services worker, Clifton Woodard, failed to prevent the abuse when he knew about it or should have known after visiting their new home repeatedly.

DCFS is being sued by the children's lawyers, saying the agency violated the children's civil rights by keeping an incompetent child abuse investigator on its staff.

The three children had been removed from a volatile home and placed with their aunt in Chicago in 1994. There, they suffered extreme abuse, particularly by their aunt's boyfriend, a felon.

The couple, Cornelia Anderson and Perry Robinson, were convicted for their crimes and sentenced to prison.

"This case is about Mr. Woodard's action or inaction," said attorney Peter Schmiedel with the Cook County Public Guardian's office.

"They needed Mr. Woodard to give them a hand," Schmiedel said. "The evidence will show he didn't so much as lift a finger to help them."

Lawyers from the Illinois attorney general's office, representing the DCFS worker, argue that Woodard never saw the abuse; Woodard would visit the aunt's home to see how the children were doing but didn't know what was happening. Other officials who saw the children didn't notice the abuse either, the attorneys said.

Woodard didn't see the marks and wounds because the children always had their clothes and shoes on. The beatings were targeted at places that were always covered by the clothes or shoes.

The children's father finally saw the abuse when he visited them in August 1995. Among the markings he saw were old and healing cigarette burns on his youngest daughter's arms.

All three children were malnourished, their attorneys say.

The father took his children to the police, who sent them to the hospital.

With that, the children's attorney said, the children escaped the abuse that varied according to whatever their aunt's boyfriend could lay his hands on.

"He hit them with belts, he hit them with shoes, he hit them with hangers, he hit them with sandals," said Schmiedel, who is prosecuting the case with Patrick Murphy.

A DCFS spokesman declined to comment on the case Monday.

Warmbir, S. (2001, May 15). DCFS goes on trial for missing abuse. *Chicago Sun-Times,* p. 16.

Early childhood education programs may help prevent later delinquency.
Elizabeth Crews/The Image Works

Program for Selective Service Rejectees, the Comprehensive Employment and Training Act, the Job Training Partnership Act, and the President's Youth Opportunities Campaign had the major objective of aiding youths to find employment by helping them become more readily employable. The basic assumption underlying these programs has been that employment is an important key to solving the problems of many youths.

The emphasis of youth opportunity centers is to increase employability through counseling or to provide vocational and prevocational training and work-training programs. This approach recognizes that if young people, handicapped by inadequate education and lack of occupational skills, are to become employable, they must somehow be provided with additional training. Hopefully, these young people will then be absorbed into the labor market once their performance capabilities are improved.

Similarly, the Job Corps program was directed toward youths between sixteen and twenty-one with the principal objective of providing training in basic skills and a constructive work experience. The Job Training Partnership Act of 1981 also promised new hope for young people seeking their first job when it replaced the scandal-ridden Comprehensive Employment and Training Act.

All of these programs have been geared toward providing youths with employment opportunities which will hopefully lead them to a better life. The basic, underlying assumption seems to be that youths employed in jobs for which they are suited are less likely to engage in delinquent or criminal activity than youths who are not employed and have little hope of finding any worthwhile employment.

In recent years, the federal government has given attention to the concept of mentoring. In 1992, Congress amended the Juvenile Justice and Delinquency Prevention Act of 1974 to include the Juvenile Mentoring Program (**JUMP**) because of a growing belief that positive bonds between children and adults can forge actions or behaviors essential to a healthy life (Bilchik 1998). According to the 1998 Juvenile Mentoring Program Report to Congress,

> Historically, the notion of one individual providing caring support and guidance to another individual has been reflected in a variety of arenas. In the clinical mental health field, we talk about *bonding* and the importance of a child feeling connected to a nurturing adult in the early years of life. In the adoption field, we talk about the need for *attachment.* In schools, *tutors* help support successful educational experiences. In juvenile and family court, Court Appointed Special Advocates (CASA's) provide support and advocacy for children in need of assistance. In the substance abuse field, we make use of *sponsors* to support sobriety. In the business field, we create *teams* to ensure that new employees have the support they need to be successful in the corporate organizational system. Currently, there are many types of formal mentoring programs generally distinguishable by the goals of their sponsoring organization. Most youth oriented programs recognize the importance of ensuring that each child they serve has at least one significant adult in his/her own life that can be friend, role model, guide, and teacher of values. If that person is not available in the child's family, mentors can help fill the critical gap. (p. 5)

By using the JUMP program, the federal government is hoping to modify behaviors committed by youth that can lead to juvenile delinquency, gang participation, and school dropout rates and to enhance the academic performance of the youth participating in the program. All JUMP programs have been sponsored by local community organizations with the help of federal grants for the previous two years. Research is ongoing as to the success of these programs.

The role of the federal government in programs specifically designed to prevent delinquency has been somewhat limited as a result of the belief that the primary responsibility for these programs rests with the states. Although there have been scattered efforts in the field of juvenile justice by the federal government (for example, the development of the Children's Bureau in 1912 and the development of various federal commissions and programs in 1948, 1950, and 1961), the most relevant to prevention occurred in 1968 with the Juvenile Delinquency Prevention and Control Act and in 1974 with the Juvenile

Justice and Delinquency Prevention Act. The Juvenile Delinquency Prevention and Control Act permits allocation of federal funds to the states for delinquency prevention programs, and the Juvenile Justice and Delinquency Prevention Act attempts to create a coordinated national program to prevent and control delinquency (Office of Juvenile Justice and Delinquency Prevention 1979). The Juvenile Justice and Delinquency Control Act also called for an evaluation of all federally assisted delinquency programs, for a centralized research effort on problems of juvenile delinquency, and for training programs for persons who work with delinquents. This law directs spending of funds on diverting juveniles from the juvenile justice system through the use of community-based programs, such as group homes, foster care, and homemaker services. In addition, community-based programs and services that work with parents and other family members to maintain and strengthen the family unit are recommended.

The Juvenile Justice Amendments of 1977 made it clear that, in the opinion of Congress, the evolution of juvenile justice in the United States had resulted in excessive and abusive use of incarceration under the rubric of "in the best interests of the child" and that the prohibitions of contact with adult offenders and incarceration of status offenders and nonoffenders (e.g., dependent and neglected youth) were to be taken seriously (Office of Juvenile Justice and Delinquency Prevention 1980).

A wide variety of community and state agencies have become involved in delinquency prevention. Most efforts have been independent and uncoordinated. By the 1950s the delinquency prevention effort in virtually every state and large city was like a jigsaw puzzle of services operating independently. The agencies concerned with delinquency prevention included the schools, recreation departments, public housing authorities, public welfare departments, private social agencies, health departments, and medical facilities. Davidson, Redner, and Amdur (1990), forty years later, came to the conclusion that while diversion programs can provide positive results, territorial jealousies remain difficult to overcome.

Other Diversion and Prevention Programs

While it would be impossible to list and discuss all prevention and diversion programs, we would like to mention a few more. Recreational and activity programs conducted by local police, civic, and religious groups are often aimed at preventing delinquency. The concept of **teen court** has originated as a way to keep first-time juvenile offenders who commit minor offenses and are willing to admit guilt from being processed in the formal juvenile justice system. Local civic agencies or schools in conjunction with the police department and the juvenile court sponsor most of these programs. The courts are made up of teens below the age of seventeen who process the cases by acting as prosecutor, defense counsel, bailiff, and clerk and who determine the punishment for the cases by acting as the jury. Adult attorneys act as the judge to ensure the fairness and legality of the sentencing. The offender is required to complete the sentence handed down by the teen jury. If he or she does not abide by the sentencing guidelines, he or she is referred to the juvenile court for formal processing. The goal of these programs is to hold the juveniles accountable for their actions but not to stigmatize the youth by formally processing them in the juvenile justice system while attempting to divert the youth from further delinquency.

The Office of Juvenile Justice and Delinquency Prevention has identified a number of components critical to the success of rehabilitation and treatment programs for youth. Among these components are:

1. small size
2. individualized attention
3. small caseloads
4. an emphasis on reintegration into the community
5. opportunities for youth to succeed
6. clear and consistent consequences for violation of rules
7. individual and family counseling matched to the individual needs of youth. (http://www.ncjrs.org/ojjhome.htm)

In addition to the prevention and diversion programs already mentioned, there have been a number of attempts to scare juveniles away from delinquent behavior. The best known, though not the earliest, of these programs was publicized nationally through a television film call ***Scared Straight.*** The film recorded a confrontation between juveniles brought into, and inmates housed in, Rahway State Prison in New Jersey. Such confrontation was based on the theory that inmates could frighten juveniles to the extent that they would be deterred from committing further delinquent acts. *Scared Straight* reported that of the 8,000 juveniles participating in such sessions through 1978, 90 percent had not been in trouble with the law again. Nationwide attention was focused on attempts to frighten youth out of delinquency and such programs were viewed by some as a panacea for delinquency problems (Finkenauer 1982). However, more objective evaluations of this and other such programs have yielded, at best, mixed results. It is certain that such programs are not a panacea for delinquency, and some appear to increase rather than decrease the frequency of recidivism. In fact, Lundman (1993) recommends the permanent abandonment of efforts to scare and inform juveniles "straight."

Yet another attempt at preventing delinquency and diverting delinquent youth involves the use of community policing models oriented toward juveniles. These programs operate on the assumption that community policing officers are more likely to favor problem-solving and peacekeeping roles with youth than their traditional counterparts (see chapter 7). Officers who view their roles in these terms may be more likely to try to help youth before they get in trouble or to divert them away from the juvenile justice network (Belknap, Morash, and Trojanowicz 1987; Bazemore and Senjo 1997).

Community-based programs in Harrisburg, Pennsylvania, sponsored by the juvenile justice system of that state, attempted to reduce minority overrepresentation in the juvenile justice system by reducing rates of arrest and rearrest for clients and by reducing educational failure, dropout, and truancy. A two-year follow-up evaluation of the results of the programs showed that they were somewhat successful in reducing recidivism, but had little effect on school failure, dropout, or truancy (Welsh, Jenkins, and Harris 1999).

There are a host of other agencies providing services that complement those of the juvenile justice system. These include YMCAs and YWCAs, which often provide counseling and recreation programs. One alarming trend among these agencies is that membership fees have tended to eliminate the opportunity for some youth to use the services available. Some YMCA and YWCA programs seem to discourage rather than encourage the participation of youth who have little interaction with adults and have few resources.

In many areas, community mental health clinics provide services based on a sliding fee scale. Other agencies—such as Catholic Social Services, Vocational Rehabilitation Services, and the Boy and Girl Scouts of America—also use a sliding scale to determine fees for counseling, membership, testing, and employment referrals. Still other agencies provide essentially the same services free of charge. These agencies typically include community centers, Big Brother/Sister Volunteer Programs, alcohol and drug clinics, and hotline programs. In addition, many colleges and universities offer counseling services free of charge or based upon a sliding scale.

Straight, Inc., was a private chemical dependency program that originated in Florida in 1976. The program served hundreds of clients in several cities. It was designed to deal with individuals ranging in age from early teens through early twenties by isolating such individuals from outside influences during initial treatment stages. Newcomers could receive no mail or phone calls initially, but the program moved to counseling sessions involving youth and their parents and assumed that chemical dependency is a family problem. Treatment usually took about a year and cost more than $11,000. Program practices were criticized as being authoritarian, and selection procedures have been questioned as well. Straight, Inc., made changes in these areas, but staff personnel indicated the program may be unsuitable for some youth (Tarpy 1989). In April of 1993, the program closed its center in St. Petersburg, Florida, amid alleged complaints of client abuse. In 1992, Straight, Inc., closed its center in Washington, D.C., after Virginia officials announced plans not to renew the center's license because the program has allegedly failed to provide proper education for youth, allowed clients to be improperly physically restrained, and made mistakes in evaluating clients' needs (Krueger 1993). Miller Newton, a psychologist who once helped lead Straight, Inc., later became president of Kids of North Jersey. This program, too, came under fire for improper restraint of clients and insufficient staffing. In 1996, the New Jersey program paid $45,000 to the federal government to settle a claim alleging that Newton and the program improperly submitted 254 insurance claims. Both the program and Newton denied any wrongdoing, but the program closed in 1998 (Krueger 1999).

Not all diversion and prevention programs originate in urban areas. There are many programs that have been implemented effectively in rural areas as well. One example is mentoring programs that highlight the importance of a caring adult in helping to prevent delinquency, increasing the likelihood of school success, and developing relationship skills. Mentors provide tutoring, job skills, and informal counseling and also make referrals to agencies as necessary. Big Brother/Big Sister programs are among the best known mentoring programs, and they have branches in rural as well as urban areas around the country. Teen courts are also spreading to small towns and rural areas, as is the notion of restorative justice in general.

SOME CRITICISMS

As we have indicated previously, delinquency prevention programs usually employ one of two strategies, either reform of society or individual treatment. Both strategies as generally employed have had difficulties. Programs oriented toward reforming society have been quite costly in terms of the results produced, depending on whether results are measured in terms of alleviating educational, occupational, or economic difficulties or in terms of reducing delinquency. Lack of coordination among various programs, interprogram jealousy, considerable duplication, and mismanagement have seriously hampered the effectiveness of these programs. As a result, much of the money intended for youth with problems ends up in staff salaries, and many of the personnel hired to help supervise, train, and educate these youths are tied up dealing with administrative red tape. In addition, programs attempting to improve societal conditions may take a long time to show results. The extent to which any results can be attributed to a specific program is extremely difficult to measure. As a result, the public is frequently hesitant to finance prevention programs, since they have no immediately visible payoff. In fact, it may be that diversion programs simply do not work either because the concept is flawed or because the current system does not provide an opportunity for them to work. Some see diversion as an interesting concept with "unanticipated negative consequences" (Mays and Winfree 2000, p. 116).

There are two basic types of prevention programs directed at providing individual treatment. The first deals with youth who have already come into contact with the juvenile justice system and attempts to prevent further contact. As noted previously, there are inherent difficulties in attempting to reform or rehabilitate youth after they have become delinquent. Many of the basic assumptions about programs directed toward preventing future delinquent acts by those already labeled *delinquent* are highly questionable. For example, it is doubtful whether individual therapy will be successful if the juvenile's problems involve family, school, or peers. Similarly, the belief that recreational or activity programs, in and of themselves, are beneficial in reducing delinquency seems to be more a matter of faith than fact at this time.

The second type of individual treatment program attempts to identify juveniles who are likely to become delinquent before a delinquent act is committed. These programs may be called *early identification programs* or *predelinquency detection programs.* While these programs are clearly intended to "nip the problem in the bud," they may be criticized for creating the very delinquency they propose to reduce; that is, identifying a juvenile as predelinquent focuses attention on the juvenile as a potential problem youth and, therefore, labels him or her in much the same way official juvenile justice agencies label youth delinquent. In one sense, then, the juvenile is being treated (and sometimes punished) for something which he or she has not yet done. Programs directed toward pure prevention may, unintentionally, lead juveniles to be labeled earlier by identifying them at an earlier stage. This phenomenon is often referred to as *net widening* (discussed earlier in this chapter).

Some time ago, Edwin M. Schur (1973) encouraged the development of an approach to delinquency prevention. We believe (and have suggested at other points in this book) that it has considerable merit. His approach is called *radical nonintervention.* According to Schur, "the primary target for delinquency policy should be neither the individual nor the local community setting, but rather the delinquency-defining processes themselves" (154). Rather than consistently increasing the number of behaviors society refuses to tolerate, policies should be developed that encourage society to tolerate the "widest possible diversity of behaviors and attitudes." Much of the behavior currently considered delinquent is characteristic of adolescence, nonpredatory in nature, and is offensive only because it is engaged in by juveniles. Since, in one sense, it is rules that produce delinquents, it may make more sense to change the rules (as we have done at the adult level in terms of alcohol consumption, abortion, and homosexuality) than to attempt to change juveniles or the entire society overnight. One approach, then, would be to make fewer activities delinquent and to concentrate on enforcing rules for violations that may actually be harmful to the juvenile or to society or both. In other cases, our best strategy may be simply to "leave kids alone wherever possible" (154).

Supporting Schur's contention is the fact that the Office of Juvenile Justice and Delinquency Prevention (1979) found that a number of programs have no defensible basis whatsoever (e.g., those based on presumed personality differences or biological differences), others are poorly implemented (e.g., behavior modification programs in treatment settings without community follow-up), and still others of questionable merit are only based upon preliminary evidence (most predelinquency identification programs).

Finally, Sherman et. al. (1997), in a systematic review of literature on crime prevention, conclude that some programs seem to work, but many do not. More importantly, perhaps, the authors conclude that the programs that work best are those in communities that need them least and that true prevention probably lies outside the realm of criminal justice. Indeed, many programs seem to work where schools and families are stable, but few appear to be successful where schools and families are torn apart by drugs, crime, and violence. Walker (1998, p. 279), in reviewing this and other studies, concludes: "We found that most current crime [delinquency] policies and proposed alternatives are not effective. We found that both conservatives and liberals are guilty of peddling nonsense with respect to crime policy. . . . The truth about crime policy seems to be that most criminal justice–related policies will not make any significant reduction in crime." Thus, as we have indicated earlier in this book, if we wish to prevent at least some crime and delinquency, we must seek solutions in the broader social structure by focusing on unemployment, discrimination, maintaining stable families (whatever their structure), and providing meaningful education for all youth.

CHILD ABUSE AND NEGLECT PREVENTION PROGRAMS

Many of the specific programs we have discussed are oriented toward diverting delinquents and preventing delinquency. There are also numerous programs aimed at preventing child abuse and neglect. We will examine a few of these programs here.

Illinois has recently instituted a program to provide in-home assistance to families in which children have been mildly abused in order to prevent foster home placement. Mild abuse has been defined as including things such as overspanking or bruising of the child which does not result in serious injury to the child. Under the plan, when a report of abuse is filed, investigators from the Department of Children and Family Services talk with the family in order to determine whether the child is safe in the home and whether the family is likely to benefit from the plan (Perkiss 1989).

In the state of Minnesota, politicians have made childhood assistance a clear priority in their campaigns. Among the programs already underway is the Child Care Fund, which helps subsidize the cost of day care. The Children's Health Plan provides benefits to poor children under the age of eight and may be expanded to help poor children up to age eighteen (Madigan 1989).

Operation K.I.D. (Kids Identification), initiated by the Edmond Police Department and Edmond Memorial Hospital, is a program addressing the issue of missing children. The program provides tips for preventing abduction of children, provides fingerprints and dental records for parents to be used in the event a missing child who cannot be identified is found, and also provides a profile sheet of information about the child (Russi 1984).

St. Luke's Hospital in Cedar Rapids, Iowa, opened a Child Protection Center in 1987. The center provides centralized access to services for sexually and physically abused children and coordinates efforts to identify, treat, and prevent child abuse. Specially trained personnel conduct examinations of abused children and collect evidence for prosecution based on briefings provided by police investigators (Hinzman and Blome 1991).

These are only a few of the many programs currently being used to prevent abuse and neglect. As is the case with delinquency prevention programs, none of them are foolproof, none a panacea.

Career Opportunity—Big Brother Big Sister Caseworker

Job Description: Work with children and their families interested in forming a relationship with an adult mentor; work with adult volunteers who choose to develop a mentoring relationship with a child; interview, assess, and train volunteers, youth, and families; supervise and monitor adult to child mentoring matches; facilitate support groups; responsible for recruiting youth and adult mentors from the community.

Employment Requirements: Must have a minimum of a bachelor's degree in social work, counseling, guidance, psychology, or a related field. Must have experience in working directly with youth within a social service agency or similar surroundings, excellent oral and written communication skills, assessment and counseling skills, problem-solving skills, and experience with diverse populations, and usually some experience in public speaking. Required to work some evenings and, on occasion, weekends.

Salary and Benefits: Salary ranges from $20,000 to $30,000. Benefits vary by geographical location, but typically include paid medical, dental, vacation, and 401(k).

Summary

All practitioners interested in the welfare of juveniles with problems should be familiar with the wide range of programs available in most communities. Teachers should not hesitate to consult personnel from children and family services or law enforcement officials when appropriate or to enter into long-term agreements about sharing information in the interests of intervening appropriately with youth in trouble. It is important to remember that the goal of each of these agencies is the same—provide for the best interests of youth. Territorial jealousy must be eliminated and practitioners must learn to share their expertise with those outside their agency. It is not a sign of failure or weakness to recognize and admit that a particular problem could be dealt with more beneficially by personnel from an agency other than one's own. Concerned practitioners should provide direct services when it is possible and should not hesitate to make referrals when it is necessary or desirable.

Probably the best way to combat delinquency and child abuse is to prevent them from occurring in the first place. There are at least three ways to accomplish some form of prevention. These include changing juvenile behavior, the rules governing that behavior, or societal conditions leading to that behavior. While the latter probably holds the most promise for success, it is also the least likely to occur.

By establishing good working relationships among schools, families, and juvenile justice practitioners, early detection of serious juvenile problems may be facilitated and proper referrals may be made. Clearly, if the old adage "an ounce of prevention is worth a pound of cure" is true, early detection and the support of the family as the primary institution influencing juvenile behavior are crucial to prevention programs. It is true that educational and vocational projects, community treatment programs, and the use of volunteers and nonprofessionals show some effectiveness. Recreation, individual and group counseling, social casework, and the use of detached workers (gang workers) may also be effective under some conditions.

At the same time, it is clear that many juvenile offenses are of a nonserious nature and that the statutes creating these offenses might be changed. We need to assess the necessity or desirability of many statutes and move to change those that serve no useful purpose and those which do more harm than good.

Practitioners are also in an excellent position to detect and report types of behavior which, in their experience, frequently lead to the commission of serious delinquent acts. Use of their experiences in combination with well-designed research projects will hopefully lead to modified, more satisfactory theories of causation. Recognizing the variety of factors involved, the range of alternative programs available, and the strengths and weaknesses of prevention programs should lead to greater success in dealing with both categories of juveniles.

Preventing delinquency and abuse is more desirable than attempting to rehabilitate delinquents or salvage battered and neglected youth, from an economic viewpoint, from the viewpoint of the juveniles involved, and from society's viewpoint. Hopefully, commitment by both government and the private sector will facilitate more effective prevention and lead to the abandonment of ineffective programs. Examination of some of the basic assumptions of current prevention programs is essential.

There are a number of agencies operating programs that complement or supplement juvenile justice programs. Coordinating and organizing these programs to eliminate duplication and increase efficiency has proved difficult as the result of territorial jealousy. Nonetheless, the best way to ensure the welfare of juveniles with problems is to share knowledge through interagency cooperation and referral, and budgetary restraints are currently dictating that this be accomplished.

INTERNET EXERCISES

The juvenile court system could not function without the help of agencies and organizations who sponsor prevention and diversion programs. Prevention and diversion programs vary among states, counties, towns, and even neighborhoods. A program offered in one town may be not be offered anywhere else in the nation, thus, these programs may become very personalized to the issues or concerns of a particular geographical area. On the other hand, some prevention and diversion programs, like Drug Abuse Resistance Education, Job Corps, and alternative education programs, become nationwide practices with programming offered in nearly every community. The Big Brothers, Big Sisters mentoring program has become a nationwide prevention and diversion program. Visit the Orange County, California Big Brother, Big Sister program website at http://www.bigbrooc.org/default.htm to learn more about this type of prevention and diversion program.

1. Based upon the information provided, discuss whether you believe the Orange County Big Brother, Big Sister mentoring program is effective or ineffective. What is your decision based upon? Would you classify the Big Brother, Big Sister program more as a prevention program or as a diversion program? Why?
2. Click on Programs and review the types of curriculums offered by the agency. The Orange County Big Brother, Big Sister program offers curriculums to meet the needs of many types of children. How can the competition to get many types of children to use Big Brother, Big Sister services create territorial jealousies with other social service agencies that are offering programs for the same children?
3. Does the Big Brother, Big Sister program have the same or similar goals as the juvenile justice system? Would it be beneficial for this program to be offered by the juvenile court instead of a private agency? Why or why not? In your opinion, which type of child under the juvenile court's jurisdiction would benefit the most from the Big Brother, Big Sister mentoring program?
4. After reading the Frequently Asked Questions, discuss the fundamental characteristics of the Big Brother, Big Sister program that make it a necessary program to prevent juvenile delinquency and abuse and neglect. Are there any inherent weaknesses to the Big Brother, Big Sister program?

Useful Websites

Juvenile Justice: Diversion—*http://www2.sunysuffolk.edu/phillit/so35pap.htm*

Juvenile Forensic Evaluation Resource Center—*http://www.ilppp.virginia.edu/juv/Characteristics.html*

Mediation in Juvenile Criminal Cases—*http://www.lectlaw.com/files/cjs08.htm*

Alternative Sanctions for Juveniles: Bibliography—*http://www.library.utoronto.ca/www/libraries_crime/alternat.htm*

Center for Restorative Justice—*http:ssw.che.umn.edu/rjp*

Critical Thinking Questions

1. What are the major approaches to delinquency prevention? What are the strengths and weaknesses of each? Discuss some contemporary attempts to prevent delinquency or divert delinquents, and tell why you feel they are effective or ineffective.
2. List some of the assumptions you feel are basic to delinquency prevention and diversion programs. To what extent do you feel each of these assumptions is justified? Why is the public often unwilling to finance prevention programs and what are the consequences of this unwillingness?

4. What is territorial jealousy? Why does it occur and what are some of its consequences?
5. Discuss at least two agencies or programs with goals similar to those of the juvenile justice system. In your opinion, how successful are these agencies in achieving their goals?
6. Discuss some of the attempts currently being made to prevent child abuse and neglect? Are such programs operating in your community?

SUGGESTED READINGS

Bilchik, S. (1998). *Juvenile mentoring program: 1998 report to Congress.* Washington, D.C.: Office of Juvenile Justice and Delinquency Prevention, U.S. Department of Justice.

Botvin, G. J., Baker, E., Dusenbery, L., Botvin., E. M., & Diaz, T. (1995). Long-term follow-up results of a randomized drug abuse prevention trial in a white middle-class population. *Journal of the American Medical Association, 273,* 1106–1112.

Botvin, G. J., Schinke, S. P., Epstien, J. A., & Diaz, T. (1995). The effectiveness of culturally-focused and generic skills training approaches to alcohol and drug abuse prevention among minority youth: Two-year follow-up results. *Psychology of Addictive Behaviors, 9* (3), 183–194.

Davidson, W. S., Redner, R., & Amdur, R. L. (1990). *Alternative treatments for troubled youths: The case of diversion from the justice system.* New York: Plenum.

Esbensen, F., & Osgood, D. W. (1999). Gang resistance education and training (GREAT): Results from the national evaluation. *Journal of Research in Crime and Delinquency, 36* (2), 194–225.

Hinzman, G., & Blome, D. (1991). Cooperation key to success of child protection center. *Police Chief, 58,* 24–27.

Lundman, R. J. (1993). *Prevention and control of juvenile delinquency.* 2nd ed. New York: Oxford University Press.

McCord, J., & Tremblay, R. E. (1992). *Preventing antisocial behavior: Interventions from birth through adolescence.* New York: Guilford Press.

Schur, E. M. (1973). *Radical non-intervention; Rethinking the delinquency problem.* Englewood Cliffs, NJ: Prentice-Hall.

CHAPTER

10 Dispositional Alternatives

Chapter Learning Objectives

Upon completion of this chapter, students should be able to:

List and describe dispositional alternatives
Discuss the dispositional phase of the juvenile justice process
Discuss probation, conditions of probation, and revocation
Discuss the relationship between probation and restorative justice
List advantages and disadvantages of foster homes
List advantages and disadvantages of treatment centers
Discuss juvenile corrections, dilemmas, and consequences
Present arguments for and against capital punishment for juveniles
Address some possible solutions to the effects of incarceration

Key Terms

probation
John Augustus
National Probation Act
revocation of probation
technical violations
probation as conditional release
labeling process
electronic monitoring
intensive supervision
restorative justice
Victim Offender Reconciliation Programs
Community Response to Crime Program
Victims of Crime Impact Panels
Victim Offender Mediation Programs
foster homes
away syndrome
private detention facilities
public detention facilities
capital punishment
shock intervention
boot camps
positive peer culture

When attempts to divert youth from the juvenile justice network fail, an adjudicatory hearing is held to determine whether the youth should be dismissed or categorized as a delinquent, minor in need of supervision (or authoritative intervention), or an abused, neglected, or dependent child. After adjudication, the judge must make a decision concerning appropriate disposition. The judge uses his or her own expertise and experience, the social background investigation report, and sometimes the probation officer's or caseworker's recommendation in arriving at a decision.

Many states used a bifurcated hearing process so that the adjudicatory and dispositional hearings are held at different times. This is often preferred because different evidentiary rules

The impact of shock intervention programs is still being evaluated.
John B. Boykin/corbisstockmarket

apply at the two hearings. While only evidence bearing on the allegations contained in the petition is admitted at the adjudicatory hearing, the totality of the juvenile's circumstances may be heard at the dispositional hearing.

The alternatives available to the judge differ depending upon the category in which the youth has been placed, but in general they range from death in certain circumstances to incarceration to treatment or foster-home placement to probation. In the *Gault* case, the Supreme Court specifically declined to comment on the applicability of due process requirements during the dispositional phase of juvenile court proceedings. Thus, we must turn to state statutes or lower court decisions in analyzing this process. Keep in mind that the purpose of the dispositional hearing is to determine the best way to correct or treat the youth in question while protecting society. In order to accomplish these goals, the court must have available as much information as possible about the youth, his or her background (family, education, legal history), and available alternatives. Evidence pertaining to the welfare of the youth is generally admissible at this stage of the proceedings, and the youth should be represented by counsel.

While some nondelinquent youth, typically those found to be in need of supervision, may be confined temporarily in specifically designated facilities, the trend had been toward diverting them to other types of programs. In some cases the child is permitted to remain with the family under the supervision of the court; in others custody reverts to the state, with placement in a foster or adoptive home. The extent of state intervention has been a subject of considerable controversy, but when the welfare of the child is involved, termination of parental rights may be the only way to provide adequate protection.

Delinquent conduct always involves violation of law, unlike some of the other conduct dealt with by the juvenile court. There are numerous available dispositions for youth in this category, including probation (release after trial with court supervision) under conditions prescribed by the court, placement in a restrictive/secure facility not operated by the department of corrections, or commitment to a public correctional facility. The latter disposition is generally used as a last resort, but may be necessary to protect society. In some cases restitution is used in addition to probation, or as a disposition in and of itself. In some cases weekend incarceration or community-based correctional programs are used. These programs allow youth to remain in the community where they may attend school, work part time, and participate in supervised activities. The effectiveness of such programs is an empirical question and many are not adequately evaluated.

PROBATION

A juvenile delinquent on **probation** is released into the community with the understanding that his or her continued freedom depends upon good behavior and compliance with the conditions established by his or her probation officer and/or the judge. Probation, then, gives the delinquent a second chance to demonstrate that he or she can function in the community. The history of probation goes back to the fourteenth century when offenders could be entrusted to the custody of willing citizens to perform a variety of tasks. The founding father of probation is said to be **John Augustus** who attended criminal court proceedings in the 1850s and took selected offenders into his home in order that they might avoid prison. By 1878, the city of Boston had hired a probation officer, other cities and states followed suit, and by 1925 all states had adopted probation legislation.

The **National Probation Act,** passed in 1925, authorized federal district court judges to hire probation officers as well (Cromwell, Killinger, Kerper, and Walker 1985).

A major finding of past presidential commissions has been that the earlier and deeper an offender goes into the juvenile justice system, the more difficult it is to get out successfully. Unnecessary commitments to correctional institutions often result in "criminalized" juveniles. The revolving door of delinquency and criminality is perpetuated as a result. The fact that there may be a short-term benefit from temporarily removing some juveniles from society should be tempered with the realization that, once released, some juveniles are more likely to jeopardize the community than if they had been processed under adequate probation services in the community where they must eventually prove themselves anyway. Since the goal of the juvenile court is therapeutic rather than punitive, probation is clearly in accord with the philosophy of the court. When circumstances warrant probation, when the juveniles for whom probation is a viable alternative are carefully selected, and when adequate supervision by probation officers is available, probation seems to have potential for success. Failure to take proper precautions in any of these areas, however, jeopardizes chances of success and adds to the criticism of probation as an alternative that coddles delinquents.

Probation is clearly the most frequent disposition handed down by juvenile court judges, accounting for more than 90 percent of all dispositions in some jurisdictions. Despite pressures exerted by the mass media (in the form of coverage of some exceptionally disturbing offenses committed by probationers), juvenile court judges have generally adopted the philosophy that a delinquent youth will usually benefit more from remaining with his or her family or under the custody of other designated persons in the community than from incarceration.

In making a disposition, the juvenile court judge traditionally places heavy emphasis on the present offense, the wishes of the complainant, prior legal history, family background, personal history, peer associates, school record, and home and neighborhood. In addition, consideration is given to whether justice would be best served by granting probation or whether incarceration is necessary for the protection of the public. There are a multitude of other factors considered by judges, including the youth's attitude toward the offense and whether the youth participated in the offense in a principal or secondary capacity. The degree of aggravation and premeditation as well as mitigating circumstances are also considered. All of this information is provided to the judge in the social background investigation.

Once probation has been decided upon, certain terms and conditions are imposed on the probationer. Within broad limits, these terms and conditions are left to the discretion of the judge and/or probation officer. The requirements that the probationer obey all laws of the land, attend school on a regular basis, avoid associating with criminals and other persons of ill repute, remain within jurisdiction, and report regularly to the probation officer for counseling and supervision are general terms and conditions usually imposed by statutory decree. Other requirements the court may impose are curfews, drug testing, counseling, community service, and restorative justice programming. Although the court has broad discretion in imposing terms and conditions of probation, these terms and conditions must be reasonable and relevant to the offense for which probation is being granted. For example, a condition that a defendant cannot become pregnant while unmarried was not considered to be related to the robbery for which the female was adjudicated delinquent. The appellate court reasoned that a possible pregnancy had no reasonable relationship to future criminality (*People v. Dominquez* 1967). An order of a juvenile court requiring regular attendance at Sunday school and church was held to be unconstitutional, as "no civil authority has the right to require anyone to accept or reject any religious belief or to contribute any support thereto" (*Jones v. Commonwealth* 1946). However, a condition of probation that requires a defendant to pay costs or make restitution is generally upheld, provided that the amounts ordered to be paid are not excessive in view of the financial condition of the defendant. Any condition that cannot reasonably be fulfilled within the period fixed by the court is not likely to be upheld.

The importance of adhering to the terms and conditions of probation is stressed since violations constitute a basis for **revocation of probation** and the imposition or execution of the sentence that could have been given originally by the judge. There are generally three types of violations—technical, rearrest for a new crime or act of delinquency, and absconding or fleeing jurisdiction. A **technical violation** is usually characterized by the probationer flagrantly ignoring the terms or conditions of probation, but not actually committing a new act of delinquency. For example, deliberately associating with delinquent peers might lead to revocation if such was prohibited as a condition of probation. Typically, technical violations include minor infractions on behalf of the probationer. Technical violations are generally worked out between the probationer and probation officer and usually do not result in revocation action, unless the probationer develops a complete disregard for the terms or conditions of probation. A rearrest or new custody action due to a new act of delinquency is obviously a serious breach of probation. The seriousness of the new act of delinquency is important in determining whether revocation proceedings will be initiated. Most rearrests are viewed by probation officers as serious and usually result in the revocation of probation, although there is some room for discretion. Although absconding or fleeing the juvenile court's jurisdiction may be considered a technical violation, it is generally considered separately and may result in revocation action.

Release on probation is a **conditional release;** that is, the liberty of the probationer is not absolute but subject to the terms and conditions being met. Although the probation officer may seek a revocation of probation, the court will ultimately determine whether to revoke probation. When juveniles violate the conditions of supervised release and face revocation of probation, issues of due process with respect to right to counsel and standard of proof arise. In *Morrissey v. Brewer* (1972) the Supreme Court held that, although a parole revocation proceeding is not a part of the criminal prosecution, the potential loss of liberty involved is nevertheless significant enough to entitle the parolee to due process of law. First, the Court held that the parolee is entitled to a preliminary hearing to determine if there is probable cause to believe that a violation of a condition has occurred. Second, an impartial examiner shall conduct the hearing. Finally, notice of the alleged violation, purpose of the hearing, disclosure of evidence to be used against the parolee, opportunity to present evidence on his or her own behalf, and limited right to cross-examination are allowed under due process. Subsequently, in *Gagnon v. Scarpelli* (1973) concerning the issue of probation revocation proceedings, the Court held that a probationer was entitled to the same procedural safeguards announced in *Morrissey v. Brewer,* including requested counsel. Earlier, in *Mempa v. Rhay* (1967), the Court had held that, where the petitioner had been placed on probation and his sentence deferred, he was entitled by due process of law to the right to counsel in a subsequent revocation proceeding, since the revocation proceeding was a continuation of the sentencing process and, therefore, the criminal prosecution itself. Most courts, in the absence of statute, have held that the probation violation need only be established by a preponderance of the evidence, even if the violation is itself an offense.

There are several dispositions available in revocation hearings. If the charges are vacated, the probationer may be restored to probation or the conditions may be altered, amended, or even remain the same. The revocation may be granted with a new disposition generally resulting in commitment to a juvenile correctional institution. The juvenile may also be sentenced to a treatment center if the revocation was due to a behavior requiring treatment, such as drug or alcohol abuse.

Although the length of probation varies among states, the maximum term of probation for the juvenile is usually not beyond the maximum jurisdiction of the juvenile court. Most terms of juvenile probation are between six months to one year, with possible extensions in most states. Probation dispositions are usually indeterminate, leaving the release date up to the discretion of the probation officer. Upon successful completion of the probation period or on the recommendation of the probation officer for early discharge, termination of probation releases the juvenile from the court's jurisdiction.

Although probation serves the purpose of keeping the juvenile in the community while rehabilitation attempts are being made, there are some potential dangers built into this disposition. Learning and labeling theories indicate that proper supervision of probationers is essential if rehabilitation is to occur. Otherwise, the juvenile placed on probation may immediately return to the "old gang" or behavior patterns that initially led to that juvenile's adjudication as delinquent.

Similarly, the juvenile placed on probation, while remaining with his or her family, may end up in the same negative circumstances that initially led to delinquent behavior, except that he or she has now been labeled and is more or less expected to misbehave. The **labeling process** may exaggerate problems in family, school, and peer relations, and the juvenile may find it difficult to meet the expectations established for him or her. In many cases, the only positive role model available is the probation officer, whose caseload may preclude seeing the juvenile for more than a few minutes a week.

In attempt to remedy the problems of limited probation officer time and lack of sufficient supervision of the probationer, several strategies are being employed. The first of these is **electronic monitoring** which uses technology to track the whereabouts of the probationer. A bracelet is placed on the wrist or ankle of the youth in question and his or her whereabouts can be determined by signals transmitted and picked up by a receiver maintained by the probation officer. In some cases the youth is placed under house arrest for a specified period, in other cases the youth may be allowed to go to school or work, but must be home during certain hours. A second strategy involves intensive supervision. **Intensive supervision** is usually reserved for juveniles facing their last chance before incarceration. Probation officers working in intensive supervision programs have limited caseloads (usually no more than fifteen to twenty probationers), make frequent contacts with their charges, make contacts with the families of the probationers, contact school authorities and/or employers periodically, work with clients during other than normal working hours, and keep extensive records of their contacts. They typically review the conditions of probation regularly and adjust them as needed. Intensive supervision usually lasts six to twelve months. The assumption upon which these programs are based is that the probation officer as role model, supervisor, and disciplinarian will be more effective if he or she spends more time with each client. Empirical testing of the programs is ongoing. Another attempt at providing better probationary services for delinquents involves contracting with private agencies. The Office of Juvenile Justice and Delinquency Prevention (OJJDP) has funded a $1.7 million three-year project called the *Private Sector Probation Initiative.* This funding enables the juvenile courts to contract with private concerns to provide services (counseling, job readiness skills, structured and wilderness programs) for probationers, to supplement the public services provided. OJJDP has concluded that some services can be enhanced by transferring them to the private sector, and research on this approach continues. In 1999, the American Correctional Association conducted a survey concerning private sector involvement in juvenile corrections. The survey revealed that forty-six jurisdictions indicated they had at least one active private sector contract. The main reasons given for such a contract were that private sector vendors could provide services and expertise lacking in the jurisdictions in questions (Levinson and Chase 2000).

Restorative justice (see chapter 9) is a new philosophy quickly being adopted by juvenile courts as a supplement to probation services. The roots of restorative justice can be traced to 1974 in Ontario, Canada. The Mennonite Central Committee, through the help of a probation officer, created the first mediation program involving the basic principles of restorative justice. This program, called the **Victim Offender Reconciliation Program,** used the payment of restitution directly to the victim by the offender as its core. Traditionally, payment of restitution to the victim was handled directly by the probation office in an impersonal manner. By forcing the offender to pay the restitution directly to the victim, the process was construed as a repayment for loss and damages to an individual rather than a state-mandated court fine for a harm done to the state. The success of this program initiated interests in restorative justice in the United States and in other parts of Canada.

Elkhart, Indiana, was the first to initiate a victim-offender mediation program in the late 1970s in the United States. As the philosophy grew, a nonprofit organization called the Center for Community Justice based on the restorative justice philosophy was created in 1979. Since the 1980s restorative justice has been called by a variety of different names depending upon the agency applying its concepts. Although the name may change, the definition and core concepts of restorative justice—accountability, competency, and public safety—remain the same in all programs.

Accountability in restorative justice is used to explain how offenders are to respond to the harm they have caused to victims and the community. Accountability requires that offenders take personal responsibility for their actions, face those they have harmed, and take steps to repair harm by making amends. Much of the literature regarding restorative justice calls this process "making things right" or "repairing the harm" (Center for Restorative Justice and Mediation 1996a; Restorative Justice for Illinois 1999). "Accountability is more than the 'guilty party' stating they committed a wrongful act" (Restorative Justice for Illinois 1999, p. 1). The state of Illinois adopted the restorative justice philosophy as the basis of its juvenile court in 1999 and has been implementing restorative justice programming across the state. Many of the programs focus on accountability. The state of Minnesota has implemented the accountability concept in a **Community Response to Crime Program.** This program uses a community intervention team which meets with the offender to let him or her know how the behavior affected the community, how the community expects the offender to make amends, and how the community is willing to support the offender while he or she makes amends (Center for Restorative Justice and Mediation 1996b, p. 2).

Secondly, restorative justice requires competency on behalf of the offender. Competency is not the mere absence of bad behavior. It is providing the resources for persons to make measurable gains in educational, vocational, social, civic, and other abilities that enhance their capacity to function as productive citizens (Restorative Justice for Illinois 1999; Bazemore and Day 1998). Restorative justice suggests that programs be designed to promote empathy in offenders, to teach effective communication skills to offenders, and to develop conflict resolution skills in offenders. Programs such as **Victims of Crime Impact Panels** (VCIP), **Victim Offender Mediation Programs** (VORP), and those programs sponsored by community-run self-help groups like Mothers Against Drunk Driving (MADD) strive to teach competency to offenders. One competency program is being used in southeast Missouri for juvenile offenders. This program uses a Victims of Crime Impact Panel to increase empathy levels in juvenile offenders by having victims of crime tell offenders how the crime has impacted their lives. Mothers Against Drunk Driving (MADD) offers a similar program. MADD also offers victims panels on a nationwide basis for empathy development in offenders of drunk driving. Minnesota is using a "crime repair crew" in Dakota County which is "made up of offenders who are called to scenes of property crimes to fix and clean up the damage. The crime repair crew gives offenders the opportunity to 'give back' to the community while learning skills in construction and painting." (Center for Restorative Justice and Mediation 1996b, p. 2).

Public safety is the last area of restorative justice. "Public safety is a balanced strategy that cultivates new relationships with schools, employers, community groups, and social agencies" (Restorative Justice for Illinois 1999, p. 1). Public safety also facilitates new relationships with victims. "The balanced strategy of restorative justice invests heavily in strengthening a community's capacity to prevent and control crime" (Bazemore and Day 1998, p. 7). The concept of public safety relies heavily on the community. The community, according to restorative justice, should make "sure that the laws which guide citizens' behaviors are carried out in ways which are responsive to our different cultures and backgrounds—whether racial, ethnic, geographic, religious, economic, age, abilities, family status, sexual orientation, and other backgrounds—and all are given equal protection and due process" (Center for Restorative Justice and Mediation 1985, p. 1). Restorative justice also proclaims that crime control is not the sole responsibility of the criminal justice system but is the responsibility of the members of the community. Sentencing circles, reparative boards, and citizens councils are examples of the public safety concept in application. A program in Northern Canada uses "sentencing circles which are groups of community members who decide how a crime will be resolved. Originally used in Aboriginal or Native communities . . . the circles seek to get everyone involved and the perspective of the victim is valued. They often include 'law and order' [i.e., criminal justice personnel] participants and the plan for repairing the harm nearly always includes a community-based solution" (Center for Restorative Justice and Mediation 1996a, p. 2). Currently, there are few statistics available showing that these early nonretributive efforts are effective.

The participants in a balanced and restorative justice system are crime victims, offenders, and the community. Crime victims are essential to the success of the restorative justice process because they are involved in the healing and reintegration, of the offender and themselves. Crime victims receive support, assistance, compensation and restitution. The offenders participating in restorative justice programs provide repayment to their communities and are provided work experience and social skills necessary to improve decision making and citizen productivity. The community is involved by providing support to the offender and the crime victim. The community provides individuals, besides criminal justice personnel, to act as mentors to the offender and provides employment opportunities for the offender.

Juveniles placed on probation with families or support persons who are concerned and cooperative may benefit far more from this disposition than from placement in a correctional facility. In an attempt to provide this solid foundation for juveniles whose own families are unconcerned, uncooperative, or the source of the delinquent activity or abuse or neglect in question, the juvenile court judge may place his or her client on probation in a foster home.

Foster Homes

When maintenance of the family unit is clearly not in the juvenile's best interests (or in the family's best interests, for that matter), the judge may place a juvenile in a foster home. Typically, **foster homes** are reserved for children who are victims of abuse or neglect. Delinquent children may spend a short time in a foster home, but these children seem more suited for treatment facilities and the services offered by treatment facilities. Ideally, foster homes are carefully selected through state and local inspection and are to provide a concerned, comfortable setting in which the delinquent's behavior may be modified or in which abused or neglected children can be nurtured in safety. Foster parents provide the supervision and care that is often missing in the youth's own family and provide a more constant source of supervision and support than the probation officer. As a result, the juvenile's routine contacts should provide a more positive environment for change than would be the case if the youth were free to associate with former delinquent companions or unconcerned, abusive, or criminal parents. Foster homes are frequently used as viable alternatives for minors who have been abused or neglected or who are dependent or in need of supervision because many of these youths are caught up in dangerous situations at home. It is often clearly in their best interests to be removed from their natural families.

The foster home clearly has a number of advantages for youth who are wards of the court, provided the selection process for both foster parents and the youth placed with them is adequate. Unfortunately, some couples apply for foster parent status in the belief that the money paid by the state or county for housing the delinquent will supplement their income. If this added income is the basic interest of potential foster parents, limited guidance and assistance for foster children can be expected. In addition, many of these couples soon find that the money paid per foster child is barely adequate to feed and clothe the youth and therefore does nothing to enhance their income. Thus careful selection of foster parents is imperative. The number of foster children is growing more rapidly than the number of foster parents willing to take on the responsibility.

No matter how careful the juvenile court judge is in selecting youths for foster home placement, some placements are likely to involve youths whose behavior is difficult to control. Raising any adolescent presents problems, and caring for delinquent and abused youths frequently adds to these problems. As a result, the number of couples willing to provide foster care for delinquent and abused youths is never as great as the need. Foster families must be carefully screened through onsite visitations and interviews and have those physical and emotional attributes which will be supportive for any youth placed with them. Assuming responsibility for a delinquent, abused, or neglected youth placed in one's home requires a great deal of commitment, and many juveniles who might benefit from this type of setting cannot be placed due to the lack of available families. Alternatives available to the judge in such cases include placement in a treatment center, group homes or incarceration in a juvenile correctional or shelter care facility.

TREATMENT CENTERS

Throughout this book, it has been indicated that juveniles should be diverted from the juvenile justice system when the offense involved is not serious and when viable alternatives are available. Status offenders, abused, neglected, and dependent youths clearly should not be incarcerated. There may, of course, be times when the only option available to the court is to provide temporary placement in shelter care facilities, foster homes, or group homes when conditions preclude a return to the family. In cases where the juvenile in question may present a danger to him- or herself or to others, or may flee, temporary placement may be necessary.

Placement may also be necessary in cases where the juvenile's family is completely negligent or incapable of providing appropriate care and/or control. Temporary custody of dependent, neglected, and in-need-of-supervision juveniles, as well as nonserious delinquents, should be in an environment conducive to normal relations and contact with the community. Numerous private and public programs directed at such youths have emerged in the past decade.

For example, the Missouri Division of Youth Services has developed programs aimed at safeguarding Missouri citizens by establishing community partnerships to provide services to help delinquent youths avoid further delinquency. The focus of the program is on the individual needs of the delinquents involved and the eventual return of the delinquent to home and community as a productive citizen (Steward 1997). The program seems to hold considerable promise, but further evaluation needs to be accomplished.

Sentencing a child to a treatment center is often used in conjunction with probation, but can be used alone. Children are sent to treatment programs for a variety of reasons including chemical dependency, behavioral or emotional problems, sexual assault counseling, problems resulting from previous abuse or neglect, and attitudinal or empathy therapy. Facilities such as Boys Town of America specialize in treating children with behavioral problems. This facility uses small family-oriented cottages focused on behavior modification to teach delinquent children how to control impulsive behaviors that may lead to criminal acts. Other treatment centers use "positive peer culture" treatment programs, play therapy programs, anger management therapy, conflict-resolution programs, and life-skills programs, to name only a few. Treatment centers are rarely administered by the state so the juvenile court contracts with private institutions to provide these services that the state cannot provide. Most delinquent children sentenced to terms in treat-

The most severe dispositional alternative typically used is commitment to a correctional facility.
Robert King/Newsmakers/Getty Images

ment centers are one step away from being sentenced to a correctional institution. Thus, successful completion of the treatment program determines if the delinquent child will return to society or go to a correctional institution.

Juvenile Corrections

The most severe dispositional alternative available to the juvenile court judge considering a case of delinquency is commitment to a correctional facility. There are clearly some juveniles whose actions cannot be tolerated by the community. Those who commit predatory offenses or whose illegal behavior becomes progressively more serious may need to be institutionalized for the good of society. For these delinquent youth, alternative options may have already been exhausted, and the only remedy available to ensure protection of society may be incarceration. Since juvenile institutions are often very similar to adult prison institutions, incarceration is a serious business with a number of negative consequences for both juveniles and society that must be considered prior to placement.

THE DILEMMAS OF JUVENILE CORRECTIONS

While incarcerating juveniles for the protection of society is clearly necessary in some cases, correctional institutions frequently serve as a gateway to careers in crime and delinquency. The notion that sending juveniles to correctional facilities will result in rehabilitation has proved to be inaccurate in most cases. In 1974, Robert M. Martinson completed a comprehensive review of rehabilitation efforts and provided a critical summary of all studies published since 1945. He concluded that there was "pitifully little evidence existing that any prevailing mode of correctional treatment had an appreciable effect on recidivism." Bernard (1992, p. 587) arrived at the same conclusion several years later. In spite of the fact that most of the research on the effects of juvenile correctional facilities substantiates the conclusions of these authors, we have developed and frequently implement what may be termed an **"away syndrome."** When confronted with a youth who has committed a delinquent act, we all too frequently ask "Where can we send him?" This away syndrome represents part of a more general approach to deviant behavior that has prevailed for many years in America. The away syndrome applies not only to juveniles, but also to the mentally ill, the retarded, the aged, and the adult criminal. This approach frequently discourages attempts to find alternatives to incarceration, frequently arises when we become frustrated by unsuccessful attempts at rehabilitation, and is frequently accompanied by an out-of-sight, out-of-mind attitude. Our hope seems to be that if we simply send deviants far enough away so they become invisible, then they and their problems will disappear. However, walls do not successfully hide such problems nor will they simply go away. Not only do "graduates" from correctional institutions reappear, but their experiences while incarcerated often seem to solidify delinquent or criminal attitudes and behavior. Most studies of recidivism among institutionalized delinquents lead to the conclusion that while some programs may work for some offenders some of the time, most institutional programs produce no better results than the simple passage of time.

There are a number of alternative forms of incarceration available. For juveniles whose period of incarceration is to be relatively brief, there are many public and private detention facilities available. Treatment programs and security measures vary widely among these institutions. Both need to be considered when deciding where to place a juvenile. Generally speaking, **private detention facilities** house fewer delinquents and are less oriented toward strict custody than facilities operated by the state department of corrections. Many of these private facilities provide treatment programs aimed at modifying undesirable behavior as quickly as possible in order to facilitate an early release and to minimize the effects of isolation. The cost of maintaining a delinquent in an institution of this type may be quite high, and not every community has access to such facilities.

Public detention facilities frequently are located near larger urban centers and often house large numbers of delinquents in either a cottage or dormitory setting. As a rule, these institutions are used only when all other alternatives have been exhausted or when the offense involved is quite serious. As a result, most of the more serious delinquents are sent to these facilities. In these institutions, concern with custody frequently outweighs concern with rehabilitation. A number of changes have occurred in juvenile correctional facilities in the last half-century. Cottage-type facilities have been replaced by institutional-type settings and the number of juveniles incarcerated has increased, as has the severity of their offenses (Gluck 1997).

As the discussion of learning and labeling theories indicates, current correctional environments are not the best places to mold juvenile delinquents into useful law-abiding citizens. Sending a delinquent to a correctional facility to learn responsible, law-abiding behavior is like sending a person to the desert to learn how to swim. If our specific intent is to demand revenge of youthful offenders through physical and emotional punishment and isolation, current correctional facilities will suffice. If we would rather have those incarcerated return to society rehabilitated, a number of changes must be made.

First, we need to be continually aware of the negative effects resulting from isolating juveniles from the larger society, especially for long periods of time. This isolation, while clearly necessary in certain cases, makes reintegration into society difficult. The transition from a controlled correctional environment to the relative freedom of society is not easy to make for those who have been labeled delinquent. That this is so has been demonstrated by Krisberg, Austin, and Steele (1989), who found recidivism rates of 55 to 75 percent among juvenile parolees.

Second, it is essential to be aware of the continual, intense pressure to conform to institutional standards, which characterizes life in most correctional facilities. Although some juvenile institutions provide environments conducive to treatment and rehabilitation, many are warehouses concerned only with custody, control, and order maintenance. Correctional personnel frequently deceive the public, both intentionally and unintentionally, about what takes place in their institutions by providing tours that emphasize orderliness, cleanliness, and treatment orientation. Too often we fail to see or consider the harsh discipline, solitary confinement, and dehumanizing aspects of correctional facilities. We often fail to realize that the skills needed to survive in the institution may be learned very well, but these are not the same skills needed to lead a productive life on the outside. It has been recommended that concerned citizens, prosecutors, public defenders, and juvenile court judges spend a few days in correctional facilities to see if the state is really acting in the best interests of the juvenile.

Third, the effects of peer group pressure in juvenile correctional facilities must be considered. There is little doubt that behavior modification will occur, but it will not necessarily result in the creation of a law-abiding citizen. The learning of delinquent behavior may be enhanced if contact frequency with those holding favorable attitudes toward law violation is increased. Juvenile correctional facilities are typically characterized by the existence of a delinquent subculture, which enhances the opportunity for dominance of the strong over the weak and gives impetus to the exploitation of the unsophisticated by the more knowledgeable.

Into this quagmire we sometimes thrust delinquents who become involved in forced homosexual activities, who learn to settle disputes with physical violence or weapons, who learn the meaning of shakedowns and "the hole," and who discover how to "score" for narcotics and other contraband. Juvenile institutions have long been cited in cases of brutal beatings and other inhumane practices between residents (inmates) and between staff and residents. We are then surprised when juveniles leave these institutions with more problems than they had prior to incarceration.

It is clearly counterproductive to send juveniles to educational or vocational training six to eight hours a day only to return them to a cottage or dormitory where "anything goes" except escape. Juveniles who are physically assaulted or gang raped in their cottage at night are seldom concerned about success in the classroom the next day. The delinquent subculture existing in juvenile correctional facilities is based upon toughness and the ability to manipulate others. Status is largely determined by position within this delinquent subculture, which often offsets the efforts of correctional staff to effect positive attitudinal and/or behavioral change. Since, as we have seen earlier, the behavior demanded within the delinquent subculture is frequently contrary to behavior acceptable to the larger society, techniques must be found for minimizing the negative impact of that subculture.

A fourth problem frequently encountered in juvenile correctional facilities is the assignment to cottages and/or existing programs based on vacancies rather than on the benefit to the juvenile. Juveniles who need remedial education may end up in vocational training. Any benefits to be derived from treatment programs are therefore minimized.

A fifth problem involves mutual suspicion and distrust among staff members who see themselves as either rehabilitators or as custodians. Rehabilitators often believe that custodians have little interest and expertise in treatment, while custodians often believe that rehabilitators are "too liberal" and fail to appreciate the responsibilities of custody. The debate between these factions frequently makes it difficult to establish a cooperative treatment program. In addition, juveniles frequently use one staff group against the other. For example, they may tell the social worker that they have been unable to benefit from treatment efforts because the guards harass them physically and psychologically, keeping them constantly upset. This kind of report often contributes to the feud between guards and caseworkers, who occasionally become so concerned with staff differences that the youth are left to do mostly as they please.

Finally, the development of good working relationships between correctional staff and incarcerated juveniles is difficult. The delinquent subculture, the age difference, and the relative power positions of the two groups work against developing good rapport in most institutions. Frankly, there is often little contact between treatment personnel and their clients. It is very difficult for the caseworker, who sees his or her clients thirty minutes a week, to significantly influence juveniles, who spend the remainder of the week in the company of custodial staff and their delinquent peers. Since the custodial staff enforces institutional rules, there is a built-in mistrust between the staff members and their charges. Nonetheless, guards deal with the day-to-day problems of incarcerated youth most frequently, even though they are generally not regarded by caseworkers as particularly competent.

Under these circumstances, it is not difficult to see why rehabilitative efforts often end in failure. Finding solutions to these problems is imperative if we are to improve the chances of rehabilitating youth who must be incarcerated.

Capital Punishment and Youthful Offenders

Clearly there are some youth who are extremely dangerous to others and who do not appear to be amenable to rehabilitation. Thus, all states have established mechanisms for transferring or waiving jurisdiction to adult court in such cases (as we indicate in chapter 5). Once such transfer occurs, the accused loses all special rights and immunities and is subject to the full range of penalties for criminal behavior. This includes, in some jurisdictions, "absolute" sentences such as **capital punishment** and life in prison without parole (Dorne and Gewerth 1998, p. 203; Cothern 2000, p. 1). "Currently, 38 states authorize the death penalty, 23 of these permit the execution of offenders who committed capital offenses prior to their 18th birthdays. . . . Since 1973 . . . 17 men have been executed for crimes they committed as juveniles . . . and 74 people in the United States currently sit on death row for crimes they committed as juveniles." (Cothern 2000, p. 1; Streib 2000).

The first recorded juvenile execution in America occurred in 1642. Since that time, 361 individuals have been executed for crimes they committed as juveniles (Cothern 2000, p. 3; Streib 2000). The first case the Supreme Court heard on the death penalty for youth was *Eddings v. Oklahoma* (455 U.S. 104 [1982]). In this case, the Court did not rule on the constitutionality of the death penalty for minors, but did hold that the age of the minor is a mitigating factor to be considered at sentencing. The U.S. Supreme Court in *Thompson v. Oklahoma* (487 U.S. 815 [1988]) found that the death penalty did not constitute cruel and unusual punishment in this particular case, though the justices were deeply divided over the issue. The Court reaffirmed this ruling in *Stanford v. Kentucky* (492 U.S. 361 [1989]) and *Wilkins v. Missouri* (492 U.S. 361 [1989]). Nonetheless, the American Bar Association has proposed a moratorium on the death penalty for juveniles (as well as others), recommending instead that the focus on prevention be stepped up (Streib 1998). Currently, the presence on death row of seventy-four males who committed their crimes as juveniles (Cothern 2000, p. 4) is attracting considerable attention, and a number of legislatures and other groups are now reviewing the laws regarding execution of youth and execution in general (see In Practices 10.1 and 10.2).

Some Possible Solutions

All rehabilitative programs are based on some theoretical orientation to human behavior, running the gamut from individual to group approaches and from nature to nurture. Knowledge of these various approaches is critical for all staff working in juvenile correctional facilities. Nearly all juvenile institutions use some form of treatment program for the youth in custody—counseling on an individual or group basis, vocational and educational training, various types of therapy, recreational programs, and religious counseling. In addition, they provide medical and dental programs of some kind, as well as occasional legal service programs. The purpose of these various programs is to rehabilitate the youths within the institutions—to turn them into better-adjusted individuals and send them back into the community to be productive citizens. Despite generally good intentions, however, the goal of rehabilitation has been elusive, and it may be argued that it is better attained outside the walls of institutions.

Solving the problems created by the effects of isolation on incarcerated juveniles is a difficult task. We need to be certain that all available alternatives to incarceration have been explored. We must remember that virtually all juveniles placed in institutions will eventually be released into society. If those juveniles are to be released with positive attitudes toward reintegration, we must orient institutional treatment programs toward that goal. This can be accomplished through educational and vocational programs brought

In Practice 10.1

Rally Calls for Stay of Executions; Death Penalty Opponents Seek State Moratorium

Michael Stroh

Concerned that Maryland could put to death more people next year than it has during the past 34, opponents of capital punishment urged Gov. Parris N. Glendening yesterday to impose a moratorium on executions in the state.

"Maryland is starting to look more like Texas or Virginia. Obviously, something's wrong, something's broken," says Michael Stark of the Campaign to End the Death Penalty, which organized a rally of more than 100 demonstrators in front of the Supermax prison on East Madison Avenue in Baltimore.

Three people have been executed in Maryland since 1976, when capital punishment was reinstated by the U.S. Supreme Court.

But in an unusual coincidence, there's a chance that four men on death row, all in the final stages of their appeals, could go to the state's execution chamber next year.

Death penalty foes have seized on this possibility to draw attention to issues such as racial bias and wrongful convictions of death-row inmates.

Questions about the legitimacy of the death penalty have been growing in Maryland and across the country, although perhaps not as quickly as advocates would like.

"We're at a crossroads," says Jeanette Ravendhran, a protester from Eldersburg. "The death penalty is under fire like it never has been before."

In January, Illinois Gov. George H. Ryan, a death penalty supporter, declared a moratorium on executions in his state after doubts emerged about the guilt of several condemned inmates.

Some Maryland legislators are calling for a similar action. Del. Dana Lee Dembrow, a Montgomery County Democrat, has said he plans to sponsor a bill to abolish the death penalty. Several past attempts by legislators have failed.

Glendening this year agreed to a $225,000 study of whether racial bias plays a role in death penalty cases in Maryland. Of the 16 convicts now sentenced to die, 11 are black, giving the state one of the highest proportions of African-Americans on death row in the nation.

The study, which is to be completed next summer, is the third to examine the issue in the past decade.

But for now the governor is not considering a moratorium on executions, spokesman Michael Morrill said yesterday.

"What he is doing is examining each case on its own individual merits," Morrill said. "He spends a lot of time on each one."

In June, the governor granted clemency to Eugene Colvin-el, 55, who was sentenced to die for the 1980 stabbing death of Lena Buckman, 82, in Pikesville. Colvin-el is serving life without parole.

Morrill said he's not sure how the governor or the public will react if the four men facing the death penalty go to the execution chamber at about the same time.

Wesley Baker was sentenced to death for killing Jane Tyson in the parking lot of Westview Mall in 1991.

Steven Oken was convicted of sexually assaulting Dawn Marie Garvin in her White Marsh home, then shooting her twice in the head in 1987.

Vernon Lee Evans Jr. and Anthony Grandison Sr. were sentenced to die for their roles in a 1983 murder-for-hire scheme.

Stroh, M. (2000, December 10.). Rally calls for stay of executions: Death penalty opponents seek state moratorium. *The Baltimore Sun,* p. 3B.

In Practice 10.2

IS EXECUTION THE ULTIMATE PUNISHMENT?

Edwin A. Roberts, Jr.

One of the issues raised against George W. Bush during the campaign was the extraordinary number of murderers executed in Texas, although his responsibility in that regard was, under the law, far from central. It was difficult to discern, moreover, whether the morbid scorecard reflects an overabundance of vicious killers in Texas or a unique enthusiasm for the death penalty in that robust state.

Polls show most Americans favor capital punishment for those who commit the worst of crimes. Why? Because most Americans believe death is the harshest of punishments.

That could be more easily argued, I have come to believe, in the days of the hangman's noose and the electric chair, and it could be argued more powerfully still in the days of Henry VIII, when the lusty monarch condemned those who fell out of favor to kneel beneath the headsman's ax, while those he very seriously disliked were forced to suffer disembowelment prior to being burned at the stake.

WHAT HISTORY REVEALS is the gradual easing of the duration and severity of the physical pain associated with the death penalty. Indeed, in many countries that penalty has been abolished altogether, but not in America, where most states still have it on the books, and certainly not in Texas, where it retains a conspicuous rhythm.

When I was growing up, the executions at Sing Sing Prison occurred on Thursday nights, and New York's more rollicking newspapers covered them with a fine eye for grotesque detail. The time between sentencing and punishment was much shorter then, so the miscreants' deeds were still fresh in the public mind. I can remember middle-class mothers, gentlewomen all, discussing over a nice cup of tea how a murderer was "fried" the night before and was now burning in hell, thank God.

We live in a different era, when the preferred method of exacting retribution is lethal injection. Lethal injection! Henry VIII would think us mad. Putting people to sleep so they feel no pain when they are dispatched is, Henry would surely proclaim, a chicken-hearted way to conduct an execution.

It seems we have reached that point in the development of Western civilization when there is a widening concern about the morality of what opponents describe as state-mandated murder. As a result, jurisdictions still employing capital punishment have acted to soften the look of it.

Even so, the apprehension of death is ever present during the long period of appeals, an interlude perhaps constituting the more racking punishment. In that light, the execution itself can assume the color of escape.

Which is the more terrible sentence: exiting fearfully but painlessly or spending the rest of one's life in the society of brutal prison inmates? Just knowing that such confinement, devoid of all natural joys, is permanent certainly must strike many people as coming very close to rivaling execution as the ultimate penalty.

NEVERTHELESS, SUPPORTERS of capital punishment have rational arguments. Why would a lifer hesitate to kill a guard if he wouldn't thereby greatly worsen his outlook?

—Continued on page 228

—*Continued from page 227*
Why would a robber hesitate to shoot a witness or police officer if the fear of execution were eliminated?

In addition, the emotion factor is large. Only a very small percentage of Florida's murderers are sentenced to death, and those have been found guilty of crimes so hideous that a prison sentence, however long, doesn't quickly quiet society's rage.

But what of the possibility, somewhat lessened by DNA testing, of misidentification, of executing an innocent person?

There are people on both sides of the issue who are wholly confident of the rightness of their moral vision.

I envy their certainty.

Roberts, E. A., Jr. (2001, January 14). Is execution ultimate punishment? *The Tampa Tribune,* p. 1.

into the institution from the outside and through work or educational release programs for appropriate juveniles. In addition, attempts to facilitate reintegration through the use of halfway houses or prerelease guidance centers seem to be somewhat successful.

Unfortunately, in many instances correctional staff members begin to see isolation as an end in itself. As a result, attempts at treatment are often oriented toward helping the juvenile adapt to institutional life rather than preparing the juvenile for reintegration. Ignoring life on the outside and failing to deal with problems that will be confronted upon release simply add to the problem. Provision of relevant educational and vocational programs, employment opportunities upon release, and programs provided by interested civic groups should take precedence over concentrating on strict schedules, mass movements, and punishment. The out-of-sight, out-of-mind attitude should be eliminated through the use of programs designed to increase community contact as soon as possible. This is not meant to belittle the importance of institutional educational, vocational, and recreational programs for the juvenile delinquent. However, they will fail unless they are supported by an intensive, continual orientation to success outside the walls of the institution. This will require both correctional personnel and concerned citizens to pull their heads out of the sand in a cooperative effort to serve the best interests of both incarcerated juveniles and society.

One example of a program aimed at rehabilitating youth is the Texas Youth Commission. The commission has made incarceration a tough and demanding experience for the chronic and violent offenders it deals with, thus attempting to convince youthful offenders that a return to incarceration is undesirable. At the same time, dedicated employees are implementing and perfecting resocialization programs to make the transition from prison to the larger society more successful (Robinson 1999).

In some instances, it appears that no matter what correctional officials have attempted in traditional programs, some youths just don't get the message. In an attempt to get the attention of such youths, programs using **shock intervention** or **boot camp** principles have been introduced. These programs are usually relatively short in duration (three to six months) with an emphasis on military drill, physical training, and hard labor coupled with drug treatment and/or academic work (Inciardi et al. 1993; Klein-Saffran, Chapman, and Jeffers 1993). Drill sergeant–like supervisors scream orders at the youth, demand strict obedience to all rules, and otherwise try to shock young offenders out of crime while imposing order and discipline. While these programs have received a good deal of media attention, there is some doubt about their overall effectiveness. While some maintain they build self-esteem and teach discipline, others argue that serious delinquents are unlikely to change their behavior as the result of marching, physical exertion, and shock tactics (MacKenzie and Souryal 1991).

Changes are needed in rehabilitation and treatment programs within the walls of the institution as well. Some programs are based upon faulty assumptions. Others fail to consider the problems arising from the transition between the institution and the community upon release. Some further examples should help to illustrate the advantages and disadvantages of different types of treatment programs.

Many institutions rely upon individual counseling or psychotherapy as treatment modalities. Treatment of this type is quite costly and contact with the therapist is generally quite limited. In addition, treatment programs of this type rest on two highly questionable assumptions: that the delinquents involved suffer from emotional or psychological disorders and that psychotherapy is an effective means of relieving such disorders. Most delinquents have not been shown to suffer from such disorders. Whether or not those who do are suffering from some underlying emotional difficulty or from the trauma of being apprehended, prosecuted, adjudicated, disposed of, and placed in an institution is not clear. Finally, whether psychotherapeutic techniques are effective in relieving emotional or psychological problems when they do exist is a matter of considerable disagreement.

Another type of program involves the use of behavior modification techniques. In programs of this type, the delinquent is rewarded for appropriate behavior and punished for inappropriate behavior. Rewards may be given by the staff, by peers, or by both, and rewards given by both show the best results. Research on behavior modification programs has shown encouraging results. It is reasonable to assume that most delinquent behavior can be modified under strictly controlled conditions. While it is possible to control many conditions within the walls of the institution, such controls cannot be applied to the same degree following release. In addition, as indicated earlier, behavior that is punished within the institution may be rewarded on the outside, and vice versa. Again, transition from the institutional setting to the community is crucial. There are also ethical issues to consider that concern granting institutional staff the power to modify behavior while still protecting the rights of the juveniles.

Other treatment techniques frequently employed in juvenile detention facilities center on change within the group. These include the use of reality therapy, group-counseling sessions, psychodrama or role-playing sessions, transactional analysis, activity therapy, guided group interaction, and self-government programs. All of these techniques are aimed at getting the juveniles to talk through their problems, to take the role of other people in order to better understand why others react as they do, and to assume part of the responsibility for solving their own problems. All of these seem to be important, since lack of communication, lack of understanding other people's views, and failure to assume responsibility for their own actions characterize many delinquents. Continuing access to behavior modification programs after release could provide valuable help during and after the period of reintegration.

Assuming that we have worthwhile rehabilitation programs in juvenile institutions, serious attempts should be made to match juveniles with appropriate programs and to stop convenience assignments such as those based upon program vacancies and ease of transfer. It is important to classify offenders into treatment-relevant types based upon youths' present behavior, self-evaluations, and past history. Assignment of youthful offenders to specific programs and living areas based on these categories must be associated with specific types of treatment and training programs. Treatment programs will vary according to the juvenile's behavioral characteristics, maturity level, and psychological orientation. Whereas one behavioral type may benefit from behavior modification based on immediate reinforcement (positive-negative), another behavioral type may benefit more through increasing levels of awareness and understanding. Inappropriate behavior will result in a loss of privileges or points toward a specific goal. While it may be risky to assume that there are clearly delineated behavioral categories with accompanying treatment for each category, systematic attempts along these lines would appear to be a step in the right direction (Harris and Jones 1999).

Since the peer group plays such an important role in correctional facilities, some way must be found to use its influence in a positive manner. Some institutions have adopted a **positive peer culture** orientation in which peers are encouraged to reward one another for appropriate behavior and to help one another eliminate inappropriate behavior. While correctional staffs frequently feel that these programs are highly successful, in many cases juveniles simply learn to play the game; that is, they make appropriate responses when being observed by staff members, but revert to undesirable behavior patterns upon their return to the dorm or cottage. This frequently happens because correctional personnel get taken in by their own institutional babble. They sometimes begin to believe that the peer culture they see is positive when it is actually mostly negative. One way to avert this problem is to view rehabilitation as more than an eight-to-five job. Unfortunately, the problems that confront incarcerated juveniles do not always arise at convenient times for staff members. Assistance in solving these problems should be available when it is needed.

Another beneficial step taken in some institutions has been to move away from the dormitory or large cottage concept to rooms occupied by two or three juveniles. These juveniles are carefully screened for the particular group in which they are included in terms of seriousness of offense, type of offense, past history of offenses, and so forth. This move holds some promise of success, since "rule by the toughest" may be averted for most inmates. In this way, nonviolent offenders, such as auto thieves or burglars, run less risk of being "contaminated" by their more dangerous peers, those who commit offenses involving homicide, battery, or armed robbery, for example.

Finally, relationships between therapeutic and custodial staff members and between all staff members and inmates need to be improved. The solution is obvious. All staff members in juvenile correctional facilities should be employed on the basis of their sincere concern with preparing inmates for their eventual release and reintegration into society. Distinctions between custodial and treatment staffs should be eliminated, rehabilitation should be the goal of every staff member, and every staff member should be concerned about custody when necessary. Training and educational opportunities should be available to help staff members keep up with new techniques and research.

Providing concerned and well-trained correctional personnel will not guarantee better relationships with all incarcerated youths, but should improve the overall quality of relationships considerably. While initial costs of employment may be somewhat higher, the overall costs will not exceed those now incurred by taxpayers who often pay to have the same juvenile rehabilitated time and time again. The National Juvenile Corrections and Detention Forum, according to Hibbler, addressed this issue, recognizing that new laws dealing with juveniles have often led to a distancing from the use of appropriate intervention techniques which might help youth to grow into responsible adults. Forum participants conclude that incarcerated juveniles should be taught to understand and respect societal rules, that vocational training should be included in their correctional programs, and that bridge programs should be developed to help incarcerated youths complete the transition to society (Hibbler 1999).

We have focused for the most part on dispositional alternatives available to delinquents. There are other types of alternatives available to dependent, addicted, abused, and neglected minors as well. These include, in addition to foster home placement, placement in their own homes under court supervision (protective supervision), the use of orders of protection which detail when, where, and under what circumstances parents or guardians may interact with the juveniles in question, and commitment to drug rehabilitation or mental health programs.

Career Opportunity—Recreation Officer I or II

Job Description: Responsible for facilitating and implementing planned recreational activities for incarcerated youths. Activities include indoor and outdoor supervised sports, conducting group games, organizing field trips, and other recreational programs that meet the varied interests, abilities, and needs of the youths. Maintain facility policies and enforce behavior management strategies in the course of their recreational programs.

Employment Requirements: Four-year degree with a specialization in recreation, physical education, leisure management, or a closely related field. If without a college education, must possess four years of diversified experience in the field of group recreation or physical education and have graduated from high school, and must have been responsible for organizing, implementing, scheduling, and overseeing recreation activities. General college education may be substituted for up to two years of experience.

Salary and Benefits: Ranges from $22,000 to $36,000 yearly. Benefits provided according to the state benefit program, which usually includes health and life insurance, paid vacations and holidays, and retirement programs.

Summary

It is clear that careful consideration should be given to available alternatives to incarceration of juveniles. Probation, whether within the juvenile's own family or in a foster home, has the advantage of maintaining ties between the juvenile and the community. Proper supervision and careful selection procedures to determine whether a youth can benefit from probation, if at all, are essential. When incarceration is necessary to protect society, programs directed toward the eventual return of the juvenile to society should be stressed.

Changes are required in society's belief that juveniles who are out of sight will automatically remain out of mind. Almost all of these youths will be returning to society, and efforts must be made to ensure that time spent in institutions produces beneficial, not negative results. Thus, juveniles should not be randomly assigned to correctional treatment programs nor can the negative effects of the delinquent subculture that develops in most institutions be ignored. All programs should be routinely evaluated to determine whether they are meeting their goals and the more general goals of rehabilitating youth while protecting society.

INTERNET EXERCISES

Restorative justice is one dispositional alternative available to juvenile courts. Restorative justice comes in a variety of applications such as mediation panels, community service, circles, and so on. The type of program used by the juvenile court will depend on the type of restorative justice program offered in their geographical area. It is important, however, to understand all of the various restorative justice applications because this philosophy is quickly being adapted in jurisdictions across the United States. In order to more fully understand restorative justice, please visit the Center for Restorative Justice and Peacemaking at http://ssw.che.umn.edu/rjp/.

1. Restorative justice can be used in conjunction with probation. Explain how the two concepts can coexist and the strengths and weaknesses of the combined programs.
2. Click on Research Findings and read two or three articles on the various restorative justice practices. What are the major differences and similarities among the programs?
3. The Center for Restorative Justice and Peacemaking provides a variety of statistics regarding the effectiveness of restorative justice. What types of statistics are provided on the website regarding the effectiveness of restorative justice programs? What are the inherent problems with these types of statistics? If the website provides primarily unofficial statistics, what information is not being provided by the restorative justice statistics? If the website provides primarily official statistics, what information is not being provided by the restorative justice statistics?
4. From the homepage, click on BARJ/FA to read about the Balanced and Restorative Justice (BARJ) Project. According to this project, what is the emphasis of restorative justice? How is this emphasis different than that of the current juvenile justice system? What are the similarities of the BARJ project and the traditional juvenile justice system?
5. The restorative justice system provides dispositions to juveniles who come before the program. How are these dispositions different from or similar to the dispositions currently used within the juvenile justice system? Do these dispositions have different goals than those currently used by the juvenile justice system? If so, how are the goals different?
6. Can restorative justice be used with any of the other dispositions discussed in chapter 10 of your textbook? If so, discuss which dispositions restorative justice can be combined with and how the goals of the dispositions may change when restorative justice is combined with them. If you do not believe that restorative justice can be combined with dispositions used in the traditional juvenile justice system, explain why.

USEFUL WEBSITES

American Probation and Parole Association—*http://www.csg.org/appa*

Juvenile Intensive Probation Supervision—*http://www.supreme.state.az.us//jjsd/jips.htm*

Juvenile Corrections Resource Center—*http://www.geocities.com/Pentagon/9076*

U.S. probation history—*http://www.flmp.uscourts.gov/History/history.htm*

The Corrections Connection—*http://www.corrections.com*

Federal Bureau of Prisons—*http://www.bop.gov/bopmain.html*

CRITICAL THINKING QUESTIONS

1. What are some of the possible negative consequences of placing youths in correctional facilities? In your opinion, what circumstances would warrant such placement? Why?
2. What are the major advantages and disadvantages of probation as a disposition? How are these advantages and disadvantages modified by foster-home placement? Why has so much criticism been aimed at probation as a disposition?
3. What is restorative justice? What are the three primary concepts used in restorative justice? Who is involved in the implementation of restorative justice programs?
4. If you were superintendent of a juvenile correctional facility today, what steps would you take to ensure that juveniles would be better prepared for their return to society? Why would you take these steps?
5. What are intermediate sanctions? What is shock intervention? How likely do you think the latter is to help rehabilitate serious delinquents?

SUGGESTED READINGS

Bazemore, G., & Day, S. E. (no date). *Restoring the balance: Juvenile and community justice, 3* (1): Washington, D.C.: U.S. Department of Justice, Office of Juvenile Justice and Delinquency Prevention.

Center for Restorative Justice and Mediation. (1996). *Restorative justice: For victims, communities and offenders. What is restorative justice?* St. Paul, MN: School of Social Work, University of Minnesota.

Center for Restorative Justice and Mediation. (1996). *Restorative justice: For victims, communities, and offenders. What is the community's part in restorative justice?* St. Paul, MN: School of Social Work, University of Minnesota.

Center for Restorative Justice and Mediation. (1985). *Principles of restorative justice.* St. Paul, MN: School of Social Work, University of Minnesota.

Cothern, L. (2000, November). *Juveniles and the death penalty.* Washington, D.C.: Coordinating Council on Juvenile Justice and Delinquency Prevention. U.S. Department of Justice.

Levinson, R. B., & Chase, R. (2000). Private sector involvement in juvenile justice. *Corrections Today, 62* (2), 156–159.

Mennonite Central Committee. (1990). Mediating the victim-offender conflict. Online publication. http://www.mcc.org.

Real Justice Conferencing. (2000). An ideal practice for balanced and restorative justice. Online publication. http://www.realjustice.org.

Restorative Justice for Illinois Newsletter. (1999). What is restorative justice? LSSI/Prison and Family Ministry, Des Plaines, IL.

Wilkinson, R. A. (1997, December). Back to basics. *Corrections Today, 59,* 6–7.

Zehr, Howard. (1990). *Changing lenses.* Scottdale, PA: Herald Press.

CHAPTER

11

CHILD ABUSE AND NEGLECT

CHAPTER LEARNING OBJECTIVES

Upon completion of this chapter, students should be able to:

Discuss domestic violence
Define and discuss physical abuse of juveniles
Discuss the importance of mandated reporting
Define and discuss child neglect
Discuss the vicious cycle of child abuse
Enumerate the consequences of psychological/emotional abuse of juveniles
Define and discuss sexual abuse of juveniles
Discuss intervention strategies

KEY TERMS

domestic violence
Abused and Neglected Child Reporting Act
child neglect
types of neglect
emotional or psychological abuse
latchkey children
sexual abuse
criminal sexual abuse
criminal sexual assault
sexual exploitation
intervention
White v. Illinois
Munchausen's Syndrome by Proxy
child death review teams

Over the past three decades studies of the family have touched upon an aspect of the family which was rarely discussed before—**domestic violence** (spousal and/or child abuse). The family, which had traditionally been viewed as an institution characterized by love, compassion, tenderness, and concern, proved to be an institution in which members are at considerable risk due to increasing reported episodes of physical abuse and violence among members. In fact, the FBI (1993) reported that 913 wives, 383 husbands, 325 sons, 235 daughters, 169 fathers, 167 brothers, 121 mothers, and 42 sisters were killed by other family members in 1992. Further, some 22,000 babies were abandoned in hospitals in the United States in 1991 (Dixon 1993). Although the privacy of the home and family has made research on this topic difficult, there is now little doubt that the seeds of violence are frequently sown in this setting or that one cause of violence among juveniles is that of being reared in a violent family (Scudder, Blount, Heide, and Silverman 1993). The privacy of the home and the fear of retaliation and/or exposure make identifying and helping maltreated youths (which includes abused and neglected youths) extremely difficult. And, quite frankly, many juvenile court judges who

Child abuse knows no socioeconomic boundaries.
Courtesy of National Court Appointed Special Advocate Association (CASA)

hear cases of suspected child abuse are hesitant to break up the family by removing the child to other circumstances, a trait not difficult to understand in light of the emphasis of most juvenile court acts on preserving the integrity of the family. It may be, however, that preserving the family also preserves child abuse and perpetuates violence on the part of some abused children as they grow into adulthood.

High divorce rates, increasing numbers of stepparents, increasing numbers of children reported as abused, the development of coalitions against domestic violence, and changes in state statutes dealing with domestic violence all indicate that family life is often problematic and sometimes violent.

PHYSICAL ABUSE

On the basis of a nationwide sample, Straus and Gelles (1986) concluded that 1.4 to 1.9 million children between the ages of three and seventeen, who were living with parents, were bitten, kicked, punched, beaten, threatened with a gun or knife, or actually had a gun or knife used against them. Between 1980 and 1985, homicide was the leading cause of injury-related death among children under one year of age. Estimates for 1989 indicated that over two million children were abused or neglected (*Criminal Justice Newsletter* 1990, p. 3). Additionally, 40 percent of those murdered were killed by family members. In 1991, a survey conducted by The National Committee for Prevention of Child Abuse found that 2.7 million cases of abuse and neglect were reported by child protective service agencies (National Resource Center on Child Sexual Abuse [NRCCSA] 1992, p. 5). Authorities estimate that seven children die each day from abuse and another twelve suffer some brain damage. More children under the age of five die from mistreatment by parents than from tuberculosis, whooping cough, polio, measles, diabetes, rheumatic fever, and appendicitis combined. "In 1997, the National Center for Health Statistics listed homicide as the fourth leading cause of death for children ages 1 to 4, third for youth ages 5 to 14, and second for persons 15 to 24" (Snyder and Sickmund 1999). Of all persons murdered in 1997, 11 percent were under the age of eighteen. Of these 2,100 juvenile murder victims in 1997, 33 percent were under age six and 50 percent were ages fifteen through seventeen (Snyder and Sickmund 1999). These deaths are simply the tip of the iceberg. Children who are brain damaged or maimed are less visible but far more frequent. Nationwide, child abuse deaths rose 3 percent between 1988 and 1989, and it is estimated that over one thousand eight hundred children are abused daily (Blau and Recktenwald 1990).

A recent report by Finkelhor and Ormrod (2001, p. 1) indicates that in 1999, about one thousand eight hundred juveniles (a rate of 3 per 100,000) were victims of homicide in the United States, "a rate substantially higher than that of any other developed country." This report, like those discussed above, notes that most homicides of young children are committed by family members. Although the number of boys and girls victimized is approximately the same, offenders include a disproportionate number of women. Finkelhor and Ormrod (p. 2) also found that homicides of young children may be seriously undercounted.

As a result of the frequency of occurrence of child abuse, legislatures in all fifty states have enacted child abuse reporting laws. In Illinois, the **Abused and Neglected Child Reporting Act** (*ILCS.* ch. 325, art 5, sec. 5/1-11: 1998) not only designates the state agency for investigating reports made under the act, but also lists persons mandated to report such acts. Other states have similar acts mandating reporting for medical, social service, school, and law enforcement personnel. Civil immunity for persons reporting in good faith as well as waiver of the spousal and physician/patient privilege is typically spelled out in these acts.

Generally speaking, child abuse occurs when a child under a specific age (typically eighteen) is mistreated by a parent or immediate family member or any person responsible for the child's welfare (see chapter 5). Often referred to as child maltreatment, child abuse includes physical, sexual, and emotional abuse, and physical, emotional, and educational neglect by a caretaker. While legal definitions of physical abuse are quite specific, it is important to realize that, in practical terms, what constitutes abuse differs considerably depending upon time, place, and audience and that the line between abuse and discipline is often vague. Does spanking a four-year-old child with an open hand on the buttocks constitute child abuse? What if the child is two years of age? Suppose a belt is used instead of the hand? Suppose the child is struck on the torso instead of the buttocks? On the head? What kind of behavior are we talking about here? Most people in a given society can agree that certain behaviors are unreasonable—for example, kicking, biting,

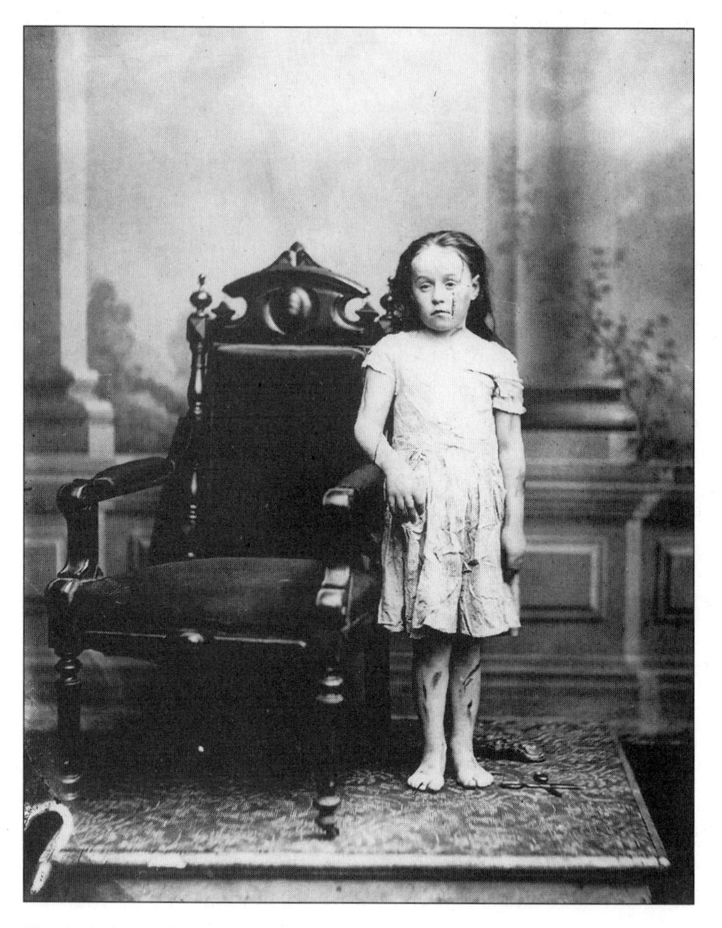

Physical abuse of children must be taken seriously in the interests of both current and future generations.
The New York Society for the Prevention of Cruelty to Children

cutting, burning, strangling, shooting, etc.—when it comes to dealing with children. Cases involving these behaviors are relatively clear-cut, and though not problem free, present the lowest degree of difficulty for intervening authorities. It is the more frequent, less clear-cut cases which are most difficult to resolve.

Physical abuse can be defined as any physical acts that cause or can cause physical injury to a child (Snyder and Sickmund 1999). Physical abuse can be described as a vicious cycle involving parents with unrealistic expectations for their children and, often, feelings of insecurity. The result is conflict between the two parties or perhaps perceived conflict in the case of infants. For example, the parent wants a young child to eat nicely in the presence of guests. As is often the case with young children, the child does not eat, plays with his food, and eventually ends up wearing a good deal of it. The parent may regard this as a direct reflection of her child-rearing abilities and may discipline the unruly child as a result. The extent of discipline depends upon the extent of anger and frustration present in the parent, the level of parenting skills involved, the age of the child, the nature of the audience, and so on. With older children who have clearly defined goals in the interactive process, the conflict may be more intentional as when an adolescent chooses to go out with friends rather than respect his parents' wishes to stay home and clean his room. In the negotiations that follow, physical abuse is one of several options available to the parent and is more likely under certain circumstances. These circumstances often exist in situations in which a teenage single parent attempts to raise children in conditions bordering on poverty. The young parent may not have learned how to care for an infant, may not know what realistic expectations are for the child, and may be frustrated by having to raise a dependent child alone, thereby reducing his or her own life chances. If the child fails to meet the expectations which the parent has established (or which have been mutually established in the case of older children), disappointment results. When this is expressed by the parent, it may lead to lower self-esteem on behalf of the child and may lead to underachievement and further failure to meet parental expectations. The parent(s), disappointed and fearing that she may be perceived as a failure, may respond with emotional or physical abuse or both and the cycle begins again (Crosson-Tower 1999; DePaul and Domenech 2000; DiLillo, Tremblay, and Peterson 2000).

It is important to point out that child abuse occurs among all social class, racial, and ethnic groups. Still, some researchers have found relationships between child abuse and such factors as age of mother and socioeconomic, educational, and employment factors (Brown, Cohen, and Johnson 1998; Paxson and Waldfogel 1999; Cadzow, Armstrong, and Frazer 1999). The disproportionate number of official cases involving those youths in lower socioeconomic circumstances may be as much a result of differing ability to pay for medical services as that of actual behavior. Available data indicate that abusers are more likely to be women, perhaps because they spend more time with youths (Livingston 1996, p. 211). At least three out of four abusers are parents of the children involved, with other family members constituting the next largest group. Babysitters, friends of the family, and others account for a small proportion of child abuse (Knudsen 1992).

CHILD NEGLECT

Child neglect generally involves those under the age of eighteen whose parent or other person responsible for the child's welfare does not provide the proper or necessary support, education as required by law, or medical or other remedial care recognized under state law as necessary, including adequate food, shelter, clothing, or who is abandoned (see chapter 5). There are three **types of neglect**—physical, emotional, and educational neglect. Physical neglect includes abandonment, expulsion from the home (thrownaway children), failure to seek medical help for the child, delay in seeking medical care, inadequate supervision, or inadequate food, clothing, and shelter. Emotional neglect consists of inadequate nurturing or affection, permitting maladaptive behavior such as illegal drug or alcohol use, and inattention to emotional and developmental needs. Educational neglect happens when a parent or caretaker permits chronic truancy or ignores educational or special needs (Snyder and Sickmund 1999). While the impact of neglect may be less obvious than that of abuse, the long-term consequences for the child may be equally harmful (Brown, Cohen, and Johnson 2000). Emotional, behavioral, and physical development may be impaired, the youth may drop out of school, medical problems may ensue, and encounters with the juvenile and/or criminal justice system(s) may result.

EMOTIONAL ABUSE OF CHILDREN

Emotional abuse occurs in families where the child's opinions don't count or where they are never sought. It occurs in families where the adult members fail to spend quality time with their children, where children's requests are met with responses such as "not right now," "maybe later," "we'll see," and "after while." This type of abuse occurs in families fighting for economic survival, in families where drugs and their pursuit are more important than children, and in dual career families where there just never seems to be enough time to do things with the children, where the videocassette recorder is a constant, built-in babysitter, and where giving the latest toy or electronic game takes the place of giving time. Estimates are that there are up to ten million **latchkey children** who leave from and/or return to an empty house (Willwerth 1993).

Some states include emotional or **psychological abuse** within the general definition of abuse (*Fla. State. Ann.* 415, 503(9)(a), (12) Supp: 1991). Wyoming's statute, for example, defines mental injury as "an injury to the psychological capacity or emotional stability of a child as evidenced by an observable or substantial impairment in the ability to function within a normal range of performance and behavior with due regard to their culture" (*Wyo. Stat.* sec. 14-3-202(a)(ii): 1987). Emotional abuse can more generally be defined as "an act (including verbal or emotional assault) or omissions that caused or could have caused conduct, cognitive, affective, or other mental disorders" (Snyder and Sickmund 1999, p. 40). Ambiguous definitions of emotional abuse often preclude protective agencies from intervening in suspected emotional abuse cases (Hamarman and Bernet 2000).

SEXUAL ABUSE OF CHILDREN

Sexual abuse of children is "involvement of the child in sexual activity to provide sexual gratification or financial benefit to the perpetrator, including contacts for sexual purposes, prostitution, pornography, or other sexually exploitative activities" (Snyder and Sickmund 1999, p. 41). Under most statutes it includes incest (generally, sexual relations with family members), criminal sexual abuse, and criminal sexual assault. Generally speaking, **criminal sexual abuse** involves the intentional fondling of the genitals, anus, or breasts, or any other part of the body, through the use of force or threat of force or of a victim (child) unable to understand the nature of the act, for the purpose of sexual gratification. **Criminal sexual assault** involves contact with or intrusion into the sex organs, anus, mouth, or other body part by the sex organ of another or some other object wielded by another with accompanying force, threat of force, or of a victim (child) unable to understand the nature of the act.

Some states include **sexual exploitation** in an expanded statutory definition of sexual abuse. Such statutes typically include references to exploitation for pornographic purposes and to prostitution (*Md. Ann. Code.* art. 27, sec. 35A9a)(2): 1992; *Fla. Stat. Ann.* 415. 503(9)9b), (17)(g) Supp: 1991).

Prevalence estimates of child sexual abuse based upon a review of available studies range from 2 percent to 62 percent, leading Bolen and Scannapieco (1999) to conclude that child sexual abuse is a problem of epidemic proportions. There were about 300,000 cases of child sexual abuse reported in 1993 to the National Center on Child Abuse and Neglect according to the 1999 national report from the Office of Juvenile Justice and Delinquency Prevention. "The incidence of sexual abuse was almost three times greater among females than males in 1993" (Snyder and Sickmund 1999, p. 41). According to the Office of Juvenile Justice and Delinquency Prevention report, one in every three sexual assault victims was under the age of twelve. In addition, "while just 4% of adult sexual assault victims were male, as were 8% of victims ages 12 to 17, 26% of sexual assault victims under age 12 were male" (Snyder and Sickmund 1999, p. 30). Victims typically range in age from about three to seventeen, although there are numerous cases of infant abuse reported as well. Indications are that sexual abuse of children by perpetrators known to them involves multiple incidents of abuse over a relatively long period of time (up to six or eight years, at least). Further, the vast majority (75 to 80 percent) of children who are sexually abused are abused by a parent or stepparent. In most cases the abuser is an adult male and the victim a female child, but all other combinations are reported as well. In many instances, the nonoffending spouse is aware of the sexual abuse but does little to prevent it. The nonoffending spouse may even take the side of the perpetrator possibly defending the perpetrator's innocence in court (see In Practice 11.1).

In Practice 11.1

In Molestations, Mothers Often Defend Perpetrators; Lack of Belief Hurts the Abused Child Deeply, Experts Say

Michele Munz

She wiped away her tears with a handkerchief as her husband was sentenced Thursday to 15 years in prison for molesting her daughter. As he was about to be led away in handcuffs, the woman got an opportunity to speak before the judge.

Her statement wasn't one of wrath, however; it was one of mercy.

"This is my daughter we're talking about here, and she told me he didn't do this!" she cried.

St. Charles County Circuit Judge Lucy Rauch immediately cut the woman off and made her sit down. Statements are allowed only on the behalf of victims at sentencing.

Prosecutors and counselors say the scenario is typical in cases where a child is molested by a stepfather or mother's boyfriend. The mother supports the perpetrator and doesn't believe her daughter, often resulting in the child's recanting the allegation.

—Continued on page 242

—*Continued from page 241*

"When the mother, who is the most important person in a child's life, says, 'You're ruining my life by making this allegation,' the child is going to roll over," said St. Charles County Assistant Prosecuting Attorney Matthew Thornhill, who prosecutes sex-abuse cases. "The child has more of a protecting instinct than their mother."

Maggie Lipman, the director of the St. Charles Regional Child Assessment Center in Wentzville, said a child who had been abused would take the blame for his or her mother's sadness over the ordeal.

"It's hard for a child to take on that burden. When you have a parent taking the side of the perpetrator, it's very overwhelming," Lipman said. "A child will recant because, as bad as it is, it's familiar . . . Whether good or bad, a child needs connection, to be part of something. To maintain that, a child will be silent."

The man who was sentenced in St. Charles County Circuit Court on Thursday had admitted in court to molesting his stepdaughter, now age 10, over a period of two years. He pleaded guilty of first-degree statutory sodomy and first-degree child molestation and agreed to serve 15 years in prison as part of a plea agreement worked out with prosecutors. Seven other sex offense charges against him were also dismissed as part of the agreement.

His stepdaughter had testified about the allegations at a preliminary hearing. And he had made a written confession saying that he had been drunk and had gone into the girl's room but wasn't sure what had happened.

He told his wife he pleaded guilty because he thought he would get more prison time if he went to trial, prosecutors said. His wife believes him.

"The mothers don't perceive it as taking sides. They perceive it as: 'I'm going to lose everything, I can't believe this is happening to me, or I don't know who to believe,' " Thornhill said. "But either one has an adverse affect on the kid. They automatically perceive they are hurting their mom."

Thornhill said that despite a written confession or the child's testimony, the mother of the child was against the accused perpetrator in only 20 percent of his cases. The remaining 80 percent have a range of support from ambivalent to thwarting prosecution, he said.

"Most often the women don't even form a judgment. They just try to stay completely out of it, be neutral," he said. "But by not favoring the child, they are throwing their support to the defendant . . . When you tell a kid: 'I don't know if I can believe you. I'm going to bond my husband or boyfriend out of jail,' that sends a wrong message to the kid."

On the other end of the spectrum, he said, he sees mothers who try to move the child out of state to keep her from testifying or who tell the child to take back the allegation.

In one case, Thornhill said, he had a mother tell him that her daughter didn't want to testify. But when he talked to the

Detection of child sexual abuse is difficult for a variety of reasons. First and foremost, sexual interaction with children is a very complex phenomenon. A great deal of ambiguity exists about what is and what is not appropriate behavior, especially in the mind of the child. In Practice 11.2 demonstrates the ambiguity surrounding what is or is not considered to be appropriate behavior with children.

girl, she was adamant about wanting to go to court and testify at a trial.

A man who has a case pending in St. Charles County involving his daughter said his ex-wife was another example. His daughter, 8, has accused her stepfather of molesting her, and her mother does not believe her. The stepfather has been indicted by a grand jury and his case is pending.

The real father and daughter will be referred to as Ben and Suzy to protect the girl's identity.

Ben said his ex-wife placed subtle pressure on Suzy, including being nicer to Suzy's brother and making shameful comments, he said.

Suzy was visiting her mother on a recent weekend, Ben said, and her mother told her, "You know, (the defendant) can go away for a long time, and I'm not happy with that."

Suzy "felt blame when her mom said what she said," he said. "She was hurt by it. She was really depressed when she came home."

Ben said he wasn't sure what his ex-wife's husband told her about the allegations. But he thought that once his ex-wife saw a video tape of Suzy telling her story to a counselor at the Child Assessment Center, his ex-wife would believe their daughter.

"I thought maybe she would come around if she saw if from (Suzy's) own mouth," he said. "It shocked me she still feels this way after seeing this."

Suzy is seeing a counselor to help her cope with the situation, Ben said. He and his wife are also trying to support her as much as possible.

"I don't tell (Suzy) that her mom is calling her a liar," he said. "I tell her that her mom is trying to find a reason not to believe her so she doesn't have to believe that her husband is a big, fat jerk."

But he's worried, he said, about the long-term effects. When Suzy gets older and understands more, he said, it will appear to her as if her mother betrayed her.

Ben said at this point, he does not think his daughter will recant the allegation. In addition to the support from him, she is also a gifted student and a dancer, so she has a lot of self-confidence, he said.

"But I feel sorry for those girls that have single moms and don't have anyone to support them," he said.

Thornhill said that was often the case. The children who are the targets of abuse are usually withdrawn, shy and self conscious, he said.

Ben said he just tries to encourage his daughter to tell the truth.

Ben said, "I asked her, 'Do you think if you didn't tell, it would stop?' And she said, 'No.' I asked her, 'Do you think it could happen to someone else?' And she said, 'Yes.' I told her she's doing the right thing, and it doesn't matter what other people think."

If a child recants an allegation in a case where a mother appears meddlesome, Thornhill said, prosecutors still pursue the case. "We fight the mother if we have to protect the child," he said.

Munz, M. (2000, December 27). In molestations, mothers often defend perpetrators; Lack of belief hurts the abused child deeply, experts say. *St. Louis Post-Dispatch,* p. 1.

In determining inappropriate behaviors we must ask at what point do touching, fondling, kissing, and stroking become sexual? Cases which might appear clear-cut to an adult are often far less so to a child, particularly when the adult involved is an authority figure (parent) who assures the child that the behavior is alright if it is kept secret. Second, once the child begins to question the appropriateness of the sexual behavior, several difficult alternatives

In Practice 11.2

Mom Who Breast-Fed Boy, 5, Seeks Custody

Scott Fornek

A mother in Champaign is fighting to regain custody of her son from state child welfare officials who accuse her of sexual molestation by breast-feeding the boy against his will at the age of 5.

The state Department of Children and Family Services calls it an obvious case of abuse because the boy wanted the activity to stop—and the mother is not lactating.

"The fundamental issue on this is that the child did not want to do it, and I think that's one of the key reasons this is a problem," said Jess McDonald, DCFS director.

The woman, a 32-year-old single mother and part-time liquor store clerk, calls it an attack on her parenting choices. She said she never forced the boy to nurse, and "I very much dispute their charges" of abuse.

The woman insists she is producing milk and said she believes in child-led weaning, which lets the child determine when to quit.

"I've been nominated to join that exclusive sorority of breast-feeding mothers who are accused of abusing their child by practicing a nurturant behavior," she said.

After a tip, DCFS removed the boy from the home in July, when he was 5. He is now 6. A hearing is set for Monday in Champaign.

The agency's investigators say the woman also slept naked with the boy on at least one recent occasion. But they say the primary reason they put the child in protective custody was because they feared the suckling would continue.

"He indicated during the investigation that he did not want it to continue," said Deborah Kennedy, the agency's central region administrator. "He told his mother that. . . . It's after she said he had never said that to her—and we believed she would continue that activity—that he was removed."

The Chicago Sun-Times interviewed the woman by telephone. Her name is being withheld to protect the child's identity.

"When my son was taken, he was generally nursing 10 minutes a night," she said. "He would remove himself from my breast, and roll over and go to sleep."

She said DCFS investigators never asked her if she was lactating nor had her examined.

Martha Allen, a DCFS spokeswoman, could not say how the agency reached its conclusion, but said "the records indicate that she was not lactating."

The woman said she slept with the child until he was taken from her, but she said she had not slept in the nude for two to three years.

"Even when it did occur, it was a very occasional thing—once or twice a year," she said, adding that she stopped after her son "looked over one morning and said 'Mom, put some clothes on.' "

The woman said her beliefs are in accord with La Leche League International, an advocacy group in Schaumburg. On its Web site, Miami lawyer Elizabeth N. Baldwin argues that the worldwide average to wean children is 4.2 years.

"There is no evidence that breast-feeding a child beyond infancy is harmful," Baldwin writes. "Quite the opposite is true."

But McDonald said: "I think those same experts would say that if the child did not want to continue suckling the mother's breast, it would be inappropriate for that to be forced.

"The question is: Whose needs are being met?"

Fornek, S. (2000, December 10). Mom who breast-fed boy, 5, seeks custody. *Chicago Sun-Times*, p. 14.

emerge. Does the child tell the nonoffending parent? Will that parent or any other adult believe the child? What will the adult to whom the report is made think of the child? What will happen to the child if the offending adult is arrested, or, perhaps worse, confronted but not arrested? How important is the love of the offending adult to the child? Is the child in some way responsible for what has happened? These and other questions make it difficult for the child to disclose sexual behavior considered inappropriate and therefore make child sexual abuse difficult to detect. Clearly many of these questions are related to the possibility of creating conflict within the interactive patterns of the family and a desire to avoid doing so.

Sometimes children do not perceive sexual acts by a member of the family or family friend as abuse, because children may not think that such a person can abuse them. At least two studies have found that the identity of the perpetrator makes a difference in whether sexual abuse is reported, finding that cases involving strangers are more likely to be reported than those involving adult's known to the child (Hanson, Resnick, and Saunders 1999; Stroud, Martens, and Barker 2000). Public exposure of such abuse may help to prevent further abuse, yet publicity, medical evaluation, court appearances, interviews by investigators, and unnecessary visibility may not be in the interests of the child. Very young children don't know that incest is bad or wrong at the same level that older children and adolescents know it (Yates and Comerci 1985, pp. 135–144). A sense of guilt may develop and is buried in the subconscious of the child, which may surface in later years, often in teens, when the child is approaching adulthood. Acting out behavior—running away, suicide attempts, becoming sexually promiscuous, being on drugs and a high level of apathy—tend to occur more among older children (*Health Facts* 1991).

INTERVENTION

Child abuse cases have typically been difficult to litigate for several reasons including:

1. establishing the competency and credibility of the child victim/witness;
2. questions concerning the admissibility of the child's out-of-court statements;
3. questions concerning the applicability of husband/wife, physician/patient, and clergyman/penitent privileges;
4. the use of character-witness evidence either in the form of evidence of prior acts of abuse or expert testimony on the "battered child" or "battering parent" syndrome; and,
5. the difficulty of the child victim confronting the alleged perpetrator in court.

Intervention begins with someone reporting the abuse or suspected abuse, moves into the investigatory stage which typically involves a home visit and interviews with the parties involved, and then to risk assessment and a decision concerning what type of action to take (see chart 11.1). When charges appear to be substantiated, the question of removing the child from the home must be considered, as must the propriety of arresting the suspect(s). Sometimes a medical team becomes involved either as the result of emergency needs on behalf of the child or to attempt to determine whether abuse has occurred. If it is determined that abuse has occurred, the police as well as the investigator for the child protection agency involved take up the case and present it to the prosecutor for further action. Along the way, educators and mental health professionals often become involved as well in an attempt to ensure the well-being of the child (Crosson-Tower 1999).

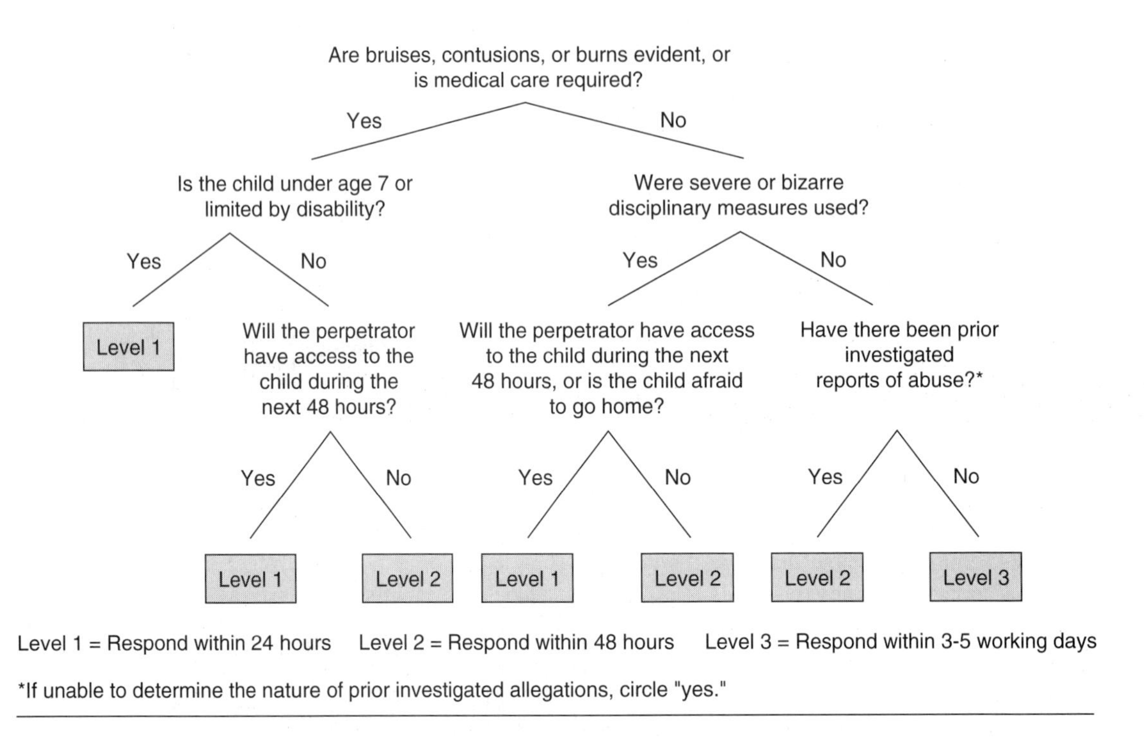

Chart 11.1 Response Priority Decision Tree: Physical Abuse Cases (Example)

Source: Children's Research Center, 2001. Adapted from: Wiebush, R., Freitag, R., & Borril, C. (2001, July). Preventing delinquency through improved child protection services. *Juvenile Justice Bulletin,* Washington, D.C.: U.S. Government Printing Office, p. 7.

In 1990, the United States Supreme Court gave tacit approval to procedures designed to protect the child victim in abuse cases. These procedures include the use of videotaped testimony, testimony by one-way closed-circuit television, and testimony by doctors and other experts in child abuse (Carelli 1990).

Some time ago, Illinois instituted a program to provide in-home assistance to families in which children have been mildly abused in order to prevent foster home placement. Mild abuse has been defined as including things such as overspanking or bruising of the child which does not result in serious injury to the child. Under the plan, when a report of abuse is filed, investigators from the Department of Children and Family Services talk with the family in order to determine whether the child is safe in the home and whether the family is likely to benefit from the plan (Perkiss 1989).

In spite of these court decisions and other attempts to improve the way in which we deal with abused youth, a recent study in Boston, which compared court data from the mid-1980s with data from 1994 found few differences: children are still in the protective system an average of five years, and court cases still require about 1.6 years to complete. Half of those children permanently removed from parental custody were still in so-called temporary foster care four years later (Bishop, Murphy, and Hicks 2000).

In the state of Minnesota, politicians have made childhood assistance a clear priority in their campaigns. Among the programs already underway is the Child Care Fund which helps subsidize the cost of day care. The Children's Health Plan provides benefits to poor children under the age of eight and may be expanded to help poor children up to age eighteen (Madigan 1989).

Operation K.ID. (Kids Identification), initiated by the Edmond Police Department and Edmond Memorial Hospital, is a program addressing the issue of missing children. The program provides tips for preventing abduction of children, provides fingerprints and dental records for parents to be used in the event a missing child who cannot be identified is found, and a profile sheet of information about the child (Russi 1984).

St. Luke's Hospital in Cedar Rapids, Iowa, opened a Child Protection Center in 1987. The center provides centralized access to services for sexually and physically abused children and coordinates efforts to identify, treat, and prevent child abuse. Specially trained personnel conduct examinations of abused children and collect evidence for prosecution based on briefings provided by police investigators (Hinzman and Blome 1991).

In 1992, the United States Supreme Court took another step in facilitating the intervention process. In ***White v. Illinois*** (112 S.Ct. 736 [1992]), the Court affirmed the use of hearsay statements in child sexual abuse cases. In this case the four-year-old child victim did not testify, but others (her mother, doctor, nurse, police officer) to whom she had talked about the assault were allowed to testify (*NRCCSA News* 1992: 3).

More and more police agencies are recognizing the importance of using specially trained investigators to conduct initial interviews with victims of abuse. Many investigations are now carried on jointly between the police and child protective agencies (Heck 1999). Investigators have been briefed concerning the needs of all the various agencies involved in such cases (see chart 11.2), eliminating the need for repeated interviews, which sometimes result in conflicting testimony resulting from fear of the interviews themselves, poor recall, new settings for the interviews, and different responses to questions which are worded differently though they are addressing the same issue (c.f. Peters 1991).

Special investigative techniques have been used by police in the investigation of a form of child abuse known as **Munchausen's Syndrome by Proxy** (MSBP). In this form of abuse, the abuser fabricates (or sometimes creates) an illness in the child victim. The child is then taken, usually by the mother, to a physician knowing that hospitalization for tests and observation is likely to be recommended since the symptoms are described as severe but no apparent cause exists. Tests, especially those that may be painful for the child, are welcomed by the apparently concerned parent. In addition, the parent may inject foreign substances (e. g., feces) into the hospitalized child and there are documented reports of attempts by the parent to suffocate the hospitalized child. Perpetrators have been apprehended with the cooperation of medical staff and the use of hidden video cameras, and prevention has been accomplished through placing the child in an open ward where medical staff are in constant attendance. The former alternative is desirable because if the perpetrator is not arrested, she may relocate and further injure or kill the child (Hanon 1991).

Other prevention initiatives include **child death review teams** (consisting of experts with medical, social services, or law enforcement backgrounds), established in most states to review suspicious deaths of children and statutory changes facilitating the prosecution of those involved in child maltreatment (Finkelhor and Ormrod 2001, 11).

It would be inappropriate to conclude our discussion of violence against youths without emphasizing the difficulties involved in dealing with them as victims. Effective advocacy for such youths is imperative for a variety of reasons. First, as we have seen they are

Far too often police investigating a child's injuries will let their emotions interfere. It should be remembered that the child abuse investigation process, if performed correctly, will ultimately determine which injuries were nonaccidental. The following are some important questions and issues to be considered when investigating a suspected case of child abuse.

- ❑ Begin by asking questions about the child's family history, substance abuse or other environmental factors in the home, and the parents' marital status, employment history, or unrealistic expectations of the child.
- ❑ How could the child's behavior or the caretaker's stress have contributed to the crisis?
- ❑ Could the child do what the caretakers told you he or she did?
- ❑ Is the child a "target" child (a child perceived by the parent(s) as having negative characteristics), or are there target children present?
- ❑ Was there any delay in treatment or was hospital "shopping" involved?
- ❑ What are the locations, configurations, and distributions of the bruises, welts, lacerations, abrasions, or burns?
- ❑ Do the injuries appear to have been caused by the hands or an instrument? Can you determine what instrument might have been used?
- ❑ Are multiple injuries (in various stages of healing) present?
- ❑ Are the injuries within the primary target zone (the back, from the neck to the back of the knees and including the shoulders and arms) and on more than one leading edge (the outside of the arm or leg, etc.) of the body?
- ❑ Can you determine the positions of the offender and the child during the attack?
- ❑ Is there any evidence of attempts to hold the child in a certain position or at a certain angle during the attack? Are there such control marks on the wrists, forearms, or biceps?
- ❑ Was a careful check made for injuries on the head, mouth, ears, and nose?

Chart 11.2 Investigator's Checklist for Use in Suspected Cases of Physical Child Abuse

Source: U.S. Department of Justice, (2000). Recognizing when a child's injury or illness is caused by abuse. Washington, D.C.: U.S. Government Printing Office, p. 18.

often ashamed, unable, or afraid to tell anyone about their plight. In many cases, even though they are being regularly and severely abused, children will not tell others because of the fear (sometimes instilled by the abuser) that their parents will be taken away from them if they do seek help. For many young children, this prospect is more frightening than their fear of continued abuse. Second, in many cases that do reach the courts, youth are unable to testify effectively due to fear and/or an inability to express themselves adequately. There are now adequate means available to deal with this problem, but these means are of little value unless they are recognized and used. Third, even when youth are able to adequately express themselves, perhaps as a result of the hesitancy to break up the family discussed earlier, judges may not remove them from the home. We are aware of cases where the evidence of abuse was overwhelming, based upon the testimony of teachers, caseworkers, and physicians, in which judges have returned the child to the home in which he or she was being abused. In several such cases, the abuse continued, and in at least one the child involved was killed by the abusing parents following the judge's decision not to remove him from the home. To avoid such occurrences, it is crucial that the rights of child abuse victims be ensured by making certain that they have proper representation and counseling and that their testimony is taken seriously. A recent study in Denver revealed that less than 3 percent of the allegations of sexual abuse made by children were demonstrated to be erroneous. The conclusion of the authors is that erroneous concerns about sexual abuse by children are rare (Oates, Jones, and Denson 2000).

If some parents are bent on destroying their own children, it is imperative that the state exercise the right of *parens patriae* to protect such children. Last but not least, the state should proceed as rigorously as possible in the prosecution of abusers, if only to prevent them from abusing their own spouses or children again. "The extent and complexity of the problem and the fact that the juvenile homicide rate in the United States continues to be substantially higher than in other modern democracies suggest that much remains to be done" (Finkelhor and Ormrod, 2001, p. 11).

SUMMARY

With respect to violence committed against youths, we must be aware that the incidence of such violence is great even by the most conservative estimates. All suspected cases should be treated as serious and given immediate attention in order to protect the youths involved, in order to prevent the youths from learning violent behavior which they may duplicate later in life, and in order to attempt to seek treatment or prosecution of the offenders.

Although family integrity is important, maintaining such integrity in cases of domestic violence or child abuse may be less important than saving life and limb (of either children or parents). Most states now have legislation in place that enables the state to protect children from abuse, but many practitioners remain hesitant to take official action that would break up the family. One need only read any newspaper with a large circulation to note the sometimes deadly consequences of failure to remove abused children from the home of the abuser. The failure to remove abused children from the homes in which they are abused is sometimes rationalized by pointing to the uncertainty of appropriate foster home or shelter-care placement. While it is true that such placement is sometimes problematic, leaving a child who has been or is being physically or sexually abused in the home of the abuser is unconscionable.

Violence against youths has received considerable attention over the past decade or so. Violence committed against youths appears to be on the increase in the United States and is considered epidemic by some. Clearly child abuse in its various forms is a relatively common occurrence, although only a small proportion of abuse cases are reported or discovered. Child abuse is particularly alarming because of the physical and psychological damage done to children, because most research indicates that at least some parents who were abused as children go on to abuse their own children, and because, in spite of numerous programs designed to help prevent or halt child abuse, child abuse is by nature difficult to detect and control.

INTERNET EXERCISES

Abused and neglected children fall under the jurisdiction of the juvenile court according to the Uniform Juvenile Court Act of 1968. These children, in most cases, are taken under the care of a state-appointed children and family services department. These departments provide prevention and diversion programs to the children and the families referred to them.

These programs are aimed at stopping child abuse and neglect and at correcting the conditions that caused the abuse and neglect in the first place. The Children's Bureau is a federal agency with the Department of Health and Human Services that works directly with children and family services departments throughout the nation. You can learn more about this office by visiting their website at http://www.acf.dhhs.gov/programs/cb/index.htm and doing the following exercise.

1. At the menu, click on About CB and read about the mission and organizational structure of the Children's Bureau. Using this information, explain why there is a need for a national clearinghouse of information on child abuse and neglect.
2. Next, click on the Laws and Policies section. At the menu, choose Strengthening Abuse and Neglect Courts Act of 2000. Why did Congress choose to strengthen abuse and neglect courts? What qualities were lacking in the traditional court system?
3. Based upon your knowledge of the key figures of the juvenile court system, which key figures do you believe are essential in the resolution of abuse and neglect cases? Why?

USEFUL WEBSITES

National Clearinghouse for Child Abuse—*http://www.calib.com/nccanch*

National Organization for Victim Assistance—*http://www.access.digex.net/~nova*

General Victims Assistance Information—*http://www.ncjrs.org/victhome.htm*

Domestic violence—*http://www.feminist.org/other/dv/dvhome.html*

CRITICAL THINKING QUESTIONS

1. It is often said that child abuse is intergenerational. Does available evidence support this claim? Why or why not? Why is child abuse so difficult to deal with? What, in your opinion, would be required for us to deal more effectively with such abuse?
2. How much progress have we made in dealing with those who abuse children? In protecting children from abuse?
3. What is emotional abuse? Does it always occur when physical abuse occurs? Does it occur independent of physical abuse? Can you provide some examples of emotional abuse without accompanying physical abuse?

SUGGESTED READINGS

Bishop, S. J., Murphy, J. M., & Hicks, R. (2000). What progress has been made in meeting the needs of seriously maltreated children? The course of 200 cases through the Boston Juvenile Court. *Child Abuse & Neglect, 24* (5), 599–610.

Crosson-Tower, C. (1999). *Understanding child abuse and neglect.* 4th ed. Boston: Allyn and Bacon.

Ernst, J. S. (2000). Mapping child maltreatment: Looking at neighborhoods in a suburban county. *Child Welfare, 79* (5), 555–572.

Finkelhor, D., & Ormrod, R. (2001, October). Homicides of youth and children. *Juvenile Justice Bulletin.* Washington, D.C.: Office of Juvenile Justice and Delinquency Prevention.

Hannon, K. A. (1991, December). Child abuse: Munchausen's Syndrome by Proxy. *FBI Law Enforcement Bulletin,* 8–11.

Hanson, R. F., Resnick, H. S., & Saunders, B. E. (1999). Factors related to the reporting of childhood rape. *Child Abuse & Neglect, 23* (6), 559–569.

McGowan, B. G., & Walsh, E. M. (2000). Policy challenges for child welfare in the new century. *Child Welfare, 79* (1), 11–27.

Meyers, J. E. B. (1996, April). Societal self-defense: New laws to protect children from sexual abuse. *Child Abuse & Neglect, 20,* 255–258.

Scudder, R. G., Blount, W. R., Heide, K. M., & Silverman, I. J. (1993). Important links between child abuse, neglect, and delinquency. *International Journal of Offender Therapy and Comparative Criminology, 37* (4), 310–323.

Smart, C. (2000). Reconsidering the recent history of child sexual abuse, 1910–1960. *Journal of Social Policy, 29,* 55–71.

Snyder, H., and Sickmund, M. (1999). Juvenile Offenders and Victims: 1999 National Report. Office of Juvenile Justice and Delinquency Prevention. National Center for Juvenile Justice. Washington, D.C.

U.S. Department of Justice. (1991, March). *Violent crime in the United States.* Washington, D.C.: U.S. Government Printing Office.

CHAPTER

12 Violent Youths and Gangs

Chapter Learning Objectives

Upon completion of this chapter, students should be able to:

Discuss the history and current status of gangs in the United States
Assess the various theories of gang development/membership
Recognize the relationships among gangs, violence, and drugs
Understand the role of firearms in youth violence
Understand the relationship between delinquency and gang membership
Discuss the characteristics of gang members in terms of age, race/ethnicity, gender, monikers, jargon, and graffiti
Discuss a variety of public and private responses to gang activities
Assess various alternatives to incarceration for violent youth

Key Terms

delinquent subculture
sociological factors
psychological factors
social disorganization
get tough approach
Violent Crime Index Offenses
Neo-Nazism
politicized gangs
street gangs
El Rukn
Bloods
Crips
Blackstone Rangers
wilding
narcotics trafficking
Black Disciples
folks
Vice Lords
Latin Kings
people
Simon City Royals
wannabees
streetcorner family
Vice Queens
monikers
graffiti
jargon
Spergel Model
alternatives to incarceration

Although there are a number of theoretical attempts to explain why juveniles engage in antisocial conduct, it is well known that many delinquent acts are committed in the company of others. As a result, much attention has been given to the role of the gang. Research has focused basically upon two areas—the factors that direct or encourage a youth to seek gang membership, and the effects of the gang on the behavior of its membership.

Albert Cohen (1955) concluded that much delinquent behavior stems from attempts by lower socioeconomic class youth to resolve status problems resulting from trying to live up to middle-class norms encountered in the educational system. Youths who determine they cannot achieve in this system often seek out others like themselves and form what Cohen calls a **delinquent subculture.** According to Cohen, it is in the company of these "mutually converted" associates that a great deal of delinquency occurs.

According to many scholars (Klein 1967; Bursik and Grasmick 1995; Wooden and Blazak 2001), there are numerous factors that bring youths into gangs. **Sociological** and physical **factors** include place of residence, the school attended, location of parks and hangouts, age, race, and nationality. **Psychological factors** include dependency needs, family rejection, impulse control, and so forth. Still other factors are related to the structure and cohesiveness of the gang and peer group pressure. In the early appraisals of gangs, causation was tied to the theories of the slum community and its inherent attributes of **social disorganization.** During the 1920s and 1930s, a group of sociologists at the University of Chicago including Frederick Thrasher, Frank Tannenbaum, Henry McKay, Clifford Shaw, and William Whyte conducted a number of studies of gangs in Chicago. According to Frederick Thrasher (1927), the gang is an important contributing factor facilitating the commission of crime and delinquency. The organization of the gang, and the protection it affords, makes it a superior instrument for execution of criminal enterprises.

Interest in the relationship between gangs and delinquency waned in the 1960s and 1970s, but increased in the late 1980s and early 1990s with reports of gang activities among minority groups both in and out of correctional facilities. Chicano gang activity on the West Coast and Chinese and Vietnamese gang activity have received media attention recently, as well as attention from the National Institute of Justice. It has been suggested that the amount of attention gangs receive is directly related to the ideology of the political party in power, to economic concerns of citizens, and to fear of victimization (Bookin and Horowitz 1983). Fear of victimization in the form of random and drive-by shootings has captured the attention of the media, the public, and Congress. The gangs of the late 1980s and 1990s appear to be better armed, more violent, and more mobile than their predecessors, and research on gangs is once again in vogue (Mays 1997; Bilchik 1999, Wooden and Blazak 2001).

Over the past two decades, violent crimes committed by juveniles have again received a great deal of attention, much of which has focused on juvenile gangs and the crimes of violence they perpetrate (see In Practice 12. 1 below).

In Practice 12.1

AMERICA UNDER THE GUN

In Pearl, Mississippi, a sixteen-year-old boy allegedly killed his mother, then went to school and shot nine students, two fatally. Three students were killed and five others were wounded in a high school in West Paducah, Kentucky; a fourteen-year-old student pleaded guilty. During a false fire alarm at a middle school in Jonesboro, Arkansas, four girls and a teacher were shot to death and ten individuals were wounded when two boys, eleven and thirteen years old, allegedly opened fire from the woods. A science teacher was shot to death in front of students at an eighth-grade dance in Edinboro, Pennsylvania; a fourteen-year-old awaits trial. Two teenagers were killed and more than twenty individuals were hurt when a fifteen-year-old boy allegedly opened fire at a high school in Springfield, Oregon. The deadliest incident of school violence recently occurred at a high school in Littleton, Colorado, when two young male students went on a killing spree and then committed suicide. (America under the gun, *New York Times* April 26, 1999).

"Although the violent juvenile crime rate has been decreasing dramatically since 1994, high-profile incidents such as school shootings serve to keep the problem of juvenile violence at the forefront of national attention" (Bilchik 1999, p. iii). As we have noted in earlier chapters, one result of this emphasis on juvenile violence is that all states now have laws making it easier to try violent juveniles in adult courts and making it possible to prescribe more severe penalties for such youth. To what extent are the concerns about growing violence by youth based in fact? What, if anything, can be done to effectively reduce violence by youth? In the following sections, we will examine these and other questions concerning the involvement of youth in violent activities.

VIOLENT YOUTHS

"Prosecutor Gets Tough with Violent Youths" states the headline in the *Miami Herald* (July 30, 2000). "Violent Youths" (*Los Angeles Times,* October 30, 2000), "To Stop School Violence, Focus on Kids, Not Guns" (*Pasco Times,* November 3, 2000), and "Children, Violence and Sex" (*Los Angeles Times,* October 8, 2000) are other headlines focusing on reports of violent youths in America. Such reports are widespread and are regular parts of newspaper/magazine headlines, television specials on youthful violence, comments on behalf of political officials promising a **get tough approach** (increasing the severity of punishment) to young offenders, and citizen action groups concerned about juvenile violence. Many of these articles and comments are based upon analyses of official statistics, which, as we have pointed out elsewhere, can be highly misleading or misinterpreted when it comes to assessing juvenile delinquency. But are these statistics currently being misinterpreted? If we consider violent juvenile offenders to be those who commit (and, in terms of official statistics, are arrested for) criminal homicide, rape, robbery, or aggravated assault/battery, what has been the trend in recent years?

In its report, *Juvenile Arrests 1999,* the Office of Juvenile Justice and Delinquency Prevention (2000), based upon FBI statistics, indicated that juveniles accounted for 16 percent of all arrests for violent crimes in 1999. "The substantial growth in juvenile violent crime arrests that began in the late 1980's peaked in 1994. In 1999, for the fifth consecutive year, the rate of juvenile arrests for **Violent Crime Index Offenses**—murder, forcible rape, robbery, and aggravated assault—declined. Specifically, between 1994 and 1999, the juvenile arrest rate for Violent Crime Index Offenses fell 36%. As a result, the juvenile violent crime arrest rate in 1999 was the lowest in a decade. The juvenile murder arrest rate fell 68% from its peak in 1993 to 1999, when it reached its lowest level since the 1960's" (Snyder 2000, p. 1).

Prior to these recent reports, the picture of juvenile violence looked considerably different. Between 1965 and 1990, the overall murder arrest rate for juveniles increased 332 percent, accompanied by a 79 percent increase in the number of juveniles who committed murder with guns. Juvenile arrests for murder also showed an increase between 1987 and 1993, when 3,800 juveniles were arrested for murder. By 1999, the number of juvenile arrests for murder had declined to 1,400 (Snyder 2000, p. 1). All in all, about one-third of 1 percent of juveniles aged ten to seventeen was arrested for violent crimes in 1999 (Snyder 2000, p. 6)

The forcible rape juvenile arrest rates increased by 44 percent between 1980 and 1991, but declined between 1991 and 1999 to the 1980 rate. Aggravated assault arrest

Violence in the schools has attracted national attention.
Steve Nagy/Wide World

rates more than doubled between 1983 and 1994, then declined to 24 percent below the 1994 peak, but remained 69 percent above its 1983 low point. And, the juvenile arrest rate for robbery increased 70 percent between 1988 and 1994, but then declined in 1999 to its lowest levels since as least 1980 (Snyder 2000, p. 8). Even with the clear decline in official violence by juveniles, fear of such violence persists and is fed by events such as the school shootings described above.

FIREARMS AND JUVENILE VIOLENCE

American researchers consistently find that the most common weapons used in juvenile homicides are firearms. Sickmund et al. (1997) found that 79 percent of victims of juvenile homicide offenders were killed with a firearm. Lizotte et al. (1994) identified two types of juvenile gun owners—low-risk and high-risk. High-risk youths who owned guns were more likely to carry guns regularly, own guns for protection, seek respect from others by carrying guns, own handguns and sawed-off long guns, and associate with peers who owned guns for protection. Further, high-risk gun owners reported higher rates of antisocial behavior and bullying than did low-risk gun owners.

"The kids who get picked on now too have a weapon: fear. Goths, punks, geeks, drama clubbers, bandies, and the math club all have a tool against the popular cliques in the *threat* of gun violence" (Wooden and Blazak 2001, p. 114). Still, the Annual Report on School Safety (1998) showed a decline in the number of high school students who brought weapons to school over the period 1993–1997 from 8 percent to 6 percent. The percentage of youth who reported bringing a gun to school within the four weeks prior to the survey remained constant at 3 percent (Department of Justice 1998).

A USA Today/CNN/Gallup Poll conducted in 1993 found that respondents believed male teenagers were the people most likely to commit crime, and in high crime areas 71 percent of the respondents indicated male teens were most likely to commit a crime (Meddis 1993). Bilchik (1999, pp. 8–9) concludes: "Twenty years of research repeatedly has shown that in any city or neighborhood a small percentage of offenders are responsible for committing a large proportion of the crime that occurs there. . . . Overall, juvenile violence is committed primarily by males and often intraracially among minority males. While some younger adolescents do commit violent offenses, the majority of juvenile offenders and victims are sixteen- and seventeen-year-olds. An examination of neighborhood factors indicates that many violent juvenile offenders live in disruptive and disorganized families and communities. However, as the surveys with the children living in high-risk neighborhoods show, the majority of youth who live in such environments are not involved in serious delinquency."

The comments above should not be interpreted to mean that juvenile females are not involved in violent offenses. While the percentage of female offenders has remained relatively constant over time, the types of offenses for which females are arrested and incarcerated have changed. The heightened involvement of females in violent offenses has been attributed to prior victimization of females. The suggestion is that females become violent perpetrators in response to their own victimization, though substance abuse, economic conditions, and dysfunctional family life have also been linked to violent offending by females (Acoca 1998; Peters and Peters 1998).

Some violent crimes have been attributed to the rebirth of **Neo-Nazism** in the form of skinhead groups such as the Nazi Low Riders, White Aryan Resistance, Hammer Skins, the World Church of the Creator, and other groups who perpetrate hate crimes (Hamm 1993; Wooden and Blazak 2001, p. 131). Whether or not these groups can be legitimately defined as gangs is a matter of perspective, but they are often excluded from the traditional definition because they are typically organized around the overt ideology of racism, rather than as the result of shared culture and experiences (Hamm 1993). Still, they may be considered as **politicized gangs** because they use violence for the purpose of promoting political change by instilling fear in innocent people. Perhaps they are best considered as a terrorist youth subculture as Hamm (1993) suggests.

The debate rages as to whether violent crimes are related to violence in the media (Centerwood 1992; Wooden and Blazak 2001, pp. 113–114). As a result of the latter, there has been considerable pressure and some success in getting television networks to tone down violence and to label programs with violent content as such.

Many of the violent crimes attributed to youths are drug-related involving gang disputes over drug territories or attempts to steal to get money to buy drugs. And, of course, a great deal of violence is associated with traditional street gangs as well as with skinheads.

Graffiti is characteristic of gang territories.
Jane Tyska/Stock Boston

Gangs

"Gangs pose a serious social problem in the United States. It is no secret that in U.S. communities, large and small, the fear wrought by teen gangs has spread rapidly. With gang victimizations reported daily, many people have become virtual prisoners in their own homes. The trepidation caused by gang driveby shootings causes schools to practice 'ducking drills' and people to huddle in their darkened homes, hide their children in bathtubs, and be afraid to let their children play outside" (Peak 1999, p. 51).

It should be noted that while we once could have referred to gangs as "juvenile" gangs, such a distinction is no longer totally appropriate since many gangs now include older adults among their membership. The "turf" gangs of yesteryear have been replaced in many instances by sophisticated criminal organizations involved in drug trafficking, extortion, murder, and other illegal activities. These **street gangs** destroy entire neighborhoods, maiming and killing their residents. They destroy family life, render school and social programs ineffective, deface property, and terrify decent citizens. Last, but not least, they have grown into national organizations that support and encourage criminal activities not only in local neighborhoods, but across the country and internationally. Some 800,000 gang members were thought to be active in over 30,000 gangs across the United States in 1997. Every city with a population of 250,000 or more reported the presence of gangs (Bilchik et al. 1999, p. iii). The number of gang members in rural counties increased by 43 percent between 1996 and 1998 (Wilson 2000). Nationally, in 1998, 46 percent of all gang members were thought to be Hispanic, 34 percent African American, 12 percent Caucasian, and 8 percent Asian or other. Over one-third of all youth gangs were thought to have memberships including members of two or more racial groups. The largest proportion of gang members involved in burglary or breaking and entering was reported in rural counties (Wilson 2000, p. xv).

A Brief History of Gangs

Thrasher's classic study of juvenile gangs was published in 1927 and included information based on over thirteen hundred gangs in the Chicago area, including fraternities, play groups, and street-corner gangs. His study was the first to emphasize the organized, purposeful behavior of youth gangs. He found that gangs emerged from the interstitial areas as a result of social and economic conditions, became integrated through conflict, gradually developed an esprit de corps or solidarity, and protected their territory against outsiders, much like today's gangs.

According to Thrasher, gangs originate naturally during the adolescent years from spontaneous play groups, which eventually find themselves in conflict with other groups. As a result of this conflict, it becomes mutually beneficial for individuals to band together in a gang to protect their rights and to satisfy needs that their environment and family cannot provide. By middle adolescence, the gang has distinctive characteristics including a name, geographical territory, mode of operation, and usually an ethnic or racial distinction. Thrasher not only analyzed gang behavior and activity, but was also concerned about the effect of the local community on the gang. He found that if the environment is permissive and lacks control, gang activity will be facilitated. If there is a high presence of adult crime, then a form of hero worshiping occurs with high status given to the adult criminal. This type of environment is conducive to, and supportive of, gang behavior. While Thrasher did his analysis more than fifty years ago, his conclusions appear to be borne out in terms of contemporary gang and neighborhood activities. Gangs clearly flourish where control of streets and children has been lost and under circumstances in which role models are basically older males involved in criminal activity.

The Chicago school spurred other studies of gangs that generally supported the earlier images of that school. Clifford Shaw and Henry McKay (1942) found that most offenses were committed in association with others in gangs and that most boys were socialized into criminal careers by other offenders in the neighborhood.

As indicated earlier, Albert Cohen (1955), in his book *Delinquent Boys,* emphasized that gang youths have a negative value system by middle-class standards. This results in a "status frustration" that is acted out in a "nonutilitarian, negativistic" fashion through the vehicle of the gang.

Lewis Yablonsky (1962) had indicated that the violent gang, at least, is not as well organized and highly structured as some theorists have supposed. In addition, Yablonsky indicated that the police, the public, and the press may help to create and to unify the gang by attributing to the gang numerous acts that the gang did not commit. Strong support for Yablonsky's conclusions can be found in David Dawley's (1973) book, *A Nation of Lords,* which is an autobiography of sorts about the Vice Lords in Chicago. Over the past decade, however, violent gangs have unquestionably become more organized with gangs like **El Rukn,** the **Bloods,** and the **Crips** illustrating that such organization extends even into prisons. Other gangs are also demonstrating the ability to organize mobile units and maintain branch units in scattered cities, largely in response to drug markets.

Albert Cohen, Walter Miller, and others (see chapter 4) further developed theories of gang delinquency in the 1950s and 1960s. During this period, delinquency came to be regarded as a product of social forces rather than individual deviance. Gang members were viewed as basically normal youths who, under difficult circumstances, adopted a gang subculture to deal with their disadvantaged socioeconomic positions. Gangs attracted a good deal of attention as a result of their apparent opposition to conventional norms and sometimes were romanticized, as in the popular *West Side Story*.

By the late 1960s and early 1970s, the United States was in a period of social upheaval marked by civil disturbances, racial protests, antiwar demonstrations, and student protests. Gangs were largely forgotten by the media and sociologists. Definitions of crime and delinquency came into question. Political liberals focused on abuse of power and crimes by the wealthy. Labeling theory came into vogue, postulating that members of the lower social class are more likely to be labeled *deviant* than those in the middle and upper classes as a result of the balance of power resting with the latter. Gangs were viewed as a response to injustice and oppression. Conservatives, however, viewed crime and delinquency as products of immorality, poor socialization, or lack of sufficient deterrence. Control theory was popular with this political faction because it postulated that delinquency was largely an individual matter, developing early in life, and occurring due to a lack of internal as well as external controls. Failure of institutions such as the family, police, and corrections became the focal point of those representing the conservative viewpoint, obviating the need to deal with the social structure and conditions that were the focus of the liberal camp. The latter group continued to view gang members as youths in need of help rather than punishment. While these groups argued over the source of responsibility for crime and delinquency in general, developments were occurring that would soon lead society to take another look at the gang phenomenon.

In the 1960s, a Chicago gang known as the **Blackstone Rangers** (later called the Black P Stone Nation, and later known as El Rukn) emerged as a group characterized by a high degree of organization and considerable influence. The Blackstone Rangers sought and were granted federal funds as well as funds from private enterprises to support their activities. This funding gave the gang an appearance of political and social respectability. Street gangs in America were becoming politicized. As Miller (1974 p. 210) stated, the notion of "transforming gangs by diverting their energies from traditional forms of gang activities—particularly illegal forms—and channeling them into 'constructive' activities is probably as old, in the United States, as gangs themselves. Thus, in the 1960s when a series of social movements aimed at elevating the lot of the poor through ideologically oriented, citizen-executed political activism became widely current, it was perhaps inevitable that the idea be applied to gangs." Jacobs (1977, p. 145) offered three explanations as to why Chicago street gangs, as well as those in many other urban areas, became politicized in the 1960s:

1. Street gangs adopted a radical ideology from the militant civil rights movement;
2. Street gangs became committed to social change for their community as a whole;
3. Street gangs became politically sophisticated, realizing that the political system could be used to further their own needs—money, power, and organized growth.

Jacobs maintains that the third explanation is applicable to the Blackstone Rangers and many other large gangs in metropolitan areas. The leadership learned how to use the system to provide capital for their illegal activities. Gangs showed increased sophistication in organizing their activities along the lines of organized crime. Individual felonies were replaced by major criminal activity involving drugs, weapons, extortion, prostitution, and gambling. Fistfights were replaced by violent acts involving the use of weapons. In Practice 12.2 indicates many of the problems discussed by Jacobs and others concerning the politicized gangs that continued to confront authorities in the 1990s and into the new century.

In the 1980s, society became increasingly concerned with violence and prescriptions for crime control, and this concern carried over into the 1990s and the new century (Bilchik et al. 1999). Attention has once again focused on crime and delinquency resulting from failures of social institutions, inadequate deterrence, and insufficient incapacitation. Deterrence research has become popular, focusing on police, probation, and corrections activities rather than on gang dynamics. Current emphasis is on preventing youths

In Practice 12.2

HOOVER FOLLOWS CAPONE LEGACY

Steve Neal

Al Capone and Larry Hoover have a great deal in common.

Chicago's most notorious kingpins of organized crime both knew how to take advantage of prohibition. Capone made his fortune from bootlegging, while Hoover reaped millions from his drug empire. Both were cold-blooded in eliminating their gangland rivals. Just as Capone achieved political influence, Hoover also has sought to help elect allies to the City Council. Hoover is doing time for murder, but has maintained influence from prison. Capone did time for tax evasion, and his influence gradually diminished. Like Capone, Hoover is a national embarrassment for the city.

In a compelling new book, *Drug Crazy* (Random House, $23.95), Mike Gray draws many parallels between the bloody streets left by Capone and Hoover. Gray, who was the producer of an award-winning documentary about the police slaying of former Black Panther leader Fred Hampton, is appalled that Hoover could build an empire that might even be more powerful than Capone's.

"It's just like the old mob days," Chicago police Detective Frank Goff told Gray. "We're talking about a street gang that can intimidate people, put up your fliers, tear down all the other people's fliers, get people to vote and register and come to the polls. This group can control a lot of votes. They finally realized that."

Studs Terkel, who has spent much of his life recording the city's history, told Gray that the last time the streets were this bloody from gangland hits was in the Capone era.

"If you look at a gangland map of Chicago from the 1920s, you find a chilling similarity with the map of today," Gray writes. "On the Near North Side where the O'Banion gang once slugged it out with the Terrible Gennas, you now find the Vice Lords facing off with the Latin Kings. . . . And there can be no doubt who is the successor to Big Al. The vast territory that sweeps from the South Side and arcs around the Loop to the west is owned and operated by Larry Hoover and the Gangster Disciples."

from joining gangs through community education and involvement, and bringing to a halt the violent activities of gangs through stricter laws, better prosecution, more severe sanctions, and negotiated peace agreements between feuding gangs.

"The last quarter of the 20th century was marked by significant growth in youth gang problems across the United States. In the 1970's, less than half of the States reported youth gang problems, but by the late 1990's, every State and the District of Columbia reported youth gang activity" (Miller 2001, p. iii). The states with the largest number of gang-problem cities in 1998 were California, Illinois, Texas, Florida, and Ohio (Wilson 2000, p. ix). While gang problems continue to be a big-city problem as we enter the twenty-first century, they are by no means confined to such cities. In fact, the number of

Capone lost his grip on Chicago when Prohibition ended. The Volstead Act, which prohibited the manufacture or sale of liquor in the United States, went into effect in January, 1920. But as Capone reaped an estimated $50 million annually from bootlegging, some high-minded people began reconsidering what they had done. Pauline Morton Sabin, a socially prominent Republican, formed the Women's Organization for National Prohibition Reform at the Drake Hotel in the spring of 1929. "Many of our members are young mothers—too young to remember the old saloon," Sabin said then. "But they are working for repeal because they don't want their babies to grow up in the hip-flask speakeasy atmosphere that has polluted their youth."

The public eventually soured on the Volstead Act. Polling indicated that 73 percent favored repeal in 1932 when Franklin D. Roosevelt won the presidency on a platform that promised this reform. Gray notes that Sabin's conference at the Drake marked a turning point in the effort to help break Capone's influence.

Gray shows how the federal government often has fumbled in its effort to fight drugs. Hamilton Wright, who helped shape the Harrison Narcotic Act of 1914, unfairly targeted doctors who prescribed pain relievers. Harry Anslinger, who led the Treasury Department's Federal Bureau of Narcotics in the middle third of the century, was more interested in protecting his turf than in listening to medical and health professionals. Like J. Edgar Hoover of the FBI, Anslinger became part of the problem rather than the solution.

Gray believes that existing drug policies have produced the opposite of what was intended. His argument is that drug prohibition has helped the bad guys get richer, while failing to deal with a serious medical problem. He cites California's recent vote to allow the medical use of marijuana as a potential breakthrough. Gray is hopeful that other states will follow California's lead in challenging failed policies.

His criticism is thoughtful and constructive.

"Prior to the Harrison Narcotics Act, if people wanted drugs they at least had to go to a drugstore," Gray notes. "Now they can get anything they want from the neighbor's kid. It would seem that if Americans are to have any say at all in what their teenagers are exposed to, they will have to take the drug market out of the hands of the Tijuana Cartel and the Gangster Disciples, and put it back in the hands of the doctors and pharmacists where it was before 1914."

Neal, S. (1998, September 13). Hoover follows Capone legacy. *Chicago Sun-Times,* p. 40.

cities with populations between 1,000 and 5,000 reporting gang activities increased twenty-seven times, and the number of cities with populations between 5,000 and 10,000 reporting gang activities increased more than thirty-two times (Miller 2001, p. x).

The Nature of Street Gangs

Generally speaking, street gangs may be identified by the following characteristics:

1. They are organized groups with recognized leaders who command the less powerful
2. They are unified at peace and at war
3. They demonstrate unity in obvious, recognizable ways (i.e., wearing of colors, certain types of graffiti, use of gang signs)
4. They claim a geographic area and economic and/or criminal enterprise (i.e., turf, drugs)
5. They engage in activities that are delinquent and/or criminal, or are somehow threatening to the larger society.
   (Illinois Department of Corrections Training Manual 1985)

Short and Strodtbeck (1965) developed a somewhat similar set of criteria for gang members:

1. Recurrent congregation outside the home
2. Self-defined inclusion/exclusion criteria
3. A territorial basis consisting of customary hanging and ranging areas, including self-defined use and occupancy rights
4. A versatile activity repertoire
5. Organizational differentiation, e.g., by authority, roles, prestige, friendship, etc.

Delinquent and Criminal Gang Activities

Antisocial and criminal conduct by members of juvenile gangs is not a new phenomenon. Early immigrant groups arriving in this country frequently found themselves located in the worst slums of urban areas, and gangs soon emerged. Among the earliest juvenile gangs were those of Irish background, followed later by Italian and Jewish gangs, and eventually gangs of virtually all ethnic and racial backgrounds. Typically, members of these gangs left gang activities behind as they grew older, married, found employment, and raised families. Some, however, gravitated to adult gangs and into organized criminal activities. The path from juvenile gang membership to adult crime seems to have broadened in recent years, so while it is true that some street gangs are still little more than collections of neighborhood youths with penchants for macho posturing, many are emerging as drug-terrorism gangs that terrify residents of inner-city neighborhoods.

Street gangs violate civilized rules of behavior, engaging in murder, rape, robbery, intimidation, extortion, burglary, prostitution, drug trafficking, and, in the late 1980s, in a phenomenon known as **"wilding,"** in which gang members attack individuals at random, committing any of the above mentioned offenses. In the 1990s, drive-by shootings became another tool of gang members who were seeking retribution but unconcerned about the lives of innocent bystanders often shot in the process. The activities of gangs have become increasingly serious, more sophisticated, and more violent, and are more likely to involve the use of weapons. Gangs have become problematic in California: the legislature there has passed a law making it a felony to belong to a gang known to engage in criminal activities and other jurisdictions are in the process of establishing similar legislation. While the constitutionality of these laws has yet to be established, their mere existence indicates how serious the gang problem is perceived to be. *Newsweek* magazine (1988) describes the drug gangs found in urban ghettos and barrios as consisting of young men

> whose poverty and deprivation have immunized them to both hope and fear. The result is a casual acceptance of—and sometimes enthusiasm for—torture and murder, 'drive-by shootings' and public mayhem. 'If they don't kill you, they'll kill your mother.' The days when rival gangs fought each other over 'turf' and 'colors' are fading fast. Today, gang conflicts are more of the form of urban-guerrilla warfare over drug trafficking. Gang turf is now drug sales territory. Informers, welchers, and competitors are ruthlessly punished or assassinated. Street warfare and the bloody rampage of gang violence is the norm in many inner cities. (20–29)

As an illustration of these points, it is estimated that 3,340 member-based gang homicides were committed in 1997 (Bilchik et al. 1999, p. 15).

Gang members commit a disproportionate share of crime for their numbers. Statistical data indicate that although gang membership in a given jurisdiction may not be high, and gang members constitute a small percentage of all criminals, they typically commit more offenses than their nongang-member criminal counterparts. In 1997, youth gangs were involved in 18 percent of homicides nationwide. Gang violence is increasing in intensity and spreading throughout the country. In large metropolitan areas such as Chicago, New York, Miami, and Los Angeles, gang-related homicides number in the hundreds annually (Bilchik 1999, pp. 15, 20). Many of these homicides result from gang wars and retaliations, and often the victims are innocent bystanders or those unable to defend themselves. The macho image of gang members confronting each other in open warfare is largely a creation of the media. More often, gang killings occur on the streets, in the dark, as a result of gang members, in a speeding vehicle, firing shots at their intended victim(s).

Major gangs have made **narcotics trafficking** (sale and distribution of drugs) an important source of income, and activities in this area have become even more lucrative with the advent of a street market for cocaine and crack. Some of the increase in gang violence is a result of competition over turf ownership related to the sales of these products. Gangs involved in profit-oriented schemes frequently resort to violence to protect their illicit businesses. With this shift to more business-oriented activities, some gangs have gone underground—members no longer openly display colors or graffiti, sometimes leading to the mistaken assumption that gang activity in a particular area has ceased. On other occasions, even when officials know gangs are behind a good deal of the illegal activity occurring in their jurisdictions, for political reasons they deny the importance of gangs. Political officials, including some police chiefs, would prefer not to make themselves look bad by admitting that gang activity in their areas is uncontrollable. It is estimated that 42 percent of youth gangs are involved in the street sale of drugs for the purpose of making a profit for the gang, and 33 percent of youth gangs in the United States are estimated to be involved in the distribution of drugs. Crack cocaine and marijuana were thought by law enforcement agencies to lead the list of drugs sold (Bilchik 1999, pp. 22, 25, 28).

An illustration of the drug-gang problem can be seen in south central Los Angeles where the Bloods and Crips reign. These gangs consist of confederations of neighborhood

Automatic weapons, such as these confiscated by the police, are used routinely in gang wars.
Gregory Smith/AP/Wide World

gangs, each with a relatively small number of members. The gangs have traditionally been involved in robbery, home invasion, burglary, and homicide, but became involved in drug trafficking as a major enterprise with the production of crack cocaine. The Bloods (whose color is red) and the Crips (whose color is blue) date back to the late 1960s and early 1970s, and consist of "rollers" or "gang bangers" who are in their twenties and thirties, gang veterans who have made it big in the drug trade. These veterans supervise and control the activities of younger members who are involved in drug trafficking and operating and supplying crack houses, activities that bring in millions of dollars a week. The drug trafficking of the Bloods and Crips spread into other cities including Seattle, Portland, Denver, Kansas City, Des Moines, and even Honolulu, and Anchorage (Hieb 1992). That these gangs are alive and well in New York is demonstrated by what has been called a "bloody gang war" now raging in Brooklyn. Police sources there say there have been some sixty-four gang-related shootings and thirty-four gang-motivated gun battles between the Bloods and the Crips since January 2000 (McPhee 2000).

Similar gangs exist in other major cities. In Chicago, for example, major street gangs include the **Black Disciples**/Black Gangster Disciple Nation/Brothers of the Struggle (B.O.S.) who are collectively known as "**folks.**" They are in competition with the **Vice Lords,** also known as the Conservative Vice Lord Nation, who have aligned themselves with other groups such as the **Latin Kings** (Main and Spielman 2000; Main 2001). These gangs are collectively referred to as **"people"** (Babicky 1993; Dart 1992). (See In Practice 12.4.) Splinter gangs of "people" and "folks" are now found in Minneapolis, Des Moines, Green Bay, and the Quad cities area in Illinois. Activities include extortion, drug trafficking, and violent crime in the form of homicide, robbery, drive-by shooting, and battery.

While street gangs are predominantly black and Hispanic, the **Simon City Royals** ("folks") are a white gang originating in Chicago in the early 1960s. Originally formed to stop the "invasion" of Hispanic gangs into their area of the city, the Royals became actively involved in burglaries and home invasions in the 1980s. As leaders of the gang were imprisoned, they formed alliances with the Black Gangster Disciples for protection and the alliances continue today (Babicky 1993).

Hispanic gangs exist in every major urban area and many suburban areas as well. Many of these become family affairs with the youngest members or "pee wees" being directed by the older, hard core "veteranos" (Peak 1999, p. 54) Asian gangs exist in Chinese, Filipino, Vietnamese, and Cambodian communities and are involved in a variety of illegal activities such as extortion, protection of illegal enterprises, and summary execution of members of rival gangs (Peak 1999, pp. 53–54).

Gangs engage in a wide variety of activities, including the following:

1. Vandalism—graffiti, wanton destruction
2. Harassment and intimidation—to recruit members, to exact revenge on those who report their activities, etc.
3. Armed robbery and burglary—targets include the elderly and, more recently, suburban communities
4. Extortion of:
   a. Students in schools (protection money)
   b. Businesses—protection money to avoid burglaries, fires, vandalism, general destruction
   c. Narcotics dealers—protection money to operate in a specific geographic area and a percentage of the "take"
   d. Neighborhood residents—who pay for the ability to come and go without being harassed and for the "privilege" of not having their property destroyed

Gang crime continues to grow in smaller suburban and even rural communities, which are frequently perceived as easy marks for theft, burglary, robbery, and shoplifting, among other crimes. In other cases, gangs migrate to these areas to avoid the intense competition of drug trafficking in the cities. (See In Practice 12.3.)

Almost every community has experienced **"wannabes"** or youth who may wear gang colors and post graffiti in an attempt to emulate big-city gang members. Yet in many communities, gangs have been largely ignored. Part of the reason for the continued expansion of gang activities is the view that such activity is not our problem. Since many street gangs are ethnically oriented, it is easy to perceive the problem as affecting only certain groups or neighborhoods. Since members of traditional gangs are predominantly from the lower social class, gangs are perceived as problematic basically in lower social class areas. However, if gang activity is not dealt with quickly, the consequences soon spread to the larger community, including middle-class neighborhoods, and the problem may become unmanageable (Pattillo 1998). Osgood and Chambers (2000) analyzed juvenile arrest rates for 264 nonmetropolitan counties in four states. They conclude that juvenile violence in nonmetropolitan

In Practice 12.3

DELINQUENCY IN THE SUBURBS

The ominous signs are everywhere: kids bringing guns onto junior high and high school campuses and shooting each other; teenagers forming sex posses and racking up "body counts" of the number of girls they have "scored with" or "sacked;" mall rats rampaging through suburban shopping arcades, "streaming" as they call it, through the aisles of department stores and grabbing stacks of clothing before making a quick getaway; tagger crews "mapping the heavens," spray painting their three letter monikers on overhead freeway signs. . . . Racist skinheads plot revenge on unsuspecting fellow students at suburban high schools for no other reason than that they dislike them because of their skin color, nationality, or presumed sexual orientation. White youthful, stoner gang members wander aimlessly with their suburban "homies," or homeboys, looking for the next high, surviving on dope and booze. Juvenile Satanists, participating in a fad, find themselves caught up in a cult. (Wooden and Blasjak 2001, p. 1)

areas is associated with residential instability, family disruption, ethnic heterogeneity, and population size. Evans, Fitzgerald, and Weigel (1999) found no significant differences in gang membership or pressure to join gangs between rural and urban youth. Urban subjects, however, were more likely to report having friends in gangs and being threatened by gangs than their rural counterparts.

Gang Membership

Among the generally accepted reasons for gang development and membership are the following:

1. The gang provides peer support during the transition from adolescence to adulthood
2. The gang results from a lower-class cultural reaction to the values or goals of the dominant society
3. The gang provides the opportunity to attain goals adopted by the larger society, but through alternative (illicit) means
4. The gang provides self-esteem, economic opportunities, a sense of belonging, affection, and so on, which are missing from the lives of many youth

Further, individual motivations for joining gangs may be categorized as follows:

1. *Identity/recognition.* Allows the member to achieve a status he or she believes is impossible outside the gang. Many are failures in legitimate endeavors such as academics, athletics, and so on.
2. *Protection/survival.* Many feel it is impossible to survive living in a gang-dominated area without becoming a member.

3. *Intimidation.* Youths are told and shown (through beatings, etc.) by gang members that membership is essential.
4. *Fellowship and brotherhood.* The gang offers psychological support to its members and provides the companionship that may be lacking in the home environment.

As Jacobs (1977, p. 150) explained, "Time and again gang members explained that, whether on the street or in prison, the gang allows you to feel like a man; it is a family with which you can identify. Many times young members have soberly stated that the organization is something, the only thing, they would die for." Bloch and Neiderhoffer (1958) believed that gangs were cohesive and organized and therefore satisfied deep-seated needs of adolescents. Whyte (1943) portrayed the gang as a **"streetcorner family."** "Gangs are residual social subsystems often characterized by competition for status and, more recently, income opportunity through drug sales" (Curry and Spergel 1988).

Characteristics

Generally, gang membership can be divided into three categories; leaders, hard-core members, and marginal members. The leaders within gangs usually acquire their positions of power through one of two methods—either by being the baddest/meanest member or by possessing charisma and leadership abilities. In addition, the leaders tend to be older members who have built up seniority. Hard-core members are those whose lives center around the totality of gang activity. They are generally the most violent, streetwise, and knowledgeable in legal matters. Marginal or fringe members (sometimes referred to as "juniors" or "peewees") drift in and out of gang activity. They are attached to the gang, but have not developed a real commitment to the gang lifestyle. They associate with gang members for status and recognition and tend to gravitate toward hard-core membership if no intervention from outside sources occurs (Babicky 1993; Mays and Winfree 2000, p. 302).

Age

Gang members generally range from eight to fifty-five years of age. For many younger youth, gang members serve as role models whose behavior is to be emulated as soon as possible in order to become full-fledged "gang-bangers." Consequently, these children are often exploited by members of gangs, manipulated into committing offenses such as theft and burglary in order to benefit the gang as part of their initiation or rite of passage. As gang crimes become more profitable, as in the case of drug franchises, the membership tends to be older. As members become older, they move away from street crime and move up in stature within the gang hierarchy. The younger members maintain the turf-oriented activities and the adults move into more organized and sophisticated activities.

Gender

Street gangs are predominantly male. Although girls have been a part of gangs since the earliest accounts from New York in the early 1800s, their role has traditionally been viewed as peripheral. Thrasher (1927) in his classic study of gangs discussed two female gangs in Chicago. Females have been described in the literature primarily as sex partners for male gang members or as members of auxiliaries to male gangs (Campbell 1995). Yet as we have indicated throughout this book, involvement in crime, including violent crime, among juvenile females has clearly increased over the past decade. In fact, a study by Bjerregaard and Smith (1993) found that rates of participation in gangs are similar for males and females.

With respect to female gang membership, Campbell (1997, pp. 129, 146) has noted:

> Although there is evidence that young women have participated in urban street gangs since the mid-nineteenth century, it is only recently that they have received attention as a topic of study in their own right. . . . Previous work on female gang members has placed considerable emphasis upon their sexuality either as [an] area for reform through social work, as a symptom of their rejection of middle-class values, or as the single most important impression management problem they face. . . . These young women are stigmatized by ethnicity and poverty as well as gender. . . . Without the opportunity to fulfill themselves in mainstream jobs beyond the ghetto, their sense of self must be won from others in the immediate environment. . . . Their association with the gang is a public proclamation of their rejection of the lifestyle which the community expects from them.

Clearly, a good deal more research is required to understand female participation in gang behavior.

The research that does exist focuses largely on Hispanic girls in gangs, with less attention given to black, white, and Asian female gang members. An exception to this trend is Fishman's ethnographic study (1995) of the black **Vice Queens** in Chicago. Fishman notes that female gangs are moving closer to being independent, violence-oriented groups. The Vice Queens were routinely involved in strong arming and auto theft, and they frequently engaged in aggressive and violent behavior, activities viewed as traditionally performed almost exclusively by males. Esbensen, Deschenes, and Winfree (1999) also found that gang girls are involved in a full range of illegal activities, although perhaps not as frequently as males. Harper and Robinson (1999) found that involvement of black juvenile females in sexual activity, substance abuse, and violence was clearly related to membership in gangs. Thus the relationship between gang membership and a variety of delinquent and criminal behaviors appears to be similar for girls and boys.

Campbell (1995) has argued that in order to account for female gang membership, we must consider the community and class context within which the girls involved live, the problems that face poverty-class girls, and the problems for which they seek answers in gangs. Among these problems are:

1. a future of meaningless domestic labor with little possibility of escape;
2. subordination to the man of the house;
3. sole responsibility for children;
4. the powerlessness of underclass membership.

Further, many of these girls "will be arrested and the vast majority will be dependent on welfare. The attraction of the gang is no mystery in the context of the isolation and poverty that awaits them" (Campbell 1995, pp. 75–76). "Without the opportunity to fulfill themselves in mainstream jobs beyond the ghetto, their sense of self must be won from others in the immediate environment. . . . Their association with the gang is a public proclamation of their rejection of the lifestyle which the community expects from them" (Campbell 1997, p. 146). Curry (1998) agrees finding that gang membership in these circumstances can be a form of liberation. Finally, Esbensen, Deschenes, and Winfree (1999) found that female gang members have lower levels of self-esteem than male gang members, lending further support to Campbell's conclusions that the gang provides a source of support and feelings of self-worth.

Of course, not all female gang members are found in urban areas as we have seen in chapter 3. Gangs have begun to appear in both suburban and rural areas, previously thought to be immune from gang activity (Bjerregaard and Smith 1993).

Monikers

Many gang members have **monikers** or nicknames that are different from their given names. Generally these monikers reflect physical or personality characteristics or connote something bold or daring. Often gang members do not know the true identities of other members, making detection and apprehension difficult for law enforcement officials.

Graffiti

Street-gang graffiti is unique in its significance and symbolism. **Graffiti** serves several functions: it is used to delineate gang turf as well as turf in dispute, it proclaims who the top-ranking gang members are, it issues challenges, and it proclaims the gang's philosophy. Placing graffiti in the area of a rival gang is considered an insult and a challenge to the rival gang, which inevitably responds. The response may be anything from crossing out the rival graffiti to drive-by shootings or other forms of violence. The correct interpretation of graffiti by the police can offer valuable information as to gang activities. Symbols which represent the various gangs are typically included in graffiti and are known as "identifiers." The identifiers in In Practice 12.4 are those of the People Nation (Black P-Stone, Latin Kings, Vicelords, Spanish Kings, El Rukns, and others) and the Folk Nation (Black Gangster Disciples, Black Disciples, Gangster Disciples, and Simon City Royals, among others).

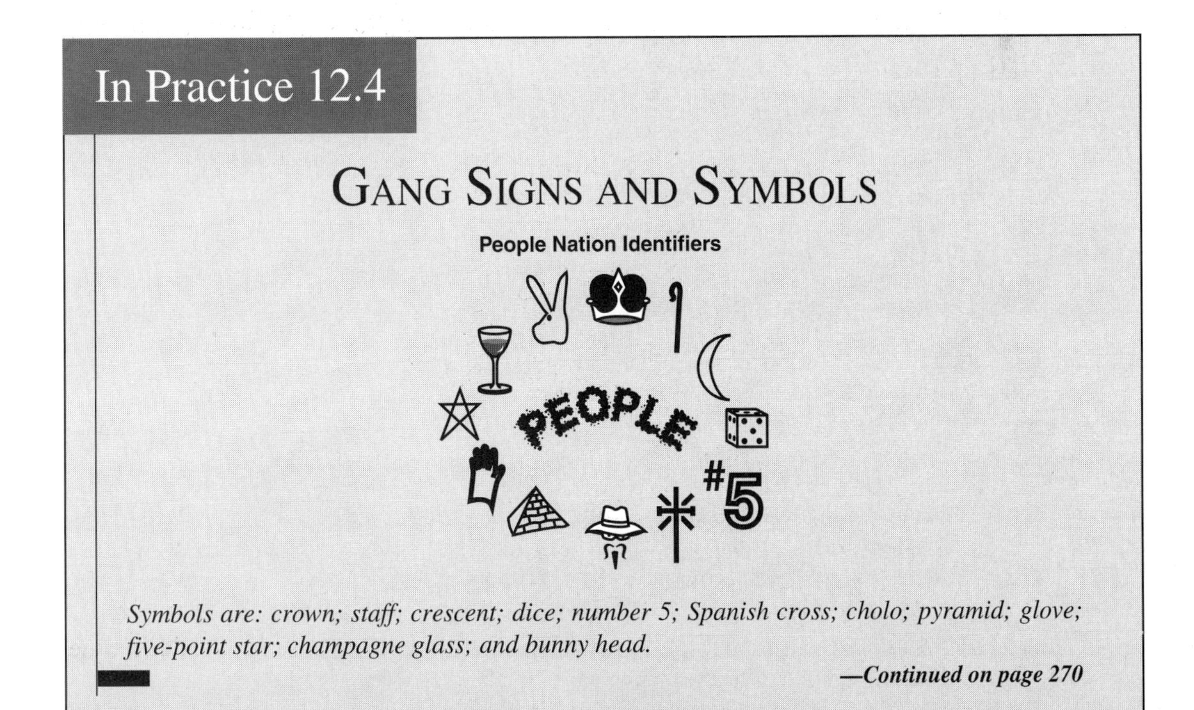

Symbols are: crown; staff; crescent; dice; number 5; Spanish cross; cholo; pyramid; glove; five-point star; champagne glass; and bunny head.

—Continued on page 270

—Continued from page 269

Members of **People Nation** sets are known to use these symbols:

Five-point star and Champagne Glass

Five-point crown example (from tattoo)

The number 5

Pyramid

Cane and Top Hat

Crescent Moons

In addition to these symbols, the People Nation groups also use **left identifiers.** For example they:

- Form their hand signs with the left hand.
- Wear their hats cocked or tilted to the left.
- Roll up the left pant leg.
- May untie the **left** shoe.
- They rest their hand in the left pocket.
- Wear jewelry to the left.

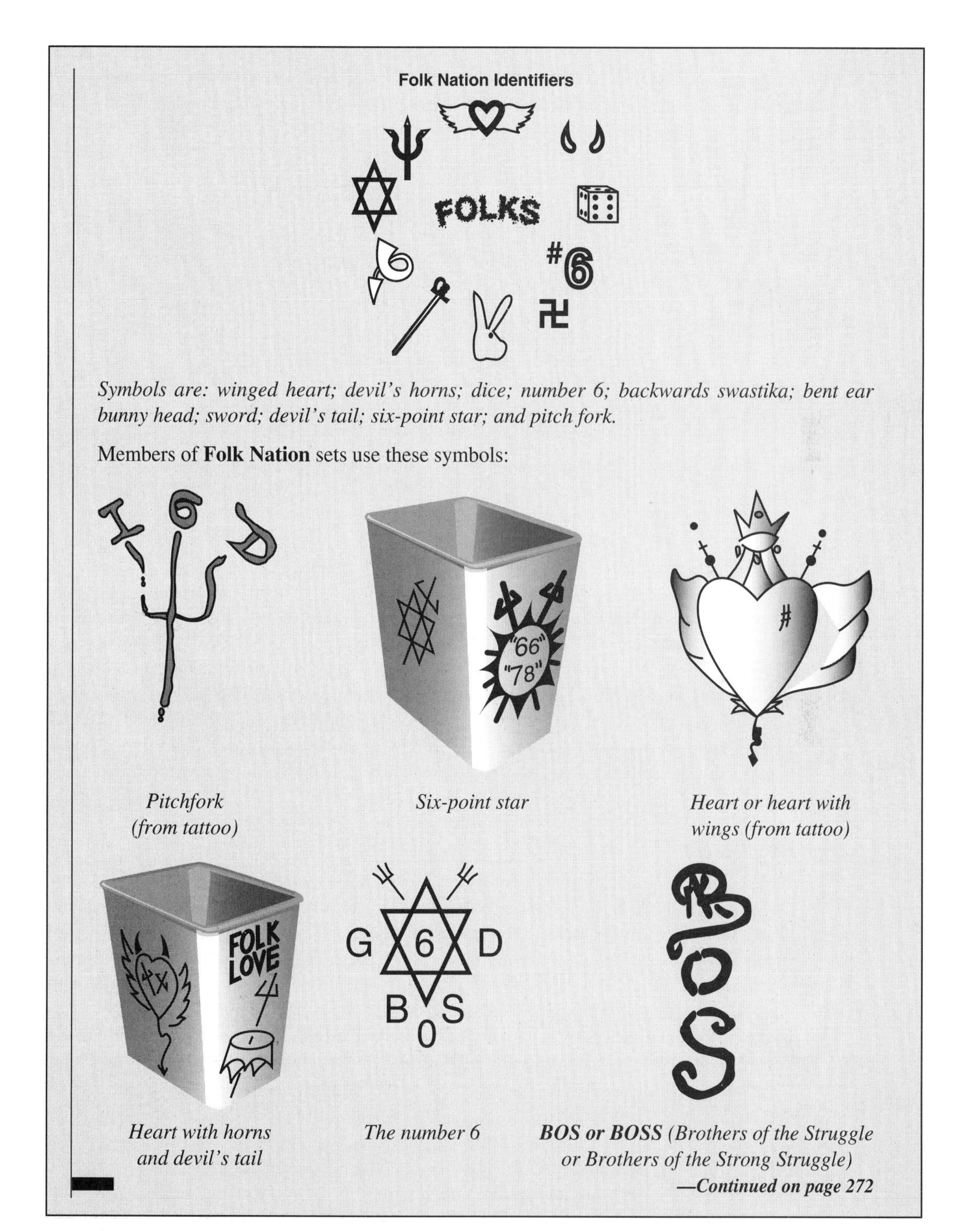

Folk Nation Identifiers

Symbols are: winged heart; devil's horns; dice; number 6; backwards swastika; bent ear bunny head; sword; devil's tail; six-point star; and pitch fork.

Members of **Folk Nation** sets use these symbols:

Pitchfork (from tattoo)

Six-point star

Heart or heart with wings (from tattoo)

Heart with horns and devil's tail

The number 6

***BOS or BOSS** (Brothers of the Struggle or Brothers of the Strong Struggle)*

—Continued on page 272

—*Continued from page 271*

Folk Nation group members use **right identifiers** to distinguish themselves from the People Nation groups. Right identification is displayed by the following:

- Wearing articles of clothing to the right, such as caps, bandannas, and belt buckles.
- Wearing jewelry to the right.
- Rolling up the right pant leg.

Source: Florida Department of Correction (August 29, 2001).

Jargon

Gang members frequently use **jargon** to exchange information. In fact, understanding gang jargon may be critical to obtaining convictions for gang-related crimes. In 1986, Jeff Fort and several high-ranking members of the Chicago-based El Rukn were charged with plotting acts of terrorism in the United States for a sum of $2.5 million from Libya. The FBI recorded thirty-five hundred hours of telephone conversations, most of which were in code, in this case. A former high-ranking member of El Rukn, who turned prosecution witness, translated portions of the confusing conversations for jurors. Fort was convicted and sentenced to an extended prison term.

Recruitment

Gangs continue to recruit new members in order to defend their turf and to expand criminal activities in order to increase profits. There is often intense competition among new, young gang members to prove themselves to the hardcore membership. Brutal initiation rituals in which recruits are severely beaten with fists, feet, and other objects are not uncommon (Mays and Winfree 2000, p. 300). This competition results in younger gang members (ten to thirteen years old) being very dangerous. Gang members know that youths in this age group are not likely to be prosecuted in adult court, making them particularly valuable in the commission of serious offenses. Since the young members want the approval of the older gang members, they are highly motivated to prove themselves and are likely to do whatever they are told to do. Recruitment of these new members occurs anywhere youths gather—shopping malls, bowling alleys, skating rinks, public parks, neighborhoods, and schools (Hieb 1992). There has been an increase in the recruitment of members outside major urban centers and in the number of middle-class youth approached as potential members.

Response of Justice Network to Gangs

The problems presented by juvenile gangs are not easily addressed. In large part, the origins of these problems are inherent in the social and economic conditions of inner-city neighborhoods across the United States, and the issue is complicated by the continued existence of racial and ethnic discrimination in the educational and social arenas. These conditions are largely beyond the control of justice officials, whose efforts are greatly hampered as a result. Since we appear unwilling to confront the basic socioeconomic factors underlying gang involvement, our options are limited largely to responding to the actions of gang members after they have occurred. In general, the response in these terms has been to propose, and often pass, legislation creating more severe penalties for the offenses typically involved; specifically, drug-related and weapons-related offenses (Finkelhor and Ormrod 2001). Recognizing the fact that gangs are now more mobile and that splinter gangs exist in numerous communities, law enforcement officials have attempted to respond by establishing cooperative task forces of combined federal, state, and local authorities who share information and other resources in order to combat gang-related activities.

At the federal level, several past presidents have called for a war on drug trafficking and appointed a "drug czar" to oversee efforts in this area. President Clinton appointed former Houston Police Chief and New York City Police Commissioner Lee Brown to the post. Prosecutors at the federal and state levels have become involved in extremely complex, expensive cases in order to incarcerate known gang leaders and to send a message to gangs that their behavior is not to be tolerated. Gang-crimes units and specialists have emerged in most large urban and some medium-sized city police departments. School liaison programs, previously discussed, have been implemented in the hope of reducing gang influence in the schools. Parent groups have mobilized to combat the influence of gangs on children, and media attention has focused on the consequences of ignoring gang-related crimes. Forfeiture laws have been passed, making it possible for government agencies to seize and sell or use cars, boats, planes, and homes in the pursuit of illegal activities. In short, there is now considerable effort directed toward controlling gang activities. Whether such effort is properly organized, coordinated, and directed, and whether the effort will have the desired consequences, remain empirical questions.

In 1995, the Office of Juvenile Justice and Delinquency Prevention awarded grants to five communities to implement and test the **Spergel Model** intended to reduce gang crime and violence. This model involves developing a coordinated team approach to delivering services and solving problems (Burch and Kane 1999). Strategies involved include mobilization of community leaders and residents, use of outreach workers to engage gang youths, access to academic, economic, and social opportunities, and gang suppression activities. The University of Chicago is currently conducting evaluations of the demonstration effort.

Public, Legislative, and Judicial Reaction

There is little doubt that some violent juveniles must be dealt with harshly and incarcerated for the protection of society, in spite of the fact that processing these juveniles as adults clearly violates the philosophy of the juvenile court network by labeling them as criminals at an early age and by placing them in incarceration with automatic transfer to adult facilities at the age of majority. As we have seen, public perception that there was a dramatic increase in violent and serious crime by juveniles during the 1980s and 90s resulted in considerable pressure on legislators to pass new, more stringent laws relating to the prosecution and incarceration of violent juvenile offenders. As we have previously noted, the juvenile court acts of many states have been amended to remove juveniles charged with criminal homicide, rape, and armed robbery from the jurisdiction of the juvenile court if they are over a certain age at the time they commit the offense.

However, legislative attempts to solve crime problems by passing tougher laws such as mandatory sentencing laws (for drug crimes, for instance) and "three strikes" laws (after the third offense, they "throw away the key") have resulted in less than desirable outcomes. Walker (1998, p. 140), for example, concludes that "Three strikes and you're out laws are a terrible crime policy" because there is no evidence that they reduce serious crime and considerable evidence that they lead to the incarceration of many people who would not commit other crimes anyway.

Gang suppression, gang sweeps, zero tolerance policies, and loitering ordinances are tactics employed by the police to minimize gang activity. But recently attention has been focused on developing partnerships between the police and other community agencies in an attempt to intervene in gang activities. In the city of Reno, Nevada, for example, police decided to focus on the top 5 percent of gang members using a repeat-offender program to target them. At the same time, the police coordinate efforts to deal with the 80 percent of gang members who are not considered hard core. A Community Action Team (CAT) was formed to accomplish these tasks, interview and develop intelligence on gang members, deal with the families of gang wannabes, develop neighborhood advisory groups (NAGS), and implement an improved media policy. This collaborative effort has resulted in increasingly positive evaluations of police performance and reduced amounts of gang violence (Weston 1993).

Alternatives to Incarceration for Violent Juveniles

While numerous causes of youth violence have been posited, solutions have been less apparent. Should we censor the media? Are more prisons or longer sentences the answer? Would gun control help? Is the juvenile justice network, as currently conceived, out of date and ill equipped to handle violent youth?

In his study of juvenile homicide, Sorrells (1980) found that a disproportionate number of juveniles who commit this offense come from communities with a high incidence of poverty and infant mortality. He also notes that such offenders are products of "violent, chaotic families." He concludes that youths who kill are likely to fall into one of three categories:

1. Youngsters who lack the capacity to identify with other human beings
2. Prepsychotic juveniles who kill as an expression of intense emotional conflicts, and who are also high suicide risks, or
3. Neurologically fearful youngsters who kill in overreacting to a genuinely threatening situation. (152)

As **alternatives to incarceration** Sorrells suggests identifying high-risk communities and pooling agency resources to combat specific problems characterizing each community, screening violent juveniles for emotional problems, developing treatment programs focusing on resolving such emotional problems, and removing children from violent, chaotic families where possible.

Other studies provide general support for Sorrells' findings and recommendations. One study of recidivism among juvenile offenders, for example, found that 100 percent of those recidivists had arrest records prior to the arrest upon which the recidivism was based, 88 percent had unstable home lives, 86 percent were unemployed, and over 90 percent had school problems (Ariessohn 1981). Another study indicates that if early intervention is not effective, somewhere between two-thirds and three-fourths of violent juvenile offenders on probation will recidivate, committing essentially the same type of offense within a few months (Buikhuisen and Jongman 1970; Ariessohn and Gonion 1973). Clearly, parents can play a major role with respect to violent youths. It is important to note, however, that they can serve as negative as well as positive role models.

Schools and teachers can also play important roles in preventing violence and gang membership. The GREAT program (discussed earlier in this book) taught by police in the schools may help youths resist gangs. Parents and teachers can work together to improve the interpersonal, cognitive problem-solving skills (ICPS) of youths. This approach focuses on modifying thinking processes rather than behaviors themselves. "I Can Problem Solve" helps children learn to solve interpersonal problems by focusing on means-ends thinking (a step-by-step approach to pursuing goals), weighing pros and cons (of carrying-out behaviors), alternative solution thinking, and consequential thinking (the ability to think about different outcomes from a specific behavior). While more research needs to be done, there is some evidence that teaching children between four and eight years of age such skills can help them "grow into thinking, feeling human beings who will be able to make good decisions when they reach adolescence and adulthood" (Shure 1999).

Taylor (1980) concluded that it may be necessary to deal with juveniles who engage in progressively more serious assaultive behavior by commitment to a detention facility for a three- to six-month period (thus preventing recidivism in the community during this very high risk period), during which time the juvenile's behavior is stabilized and brought under control. Lundman (1993, p. 255) concluded that there is little doubt that incarceration suppresses delinquency. Recognizing this, the Office of Juvenile Justice and Delinquency Prevention sponsored a two-year program to identify, select, prosecute, and enhance treatment for serious, habitual juvenile offenders. Analysis showed that such programs result in more findings of guilt and more correctional commitments; also, that linking such efforts with special correctional treatment programs for youths is highly problematic due to the necessity of subcontractual relationships between prosecutors and service providers and the unavailability of special correctional programs to meet the diverse needs of serious habitual offenders (National Institute of Justice 1988).

In 1995, the OJJDP adopted a comprehensive strategy aimed at eliminating all risk factors for delinquency and gang involvement. This strategy called for a wide spectrum of services and sanctions to be used to protect potential and current delinquents from the womb to school and beyond (National Youth Gang Center 1997).

Unfortunately, getting to and treating potentially violent juveniles is not an easy task. While the proportion of juveniles who commit violent crimes is relatively small, this group commits a sizable number of offenses. Protecting the best interests of the child is clearly an important goal of the juvenile justice network, but so is protection of society. It may well be that police, prosecutors, and judges need to deal with violent juveniles earlier and more severely than they have done in the past. While giving juveniles the benefit of the doubt in early encounters with the police and courts may be well intended, in the case of violent offenders, at least, it is also dangerous to others. It is clear that violence becomes a pattern of behavior when intervention either does not occur or is not effective. In the interests of protecting society and attempting to rehabilitate violent youths by delivering the best programs available as early as possible, violent youths must be identified, apprehended, and evaluated or judged as soon as possible.

According to Father Gregory Boyle who works with troubled youths in Los Angeles (Fremon 1991), the things that ultimately lead youths to say no to gang membership are a job, self-esteem, education, and imagining a future that is viable. From Boyle's point of view, violence in a neighborhood decreases as the number of juveniles increases. Once again, it seems many of the factors involved in improving opportunities for youths while reducing delinquency lie outside the scope of the traditional juvenile justice system. Until our society chooses to deal with these issues (discrimination, unemployment, and relevant school curricula), gangs and violence are likely to remain problems.

CAREER OPPORTUNITY—D.A.R.E. OFFICER

Job Description: Certified police officers who work full time teaching the D.A.R.E. curricula to local school children in grades five through high school; act as role models in the classroom, drawing attention to the hazards of drug and alcohol use, peer pressure, and violence as well as the issues involved in racial and gender stereotyping; trained in the D.A.R.E. curricula at a training center sponsored by the national D.A.R.E. program.

Employment Requirements: Required to be full-time, uniformed police officers with at least two years of policing experience; must have met at least the minimum training standards set by the local policing agency and must go through an oral interview during the D.A.R.E. screening process. Additionally the officers and their agencies must have an agreement with the local school district to teach the D.A.R.E. curricula at the school. Other qualities important to the position include a demonstrated ability to interact and relate well with children; good oral and written communication skills; organization skills; promptness; the ability to develop personal relationships; and flexibility and the ability to handle unexpected situations, statements and actions. Must successfully complete eighty hours of training in order to be certified to teach the core curriculum and the K-4 program. If teaching at the high school level, in the D.A.R.E. Parent Program or in special education classes, must complete an additional forty hours of training and teach the core curriculum for at least two semesters prior to the additional training.

Salary and Benefits: Vary from jurisdiction to jurisdiction. Good benefits and retirement packages are typically included.

SUMMARY

Violence by and against youths has received considerable attention over the past decade or so. Stories appearing in the mass media have led many to believe that violence committed by youths is epidemic, and current official statistics and other sources of information indicate that violent acts committed by youths have indeed increased in recent years. There is little doubt that those youths who commit violent offenses deserve our immediate attention, since research indicates that they are likely to continue to commit such acts unless early, effective intervention occurs.

Even though there have been recent declines in violent crimes by juveniles, a substantial proportion of violent crime is still attributed to them. For those juveniles who do commit violent offenses, incarceration or effective intervention very early in the offense career may well be the best means of protecting society. Evidence indicates that unless one of these two alternatives is employed, recidivism is very likely.

Careful screening of juveniles to ensure that only those who actually commit violent acts are processed according to laws intended to deal with such offenders is imperative in terms of costs to both the youths involved and society.

Our society is confronted by a multitude of problems relating to gangs. Preventing youths from becoming involved in gang activities, particularly in inner-city neighborhoods, is extremely difficult if not impossible. Youths who don't join gangs voluntarily risk their lives, as well as the lives of their family members. Thus early identification of new recruits and comprehensive knowledge concerning the membership and actions of existing gangs are essential. Identification of youths who are in the process of becoming gang members may be accomplished through a variety of means. Sudden changes in friendships; minor but chronic problems with police, school, and family; wearing the same color patterns daily (though colors now appear to be diminishing in importance as a symbol of gang membership); discovery of strange logos/insignias on their bodies, notebooks, or clothing; use of new nicknames (monikers); flashing of hand signs; and unexplained money may be signs of impending as well as actual gang involvement (Hieb 1992). Spotting the signs of pre- or early gang activity is, of course, largely up to parents and teachers who then need to take appropriate action to address the issue (Corbitt 2000).

Even early intervention does not ensure that gang influence will be reduced, since the youths in question are most likely to be returned to the neighborhoods in which the gangs operate or, in some cases, to a correctional facility which is also largely controlled by gangs. Incarceration of adult gang leaders may have some impact, but evidence indicates that these leaders often continue to control gang activities on the outside while they are in prison and frequently control the gangs within the prisons themselves.

The best available strategy is to identify the signs of gang activities as early as possible and prosecute gang members to the full extent of the law in order to send gang leaders the message that their actions will not be tolerated by a given community. These programs are often referred to as "zero tolerance" programs, meaning that no amount of gang activity will be accepted. Such action by the community and the justice network may convince gang leaders looking to expand their spheres of influence to move elsewhere. Where gangs are already clearly established, as in most metropolitan areas, a massive, coordinated effort, addressing socioeconomic conditions as well as criminal behavior, will be required if gang behavior is to be brought under some degree of control. Some such efforts are now being made, and careful evaluation of their impact is crucial.

Gang activities have a long history in the United States, but attention has been redirected recently toward gangs as a result of their involvement with drug trafficking and gunrunning, which are multimillion dollar enterprises. The complexion of gangs has changed somewhat over the years, and referring to gangs as "juvenile" gangs is not totally appropriate at this time due to the strong influence of adult gang leaders who supervise, organize, and control gang activities.

Juveniles continue to join gangs in order to attain status and prestige lacking in the domestic and educational arenas. They also continue to fight territorial wars, wear colors, extort protection money, and exclude from membership those from different racial or ethnic groups. They exist in all urban areas, have extensive organizations in most prisons, and are spreading out to medium-size and even smaller cities.

Gang involvement in violent activities, sometimes random, sometimes carefully planned, has received a good deal of attention from both media and justice officials. The latter are organizing to better combat gang activities, but their success has yet to be carefully evaluated. Similarly, get-tough legislation has been passed at all levels, but the impact of such legislative action remains in question.

INTERNET EXERCISES

Chapter 12 discusses gangs, gang membership, and gang violence. Street gangs are no longer a problem in only larger cities; small towns and communities also see the effects of gang behaviors. The Madison, Wisconsin, Police Department addresses the issue of gang violence and gang behaviors in their website at http://www.ci.madison.wi.us/police/gangfaqs.html. Please visit this site and do the following exercise to learn more about the issues discussed in chapter 12.

1. The Madison Police Department alludes to the fact that schools, families, and communities must also be aware and involved in deterring gangs. Why is school, family, and community involvement necessary to prevent gang violence?
2. There is currently a legal differentiation between gang-related incidences and juvenile violence in general. Based upon the information you've gained from the textbook and the Madison Police Department, what are the differences between gang-related crimes and juvenile offenses?
3. From the Madison Police Department website, click on Folks. Why have the terms *people* and *folks* become synonymous with gangs?

USEFUL WEBSITES

The National Youth Gang Center—*http://www.iir.com/nygc*

Gangs: A Bibliography—*http://www-lib.usc.edu/~anthonya/gang.htm*

Gangs in the Schools—*http://eric-web.tc.columbia.edu/alert/ia46.html*

Gangs: Public Enemy Number One—*http://www.acsp.uic.edu/oicj/other/cccgangs.htm*

Gang Peace—*http://www.slaw.neu.edu/public/home/clinics/uli/gang/gang.htm*

CRITICAL THINKING QUESTIONS

1. Is violence committed by youths on the increase in the United States? Support your answer. In your opinion, are adults in the United States afraid of youths? Should they be?
2. Is probation likely to be effective in deterring violent youths from recidivating? Why or why not? Are there more effective programs for deterring violent youths?
3. What are the relationships among guns, drugs, and violence? Would gun control cut down on the number of violent crimes committed by juveniles? Against juveniles?
4. Describe the conditions under which gang membership is most likely to be attractive to youths. What kinds of responses do we as a society need to make in order to help control gangs?
5. Are there major differences in reasons for joining gangs and behaviors engaged in while in gangs between male and female gang members? Are female gang members more similar or different from their male counterparts today regarding criminal activity?

SUGGESTED READINGS

Bilchik, S. et al. (1999, December). *1997 national youth gang survey.* Washington, D.C.: U. S. Department of Justice.

Burch, J., & Kane, C. (1999, July). Implementing the OJJDP comprehensive gang model. *OJJDP Fact Sheet #112.* Washington, D.C.: U.S. Government Printing Office.

Campbell, A. (1991). *The girls in the gang.* 2nd ed. New York: Basil Blackwell.

Corbitt, W. A. (2000). Violent crimes among juveniles: Behavioral aspects. *FBI Law Enforcement Bulletin, 69* (6), 18–21.

Curry, G. D., & Spergel, I. A. (1988). Gang homicide, delinquency, and community. *Criminology, 26* (3), 381–405.

Davis, N. (1999). *Youth crisis: Growing up in a high-risk society.* New York: Greenwood Press.

Dawley, D. (1973). *A nation of lords: A history of the Vice Lords.* Garden City, NY: Anchor Books.

Esbensen, F., Deschenes, E. P., & Winfree, L. T. (1999). Differences between gang girls and gang boys: Results from a multisite survey. *Youth & Society, 31* (1), 27–53.

Evans, W. P., Fitzgerald, C., & Weigel, D. (1999). Are rural gang members similar to their urban peers? Implications for rural communities. *Youth & Society, 30* (3), 267–282.

Hunter, J. A., Hazelwood, R. R., & Slesinger, D. (2000). Juvenile sexual homicide. *FBI Law Enforcement Bulletin, 69* (3), 1–9.

Mays, G. L. (1997). *Gangs and gang behavior.* Chicago: Nelson-Hall.

Miller, W. B. (2001, April). The growth of youth gang problems in the United States: 1970–1998. *OJJDP Report.* Washington, D.C.: U. S. Department of Justice.

Osgood, D. W., & Chambers, J. M. (2000). Social disorganization outside the metropolis: An analysis of rural youth violence. *Criminology, 38* (1), 81–115.

Pattillo, M. E. (1998). Sweet mothers and gangbangers: Managing crime in a black middle-class neighborhood. *Social Forces, 76* (3), 747–774.

Shure, M. B. (1999). Preventing violence the problem-solving way. *Juvenile Justice Bulletin. OJJDP.* Washington, D.C.: U.S. Department of Justice.

Wilson, J. J. (2000, November). 1998 national youth gang survey. *OJJDP Summary.* Washington, D.C.: U.S. Department of Justice.

Yablonsky, L. (1970). *The violent gang.* Baltimore: Penguin Books.

CHAPTER

13

THE FUTURE OF JUVENILE JUSTICE

CHAPTER LEARNING OBJECTIVES

Upon completion of this chapter, students should be able to:

Evaluate the extent to which the goals of the juvenile justice network have been met as we enter the twenty-first century
Suggest alternatives for the future of the juvenile justice network
Explain the restorative justice and get tough approaches to juvenile justice
Discuss the possible demise of the juvenile justice network
Discuss ways of improving upon the current juvenile justice network

KEY TERMS

restorative or balanced justice
get tough or just deserts approach
revitalized juvenile justice

Throughout this book we have discussed in varying detail the philosophies of the juvenile justice network, the procedural requirements of that network, and some of the major problems with the network as it now operates. We have seen that the juvenile justice network is subject to numerous stresses and strains from within and without and that change, trial and error, and good intentions with sometimes less than desirable results characterize the network. We have arrived at a number of conclusions, some of which are supported by empirical evidence, others of which are more or less speculative, based upon our observations and those of concerned practitioners and citizens.

The initial underlying assumption of the juvenile justice network is that juveniles with problems should be treated and/or educated rather than punished. Adult and juvenile justice networks in the United States were separated because of the belief that courts should act in the best interests of juveniles and because of the belief that association with adult offenders would increase the possibility that juveniles would become involved in criminal careers. As we enter the twenty-first century, the extent to which we have achieved the goals of the juvenile justice network continues to be debated. Where do we go from here? While it is always risky to speculate, it appears to us that there are three more or less distinct possibilities for the future of the juvenile justice network. Possibility number one is that the juvenile justice network will cease to exist as a separate entity (see In Practice 13.1).

Possibility number two is that the **restorative or balanced justice** (see chapter 10) movement will triumph and we will return to a more caring, personal approach to juvenile justice. Possibility number three is that those favoring a get tough approach will be victorious and that the goals of the juvenile justice network will change dramatically. Moon et al. (2000, pp. 38–41) best describe where we have been and where we need to go in In Practice 13.2.

Possibility number three is that the **get tough or just deserts approach** supporters will reform the juvenile justice system so that an increasing number of youths are dealt with in the adult justice network. "There is little argument that the current juvenile justice system is indeed in turmoil and lacks the foresight and preventive measures required for lasting reform. . . . The challenge before us is to move from the rhetoric to the reality of what we are going to do to save their [juveniles'] lives and our collective futures" (Hatchett 1998, pp. 83–84). If this sounds familiar, it may be because it has been the theme throughout this text.

As Ohlin (1998, p. 143) notes: ". . . confidence in the ability of our institutional system to control juvenile delinquency has been steadily eroding. Public insecurity, fear, and anxiety about youth crime are now intense and widespread, despite the juvenile court and probation system and the training schools that have evolved over the past century."

Uniformity of juvenile law has yet to be achieved. Many citizens still adopt an out-of-sight, out-of-mind attitude toward youths with problems, and both citizens and practitioners are often frustrated by our supposed failure to curb delinquency and abuse or neglect in spite of the millions of dollars invested in the enterprise. We continue to refuse to

In Practice 13.1

CAN THE JUVENILE JUSTICE NETWORK SURVIVE?

After half a century of conquest and occupation, the juvenile court has in recent years entered a valley in which it has been caught in a withering crossfire which may ultimately destroy it. From its left, the canons of the civil libertarians fired the first volleys in the form of Supreme Court decisions imposing due process requirements upon the juvenile court. From the right, the forces of law and order have moved, through legislation, to force fundamental changes in the purposes of the juvenile justice system and the substantive provisions of the juvenile law. The conflict between the principles of civil liberty and social control has long been a part of the criminal justice system. Now, apparently, it is being waged in the context of the juvenile justice system. . . . The juvenile justice system, if it survives at all, may soon become not a separate and philosophically different approach from the criminal justice system, but merely a separate criminal justice system for criminals under the age of eighteen. (Hutzler 1982, pp. 37–38)

Is the "get tough" approach the future of juvenile justice?
Jeremiah Coughlan/AP/Wide World

In Practice 13.2

Change in the Juvenile Justice Network

At the close of the nineteenth century, the United States witnessed an unprecedented movement to save its children from physical and moral harm. The "Child savers," as champions of this movement have come to be known, sought wide-reaching reforms. . . . [with] the establishment of a system of juvenile justice. Now, a century after its creation, the juvenile court has experienced a period of sustained criticism. . . .

The foundation of this system of justice was an overriding belief that juvenile delinquents could be saved. . . . Beginning in the 1960s. . . . the benevolent principles on which the system was based stood in stark and ironic contrast to the punitive reality of the juvenile justice system. . . . In the 100-year anniversary of the juvenile court, serious concerns remain about the viability of this system. . . . At the end of 1997, 17 states had redefined their juvenile court purpose clauses to emphasize public safety, certain sanctions, and/or offender accountability. . . . It is frequently suggested that the changes in the juvenile court have been precipitated by two factors: high rates of serious crime and a shift in public attitudes toward youthful offenders. . . . Contemporary discussions about youthful offenders have taken a decidedly punitive flavor in the past ten years. . . . [but] despite sweeping reforms aimed at altering the juvenile court to reflect retributive and punitive goals, it is uncertain that the public wants a juvenile justice system based exclusively, or even primarily, on punishment. (Moon et al. 2000, pp. 38–41)

address the larger societal issues of race, class, and gender as they relate to crime and delinquency (Ohlin 1998, p. 152).

There is undoubtedly room for a great deal of improvement in juvenile justice. To some extent, such improvement depends upon changes in societal conditions, such as poverty, unemployment, and discrimination. Changes in the family and in the educational network, which improve our ability to meet the needs of youth, are also crucial. Changes in the rules which govern youths may be appropriate in some instances. Making better use of the information made available to us by researchers and practitioners is yet another way to improve the network. In the end, taking a rational, calculated approach to delinquency and abuse or neglect will pay better dividends than adhering to policies developed and implemented as a result of fear and misunderstanding.

Bilchik (1998a, p. 89) concludes: "A **revitalized juvenile justice** system needs to be put into place and brought to scale that will ensure immediate and appropriate sanctions, provide effective treatment, reverse trends in juvenile violence, and rebuild public confidence in and support for the juvenile justice system." Such a system would include swift intervention with early offenders, an individualized comprehensive needs assessment, transfer of serious, or chronic offenders, and intensive aftercare. This system would require the coordinated efforts of law enforcement, treatment, correctional, judicial, and social service personnel. This approach to delinquency control represents a form of community programming which might help reintegrate troubled youth into mainstream society rather than further isolate and alienate them (Bazemore and Washington 1995; Zaslaw

In Practice 13.3

Consequences of a "Just Deserts" Model for Juvenile Justice

Few maintain that juvenile justice has lived up to its promise in the United States, and many assert that its future lies basically with a due process/just deserts orientation. If treatment and rehabilitation are abandoned, however, in favor of a just deserts policy whereby serious delinquents are punished in large, custodial institutions, several untoward consequences would probably result.

First, delinquency would deepen in seriousness and expand its sway, laying the foundation for a worsening problem among adult predatory criminals in the years ahead. Second, an important voice for humane programs in the justice system would be stilled, with the result that a monolithic retributive system and its programs would prevail not only in delinquency but in criminal justice as a whole.

and Balance 1996). In order to accomplish this goal, the resistance to change that characterizes most institutions must be overcome.

We believe the first possibility, that the complete demise of the juvenile justice network is unlikely simply because the goals of the network are worthy and not likely to be completely abandoned. In addition, the separate juvenile justice system employs a large supporting staff that is unlikely to be summarily dismissed (Klofas and Stojkovic 1995).

Based upon current trends, it appears likely that the juvenile justice network will continue to provide separate services for juveniles, but with an increase in the number of crimes for which waivers to adult court are used. Further, Klofas and Stojkovic (1995) are probably correct in stating that the juvenile court may automatically release jurisdiction for older youths who commit drug- or gang-related violent crimes. In short, it appears likely that we will have a more retribution-oriented juvenile justice system. With this in mind, the overrepresentation of racial and ethnic minorities in the network will almost surely continue and perhaps worsen as the police continue to expend disproportionate resources in poverty-ridden inner-city neighborhoods. The evidence is clear that a disproportionate number of minority youths who are arrested will be convicted and incarcerated, and the prospects for change in this area appear minimal.

It is unlikely that restorative justice advocates will withdraw from the field of battle in the juvenile justice network. They have gained momentum as we enter the twenty-first century because they have focused on caring for victims too long forgotten by those in the juvenile justice network, and that is not likely to change in the near future. And, in a way, the policies they advocate fit rather well with the just deserts model, since in addition to being processed through the courts, offenders are forced to confront their victims in the interest of making both "whole" again. To the extent, if any, that such confrontations prove uncomfortable for offenders, this may be viewed as another form of punishment in addition to, or in the place of, judicial punishment.

We might close by looking at the future of gangs and efforts to deal with them as a way of summarizing the future of the juvenile justice network. The contemporary cycle of youth gang activities is likely to continue (since members who are imprisoned manage to maintain some gang-related activities even while in prison, and since recruitment, given the conditions outlined above, is no problem). As Postman (1991, p. 19) put it, we can ill afford to "hurtle into the future with our eyes fixed firmly on the rearview mirror." Or, as according to Peak (1999, p. 61), "The future will not likely witness the diminution of gang activities unless communities resolve to seek solutions and take action." In order to address the problem most effectively, we will have to recognize that police activity alone cannot control gangs. Community programs aimed at alleviating the causes of gang membership as well as providing opportunities for those inclined to gang membership will have to be forthcoming if we hope to confront the gang problem. Support for the police is essential, but so is support for a myriad of community programs directed at high-risk youth. The best efforts of school personnel, social services professionals, and the community at large will also be necessary. Only by producing our best efforts in this regard can we hope to maintain the integrity of the juvenile justice network while providing appropriate alternatives for youths who cannot, or will not, be helped through education, treatment, care, concern, and opportunity.

Internet Exercises

In this chapter we discuss the future of the juvenile court system. As the juvenile court reached its 100th birthday, many questions were raised about the effectiveness, need for, and future vision of the juvenile court system. Currently, there are many thoughts on what the juvenile court should do and how the juveniles that fall within the juvenile court's jurisdiction should be treated. To learn more about the Office of Juvenile Justice and Delinquency Prevention's initiative to strengthen the juvenile court system, refer to their website at http://ojjdp.ncjrs.org/.

1. From the homepage, click on Programs. In the programs menu, click on Juvenile Court Centennial Initiative. Then, click on About Us.
2. After reading the mission of the Juvenile Court Centennial Initiative, explain what future changes are likely to come about in the juvenile court system as proposed by the Centennial Initiative.
3. Click on Declaration for Juvenile Justice for the 21st Century from the menu. This declaration relies heavily on rehabilitative efforts within the juvenile court system. How is this different or similar to the current practices found in juvenile court? How does this contradict recent legislative changes in juvenile law? Do you believe that the juvenile court can meet all of the expectations placed before it by the various organizations and agencies working with youths, by schools, by families, by the media, and by communities? Why or why not?

Suggested Readings

Bilchik, S. (1998). A juvenile justice system for the 21st century. *Crime & Delinquency, 44* (1), 89–101.

Colbridge, T. D. (2000). The advent of the computer delinquent. *FBI Law Enforcement Bulletin, 69* (12), 7–13.

Federle, K. H. (1999, July). Is there a jurisprudential future for the juvenile court? *Annals of the American Academy of Political & Social Science, 564,* 28–36.

Hatchette, G. (1998). Why we can't wait: The juvenile court in the new millennium. *Crime & Delinquency, 44* (1), 83–88.

Lipsey, M. W. (1999, July). Can intervention rehabilitate serious delinquents? *Annals of the American Academy of Political & Social Science, 564,* 142–166.

Moon, M. M., Sundt, J. L., Cullen, F. T., & Wright, J. P. (2000). Is child saving dead? Public support for juvenile rehabilitation. *Crime & Delinquency, 46* (1), 38–60.

Morse. S. J. (1999, July). Delinquency and desert. *Annals of the American Academy of Political & Social Science, 564,* 56–80.

Uniform Juvenile Court Act

Appendix A

The Uniform Juvenile Court Act was drafted by the National Conference of Commissioners on Uniform State Laws and approved and recommended for enactment in all the states at its annual conference meeting in its seventy-seventh year, Philadelphia, Pennsylvania, July 22—August 1, 1968. Approved by the American Bar Association at its meeting at Philadelphia, Pennsylvania, August 7, 1968.

Section 1. *[Interpretation.]* This Act shall be construed to effectuate the following public purposes:

1. to provide for the care, protection, and wholesome moral, mental, and physical development of children coming within its provisions;
2. consistent with the protection of the public interest, to remove from children committing delinquent acts the taint of criminality and the consequences of criminal behavior and to substitute therefor a program of treatment, training, and rehabilitation;
3. to achieve the foregoing purposes in a family environment whenever possible, separating the child from his parents only when necessary for his welfare or in the interest of public safety;
4. to provide a simple judicial procedure through which this Act is executed and enforced and in which the parties are assured a fair hearing and their constitutional and other legal rights recognized and enforced; and
5. to provide simple interstate procedures which permit resort to cooperative measures among the juvenile courts of the several states when required to effectuate the purposes of this Act.

Section 2. *[Definitions.]* As used in this Act:

1. "child" means an individual who is:
   i. under the age of 18 years; or
   ii. under the age of 21 years who committed an act of delinquency before reaching the age of 18 years; [or]
   iii. under 21 years of age who committed an act of delinquency after becoming 18 years of age and is transferred to the juvenile court by another court having jurisdiction over him;]
2. "delinquent act" means an act designated a crime under the law, including local [ordinances] [or resolutions] of this state, or of another state, if the act occurred in that state, or under federal law, and the crime does not fall under paragraph (iii) of subsection (4) [and is not a juvenile traffic offense as defined in section 44] [and the crime is not a traffic offense as defined in Traffic Code of the State] other than [designate the more serious offenses which should be included in the jurisdiction of the juvenile court such as drunken driving, negligent homicide, etc.];

3. "delinquent child" means a child who has committed a delinquent act and is in need of treatment or rehabilitation;
4. "unruly child" means a child who:
   i. while subject to compulsory school attendance is habitually and without justification truant from school;
   ii. is habitually disobedient of the reasonable and lawful commands of his parent, guardian, or other custodian and is ungovernable; or
   iii. has committed an offense applicable only to a child; and
   iv. if any of the foregoing is in need of treatment or rehabilitation;
5. "deprived child" means a child who:
   i. is without proper parental care or control, subsistence, education as required by law, or other care or control necessary for his physical, mental, or emotional health, or morals, and the deprivation is not due primarily to the lack of financial means of his parents, guardian, or other custodian;
   ii. has been placed for care or adoption in violation of law; [or]
   iii. has been abandoned by his parents, guardian, or other custodian; [or]
   iv. is without a parent, guardian, or legal custodian;
6. "shelter care" means temporary care of a child in physically unrestricted facilities;
7. "protective supervision" means supervision ordered by the court of children found to be deprived or unruly;
8. "custodian" means a person, other than a parent or legal guardian, who stands in *loco parentis* to the child or a person to whom legal custody of the child has been given by order of a court;
9. "juvenile court" means the [here designate] court of this state.

Section 3. *[Jurisdiction.]*

a. The juvenile court has exclusive original jurisdiction of the following proceedings, which are governed by this Act:
   1. proceedings in which a child is alleged to be delinquent, unruly, or deprived [or to have committed a juvenile traffic offense as defined in section 44;]
   2. proceedings for the termination of parental rights except when a part of an adoption proceeding; and
   3. proceedings arising under section 39 through 42.
b. The juvenile court also has exclusive original jurisdiction of the following proceedings, which are governed by the laws relating thereto without regard to the other provisions of this Act:
   1. proceedings for the adoption of an individual of any age;]
   2. proceedings to obtain judicial consent to the marriage, employment, or enlistment in the armed services of a child, if consent is required by law;
   3. proceedings under the Interstate Compact of Juveniles; [and]
   4. proceedings under the Interstate Compact on the Placement of Children; [and]
   5. proceedings to determine the custody or appoint a guardian of the person of a child.]

Section 4. *[Concurrent Jurisdiction.]* The juvenile court has concurrent jurisdiction with [———] court of proceedings to treat or commit a mentally retarded or mentally ill child.]

Section 5. *[Probation Services.]*

a. [In [counties] of over ———————— population] the [————] court may appoint one or more probation officers who shall serve [at the pleasure of the court] [and are subject to removal under the civil service laws governing the county]. They have the powers and duties stated in section 6. Their salaries shall be fixed by the court with the approval of the [governing board of the county]. If more than one probation officer is appointed, one may be designated by the court as the chief probation officer or director of court services, who shall be responsible for the administration of the probation services under the direction of the court.]
b. In all other cases the [Department of Corrections] [state] [county] child welfare department] [or other appropriate state agency] shall provide suitable probation services to the juvenile court of each [county.] The cost thereof shall be paid out of the general revenue funds of the [state] [county]. The probation officer or other qualified person assigned to the court by the [Department of Corrections] [state [county] child welfare department] [or other appropriate state agency] has the powers and duties stated in section 6.]

Section 6. *[Powers and Duties of Probation Officers.]*

a. For the purpose of carrying out the objectives and purposes of this Act and subject to the limitations of this Act or imposed by the Court, a probation officer shall:
   1. make investigations, reports, and recommendations to the juvenile court;
   2. receive and examine complaints and charges of delinquency, unruly conduct or deprivation of a child for the purpose of considering the commencement of proceedings under this Act;
   3. supervise and assist a child placed on probation or in his protective supervision or care by order of the court or other authority of law;
   4. make appropriate referrals to other private or public agencies of the community if their assistance appears to be needed or desirable;
   5. take into custody and detain a child who is under his supervision or care as a delinquent, unruly or deprived child if the probation officer has reasonable cause to believe that the child's health or safety is in imminent danger, or that he may abscond or be removed from the jurisdiction of the court, or when ordered by the court pursuant to this Act. Except as provided by this Act a probation officer does not have the powers of a law enforcement officer. He may not conduct accusatory proceedings under this Act against a child who is or may be under his care or supervision; and
   6. perform all other functions designated by this Act or by order of the court pursuant thereto.
b. Any of the foregoing functions may be performed in another state if authorized by the court of this state and permitted by the laws of the other state.

Section 7. *[Referees.]*

a. The judge may appoint one or more persons to serve at the pleasure of the judge as referees on a full or part-time basis. A referee shall be a member of the bar [and shall qualify under the civil service regulations of the County.] His compensation shall be fixed by the judge [with the approval of the [governing board of the County] and paid out of [————]].

b. The judge may direct that hearings in any case or class of cases be conducted in the first instance by the referee in the manner provided by this Act. Before commencing the hearing the referee shall inform the parties who have appeared that they are entitled to have the matter heard by the judge. If a party objects the hearing shall be conducted by the judge.
c. Upon the conclusion of a hearing before a referee he shall transmit written findings and recommendations for disposition to the judge. Prompt written notice and copies of the findings and recommendations shall be given to the parties to the proceeding. The written notice shall inform them of the right to a rehearing before the judge.
d. A rehearing may be ordered by the judge at any time and shall be ordered if a party files a written request therefor within 3 days after receiving the notice required in subsection (c).
e. Unless a rehearing is ordered the findings and recommendations become the findings and order of the court when confirmed in writing by the judge.]

Section 8. *[Commencement of Proceedings.]* A proceeding under this Act may be commenced:

1. by transfer of a case from another court as provided in section 9;
2. as provided in section 44 in a proceeding charging the violation of a traffic offense;] or
3. by the court accepting jurisdiction as provided in section 40 or accepting supervision of a child as provided in section 42; or
4. in other cases by the filing of a petition as provided in this Act. The petition and all other documents in the proceeding shall be entitled "In the interest of ———, a [child] [minor] under [18] [21] years of age."

Section 9. *[Transfer from other Courts.]* If it appears to the court in a criminal proceeding that the defendant [is a child] [was under the age of 18 years at the time the offense charged was alleged to have been committed], the court shall forthwith transfer the case to the juvenile court together with a copy of the accusatory pleading and other papers, documents, and transcripts of testimony relating to the case. It shall order that the defendant be taken forthwith to the juvenile court or to a place of detention designated by the juvenile court, or release him to the custody of his parent, guardian, custodian, or other person legally responsible for him, to be brought before the juvenile court at a time designated by that court. The accusatory pleading may serve in lieu of a petition in the juvenile court unless that court directs the filing of a petition.

Section 10. *[Informal Adjustment.]*

a. Before a petition is filed, the probation officer or other officer of the court designated by it, subject to its direction, may give counsel and advice to the parties with a view to an informal adjustment if it appears;
    1. the admitted facts bring the case within the jurisdiction of the court;
    2. counsel and advice without an adjudication would be in the best interest of the public and the child; and
    3. the child and his parents, guardian or other custodian consent thereto with knowledge that consent is not obligatory.

b. The giving of counsel and advice cannot extend beyond 3 months from the day commenced unless extended by the court for an additional period not to exceed 3 months and does not authorize the detention of the child if not otherwise permitted by this Act.
c. An incriminating statement made by a participant to the person giving counsel or advice and in the discussions or conferences incident thereto shall not be used against the declarant over objection in any hearing except in a hearing on disposition in a juvenile court proceeding or in a criminal proceeding against him after conviction for the purpose of a pre-sentence investigation.

Section 11. *[Venue.]* A proceeding under this act may be commenced in the [county] in which the child resides. If delinquent or unruly conduct is alleged, the proceeding may be commenced in the [county] in which the acts constituting the alleged delinquent or unruly conduct occurred. If deprivation is alleged, the proceeding may be brought in the [county] in which the child is present when it is commenced.

Section 12. *[Transfer to Another Juvenile Court Within the State.]*

a. If the child resides in a [county] of the state and the proceeding is commenced in a court of another [county], the court, on motion of a party or on its own motion made prior to final disposition, may transfer the proceeding to the county of the child's residence for further action. Like transfer may be made if the residence of the child changes pending the proceeding. The proceeding shall be transferred if the child has been adjudicated delinquent or unruly and other proceedings involving the child are pending in the juvenile court of the [county] of his residence.
b. Certified copies of all legal and social documents and records pertaining to the case on file with the clerk of the court shall accompany the transfer.

Section 13. *[Taking into Custody.]*

a. A child may be taken into custody:
    1. pursuant to an order of the court under this Act;
    2. pursuant to the laws of arrest;
    3. by a law enforcement officer [or duly authorized officer of the court] if there are reasonable grounds to believe that the child is suffering from illness or injury or is in immediate danger from his surroundings, and that his removal is necessary; or
    4. by a law enforcement officer [or duly authorized officer of the court] if there are reasonable grounds to believe that the child has run away from his parents, guardian, or other custodian.
b. The taking of a child into custody is not an arrest, except for the purpose of determining its validity under the constitution of this State or of the United States.

Section 14. *[Detention of Child.]* A child taken into custody shall not be detained or placed in shelter care prior to the hearing on the petition unless his detention or care is required to protect the person or property of others or of the child because the child may abscond or be removed from the jurisdiction of the court or because he has no parent, guardian, or custodian or other person able to provide supervision and care for him and return him to the court when required, or an order for his detention or shelter care has been made by the court pursuant to this Act.

Section 15. *[Release or Delivery to Court.]*

a. A person taking a child into custody, with all reasonable speed and without first taking the child elsewhere, shall:
   1. release the child to his parents, guardian, or other custodian upon their promise to bring the child before the court when requested by the court, unless his detention or shelter care is warranted or required under section 14; or
   2. bring the child before the court or deliver him to a detention or shelter care facility designated by the court or to a medical facility if the child is believed to suffer from a serious physical condition or illness which requires prompt treatment. He shall promptly give written notice thereof, together with a statement of the reason for taking the child into custody, to a parent, guardian, or other custodian and to the court. Any temporary detention or questioning of the child necessary to comply with this subsection shall conform to the procedures and conditions prescribed by this Act and rules of court.

b. If a parent, guardian, or other custodian, when requested, fails to bring the child before the court as provided in subsection (a) the court may issue its warrant directing that the child be taken into custody and brought before the court.

Section 16. *[Place of Detention.]*

a. A child alleged to be delinquent may be detained only in:
   1. a licensed foster home or a home approved by the court;
   2. a facility operated by a licensed child welfare agency;
   3. a detention home or center for delinquent children which is under the direction or supervision of the court or other public authority or of a private agency approved by the court; or
   4. any other suitable place or facility, designated or operated by the court. The child may be detained in a jail or other facility for the detention of adults only if the facility in paragraph (3) is not available, the detention is in a room separate and removed from those for adults, it appears to the satisfaction of the court that public safety and protection reasonably require detention, and it so orders.

b. The official in charge of a jail or other facility for the detention of adult offenders or persons charged with crime shall inform the court immediately if a person who is or appears to be under the age of 18 years is received at the facility and shall bring him before the court upon request or deliver him to a detention or shelter care facility designated by the court.

c. If a case is transferred to another court for criminal prosecution the child may be transferred to the appropriate officer or detention facility in accordance with the law governing the detention of persons charged with crime.

d. A child alleged to be deprived or unruly may be detained or placed in shelter care only in the facilities stated in paragraphs (1), (2), and (4) of subsection (a) and shall not be detained in a jail or other facility intended or used for the detention of adults charged with criminal offenses or of children alleged to be delinquent.

Section 17. *[Release from Detention or Shelter Care—Hearing—Conditions of Release.]*

a. If a child is brought before the court or delivered to a detention or shelter care facility designated by the court the intake or other authorized officer of the court shall immediately make an investigation and release the child unless it appears that his detention or shelter care is warranted or required under section 14.

b. If he is not so released, a petition under section 21 shall be promptly made and presented to the court.

An informal detention hearing shall be held promptly and not later than 72 hours after he is placed in detention to determine whether his detention or shelter care is required under section 14. Reasonable notice thereof, either oral or written, stating the time, place, and purpose of the detention hearing shall be given to the child and if they can be found, to his parents, guardian, or other custodian. Prior to the commencement of the hearing, the court shall inform the parties of their right to counsel and to appointed counsel if they are needy persons, and of the child's right to remain silent with respect to any allegations of delinquency or unruly conduct.

c. If the child is not so released and a parent, guardian, or custodian has not been notified of the hearing, did not appear or waive appearance at the hearing, and files his affidavit showing these facts, the court shall rehear the matter without unnecessary delay and order his release unless it appears from the hearing that the child's detention or shelter care is required under section 14.

Section 18. *[Subpoena.]* Upon application of a party the court or the clerk of the court shall issue, or the court on its own motion may issue, subpoenas requiring attendance and testimony of witnesses and production of papers at any hearing under this Act.]

Section 19. *[Petition—Preliminary Determination.]* A petition under this Act shall not be filed unless the [probation officer,] the court, or other person authorized by the court has determined and endorsed upon the petition that the filing of the petition is in the best interest of the public and the child.

Section 20. *[Petition—Who May Make.]* Subject to section 19 the petition may be made by any person, including a law enforcement officer, who has knowledge of the facts alleged or is informed and believes that they are true.

Section 21. *[Contents of Petition.]* The petition shall be verified and may be on information and belief. It shall set forth plainly:

1. the facts which bring the child within the jurisdiction of the court, with a statement that it is in the best interest of the child and the public that the proceeding be brought and, if elinquency or unruly conduct is alleged, that the child is in need of treatment or rehabilitation;
2. the name, age, and residence address, if any, of the child on whose behalf the petition is brought;
3. the names and residence addresses, if known to petitioner, of the parents, guardian, or custodian of the child and of the child's spouse, if any. If none of his parents, guardian, or custodian resides or can be found within the state, or if their respective

places of residence address are unknown, the name of any known adult relative residing within the [county], or, if there be none, the known adult relative residing nearest to the location of the court; and

4. if the child is in custody and, if so, the place of his detention and the time he was taken into custody.

Section 22. *[Summons.]*

a. After the petition has been filed the court shall fix a time for hearing thereon, which, if the child is in detention, shall not be later than 10 days after the filing of the petition. The court shall direct the issuance of a summons to the parents, guardian, or other custodian, a guardian ad litem, and any other persons as appear to the court to be proper or necessary parties to the proceeding, requiring them to appear before the court at the time fixed to answer the allegations of the petition. The summons shall also be directed to the child if he is 14 or more years of age or is alleged to be a delinquent or unruly child. A copy of the petition shall accompany the summons unless the summons is served by publication in which case the published summons shall indicate the general nature of the allegations and where a copy of the petition can be obtained.
b. The court may endorse upon the summons an order directing the parents, guardian or other custodian of the child to appear personally at the hearing and directing the person having the physical custody or control of the child to bring the child to the hearing.
c. If it appears from affidavit filed or from sworn testimony before the court that the conduct, condition, or surroundings of the child are endangering his health or welfare or those of others, or that he may abscond or be removed from the jurisdiction of the court or will not be brought before the court, notwithstanding the service of the summons, the court may endorse upon the summons an order that a law enforcement officer shall serve the summons and take the child into immediate custody and bring him forthwith before the court.
d. The summons shall state that a party is entitled to counsel in the proceedings and that the court will appoint counsel if the party is unable without undue financial hardship to employ counsel.
e. A party, other than the child, may waive service of summons by written stipulation or by voluntary appearance at the hearing. If the child is present at the hearing, his counsel, with the consent of the parent, guardian or other custodian, or guardian ad litem, may waive service of summons in his behalf.

Section 23. *[Service of Summons.]*

a. If a party to be served with a summons is within this State and can be found, the summons shall be served upon him personally at least 24 hours before the hearing. If he is within the State and cannot be found, but his address is known or can with reasonable diligence be ascertained, the summons may be served upon him by mailing a copy by registered or certified mail at least 5 days before the hearing. If he is without this State but he can be found or his address is known, or his whereabouts or address can with reasonable diligence be ascertained, service of the summons may be made either by delivering a copy to him personally or mailing a copy to him by registered or certified mail at least 5 days before the hearing.

b. If after reasonable effort he cannot be found or his post office address ascertained, whether he is within or without this State, the court may order service of the summons upon him by publication in accordance with [Rule] [Section]———[the general service by publication statutes.] The hearing shall not be earlier than 5 days after the date of the last publication.
c. Service of the summons may be made by any suitable person under the direction of the court.
d. The court may authorize the payment from [county funds] of the costs of service and of necessary travel expenses incurred by persons summoned or otherwise required to appear at the hearing.

Section 24. *[Conduct of Hearings.]*

a. Hearings under this Act shall be conducted by the court without a jury, in an informal but orderly manner, and separate from other proceedings not included in section 3.
b. The [prosecuting attorney] upon request of the court shall present the evidence in support of the petition and otherwise conduct the proceedings on behalf of the state.
c. If requested by aparty or ordered by the court the proceedings shall be recorded by stenographic notes or by electronic, mechanical, or other appropriate means. If not so recorded full minutes of the proceedings shall be kept by the court.
d. Except in hearings to declare a person in contempt of court [and in hearings under section 44], the general public shall be excluded from hearings under this Act. Only the parties, their counsel, witnesses, and other persons accompanying a party for his assistance, and any other persons as the court finds have a proper interest in the proceeding or in the work of the court may be admitted by the court. The court may temporarily exclude the child from the hearing except while allegations of his delinquency or unruly conduct are being heard.

Section 25. *[Service by Publication—Interlocutory Order of Disposition.]*

a. If service of summons upon a party is made by publication the court may conduct a provisional hearing upon the allegations of the petition and enter an interlocutory order of disposition if:
    1. the petition alleges delinquency, unruly conduct, or deprivation of the child;
    2. the summons served upon any party (i) states that prior to the final hearing on the petition designated in the summons a provisional hearing thereon will be held at a specified time and place, (ii) requires the party who is served other than by publication to appear and answer the allegations of the petition at the provisional hearing, (iii) states further that findings of fact and orders of disposition made pursuant to the provisional hearing will become final at the final hearing unless the party served by publication appears at the final hearing, and (iv) otherwise conforms to section 22; and
    3. the child is personally before the court at the provisional hearing.

b. All provisions of this Act applicable to a hearing on a petition, to orders of disposition, and to other proceedings dependent thereon shall apply under this section, but findings of fact and orders of disposition have only interlocutory effect pending the final hearing on the petition. The rights and duties of the party served by publication are not affected except as provided in subsection (c).
c. If the party served by publication fails to appear at the final hearing on the petition the findings of fact and interlocutory orders made become final without further evidence and are governed by this Act as if made at the final hearing. If the party appears at the final hearing the findings and orders shall be vacated and disregarded and the hearing shall proceed upon the allegations of the petition without regard to this section.

Section 26. *[Right to Counsel.]*

a. Except as otherwise provided under this Act a party is entitled to representation by legal counsel at all stages of any proceedings under this Act and if as a needy person he is unable to employ counsel, to have the court provide counsel for him. If a party appears without the counsel the court shall ascertain whether he knows of his right thereto and to be provided with counsel by the court if he is a needy person. The court may continue the proceeding to enable a party to obtain counsel and shall provide counsel for an unrepresented needy person upon his request. Counsel must be provided for a child not represented by his parent, guardian, or custodian. If the interests of 2 or more parties conflict, separate counsel shall be provided for each of them.
b. A needy person is one who at the time of requesting counsel is unable without undue financial hardship to provide for full payment of legal counsel and all other necessary expenses for representation.

Section 27. *[Other Basic Rights.]*

a. A party is entitled to the opportunity to introduce evidence and otherwise be heard in his own behalf and to cross-examine adverse witnesses.
b. A child charged with a delinquent act need not be a witness against or otherwise incriminate himself. An extrajudicial statement, if obtained in the course of violation of this Act or which would be constitutionally inadmissible in a criminal proceeding, shall not be used-against him. Evidence illegally seized or obtained shall not be received over objection to establish the allegations made against him. A confession validly made by the child out of court is insufficient to support an adjudication of delinquency unless it is corroborated in whole or in part by other evidence.

Section 28. *[Investigation and Report.]*

a. If the allegations of a petition are admitted by a party or notice of a hearing under section 34 has been given the court, prior to the hearing on need for treatment or rehabilitation and disposition, may direct that a social study and report in writing to the court be made by the [probation officer] of the court, [Commissioner of the Court or other like officer] or other person designated by the court, concerning the child, his family, his environment, and other matters relevant to disposition of the case. If the allegations of the petition are not admitted and notice of a hearing under section 34 has not been given the court shall not direct the making of the study and report until after the court has heard the petition upon notice of hearing given pursuant to this Act and the court has found that the child committed a delinquent act or is an unruly or deprived child.

b. During the pendency of any proceeding the court may order the child to be examined at a suitable place by a physician or psychologist and may also order medical or surgical treatment of a child who is suffering from a serious physical condition or illness which in the opinion of a [licensed physician] requires prompt treatment, even if the parent, guardian, or other custodian has not been given notice of a hearing, is not available, or without good cause informs the court of his refusal to consent to the treatment.

Section 29. *[Hearing—Findings—Dismissal.]*

a. After hearing the evidence on the petition the court shall make and file its findings as to whether the child is a deprived child, or if the petition alleges that the child is delinquent or unruly, whether the acts ascribed to the child were committed by him. If the court finds that the child is not a deprived child or that the allegations of delinquency or unruly conduct have not been established it shall dismiss the petition and order the child discharged from any detention or other restriction theretofore ordered in the proceeding.

b. If the court finds on proof beyond a reasonable doubt that the child committed the acts by reason of which he is alleged to be delinquent or unruly it shall proceed immediately or at a postponed hearing to hear evidence as to whether the child is in need of treatment or rehabilitation and to make and file its findings thereon. In the absence of evidence to the contrary evidence of the commission of acts which constitute a felony is sufficient to sustain a finding that the child is in need of treatment or rehabilitation. If the court finds that the child is not in need of treatment or rehabilitation it shall dismiss the proceeding and discharge the child from any detention or other restriction theretofore ordered.

c. If the court finds from clear and convincing evidence that the child is deprived or that he is in need of treatment or rehabilitation as a delinquent or unruly child, the court shall proceed immediately or at a postponed hearing to make a proper disposition of the case.

d. In hearings under subsections (b) and (c) all evidence helpful in determining the questions presented, including oral and written reports, may be received by the court and relied upon to the extent of its probative value even though not otherwise competent in the hearing on the petition. The parties or their counsel shall be afforded an opportunity to examine and controvert written reports so received and to cross-examine individuals making the reports. Sources of confidential information need not be disclosed.

e. On its motion or that of a party the court may continue the hearings under this section for a reasonable period to receive reports and other evidence bearing on the disposition or the need for treatment or rehabilitation. In this event the court shall make an appropriate order for detention of the child or his release from detention subject to supervision of the court during the period of the continuance. In scheduling investigations and hearings the court shall give priority to proceedings in which a child is in detention or has otherwise been removed from his home before an order of disposition has been made.

Section 30. *[Disposition of Deprived Child.]*

a. If the child is found to be a deprived child the court may make any of the following orders of disposition best suited to the protection and physical, mental, and moral welfare of the child:
   1. permit the child to remain with his parents, guardian, or other custodian, subject to conditions and limitations as the court prescribes, including supervision as directed by the court for the protection of the child;
   2. subject to conditions and limitations as the court prescribes transfer temporary legal custody to any of the following:
      i. any individual who, after study by the probation officer or other person or agency designated by the court, is found by the court to be qualified to receive and care for the child;
      ii. an agency or other private organization licensed or otherwise authorized by law to receive and provide care for the child; or
      iii. the Child Welfare Department of the [county] [state,] [or other public agency authorized by law to receive and provide care for the child;]
      iv. an individual in another state with or without supervision by an appropriate officer under section 40; or
   3. without making any of the foregoing orders transfer custody of the child to the juvenile court of another state if authorized by and in accordance with section 39 if the child is or is about to become a resident of that state.

b. Unless a child found to be deprived is found also to be delinquent he shall not be committed to or confined in an institution or other facility designed or operated for the benefit of delinquent children.

Section 31. *[Disposition of Delinquent Child.]* If the child is found to be a delinquent child the court may make any of the following orders of disposition best suited to his treatment, rehabilitation, and welfare:

1. any order authorized by section 30 for the disposition of a deprived child;
2. placing the child on probation under the supervision of the probation officer of the court or the court of another state as provided in section 41, or [the Child Welfare Department operating within the county,] under conditions and limitations the court prescribes;
3. placing the child in an institution, camp, or other facility for delinquent children operated under the direction of the court [or other local public authority;] or
4. committing the child to [designate the state department to which commitments of delinquent children are made or, if there is no department, the appropriate state institution for delinquent children].

Section 32. *[Disposition of Unruly Child.]* If the child is found to be unruly the court may make any disposition authorized for a delinquent child except commitment to [the state department or state institution to which commitment of delinquent children may be made]. [If after making the disposition the court finds upon a further hearing that the child is not amenable to treatment or rehabilitation under the disposition made it may make a disposition otherwise authorized by section 31.]

Section 33. *[Order of Adjudication—Non-Criminal.]*

a. An order of disposition or other adjudication in a proceeding under this Act is not a conviction of crime and does not impose any civil disability ordinarily resulting from a conviction or operate to disqualify the child in any civil service application or appointment. A child shall not be committed or transferred to a penal institution or other facility used primarily for the execution of sentences of persons convicted of a crime.
b. The disposition of a child and evidence adduced in a hearing in juvenile court may not be used against him in any proceeding in any court other than a juvenile court, whether before or after reaching majority, except in dispositional proceedings after conviction of a felony for the purposes of a pre-sentence investigation and report.

Section 34. *[Transfer to Other Courts.]*

a. After a petition has been filed alleging delinquency based on conduct which is designated a crime or public offense under the laws, including local ordinances, [or resolutions] of this state, the court before hearing the petition on its merits may transfer the offense for prosecution to the appropriate court having jurisdiction of the offense if:
    1. the child was 16 or more years of age at the time of the alleged conduct;
    2. a hearing on whether the transfer should be made is held in conformity with sections 24, 26, and 27;
    3. notice in writing of the time, place, and purpose of the hearing is given to the child and his parents, guardian, or other custodian at least 3 days before the hearing.
    4. the court finds that there are reasonable grounds to believe that
        i. the child committed the delinquent act alleged;
        ii. the child is not amenable to treatment or rehabilitation as a juvenile through available facilities;
        iii. the child is not committable to an institution for the mentally retarded or mentally ill; and
        iv. the interests of the community require that the child be placed under legal restraint or discipline.
b. The transfer terminates the jurisdiction of the juvenile court over the child with respect to the delinquent acts alleged in the petition.
c. No child, either before or after reaching 18 years of age, shall be prosecuted for an offense previously committed unless the case has been transferred as provided in this section.
d. Statements made by the child after being taken into custody and prior to the service of notice under subsection (a) or at the hearing under this section are not admissible against him over objection in the criminal proceedings following the transfer.
e. If the case is not transferred the judge who conducted the hearing shall not over objection of an interested party preside at the hearing on the petition. If the case is

transferred to a court of which the judge who conducted the hearing is also a judge he likewise is disqualified from presiding in the prosecution.

Section 35. *[Disposition of Mentally Ill or Mentally Retarded Child.]*

a. If, at a dispositional hearing of a child found to be a delinquent or unruly child or at a hearing to transfer a child to another court under section 34, the evidence indicates that the child may be suffering from mental retardation or mental illness the court before making a disposition shall commit the child for a period not exceeding 60 days to an appropriate institution, agency, or individual for study and report on the child's mental condition.
b. If it appears from the study and report that the child is committable under the laws of this state as a mentally retarded or mentally ill child the court shall order the child detained and direct that within 10 days after the order is made the appropriate authority initiate proceedings for the child's commitment.
c. If it does not appear, or proceedings are not promptly initiated, or the child is found not to be committable, the court shall proceed to the disposition or transfer of the child as otherwise provided by this Act.

Section 36. *[Limitations of Time on Orders of Disposition.]*

a. An order terminating parental rights is without limit as to duration.
b. An order of disposition committing a delinquent or unruly child to the [State Department of Corrections of designated institution for delinquent children,] continues in force for 2 years or until the child is sooner discharged by the [department or institution to which the child was committed]. The court which made the order may extend its duration for an additional 2 years, subject to like discharge, if:
    1. a hearing is held upon motion of the [department or institution to which the child was committed] prior to the expiration of the order;
    2. reasonable notice of the hearing and an opportunity to be heard is given to the child and the parent, guardian, or other custodian; and
    3. the court finds that the extension is necessary for the treatment or rehabilitation of the child.
c. Any other order of disposition continues in force for not more than 2 years. The court may sooner terminate its order or extend its duration for further periods. An order of extension may be made if:
    1. a hearing is held prior to the expiration of the order upon motion of a party or on the court's own motion;
    2. reasonable notice of the hearing and opportunity to be heard are given to the parties affected;
    3. the court finds that the extension is necessary to accomplish the purposes of the order extended; and
    4. the extension does not exceed 2 years from the expiration of prior order.
d. Except as provided in subsection (b) the court may terminate an order of disposition or extension prior to its expiration, on or without an application of a party, if it appears to the court that the purposes of the order have been accomplished. If a party may be adversely affected by the order of termination the order may be made only after reasonable notice and opportunity to be heard have been given to him.

e. Except as provided in subsection (a) when the child reaches 21 years of age all orders affecting him then in force terminate and he is discharged from further obligation or control.

Section 37. *[Modification or Vacation of Orders.]*

a. An order of the court shall be set aside if (1) it appears that it was obtained by fraud or mistake sufficient therefor in a civil action, or (2) the court lacked jurisdiction over a necessary party or of the subject matter, or (3) newly discovered evidence so requires.
b. Except an order committing a delinquent child to the [State Department of Corrections or an institution for delinquent children,] an order terminating parental rights, or an order of dismissal, an order of the court may also be changed, modified, or vacated on the ground that changed circumstances so require in the best interest of the child. An order granting probation to a child found to be delinquent or unruly may be revoked on the ground that the conditions of probation have not been observed.
c. Any party to the proceeding, the probation officer or other person having supervision or legal custody of or an interest in the child may petition the court for the relief provided in this section. The petition shall set forth in concise language the grounds upon which the relief is requested.
d. After the petition is filed the court shall fix a time for hearing and cause notice to be served (as a summons is served under section 23) on the parties to the proceeding or affected by the relief sought. After the hearing, which may be informal, the court shall deny or grant relief as the evidence warrants.

Section 38. *[Rights and Duties of Legal Custodian.]* A custodian to whom legal custody has been given by the court under this Act has the right to the physical custody of the child, the right to determine the nature of the care and treatment of the child, including ordinary medical care and the right and duty to provide for the care, protection, training, and education, and the physical, mental, and moral welfare of the child, subject to the conditions and limitations of the order and to the remaining rights and duties of the child's parents or guardian.

Section 39. *[Disposition of Non-Resident Child.]*

a. If the court finds that child who has been adjudged to have committed a delinquent act or to be unruly or deprived is or is about to become a resident of another state which has adopted the Uniform Juvenile Court Act, or a substantially similar Act which includes provisions corresponding to sections 39 and 40, the court may defer hearing on need for treatment or rehabilitation and disposition and request by any appropriate means the juvenile court of the [county] of the child's residence or prospective residence to accept jurisdiction of the child.
b. If the child becomes a resident of another state while on probation or under protective supervision under order of a juvenile court of this State, the court may request the juvenile court of the [county] of the state in which the child has become a resident to accept jurisdiction of the child and to continue his probation or protective supervision.
c. Upon receipt and filing of an acceptance the court of this State shall transfer custody of the child to the accepting court and cause him to be delivered to the person designated

by that court to receive his custody. It also shall provide that court with certified copies of the order adjudging the child to be a delinquent, unruly, or deprived child, of the order of transfer, and if the child is on probation or under protective supervision under order of the court, of the order of disposition. It also shall provide that court with a statement of the facts found by the court of this State and any recommendations and other information it considers of assistance to the accepting court in making a disposition of the case or in supervising the child on probation or otherwise.

d. Upon compliance with subsection (c) the jurisdiction of the court of this State over the child is terminated.

Section 40. *[Disposition of Resident Child Received from Another State.]*

a. If a juvenile court of another state which has adopted the Uniform Juvenile Court Act, or a substantially similar Act which includes provisions corresponding to sections 39 and 40, requests a juvenile court of this State to accept jurisdiction of a child found by the requesting court to have committed a delinquent act or to be an unruly or deprived child, and the court of this State finds, after investigation that the child is, or is about to become, a resident of the [county] in which the court presides, it shall promptly and not later than 14 days after receiving the request issue its acceptance in writing to the requesting court and direct its probation officer or other person designated by it to take physical custody of the child from the requesting court and bring him before the court of this State or make other appropriate provisions for his appearance before the court.
b. Upon the filing of certified copies of the orders of the requesting court (1) determining that the child committed a delinquent act or is an unruly or deprived child, and (2) committing the child to the jurisdiction of the juvenile court of this State, the court of this State shall immediately fix a time for a hearing on the need for treatment or rehabilitation and disposition of the child or on the continuance of any probation or protective supervision.
c. The hearing and notice thereof and all subsequent proceedings are governed by this Act. The court may make any order of disposition permitted by the facts and this Act. The orders of the requesting court are conclusive that the child committed the delinquent act or is an unruly or deprived child and of the facts found by the court in making the orders, subject only to section 37. If the requesting court has made an order placing the child on probation or under protective supervision, a like order shall be entered by the court of this State. The court may modify or vacate the order in accordance with section 37.

Section 41. *[Ordering Out-of-State Supervision.]*

a. Subject to the provisions of this Act governing dispositions and to the extent that funds of the [county] are available the court may place a child in the custody of a suitable person in another state. On obtaining the written consent of a juvenile court of another state which has adopted the Uniform Juvenile Court Act or a substantially similar Act which includes provisions corresponding to sections 41 and 42 the court of this State may order that the child be placed under the supervision of a probation officer or other appropriate official designated by the accepting court. One certified copy of the order shall be sent to the accepting court and another filed with the clerk of the [Board of County Commissioners] of the [county] of the requesting court of this State.

b. The reasonable cost of the supervision including the expenses of necessary travel shall be borne by the [county] of the requesting court of this State. Upon receiving a certified statement signed by the judge of the accepting court of the cost incurred by the supervision the court of this State shall certify if it so appears that the sum so stated was reasonably incurred and file it with [the appropriate officials] of the [county] [state] for payment. The [appropriate officials] shall thereupon issue a warrant for the sum stated payable to the [appropriate officials] of the [county] of the accepting court.

Section 42. *[Supervision Under Out-of-State Order.]*

a. Upon receiving a request of a juvenile court of another state which has adopted the Uniform Juvenile Court Act, or a substantially similar act which includes provisions corresponding to sections 41 and 42 to provide supervision of a child under the jurisdiction of that court, a court of this State may issue its written acceptance to the requesting court and designate its probation or other appropriate officer who is to provide supervision, stating the probable cost per day therefor.
b. Upon the receipt and filing of a certified copy of the order of the requesting court placing the child under the supervision of the officer so designated the officer shall arrange for the reception of the child from the requesting court, provide supervision pursuant to the order and this Act, and report thereon from time to time together with any recommendations he may have to the requesting court.
c. The court in this state from time to time shall certify to the requesting court the cost of supervision that has been incurred and request payment therefor from the appropriate officials of the [county] of the requesting court to the appropriate officials of the [county] of the accepting court.
d. The court of this State at any time may terminate supervision by notifying the requesting court. In that case, or if the supervision is terminated by the requesting court, the probation officer supervising the child shall return the child to a representative of the requesting court authorized to receive him.

Section 43. *[Powers of Out-of-State Probation Officers.]* If a child has been placed on probation or protective supervision by a juvenile court of another state which has adopted the Uniform Juvenile Court Act or a substantially similar act which includes provisions corresponding to this section, and the child is in this State with or without the permission of that court, the probation officer of that court or other person designated by that court to supervise or take custody of the child has all the powers and privileges in this State with respect to the child as given by this Act to like officers or persons of this State including the right of visitation, counseling, control, and direction, taking into custody, and returning to that state.

Section 44. *[Juvenile Traffic Offenses.]*

a. *Definition.* Except as provided in subsection (b), a juvenile traffic offense consists of a violation by a child of:
    1. a law or local ordinance [or resolution] governing the operation of a moving motor vehicle upon the streets or highways of this State, or the waterways within or adjoining this State; or

2. any other motor vehicle traffic law or local ordinance [or resolution] of this State if the child is taken into custody and detained for the violation or is transferred to the juvenile court by the court hearing the charge.

b. A juvenile traffic offense is not an act of delinquency unless the case is transferred to the delinquency calendar as provided in subsection (g).

c. *Exceptions.* A juvenile traffic offense does not include a violation of: [Set forth the sections of state statutes violations of which are not to be included as traffic offenses, such as the so-called negligent homicide statute sometimes appearing in traffic codes, driving while intoxicated, driving without, or during suspension of, a driver's license, and the like].

d. *Procedure.* The [summons] [notice to appear] [or other designation of a ticket] accusing a child of committing a juvenile traffic offense constitutes the commencement of the proceedings in the juvenile court of the [county] in which the alleged violation occurred and serves in place of a summons and petition under this Act. These cases shall be filed and heard separately from other proceedings of the court. If the child is taken into custody on the charge, sections 14 to 17 apply. If the child is, or after commencement of the proceedings becomes, a resident of another [county] of this State, section 12 applies.

e. *Hearing.* The court shall fix a time for hearing and give reasonable notice thereof to the child, and if their address is known to the parents, guardian, or custodian. If the accusation made in the [summons] [notice to appear] [or other designation of a ticket] is denied an informal hearing shall be held at which the parties have the right to subpoena witnesses, present evidence, cross-examine witnesses, and appear by counsel. The hearing is open to the public.

f. *Disposition.* If the court finds on the admission of the child or upon the evidence that he committed the offense charged it may make one or more of the following orders:
   1. reprimand or counsel with the child and his parents;
   2. [suspend] [recommend to the [appropriate official having the authority] that he suspend] the child's privilege to drive under stated conditions and limitations for a period not to exceed that authorized for a like suspension of an adult's license for a like offense;
   3. require the child to attend a traffic school conducted by public authority for a reasonable period of time; or
   4. order the child to remit to the general fund of the [state] [county] [city] [municipality] a sum not exceeding the lesser of $50 or the maximum applicable to an adult for a like offense.

g. In lieu of the preceding orders, if the evidence indicates the advisability thereof, the court may transfer the case to the delinquency calendar of the court and direct the filing and service of a summons and petition in accordance with this Act. The judge so ordering is disqualified upon objection from acting further in the case prior to an adjudication that the child committed a delinquent act.]

Section 45. *[Traffic Referee.]*

a. The court may appoint one or more traffic referees who shall serve at the pleasure of the court. The referee's salary shall be fixed by the court [subject to the approval of the [Board of County Commissioners]].

b. The court may direct that any case or class of cases arising under section 44 shall be heard in the first instance by a traffic referee who shall conduct the hearing in accordance with section 44. Upon the conclusion of the hearing the traffic referee shall transmit written findings of fact and recommendations for disposition to the judge with a copy thereof to the child and other parties to the proceedings.
c. Within 3 days after receiving the copy the child may file a request for a rehearing before the judge of the court who shall thereupon rehear the case at a time fixed by him. Otherwise, the judge may confirm the findings and recommendations for disposition which then become the findings and order of disposition of the court.]

Section 46. *[Juvenile Traffic Offenses—Suspension of Jurisdiction.]*

a. The [Supreme] court, by order filed in the office of the [ ] of the [county,] may suspend the jurisdiction of the juvenile courts over juvenile traffic offenses or one or more classes effective and offenses committed thereafter shall be tried by the appropriate court in accordance with law without regard to this Act. The child shall not be detained or imprisoned in a jail or other facility for the detention of adults unless the facility conforms to subsection (a) of section 16.
b. The [Supreme] court at any time may restore the jurisdiction of the juvenile courts over these offenses or any portion thereof by like filing of its order of restoration. Offenses committed thereafter are governed by this Act.]

Section 47. *[Termination of Parental Rights.]*

a. The court by order may terminate the parental rights of a parent with respect to his child if:
   1. the parent had abandoned the child;
   2. the child is a deprived child and the court finds that the conditions and causes of the deprivation are likely to continue or will not be remedied and that by reason thereof the child is suffering or will probably suffer serious physical, mental, moral, or emotional harm; or
   3. the written consent of the parent acknowledged before the court has been given.
b. If the court does not make an order of termination of parental rights it may grant an order under section 30 if the court finds from clear and convincing evidence that the child is a deprived child.

Section 48. *[Proceeding for Termination of Parental Rights.]*

a. The petition shall comply with section 21 and state clearly that an order for termination of parental rights is requested and that the effect thereof will be as stated in the first sentence of Section 49.
b. If the paternity of a child born out of wedlock has been established prior to the filing of the petition, the father shall be served with summons as provided by this Act. He has the right to be heard unless he has relinquished all parental rights with reference to the child. The putative father of the child whose paternity has not been established, upon proof of his paternity of the child, may appear in the proceedings and be heard. He is not entitled to notice of hearing on the petition unless he has custody of the child.

Section 49. *[Effect of Order Terminating Parental Rights.]* An order terminating the parental rights of a parent terminates all his rights and obligations with respect to the child and of the child to him arising from the parental relationship. The parent is not thereafter entitled to notice of proceedings for the adoption of the child by another nor has he any right to object to the adoption or otherwise participate in the proceedings.

Section 50. *[Commitment to Agency.]*

a. If, upon entering an order terminating the parental rights of a parent, there is no parent having parental rights, the court shall commit the child to the custody of the [State County Child Welfare Department] or a licensed child-placing agency, willing to accept custody for the purpose of placing the child for adoption, or in the absence thereof in a foster home or take other suitable measures for the care and welfare of the child. The custodian has authority to consent to the adoption of the child, his marriage, his enlistment in the armed forces of the United States, and surgical and other medical treatment for the child.
b. If the child is not adopted within 2 years after the date of the order and a general guardian of the child has not been appointed by the [————] court, the child shall be returned to the court for entry of further orders for the care, custody, and control of the child.

Section 51. *[Guardian ad litem.]* The court at any stage of a proceeding under this Act, on application of a party or on its own motion, shall appoint a guardian ad litem for a child who is a party to the proceeding if he has no parent, guardian, or custodian appearing on his behalf or their interests conflict with his or in any other case in which the interests of the child require a guardian. A party to the proceeding or his employee or representative shall not be appointed.

Section 52. *[Costs and Expenses for Care of Child.]*

a. The following expenses shall be a charge upon the funds of the county upon certification thereof by the court:
    1. the cost of medical and other examinations and treatment of a child ordered by the court;
    2. the cost of care and support of a child committed by the court to the legal custody of a public agency other than an institution for delinquent children, or to a private agency or individual other than a parent;
    3. reasonable compensation for services and related expenses of counsel appointed by the court for a party;
    4. reasonable compensation for a guardian ad litem;
    5. the expense of service of summons, notices, subpoenas, travel expense of witnesses, transportation of the child, and other like expenses incurred in the proceedings under this Act.
b. If, after due notice to the parents or other persons legally obligated to care for and support the child, and after affording them an opportunity to be heard, the court finds

that they are financially able to pay all or part of the costs and expenses stated in paragraphs (1), (2), (3), and (4) of subsection (a), the court may order them to pay the same and prescribe the manner of payment. Unless otherwise ordered payment shall be made to the clerk of the juvenile court for remittance to the person to whom compensation is due, or if the costs and expenses have been paid by the [county] to the [appropriate officer] of the [county].

Section 53. *[Protective Order.]* On application of a party or on the court's own motion the court may make an order restraining or otherwise controlling the conduct of a person if:

1. an order of disposition of a delinquent, unruly, or deprived child has been or is about to be made in a proceeding under this Act;
2. the court finds that the conduct (1) is or may be detrimental or harmful to the child and (2) will tend to defeat the execution of the order of disposition; and
3. due notice of the application or motion and the grounds therefor and an opportunity to be heard thereon have been given to the person against whom the order is directed.

Section 54. *[Inspection of Court Files and Records.]* [Except in cases arising under section 44] all files and records of the court in a proceeding under this Act are open to inspection only by:

1. the judge, officers, and professional staff of the court;
2. the parties to the proceeding and their counsel and representatives;
3. a public or private agency or institution providing supervision or having custody of the child under order of the court;
4. a court and its probation and other officials or professional staff and the attorney for the defendant for use in preparing a pre-sentence report in a criminal case in which the defendant is convicted and who prior thereto had been a party to the proceeding in juvenile court;
5. with leave of court any other person or agency or institution having a legitimate interest in the proceeding or in the work of the court.

Section 55. *[Law Enforcement Records.]* Law enforcement records and files concerning a child shall be kept separate from the records and files of arrests of adults. Unless a charge of delinquency is transferred for criminal prosecution under section 34, the interest of national security requires, or the court otherwise orders in the interest of the child, the records and files shall not be open to public inspection or their contents disclosed to the public; but inspection of the records and files is permitted by:

1. a juvenile court having the child before it in any proceeding;
2. counsel for a party to the proceeding;
3. the officers of public institutions or agencies to whom the child is committed;
4. law enforcement officers of other jurisdictions when necessary for the discharge of their official duties; and

5. a court in which he is convicted of a criminal offense for the purpose of a pre-sentence report or other dispositional proceeding, or by officials of penal institutions and other penal facilities to which he is committed, or by a [parole board] in considering his parole or discharge or in exercising supervision over him.

Section 56. *[Children's Fingerprints, Photographs.]*

a. No child under 14 years of age shall be fingerprinted in the investigation of a crime except as provided in this section. Fingerprints of a child 14 or more years of age who is referred to the court may be taken and filed by law enforcement officers in investigating the commission of the following crimes: [specifically such crimes as murder, non-negligent manslaughter, forcible rape, robbery, aggravated assault, burglary, housebreaking, purse snatching, and automobile theft].
b. Fingerprint files of children shall be kept separate from those of adults. Copies of fingerprints known to be those of a child shall be maintained on a local basis only and not sent to a central state or federal depository unless in the interest of national security.
c. Fingerprint files of children may be inspected by law enforcement officers when necessary for the discharge of their official duties. Other inspections may be authorized by the court in individual cases upon a showing that it is necessary in the public interest.
d. Fingerprints of a child shall be removed from the file and destroyed if:
    1. a petition alleging delinquency is not filed, or the proceedings are dismissed after either a petition if filed or the case is transferred to the juvenile court as provided in section 9, or the child is adjudicated not to be a delinquent child; or
    2. the child reaches 21 years of age and there is no record that he committed a criminal offense after reaching 16 years of age.
e. If latent fingerprints are found during the investigation of an offense and a law enforcement officer has probable cause to believe that they are those of a particular child he may fingerprint the child regardless of age or offense for purposes of immediate comparison with the latent fingerprints. If the comparison is negative the fingerprint card and other copies of the fingerprints taken shall be immediately destroyed. If the comparison is positive and the child is referred to the court, the fingerprint card and other copies of the fingerprints taken shall be delivered to the court for disposition. If the child is not referred to the court, the fingerprints shall be immediately destroyed.
f. Without the consent of the judge, a child shall not be photographed after he is taken into custody unless the case is transferred to another court for prosecution.

Section 57. *[Sealing of Records.]*

a. On application of a person who has been adjudicated delinquent or unruly or on the court's own motion, and after a hearing, the court shall order the sealing of the files and records in the proceeding, including those specified in sections 55 and 56, if the court finds:
    1. 2 years have elapsed since the final discharge of the person;

2. since the final discharge he has not been convicted of a felony, or of a misdemeanor involving moral turpitude, or adjudicated a delinquent or unruly child and no proceeding is pending seeking conviction or adjudication; and
3. he has been rehabilitated.

b. Reasonable notice of the hearing shall be given to:
 1. the [prosecuting attorney of the county];
 2. the authority granting the discharge if the final discharge was from an institution or from parole; and
 3. the law enforcement officers or department having custody of the files and records if the files and records specified in sections 55 and 56 are included in the application or motion.
c. Upon the entry of the order the proceeding shall be treated as if it never occurred. All index references shall be deleted and the person, the court, and law enforcement officers and departments shall properly reply that no record exists with respect to the person upon inquiry in any matter. Copies of the order shall be sent to each agency or official therein named. Inspection of the sealed files and records thereafter may be permitted by an order of the court upon petition by the person who is the subject of the records and only by those persons named in the order.

Section 58. *[Contempt Powers.]* The court may punish a person for contempt of court for disobeying an order of the court or for obstructing or interfering with the proceedings of the court or the enforcement of its orders subject to the laws relating to the procedures therefor and the limitations thereon.]

Section 59. *[Appeals.]*

a. An aggrieved party, including the state or a subdivision of the state, may appeal from a final order, judgment, or decree of the juvenile court to the [Supreme Court] [court of general jurisdiction] by filing written notice of appeal within 30 days after entry of the order, judgment, or decree, or within any further time the [Supreme Court] [court of general jurisdiction] grants, after entry of the order, judgment, or decree. [The appeal shall be heard by the [court of general jurisdiction] upon the files, records, and minutes or transcript of the evidence of the juvenile court, giving appreciable weight to the findings of the juvenile court.] The name of the child shall not appear on the record on appeal.
b. The appeal does not stay the order, judgment, or decree appealed from, but the [Supreme Court] [court of general jurisdiction] may otherwise order on application and hearing consistent with this Act if suitable provision is made for the care and custody of the child. If the order, judgment or decree appealed from grants the custody of the child to, or withholds it from, one or more of the parties to the appeal it shall be heard at the earliest practicable time.

Section 60. *[Rules of Court.]* The [Supreme] Court of this State may adopt rules of procedure not in conflict with this Act governing proceedings under it.

Section 61. *[Uniformity of Interpretation.]* This Act shall be so interpreted and construed as to effectuate its general purpose to make uniform the law of those states which enact it.

Section 62. *[Short Title.]* This Act may be cited as the Uniform Juvenile Court Act.

Section 63. *[Repeal.]* The following Acts and parts of Acts are repealed:
1.
2.
3.

Section 64. *[Time of Taking Effect.]* This Act shall take effect. . . .

References

Abadinsky, H., & Winfree, L. T., Jr. (1992). *Crime and justice.* 2nd ed. Chicago: Nelson-Hall.

Ackerman, W. V. (1998). Socioeconomic correlates of increasing crime rates in smaller communities. *Professional Geographer, 50* (3), 372–387.

Acoca, L. (1998). Outside/inside: The violation of American girls at home, on the streets, and in the juvenile justice system. *Crime & Delinquency, 44* (4), 561–589.

Adams, P. (1994, March 13). Child abuse, delinquency prominent in judge's world. *Peoria Journal Star,* p. 1A.

Adler, A. (1931). *What life should mean to you.* London: Allen & Unwin.

Agnew, R. (1985). A revised strain theory of delinquency. *Social Forces, 64,* 151–167.

Akers, R. L. (1964, January). Socioeconomic status and delinquent behavior: A retest. *Journal of Research in Crime and Delinquency,* 10, 38–46.

———. (1985). *Deviant behavior: A social learning approach.* 3rd ed. Belmont, CA: Wadsworth.

———. (1992). Linking sociology and its specialties: The case of criminology. *Social Forces, 71,* 1–16.

———. (1994). *Criminological theories: Introduction and evaluation.* Los Angeles: Roxbury Publishing.

———. (1998). *Social learning and social structure: A general theory of crime and deviance.* Boston: Northeastern University Press.

Alabama Code. (1995).

Alexander, D., & Deering, T. (2000, October 27). Boy charged with arson locked up: A judge orders the detention of a 10-year old accused with three other juveniles in several fires. *Omaha World-Herald,* p. 1.

Alwin, D. F., & Thornton, A. (1984). Family origins and the schooling process: Early versus late influence of parental characteristics. *American Sociological Review, 49,* 784–802.

America under the gun: Assaults in U.S. schools. (1999, April 26). *The New York Times.* http://www.nytimes.com/library/national/guns-schools.html.

American Bar Association. (1977). *Standards relating to counsel for private parties.* Cambridge, MA: Ballinger.

American Bar Association & National Bar Association. (2001, May 1). *Justice by gender.* Washington, D.C.: American Bar Association.

Anderson, E. (1990). *Streetwise.* Chicago: University of Chicago Press.

Aniskievicz, R., & Wysong, E. (1990). Evaluating DARE: Drug education and the multiple meanings of success. *Policy Studies Review, 9,* 727–747.

Ards, S., & Harrell, A. (1993). Reporting of child maltreatment: A secondary analysis of the National Incidence Surveys. *Child Abuse & Neglect, 17* (3), 337–344.

Ariessohn, R. M. (1981, November). Recidivism revisited. *The Juvenile Family Court Journal, 65.*

Ariessohn, R. M., & Gonion, G. (1973, May). Reducing the juvenile detention rate. *Juvenile Justice, 31.*

Arizona Revised Statutes Annotated. 1999.

Arkansas Code Annotated. (1999).

Associated Press. (2001, August 28). Man freed in Illinois murder retrial arrested in California racial attack.

Atkins, B., & Pogrebin, M. (1978). *The invisible justice system: Discretion and the law.* Cincinnati: Anderson.

Babicky, T. (1993, July). *Gangs fact sheets: A reference guide.* Springfield, IL: Illinois Department of Corrections.

———. (1993, September). *Gangs and gang activity.* Springfield, IL: Illinois Department of Corrections.

Barlow, H. D. (2000). *Criminal justice in America.* Upper Saddle River, NJ: Prentice Hall.

Bartollas, C. (1993). *Juvenile delinquency.* 3rd ed. New York: MacMillan.

Battistich, V., & Hom, A. (1997, December). The relationship between students' sense of their school as a community and their involvement in problem behaviors. *American Journal of Public Health, 87,* 1997–2001.

Bazemore, G., & Day, S. E. (no date). *Restoring the balance: Juvenile and community justice, 3* (1), Washington, D.C.: U.S. Department of Justice, Office of Juvenile Justice and Delinquency Prevention.

Bazemore, G., & Feder, L. (1997). Rehabilitation in the new juvenile court: Do judges support the treatment ethics? *American Journal of Criminal Justice, 21,* 181–212.

Bazemore, G., & Senjo, S. (1997). Police encounters with juveniles revisited: An exploratory study of themes and styles in community policing. *Policing: An International Journal of Police Strategy and Management, 20,* (1) 60–82.

Bazemore, G., & Washington, C. (1995, Spring). Charting the future of the juvenile justice system: Reinventing mission and management. *Spectrum, 68,* 51–66.

Becker, H. S. (1963). *The outsiders.* New York: Free Press.

Beirne, P., & Quinney, R. (1982). *Marxism and the law.* New York: John Wiley and Sons.

Belknap, J., Morash, M., & Trojanowicz, R. (1987). Implementing of community policing model for work with juveniles. *Criminal Justice and Behavior, 14* (2), 211–245.

Bell, D. J., & Bell, S. (1991). The victim-offender relationship as a determinant factor in police dispositions of family violence incidents: A replication study. *Policing and Society, 1* (3) 225–234.

Bernard, T. J. (1992). *The cycle of juvenile justice.* New York: Oxford University Press.

Bilchik, S. (1998). *Juvenile mentoring program: 1998 report to Congress.* Washington, D.C: U.S Department of Justice.

———. (1998a). A juvenile justice system for the 21st century. *Crime & Delinquency, 44* (1), 89–101. Washington, D.C.: U.S. Department of Justice.

———. (1999). *Report to Congress on juvenile violence research.* Washington, D.C.: U.S. Department of Justice.

———. (1999a, December). Juvenile justice: A century of change. *Juvenile Justice Bulletin.* Washington, D.C.: U.S. Department of Justice.

———. (1999b, August). *OJJDP research: Making a difference for juveniles.* Washington, D.C.: U.S. Department of Justice.

Bishop, S. J., Murphy, J. M., & Hicks, R. (2000). What progress has been made in meeting the needs of seriously maltreated children? The course of 200 cases through the Boston Juvenile Court. *Child Abuse & Neglect, 24* (5), 599–610.

Bjerregaard, B., & Smith, C. (1993). Gender differences in gang participation, delinquency and substance abuse. *Journal of Quantitative Criminology, 4,* 329–355.

Black, D. J., & Reiss, A. J. (1970). Police control of juveniles. *American Sociological Review, 1,* 63–77.

Blackstone, W. (1803). *Commentaries on the laws of England.* 12th ed., vol. 4. London: Strahan.

Blair, S. L., Blair, M. C. L., & Madamba, A. B. (1999). Racial/ethnic differences in high school students' academic performance: Understanding the interweave of social class and ethnicity in family context. *Journal of Comparative Family Studies, 30* (3), 539–555.

Blankenship, R. L., & Singh, B. K. (1976). Differential labeling of juveniles: A multivariate analysis. *Criminology, 13* (4), 471–490.

Blau, R., & Recktenwald, W. (1990, May 20). Child homicides soar in city and suburbs. *Chicago Tribune,* pp. 1, 16.

Bloch, H., & Neiderhoffer, A. (1958). *The gang: A study in adolescent behavior.* New York: Philosophical Library.

Blumberg, A. S. (1967). *Criminal justice.* Chicago: Quadrangle.

Bohm, R. M. (2001). *A primer on crime and delinquency theory.* 2nd ed. Belmont, CA: Wadsworth.

Bolen, R. M., & Scannapieco, M. (1999). Prevalence of child sexual abuse: A corrective metanalysis. *Social Service Review, 73* (3), 281–313.

Bookin, H., & Horowitz, R. (1983). The end of the youth gang: Fad or fiction? *Criminology, 21* (4), 585–602.

Booth, A., & Osgood, D. W. (1993, February). The influence of testosterone on deviance in adulthood: Assessing and explaining the relationship. *Criminology 31,* 93–117.

Braithwaite, J. (1989). *Crime, shame and reintegration.* New York: Cambridge University Press.

Braun, C. (1976). Teacher expectations: Sociopsychological dynamics. *Review of Educational Research, 46,* 185–213.

Breed v. Jones, 421 U.S. 519, 95 S.Ct. 1779 (1975).

Breen, M. D. (2001). A renewed commitment to juvenile justice. *Police Chief, 68* (3), 47–52.

Bridges, G. S., & Steen, S. (1998). Racial disparities in official assessments of juvenile offenders: Attributional stereotypes as mediating mechanisms. *American Sociological Review, 63* (4), 554–570.

Brown, J., Cohen, P., & Johnson, J. (1998). A longitudinal analysis of risk factors for child maltreatment: Findings of a 17-year prospective study of officially recorded and self-reported child abuse and neglect. *Child Abuse & Neglect, 22* (11), 1065–1078.

Brown, S. E. (1984). Social class, child maltreatment, and delinquent behavior. *Criminology, 22* (2), 259–278.

Brownfield, D. (1990, April/June). Adolescent male status and delinquent behavior. *Sociological Spectrum, 10,* 227–248.

Browning, K., & Loeber, R. (1999, February). Highlights of findings from the Pittsburgh Youth Study. *OJJDP Fact Sheet #95.* Washington, D.C.: U.S. Department of Justice.

Buerger, M. E., Cohn, E. G., & Petrosino, A. J. (2000). Defining the hot spots of crime. In R. W. Glensor, M. E. Corriea, & K. J. Peak (eds.), *Policing communities: Understanding crime and solving problems.* (pp. 138–150). Los Angeles: Roxbury.

Buikhuisen, W., & Jongman, R. W. (1970). A legislative classification of juvenile delinquents. *British Journal of Criminology, 10,* 109–123.

Bumphus, V. W., & Anderson, J. F. (1999). Family structure and race in a sample of criminal offenders. *Journal of Criminal Justice, 27* (4), 309–320.

Burch, J., & Kane, C. (1999, July). Implementing the OJJDP comprehensive gang model. *OJJDP Fact Sheet #112.* Washington, D.C.: U.S. Department of Justice.

Bureau of Justice Statistics. (1995). *Highlights from 20 years of surveying crime: The National Crime Victimization Survey, 1973–92.* Washington, D.C.: U.S. Department of Justice.

Bureau of Justice Statistics. (2000). *Crime and victim statistics.* http://www.ojp.usdoj.gov/bjs.

Bureau of Justice Statistics. (2000, February). *Profile of state prisoners under age 18, 1985–1997.* Washington, D.C.: U.S. Department of Justice.

Burgess, E. W. (1952). The economic factor in juvenile delinquency. *Journal of Criminal Law, 43,* 29–42.

Burgess, R. L., & Akers, R. L. (1968). A differential association-reinforcement theory of criminal behavior. *Social Problems, 14,* 128–147.

Bursik, R. J., & Grasmick, H. G. (1995). The effect of neighborhood dynamics on gang behavior, In M. Klein, C. L. Maxson, & J. Miller (eds). *The modern gang reader* (pp. 114–123). Los Angeles: Roxbury.

Butts, J. A. (1997, January). Necessarily relative: Is juvenile justice speedy enough? *Crime & Delinquency, 43,* 3–23.

Bynum, J. E., & Thompson, W. E. (1992). *Juvenile delinquency.* 2nd ed. Boston: Allyn and Bacon.

———. (1999). *Juvenile delinquency.* 4th ed. Boston: Allyn and Bacon.

Cadzow, S. P., Armstrong, K. L., & Fraser, J. A. (1999). Stressed parents with infants: Reassessing physical abuse risk factors. *Child Abuse & Neglect, 23* (9), 845–853.

California Welfare and Institutional Code, 1998.

Campbell, A. (1991). *The girls in the gang.* 2nd ed. Cambridge, MA: Blackwell.

———. (1995). Female participation in gangs. In M. W. Klein, C. L. Maxson, & J. Miller (eds.) *The modern gang reader* (pp. 70–77). Los Angeles: Roxbury.

———. (1997). Self definition by rejection: The case of gang girls. In G. L. Mays (ed.), *Gangs and gang behavior* (pp. 129–149). Chicago: Nelson-Hall.

Canter, R. (1982). Family correlates of male and female delinquency. *Criminology, 20* (2), 163.

Carelli, R. (1990, June 28). Court backs sparing children in abuse cases. *Peoria Journal Star,* p. A2.

Cauchon, D. (1993, October 11). Studies find drug program not effective. *USA Today,* pp. 1A–2A.

Cavan, R. S. (1969). *Juvenile delinquency: Development, treatment, control.* 2nd ed. Philadelphia: J.B. Lippincott Co.

Center for Restorative Justice and Mediation. (1985). *Principles of restorative justice.* St. Paul, MN: School of Social Work, University of Minnesota.

Center for Restorative Justice and Mediation. (1996a). *Restorative justice: For victims, communities and offenders. What is restorative justice?* St. Paul, MN: School of Social Work, University of Minnesota.

Center for Restorative Justice and Mediation. (1996b). *Restorative justice: For victims, communities, and offenders. What is the community's part in restorative justice?* St. Paul, MN: School of Social Work, University of Minnesota.

Centerwood, B. S. (1992). Television and violence: The scale of the problem and where to go from here. *Journal of the American Medical Association, 267,* 3059–3063.

Chambliss, W. J. (1984). *Criminal law in action.* 2nd ed. New York: John Wiley and Sons.

Chambliss, W. J., & Mandoff, M. (1976). *Whose law, what order?* New York: John Wiley and Sons.

Charton, S. (2001, July 16). Sheriff says making kids shovel manure stinks. *Chicago Sun-Times,* p. 28.

Chesney-Lind, M. (1999). Challenging girls' invisibility in juvenile court. *Annals of the American Academy of Political & Social Science, 564,* 185–202.

Chicago Tribune. (1990, January 14). Editorial: Hope for those lagging test scores. Sec. 5, p. 12.

Children out of school. (1974). Defense Fund of the Washington Research Project. Cambridge: MA.

Children's Bureau, Department of Health, Education, and Welfare. (1969). *Legislative guide for drafting family and juvenile court acts.* Washington, D.C.: U.S. Government Printing Office.

Children's Defense Fund. (2001, August 27). *In America: Facts on youth, violence, & crime.* http://www.childrensdefense.org.

Clark, J. P. & Tifft, L. L. (1966, August). Polygraph and interview validation of self-reported deviant behavior. *American Sociological Review, 4,* 516–523.

Cloward, R. A., & Ohlin, L. E. (1960). *Delinquency and opportunity.* New York: Free Press.

Cohen, A. K. (1955). *Delinquent boys: The culture of the gang.* New York: Free Press.

Cohn, A. W. (1999). Juvenile focus. *Federal Probation, 58* (2), 87–91.

———. (2000). Juvenile focus. *Federal Probation, 64* (1), 73–75.

Colbridge, T. D. (2000). The advent of the computer delinquent. *FBI Law Enforcement Bulletin, 69* (12), 7–13.

Colorado Revised Statutes Annotated. 1999.

Conklin, J. E. (1998). *Criminology.* 6th ed. Boston: Allyn and Bacon.

Connecticut General Statutes Annotated. 1995, 1999.

Consolidated Laws of New York Annotated. 1975.

Coohey, C. (1998). Home alone and other inadequately supervised children. *Child Welfare, 77* (3), 291–310.

Costello, B. J., & Vowell, P. R. (1999). Testing control theory and differential association: A reanalysis of the Richmond Youth Project data. *Criminology, 37* (4), 815–842.

Cothern, L. (2000, November). *Juveniles and the death penalty.* Washington, D.C.: Coordinating Council on Juvenile Justice and Delinquency Prevention. U.S. Department of Justice.

Covington, J. (1984). Insulation from labeling: Deviant defenses in treatment. *Criminology, 22* (4), 619–643.

Cox, S. M. (1975). Review of "Critique of legal order." *Teaching Sociology, 3* (1), 98.

Cox, S. M., & Fitzgerald, J. D. (1992). *Police in community relations: Critical issues.* 2nd ed. Dubuque, IA: Wm. C. Brown.

Cox, S. M., & Wade, J. E. (1996). *The criminal justice network: An introduction.* Boston: McGraw-Hill.

Crime in the United States, 1999. (2000). U.S. Department of Justice. Washington, D.C.: U.S. Government Printing Office.

Criminal Justice Newsletter. (1990). Child abuse prosecutions are supported by Anti-Crime Bill. 21 (22), 3.

Cromwell, P. F., Jr., Killenger, G. G., Kerper, H. B., & Walker, C. (1985). *Probation and parole in the criminal justice system.* 2nd ed. St. Paul, MN: West.

Crosson-Tower, C. (1999). *Understanding child abuse and neglect.* 4th ed. Boston: Allyn and Bacon.

Curran, D. J., & Renzetti, C. M. (1994). *Theories of crime.* Boston: Allyn and Bacon.

Curry, G. D. (1998). Female gang involvement. *Journal of Research in Crime & Delinquency, 35* (1), 100–118.

Curry, G. D., & Spergel, I. A. (1988). Gang homicide, delinquency, and community. *Criminology, 26* (3), 381–405.

Daly, K., & Chesney-Lind, M. (1988), Feminism and criminology. *Justice Quarterly, 5,* 497–538.

Dart, R. W. (1992). *Street gangs.* Chicago: Chicago Police Department.

Davidson, H. (1981). The guardian ad litem: An important approach to the protection of children. *Children Today, 10* (23), 20–23.

Davidson, N. (1990). Life without father. *Policy Review, 51,* 40–44.

Davidson, W. S., Redner, R., & Amdur, R. L. (1990). *Alternative treatments for troubled youth: The case of diversion from the justice system.* New York: Plenum.

Davis, K. C. (1975). *Police discretion.* St. Paul, MN: West.

Davis, N. J. (1999). *Youth crisis: Growing up in a high-risk society.* Westport, CN: Praeger.

Davis, S. M. (2001). *Rights of juveniles.* New York: Clark Boardman/West.

Dawkins, M. P. (1997). Drug use and violent crime among juveniles. *Adolescence, 32,* 395–405.

Dawley, D. (1973). *A nation of lords.* New York: Doubleday.

Del Carmen, R., Parker, M., & Reddington, F. P. (1998). *Briefs of leading cases in juvenile justice.* Cincinnati: Anderson.

Denno, D. W. (1994, Summer). Gender, crime, and the criminal law defenses. *Journal of Criminal Law and Criminology, 85,* 80–180.

Dentler, R. A., & Monroe, L. J. (1961, October). Early adolescent theft. *American Sociological Review, 26,* 733–743.

Department of Justice, Department of Education. (1998). *1998 annual report on school safety.* Washington, D.C.: U.S. Department of Justice.

DePaul, J., & Domenech, L. (2000). Childhood history of abuse and child abuse potential in adolescent mothers: A longitudinal study. *Child Abuse & Neglect, 24* (5), 701–713.

DiLillo, D., Tremblay, G. C., & Peterson, L. (2000). Linking childhood sexual abuse and abusive parenting: The mediating role of maternal anger. *Child Abuse & Neglect, 24* (6), 767–779.

District of Columbia Code. 1997.

Dixon, J. (1993, November 9). Thousands of babies abandoned. *Peoria Journal Star,* pp. 1–2.

Dorne, C., & Gewerth, K. (1998). *American juvenile justice: Cases, legislation and comments.* San Francisco: Austin & Winfield.

Drowns, R. W., & Hess, K. M. (1990). *Juvenile justice.* Saint Paul, MN: West Publishing Co.

Dugdale, R. L. (1888). *The Jukes: A study in crime, pauperism, disease and heredity.* New York: Putnam.

Echeburua, E., Fernandez-Montalvo, J., & Baez, C. (2000). Relapse prevention in the treatment of slot-machine pathological gambling. *Behavior Therapy, 31* (2), 351–364.

Eddings V. Oklahoma (455 U.S. 104). 1982.

Editorial. (2001, March 15). What is juvenile justice? *Milwaukee Journal Sentinel,* p. 18A.

Ehrenreich, B. (1990). The hour glass society. *New Perspectives Quarterly, 7,* 44–46.

Eitzen, D. S., & Zinn, M. B. (1992). *Social problems.* 5th ed. Boston: Allyn and Bacon.

Elliott, D., & Ageton, S. (1980). Reconciling race and sex differences in self-reported and official estimates of delinquency. *American Sociological Review, 45,* 95–110.

Ellis, R. A., O'Hara, M., & Sowers, K. (1999). Treatment profiles of troubled female adolescents: Implications for judicial disposition. *Juvenile and Family Court Journal, 50* (3), 25–40.

Ellis, R. A. & Sowers, K. M. (2001). *Juvenile justice practice: A cross- disciplinary approach to intervention.* Belmont, CA: Brooks/Cole.

Emery, R. E. (1982). Interparental conflict and the children of discord and divorce. *Psychological Bulletin, 92,* 310–330.

Empey, L. T., & Stafford, M. C. (1991). *American delinquency: Its meaning and construction.* 3rd ed. Belmont, CA: Wadsworth.

Empey, L. T., Stafford, M. C., & Hay C. H. (1999). *American delinquency: Its meaning and construction.* 4th ed. Belmont, CA: Wadsworth.

Ending disorder at the court. [Editorial]. (2000, July 6). *The Plain Dealer,* p. 10B.

Engel, R. S., Sobol, J. J., & Worden, R. E. (2000). Further exploration of the demeanor hypothesis: The interaction effects of suspects' characteristics and demeanor on police behavior. *Justice Quarterly, 17* (2), 235–258.

Ennet, S., Tobler, N. S., Ringwalt, C. L., and Flewelling, R. L. (1994). How effective is drug abuse resistance education? A meta-analysis of project DARE outcome evaluations. *American Journal of Public Health, 84* (9), 1394–1401.

Erikson, K. (1962). Notes on the sociology of deviance. *Social Problems, 9,* 301–314.

Esbensen, F., & Osgood, D. W. (1999). Gang resistance education and training (GREAT): Results from the national evaluation. *Journal of Research in Crime & Delinquency, 36* (2), 194–225.

Esbensen, F., Deschenes, E. P. & Winfree, L. T. (1999). Differences between gang girls and gang boys: Results from a multisite survey. *Youth & Society, 31* (1), 27–53.

Evans, W. P., Fitzgerald, C., & Weigel, D. (1999). Are rural gang members similar to their urban peers: Implications for rural communities. *Youth & Society, 30* (3), 267–282.

Fagan, J., & Pabon, E. (1990). Contributions of delinquency and substance use to school dropout among inner city youths. *Youth and Society, 21,* 306–354.

Faust, F. L. & Brantingham, P. J. (1974). *Juvenile justice philosophy.* St. Paul: West.

Federal Bureau of Investigation. (1993). *Crime in the United States, 1992.* Washington, D.C.: U.S. Department of Justice.

Federal Bureau of Investigation. (1997). *Crime in the United States, 1996.* Washington, D.C.: U.S. Department of Justice.

Federal Bureau of Investigation. (2000). *National incident-based reporting system (NIBRS).* http://www/fbi.gov/ucr/faqs.htm.

Federal Bureau of Investigation. (2000). *Crime in the United States–1999.* Washington, D.C.: U.S. Government Printing Office.

Feiler, S. M., & Sheley, J. F. (1999). Legal and racial elements of public willingness to transfer juvenile offenders to adult court. *Journal of Criminal Justice, 27* (1), 55–64.

Fenwick, C. R. (1982). Juvenile court intake decision making: The importance of family affiliation. *Journal of Criminal Justice, 10,* 443–453.

Ferdinand, T. N. (1991). History overtakes the juvenile justice system. *Crime and Delinquency, 37* (2), 204–224.

Finkelhor, D., & Ormrod, R. (2001, October). Homicides of children and youth. *Juvenile Justice Bulletin.* Washington, D.C.: Office of Juvenile Justice and Delinquency Prevention.

Finkenauer, J. O. (1982). *Scared straight.* Englewood Cliffs, NJ: Prentice Hall.

Fishbein, D. H. (1990, February). Biological perspectives in criminology. *Criminology, 28,* 27–72.

Fishman, L. T. (1995). The Vice Queens: An ethnographic study of black female gang behavior. In M. W. Klein, C. L. Maxson, & J. Miller (eds.), *The modern gang reader* (pp. 83–92). Los Angeles: Roxbury.

Fitzgerald, J. D., & Cox, S. M. (1994). *Research Methods in Criminal Justice: An Introduction.* 2nd ed. Madison, WI: Brown Benchmark.

Flannery, D. J., Williams, L. L., & Vazsonyi, A. T. (1999). Who are they and what are they doing? Delinquent behavior, substance abuse, and early adolescents' after-school time. *American Journal of Orthopsychiatry, 69* (2), 247–253.

Fleener, F. T. (1999). Family as a factor in delinquency. *Psychological Reports, 85* (1), 80–81.

Florida Statutes Annotated. 1991, 1999.

Florsheim, P., Shotorbani, S., & Guest-Warnick, G. (2000). Role of the working alliance in the treatment of delinquent boys in community-based programs. *Journal of Clinical Child Psychology, 29* (1), 94–107.

Fornek, S. (2000, December 10). Mom who breast-fed boy, 5, seeks custody. *Chicago Sun-Times,* p. 14.

Fox, J. A., & Levin, J. (1994). Firing back: The growing threat of workplace homicide. *Journal of Criminal Law, Criminology, and Police Science, 563,* 16–30.

Fox, R. W., Kanitz, H. M., & Folger, W. A. (1991). Basic counseling skills training program for juvenile court workers. *Journal of Addictions and Offender Counseling, 11* (2), 34–41.

Fox, S. (1984). *Juvenile courts in a nutshell.* 2nd ed. Saint Paul, MN: West Publishing Co.

Frazier, C. E., Bishop, D. M., & Henretta, J. C. (1992). The social context of race differentials in juvenile justice dispositions. *The Sociological Quarterly, 33* (3), 447–458.

Friedenberg, E. Z. (1965). *Coming of age in America.* New York: Random House.

Friend, T. (2000, June 27). Genetic map is hailed as new power. *USA Today,* p. 1A.

Gahr, E. (2001). Judging juveniles. *American Enterprise, 12* (4), 26–28.

Gallegos V. Colorado, (370 U.S. 49). 1969.

Gallico, R., Burns, T. J., & Grob, C. S. (1988). *Emotional and behavioral problems in children with learning disabilities.* Boston: Little, Brown.

Gannon v. Scarpelli, 411 U. S. 778. 1973.

Garrett, C. (1985). Effects of residential treatment on adjudicated delinquents. *Journal of Research in Crime and Delinquency, 22,* 287–308.

Garrett, M., & Short, J. F. (1975, February). Social class and delinquency: Predictions and outcomes of police-juvenile encounters. *Social Problems, 22,* 368–383.

Gates, D. F., & Jackson, R. K. (1990). The situation in Los Angeles. *Police Chief, 57* (11), 20–22.

Gavin, T., & Jacobs, W. (1987). Adolescent suicide and the school resource officer. *Police Chief, 4,* 42–44.

Georgia Code Annotated. 1999.

Gibbons, D. C. (1992). *Society, crime and criminal behavior.* 6th ed. Englewood Cliffs, NJ: Prentice Hall.

———. (1994). *Talking about crime and criminals: Problems and issues in theory development in criminology.* Englewood Cliffs, NJ: Prentice Hall.

Glaser, D. (1960). Differential association and criminological prediction. *Social Problems 8,* 6–14.

———. (1978). *Crime in our changing society.* New York: Holt, Rinehart and Winston.

Glensor, R. W., Correia, M. E., & Peak K. J. (eds.). (2000). *Policing communities: Understandinig crime and solving problems.* Los Angeles: Roxbury.

Gluck, S. (1997, June). Wayward youth, super predataor: An evolutionary tale of juvenile delinquency froms the 1950s to the present. *Corrections Today, 59,* 62–64.

Glueck, S., & Glueck, E. (1950). *Unraveling juvenile delinquency.* Cambridge, MA: Harvard University Press.

Goddard, H. H. (1914). *Feeblemindedness: Its causes and consequences.* New York: Macmillan.

Goldstein, S. L. & Tyler, R. P. (1998). Frustrations of inquiry: Child sexual abuse allegations in divorce and custody cases. *FBI Law Enforcement Bulletin, 67* (7), 1–6.

Goring, C. (1913). The *English convict.* London: H. M. Stationery Office.

Gorman-Smith, D., Tolan, P. H., & Loeber, R. (1998). Relation of family problems to patterns of delinquent involvement among urban youth. *Journal of Abnormal Child Psychology, 26* (5), 319–333.

Gough, H. G. (1948). A sociological theory of psychopathy. *American Journal of Sociology, 53,* 359–366.

———. (1960). Theory and measurement of socialization. *Journal of Consulting Psychology, 24,* 23–30.

Greenberg, D. F. (1999). The weak strength of social control theory. *Crime & Delinquency, 45* (1), 66–81.

Gresham, F. M., MacMillan, D. L., & Bocian, K. M. (1998). Comorbidity of hyperactivity-impulsivity-inattention and conduct problems: Risk factors in social, affective, and academic domains. *Journal of Abnormal Child Psychology, 26* (5), 393–406.

Griffin, B.S., & Griffin, C.T. (1978). *Juvenile delinquency in perspective.* New York: Harper and Row.

Haley v. Ohio, (332 U.S. 596). 1948.

Halleck, S. (1971). *Psychiatry and the dilemmas of crime.* Berkeley: University of California Press.

Hamarman, S., & Bernet, W. (2000). Evaluating and reporting emotional abuse in children: Parent-based, action-based focus aids in clinical decision-making. *Journal of the American Academy of Child & Adolescent Psychiatry, 39* (7), 928–930.

Hamm, M. S. (1993). *American skinheads: The criminology and control of hate crime.* Westport, CT: Praeger.

Hannon, K. A. (1991, December). Child abuse: Munchausen's Syndrome by Proxy. *FBI Law Enforcement Bulletin,* 8–11.

Hanson, R. F., Resnick, H. S., & Saunders, B. E. (1999). Factors related to the reporting of childhood rape. *Child Abuse & Neglect, 23* (6), 559–569.

Harper, G. W., & Robinson, W. L. (1999). Pathways to risk among inner-city African-American adolescent females: The influence of gang membership. *American Journal of Community Psychology, 27* (3), 383–404.

Harris, P. W., & Jones, P. R. (1999). Differentiating delinquent youths for program planning and evaluation. *Criminal Justice & Behavior, 26* (4), 403–434.

Hawkins, J. D., & Listiner, D. M. (1987). Schooling and delinquency. In E. Johnson (ed.), *Handbook on crime and delinquency prevention.* Westport, CT: Greenwood Press.

Health Facts, 16 (150). (1991). Memory loss as a survival method. New York: Center for Medical Consumers, pp. 1–6.

Healy, W., & Bronner, A. (1936). *New light on delinquency and its treatment.* New Haven: Yale University Press.

Heck, W. P. (1999). Basic investigative protocol for child sexual abuse. *FBI Law Enforcement Bulletin, 68* (10), 19–25.

Hibbler, W. J. (1999). A message from the 14th Annual National Juvenile Corrections and Detention Forum. *Corrections Today, 61* (4), 28–31.

Hieb, C. F. (1992). *Gang task force and Lakewood, CO Police Department.* Lakewood, CO: Access Publishing.

High/Scope Educational Research Foundation. (2002). *High-quality preschool program found to improve adult status.* http://www.highscope.org/research/Fact%20Sheets/Perry%20Sheet.pdf.

Hindelang, M. J., Hirschi, T., & Weis, J. G. (1981). *Measuring delinquency.* Beverly Hills, CA: Sage.

Hinzman, G., & Blome, D. (1991). Cooperation key to success of child protection center. *Police Chief, 58,* 24–27.

Hirschi, T. (1969). *Causes of delinquency.* Berkeley, CA: University of California Press,

———. & Gottfredson, M. (1993). Rethinking the juvenile justice system. *Crime and Delinquency, 39* (2), 262–271.

Holsinger, K. (2000). Feminist perspectives on female offending: Examining real girls' lives. *Women & Criminal Justice, 12* (1), 23–51.

Holzman, H. R. (1996). Criminological research on public housing: Toward a better understanding of people, places, and spaces. *Crime and Delinquency, 42,* 361–378.

Hooton, E. (1939). *Crime and the man.* Cambridge, MA: Harvard University Press.

Hurst, Y. G., & Frank, J. (2000). How kids view cops: The nature of juvenile attitudes toward the police. *Journal of Crime & Justice, 28* (3), 189–202.

Hurst, Y. G., Frank, J., & Browning, S. L. (2000). The attitudes of juveniles toward the police: A comparison of black and white youth. *Policing: An International Journal of Police Strategies & Management, 23* (1), 37–53.

Hutzler, J. L. (1982). Canon to the left, canon to the right: Can the juvenile court survive? *Today's Delinquent,* 25–38.

Illinois Complied Statutes (ILCS). (1999).

Illinois Department of Corrections. (1985). *Training manual.* Springfield, IL.

Indiana Code Annotated. (1997).

In re Gault, 387 U.S. 1, 87 S.Ct. 1428 (1967).

In re Holmes, 379 Pa. 599, 109 A 2d. 523 (1954), cert. denied, 348 U.S. 973, 75 S.Ct. 535 (1955).

In re Register, 84 N.C. App. 336, 352 S. E. 2d 889 (1987) [dictum].

In re Winship, 397 U.S. 358, 90 S.Ct. 1068 (1970).

Inciardi, J. A., Horowitz, R., & Pottieger, A. E. (1993). *Street kids, street drugs, street crime: An examination of drug use and serious delinquency in Miami.* Belmont, CA: Wadsworth.

Institute of Judicial Administration and the American Bar Association. (1980). *Standards for the Administration of Juvenile Justice.* Cambridge, MA: Ballinger.

Iowa Code Annotated. 1999.

Jacobs, J. (1977). *Stateville: The penitentiary in mass society.* Chicago: University of Chicago Press.

Jang, S. L. (1999). Age-varying effects of family, school, and peers on delinquency: A multilevel modeling test of interactional theory. *Criminology, 37* (3), 687–702.

Jarjoura, G. R. (1996). The conditional effect of social class on the dropout delinquency relationship. *Journal of Research in Crime & Delinquency, 33,* 232–255.

Jeffery, C. R. (1996, March/April). The genetics and crime conference revisited. *The Criminologist,* 1, 3.

Johnson, D. (1999). Rehabilitating criminals before they grow up. *Futurist, 33* (10), 11–12.

Johnson, J. M., & DeBerry, M. (1989). *Criminal Victimization, 1988.* Washington, D. C.: Bureau of Justice Statistics.

Johnson, M. (1999, December 7). *Lawmakers propose tougher attendance laws.* Associated Press.

Johnson, R. E. (1980). Social class and delinquent behavior. *Criminology, 18* (1), 86.

Johnson, S. (1998). Girls in trouble: Do we care? The number of delinquent girls is on the rise; only a coordinated, multiagency approach can turn the tide. *Corrections Today, 60* (7), 136–138.

Jones v. Commonwealth, 185 Va. 335, 38 S.E.2d 444 (1946).

Katkin, D., Hyman, D., & Kramer, J. (1976). *Juvenile delinquency and the juvenile justice system.* North Scituate, MA: Duxbury Press.

Kaufman, J., & Zigler, E. F. (1987, August). Do abused children become abusive parents? *American Journal of Orthopsychiatry, 40,* 953–959.

Kelley, D. H. (1977). Labeling and the consequences of wearing a delinquent label in a school setting. *Education, 97,* 371–380.

Kempf, K. L. (1992). *The role of race in juvenile justice processing in Pennsylvania.* Shippensburg, PA: Center for Juvenile Justice Training and Research.

Kent v. United States, 383 U.S. 541, 86 S.Ct. 1045 (1966).

Klein, M. W. (1967). *Juvenile gangs in context.* Englewood Cliffs, NJ: Prentice Hall.

Klein-Saffran, J., Chapman, D. A., & Jeffers, J. L. (1993). Boot camp for prisoners. *Law Enforcement Bulletin, 62* (10), 13–16.

Klockars, C. B. (1979). The contemporary crises of Marxist criminology. *Criminology, 16* (4), 477–515.

Klofas, J., & Stojkovic, S. (eds.). (1995). *Crime and justice in the year 2010.* New York: Wadsworth.

Knudsen, D. D. (1992). *Child maltreatment: Emerging perspectives.* Dix Hills, NY: General Hall.

Kowaleski-Jones, L. (2000). Staying out of trouble: Community resources and problem behavior among high-risk adolescents. *Journal of Marriage & the Family, 62* (2), 449–464.

Krasner, L., & Ullman, L. P. (1965). *Research in behavior modification.* New York: Holt, Rinehart and Winston.

Kratcoski, P. C., & Kratcoski, L. D. (1995). *Juvenile delinquency.* 4th ed. New York: McGraw-Hill.

Kretschmer, E. (1925). *Physique and character.* trans. W. Sprott. New York: Harcourt, Brace and World.

Krisberg, B., Austin, J., & Steele, P. A. (1989). *Unlocking juvenile corrections: Evaluating the Massachusetts Department of Youth Services.* San Francisco: National Council on Crime and Delinquency.

Krueger, C. (1993, April 27). State investigating Straight, Inc. drug program. *St. Petersburg Times,* p. A1.

———. (1999, August 24). Ex-Straight leader files to help kids. *St. Petersburg Times,* p. 1B.

———. (2000, December 15). Observers decry approach to delinquent girls. *St. Petersburg Times,* p. 3B.

Kvaraceus, W. C. (1945). *Juvenile delinquency and the school.* New York: World Book.

Lander, B. (1970). An ecological analysis of Baltimore. In M. E. Wolfgang et al. (eds.), *Sociology of crime and delinquency.* 2nd ed. (pp. 247–265). New York: John Wiley and Sons.

Lane, J., & Turner, S. (1999). Interagency collaboration in juvenile justice: Learning from experience. *Federal Probation, 63* (2), 33–39.

Lanier, M., & Henry, S. (1998). *Essential criminology.* Boulder, CO: Westview Press.

Lardiero, C. J. (1997, June). Of disproportionate minority confinement. *Corrections Today, 59,* 14.

Laub, J. H., & MacMurray, B. K. (1987). Increasing the prosecutor's role in juvenile court: Expectations and realities. *Justice System Journal, 12,* 196–209.

Leiber, M. J., & Stairs, J. M. (1999). Race: Contexts, and the use of intake diversion. *Journal of Research in Crime and Delinquency, 36* (1), 56–86.

Leshner, A. I. (1998). Addiction is a brain disease—and it matters. *National Institute of Justice Journal* (237), 2–6.

Levinson, R. B., & Chase, R. (2000). Private sector involvement in juvenile justice. *Corrections Today, 62* (2), 156–159.

Liddle, H. A., & Hogue, A. (2000). A family-based, developmental-ecological preventive intervention for high-risk adolescents. *Journal of Marital & Family Therapy, 26* (3), 265–279.

Life Skills Training Programs. (2001). http://www.ncjrs.org/ojjhome.htm.

Lipsey, M. W. (1999, July). Can intervention rehabilitate serious delinquents? *Annals of the American Academy of Political & Social Science, 564,* 142–166.

Livingston, J. (1992). *Crime and criminology.* 2nd ed. Upper Saddle River, NJ: Prentice Hall.

———. (1996). *Crime and criminology.* 2nd ed. Upper Saddle River, NJ: Prentice Hall.

Lizotte, A. J., Tesorio, J. M., Thornberry, T. P., & Krohn, M. D. (1994) Patterns of adolescent firearms ownership and use. *Justice Quarterly, 11,* 51–74.

Loeber, R. (1988). Families and crime. *National Institute of Justice: Crime file study guide.* U.S. Department of Justice. Washington, D.C.: U.S. Government Printing Office.

Lotz, R., & Lee, L. (1999). Sociability, school experience, and delinquency. *Youth & Society, 31* (2), 199–223.

Louisiana Children's Code Annotated. 1999.

Ludwig, F. J. (1955). *Youth and the law: Handbook on laws affecting youth.* Brooklyn: Foundation Press.

Lundman, R. J. (1993). *Prevention and control of juvenile delinquency.* 2nd ed. New York: Oxford University Press.

Lundman, R. L., Sykes, R. E., & Clark, J. P. (1978, January). Police control of juveniles: A replication. *Journal of Research in Crime and Delinquency, 15,* 74–91.

Lyerly, R. R., and Skipper, J. K. (1981). Differential rate of rural-urban delinquency. *Criminology, 19* (3), 385–399.

Lynam, D. R. (1998). Early identification of the fledgling psychopath: Locating the psychopathic child in the current nomenclature. *Journal of Abnormal Psychology, 107* (4), 566–575.

MacDonald, S. S., & Baroody-Hard, C. (1999). Communication between probation officers and judges: An innovative model. *Federal Probation, 63* (1), 42–50.

MacKenzie, D. L., & Souryal, C. C. (1991, October). Boot camp survey. *Corrections Today,* 90–96.

Madigan, C. (1989, February 5). Minnesota shows the way in childhood assistance. *Chicago Tribune,* Sec.1, p. 7.

Main, F. (2001, January 16). Gangs go global. *Chicago Sun-Times,* p. 3.

Main, F., & Spielman, F. (2000, October, 5). Gang battles terrorize schools: Students locked inside after series of shootings near campuses. *Chicago Sun-Times,* p. 1

Martens, W. H. J. (1999). Marcel: A case report of a violent sexual psychopath in remission. *International Journal of Offender Therapy & Comparative Criminology, 43* (3), 391–399.

Martin, G., & Peas, J. (1978). *Behavior modification: What it is and how to do it.* Englewood Cliffs, NJ: Prentice Hall.

Martin, J. R., Schulze, A. D., & Valdez, M. (1988). Taking aim at truancy. *FBI Law Enforcement Bulletin, 57* (5), 8–12.

Martinson, T. M. (1974). What works? Questions and answers about prison reform. *Public Interest, 35,* 22–54.

Maryland Annotated Code. 1992.

Maryland Courts and Judicial Procedures Code Annotated. 1998.

Massachusetts General Laws Annotated. 1999.

May, D. C. (1999). Scared kids, unattached kids, or peer pressure: Why do students carry firearms to school? *Youth & Society, 31* (1), 100–127.

Mays, G. L. (1997). *Gangs and gang behavior.* Chicago: Nelson-Hall.

Mays, G. L., & Winfree, L. T., Jr. (2000). *Juvenile justice.* Boston: McGraw-Hill.

McCord, J., & Tremblay, R. E. (1992). *Preventing antisocial behavior: Interventions from birth through adolescence.* New York: Guilford Press.

McKeiver v. Pennsylvania, 403 U.S. 528, 91 S. Ct. (1971).

McPhee, M. (2000, November 26). Gangs waging war on street: Crips and Bloods take their deadly battle to Brooklyn. *Daily News (New York),* p. 28.

McQueen, A. (2000, October 26). Children safer at school, says new collection of crime statistics. *The Associated Press.*

Meddis, S. V. (1993, October 29). In a dark alley, most-feared face is a teen's. *USA Today.* p. 6A.

Meehan, A. J. (1992). I don't prevent crime, I prevent calls: Policing a negotiated order. *Symbolic Interaction, 15* (4), 455–480.

Mempa v. Rhay, 389 U.S. 128 (1967).

Mercer, R., Brooks, M., & Bryant, P. T. (2000). Global positioning satellite system: tracking offenders in real time (Florida). *Corrections Today, 62* (4), 76–80.

Merton, R. K. (1938). Social structure and anomie. *American Sociological Review, 3,* 672–682.

———. (1955). *Social theory and social structure.* New York: Free Press.

Meyers, J. E. B. (1996, April). Societal self-defense: New laws to protect children from sexual abuse. *Child Abuse & Neglect, 20,* 255–258.

Michigan Compiled Laws Annotated. 1999.

Miller, W. B. (1958). Lower class culture as a generating milieu of gang delinquency. *Journal of Social Issues, 14* (3), 5–19.

———. (2001, April). *The growth of gangs in the United States: 1970–1998. OJJDP Report.* Washington, D.C.: U.S. Department of Justice.

Miranda v. Arizona, 384 U.S. 436, 86 S.Ct. 1602 (1966).

Mississippi Code Annotated. 1999.

Monk-Turner, E. (1990). The occupational achievements of community and four-year college entrants. *American Sociological Review, 55* (5), 719–727.

Montana Code Annotated. 1999.

Moon, M. M., Sundt, J. L.,Cullen, F. T., & Wright, J. P. (2000). Is child saving dead? Public support for juvenile rehabilitation. *Crime and Delinquency, 46* (1), 38–60.

Moore, J., & Hagedorn, J. (2001, March). Female gangs: A focus on research. *Juvenile Justice Bulletin.* Washington, D.C.: U.S. Department of Justice.

Morash, M. (1984). Establishment of a juvenile police record: The influence of individual and peer group characteristics. *Criminology, 22* (1), 97–111.

———. and Chesney-Lind, M. (1991). A reformulation and partial test of the power control theory of delinquency. *Justice Quarterly, 8* (3), 347–379.

Morrissey v. Brewer, 408 U.S. 471 (1972).

Morse, S. J. (1999, July). Delinquency and desert. *Annals of the American Academy of Political & Social Science, 564,* 56–88.

Moutrie, D., & Hayasaki, E. (2000, December 29). Getting young lives back on track: A 10-year old LAPD program for at-risk youths combines physical training with classes in anger management and creative arts and instruction in math and English. *Los Angeles Times,* p. 2B.

Moyer, I. (1981). Demeanor, sex, and race in police processing. *Journal of Criminal Justice, 9* (3), 235.

Munz, M. (2000, December 27). In molestations, mothers often defend perpetrtators; Lack of belief hurts the abused child deeply, experts say. *St. Louis Post-Dispatch,* p. 1.

Nadelman, E. A. (1998). Commonsense drug policy. *Foreign Affairs, 77* (1), 111–126.

National Center for Education Statistics. (1997, June 12). *Student reports of availability, peer approval, and use of alcohol, marijuana, and other drugs at school: 1993.* Washington, D. C.: NCES.

National Center for Juvenile Justice. (1991). *Desktop guide to good juvenile probation practice.* Pittsburgh, PA: National Center for Juvenile Justice.

National Institute of Justice. (1988, September-October). Targeting serious juvenile offenders for prosecution can make a difference. *NIJ Reports.* Washington, D.C.: U.S. Government Printing Office: 9–12.

National Institute of Justice. (1994, October). *The DARE program: A review of prevalence, user satisfaction, and effectiveness.* Washington, D.C.: National Institute of Justice.

National Victims Center. (1998). *Promising practices and strategies for victim services in corrections.* www.nvc.org/ADIR/Compenm.htm.

National Youth Gang Center. (1997). *1995 National youth gang survey. OJJDP.* Washington, D.C.: U.S. Department of Justice.

Neal, S. (1998, September 13). Hoover follows Capone legacy. *Chicago Sun-Times,* p. 40.

Nebraska Revised Statutes. 1998.

New Jersey Statutes Annotated. (1999).

New Mexico Statutes Annotated. 1995.

New York Family Court Act. 1999.

New York Sessions Laws. 1962.

Newsweek. (1988, November 28). Crack, hour by hour. pp. 20–29.

North Carolina General Statutes. 1999.

North Dakota Century Code. 1991, 1999.

NRCCSA News. (1992). *Statistical base still unfolding.* Huntsville, AL: The National Resource Center on Child Sexual Abuse: 1 (1), 5, 8.

Nyquist, O. (1960). *Juvenile justice: A comparative study with special reference to the Swedish Welfare Board and the California juvenile court system.* London: Macmillan.

Office of Juvenile Justice and Delinquency Prevention. (1976). *First analysis and evaluation: Federal juvenile delinquency programs.* Washington, D.C.: U.S. Government Printing Office.

Office of Juvenile Justice and Delinquency Prevention. (1979). *Delinquency prevention: theories and strategies.* Washington, D.C.: U.S. Government Printing Office.

Office of Juvenile Justice and Delinquency Prevention. (1980). *Juvenile justice: Before and after the onset of delinquency.* Washington, D.C.: U.S. Government Printing Office.

Office of Juvenile Justice and Delinquency Prevention. (1992). *Arrests of youth, 1990.* Washington, D.C.: U.S. Government Printing Office.

Office of Juvenile Justice and Delinquency Prevention. (1996, March). *Juvenile probation: The workhorse of the juvenile justice system.* Washington, D.C.: U.S. Department of Justice.

Office of Juvenile Justice and Delinquency Prevention. (1998, December). *Trying juveniles as adults in criminal court: An analysis of state transfer provisions.* Washington, D.C.: U.S. Government Printing Office.

Office of Juvenile Justice and Delinquency Prevention. (2000, September). Preventing adolescent gang involvement. *Juvenile Justice Bulletin.* Washington, D.C.: U.S. Department of Justice.

Ohlin, L. E. (1998). The future of juvenile justice policy and research. *Crime & Delinquency, 44* (1), 143–153.

Oklahoma Statutes Annotated. 1998.

Omaha World Herald, Editorial. (2001, March 23). In this church, the little children suffer.

Omaha World-Herald, p. 12.

Oregon Revised Statutes. 1995.

Osgood, D. W., & Chambers, J. M. (2000). Social disorganization outside the metropolis: An analysis of rural youth violence. *Criminology, 38* (1), 81–115.

Pagani, L., Boulerice, B., & Vitaro, F. (1999). Effects of poverty on academic failure and delinquency in boys: A change and process model approach. *Journal of Child Psychology & Psychiatry & Allied Disciplines, 40* (8), 1209–1219.

Palumbo, M. G., & Ferguson, J. (1995). Evaluating gang resistance education and training. Is the impact the same as Drug Abuse Resistance Education (DARE)? *Evaluation Review, 19* (6), 597–619.

Parker-Jimenez, J. (1997). An offender's experience with the criminal justice system. *Federal Probation, 61,* 47–52.

Parsons, A. (1998, August). Meth and cocaine: Addictive drugs alike but different. *Southeast Missourian,* p. 1.

Pattillo, M. E. (1998). Sweet mothers and gang bangers: Managing crime in a black middle-class neighborhood. *Social Forces, 76* (3), 747–774.

Paul, R. H., Marx, B. P., & Orsillo, S. M. (1999). Acceptance-based psychotherapy in the treatment of an adjudicated exhibitionist: A case example. *Behavior Therapy, 30* (1), 149–162.

Paxson, C. H., & Waldfogel, J. (1999). Parental resources and child abuse and neglect. *American Economic Review, 89* (2), 239–244.

Payne, J. W. (1999). Our children's destiny. *Trial, 35* (1), 83–85.

Peak, K. J. (1999). Gangs: Origins, status, community responses, and policy implications. In R. Muraskin & A. R. Roberts (eds.), *Visions for change: Crime and justice in the twenty-first century* (pp. 51–63). Upper Saddle River, NJ: Prentice Hall.

People ex rel. O'Connell v. Turner, 55 Ill. 280, 286 (1870).

People v. Dominquez, 256 Cal.App. 2d 623 (1967).

Perkiss, M. (1989, January 22). Program aims to help mildly abused children without foster care. *The Macomb Journal,* p. 2C.

Perlmutter, B. F. (1987). Delinquqency and learning disabilities: Evidence for compensatory behaviors and adaptation. *Journal of Youth and Adolescence, 16,* 89–95.

Peters, J. M. (1991, February). Specialists a definite advantage in child sexual abuse cases. *Police Chief,* 21–23.

Peters, S. R., & Peters, S. D. (1998). Violent adolescent females. *Corrections Today, 60* (3), 28–29.

Petition of Ferrier, 103 Ill. 367, 371 (1882).

Piliavin, I., & Briar, S. (1964). Police encounters with juveniles. *American Journal of Sociology, 70,* 206–214.

Pinkerton, J. (2000, December 21). Brownsville takes family under wing: Community provides a home for Christmas. *The Houston Chronicle,* p. 33A.

Piscotta, A. W. (1982). Saving the children: The promise and practice of parens patriae, 1838–98. *Crime and Delinquency, 28* (3), 424–425.

Platt, A. (1977). *The child savers.* 2nd ed. Chicago: University of Chicago Press.

Polk, K. (1984). The new marginal youth. *Crime and Delinquency, 30,* 462–480.

Polk, K., & Scafer, W. B. (eds). (1972). *School and delinquency.* Englewood Cliffs, NJ: Prentice Hall.

Pollock, J. M. (1994). *Ethics in crime and justice: Dilemmas & decisions.* 2nd ed. Belmont, CA: Wadsworth.

Porterfield, A. L. (1946). *Youth in trouble.* Fort Worth, IN: Potishman Foundation.

Portwood, S. G., Grady, M. T., & Dutton, S. E. (2000). Enhancing law enforcement identification and investigation of child maltreatment. *Child Abuse & Neglect, 24* (2), 195–207.

Postman, N. (1991). Quoted in D. Osborne and T. Gaebler. *Reinventing government: How the entrepreneurial spirit is transforming the public sector,* p. 19. Reading, MA: Addison-Wesley.

Poythrees, N. G., Edens, J. F., & Lilienfeld, S. O. (1998). Criterion-related validity of the Psychopathic Personality Inventory in a prison sample. *Psychological Assessment, 10* (4), 426–430.

President's Commission on Law Enforcement and Administration of Justice. (1967). *Task force report: Juvenile delinquency and youth crime.* Washington, D.C: U.S. Government Printing Office.

Prosecution in juvenile courts: Guidelines for the future. (1973). Washington, D.C.: U.S. Department of Justice.

Quinney, R. (1970). *The social reality of crime.* Boston: Little, Brown.

———. (1974). *Critique of legal order: Crime control in capitalist society.* Boston: Little, Brown.

———. (1975). *Criminology.* Boston: Little, Brown.

Reckless, W. C. (1961). A new theory of delinquency and crime. *Federal Probation, 25,* 42–46.

———. (1967). *The crime problem.* New York: Appleton-Century-Crofts.

Reddington, F. P., & Kreisel, B. W. (2000). Training juvenile probation officers: National trends. *Federal Probation, 64* (2), 28–32.

Regoli, R. M., & Hewitt, J. D. (1994). *Delinquency in society: A child-centered approach.* New York: McGraw-Hill.

Rendleman, D. R. (1974). Parens patriae: From chancery to the juvenile court. In F. L. Faust & P. J. Brantingham (eds.), *Juvenile justice* (pp. 72–117). St. Paul, MN: West.

Reno, J. (1998). Taking America back for our children. *Crime and Delinquency, 44* (1), 75–82.

Restorative Justice for Illinois Newsletter. (1999). *What is restorative justice?* LSSI/Prison and Family Ministry, Des Plaines, IL.

Rinehart, W. (1991). *Convicted child molesters.* Unpublished M.A. thesis. Macomb, IL: Western Illinois University.

Roberts, A. R. (1989). *Juvenile justice: Policies, programs, services.* Chicago: Dorsey Press.

Roberts, E. A., Jr. (2001, January 14). Is execution the ultimate punishment? *The Tampa Tribune,* p. 1.

Robinson, S. (1999). Juvenile offenders are worth the effort. *Corrections Today, 61* (2), 8.

Rodney, E. H., & Mupier, R. (1999). Comparing the behaviors and social environments of offending and non-offending African-American adolescents. *Journal of Offender Rehabilitation, 30* (1/2), 65–80.

Ross, R. R., & McKay, H. B. (1978). Behavioral approaches to treatment in corrections: Requiem for a panacea. *Canadian Journal of Criminology, 20,* 279–298.

Rubin, H. T. (1980). The emerging prosecutor dominance of the juvenile court intake process. *Crime and Delinquency, 6,* 229–318.

Rush, J. P. (1992). Juvenile probation officer cynicism. *American Journal of Criminal Justice, 16* (2), 1–16.

Russi, K. (1984, February). Operation K.ID.: A community approach to child protection. *Police Chief, 46,* 35–36.

Sanders, W. B. (1974). Some early beginnings of the children's court movement in England. In F. L. Faust & P. J. Brantingham (eds.), *Juvenile justice philosophy.* St. Paul, MN: West Publishing Co.

Sarasohn, D. (2000, June 29). Putting kids behind bars is wastiing dollars and lives: Better to be smart than just tough. *Star Tribune,* p. 21A.

Satterfield, J. H. (1987). Childhood diagnostic and neurophysiological predictors of teenage arrest rates: An eight year prospective study. In S. A. Mednick, T. E. Moffit, & S. S. Stack (eds.), *The causes of crime: New biological approaches* (pp. 146–167). Cambridge: Cambridge University Press.

Scaramella, G. L. (2000). Methamphetamines: A blast from the past. *Crime & Justice International, 16* (45), 7–8.

Schafer, W. E., & Polk, K. (eds.). (1967). *Delinquency and the schools.* In *Task force report: Juvenile delinquency and youth crime.* President's Commission on Law Enforcement and the Administration of Justice. Washington, D.C.: U.S. Government Printing Office.

Schall v. Martin, 467 U.S. 253 (1984).

Schinke, S. P., & Gilchrist, L. D. (1984). *Life counseling skills with adolescents.* Baltimore, MD: University Park Press.

Schiraldi, V., & Drizin, S. (1999). 100 years of the children's court—giving kids a chance to make better choices. *Corrections Today, 61* (7), 24.

School safety: Annual report, 1998. (1998). Washington, D.C.: U.S. Department of Justice.

Schur, E. M. (1973). *Radical non-intervention: Rethinking the delinquency problem.* Englewood Cliffs, NJ: Prentice Hall.

Schwartz, I. M., Weiner, N. A., & Enosh, G. (1998). Nine lives and then some: Why the juvenile court does not role over and die. *33 Wake Forest L. Rev,* 533.

Schwartz, I. M., Weiner, N. A., & Enosh, G. (1999, July). Myopic justice? The juvenile court and child welfare systems. *Annals of the American Academy of Political & Social Science, 564,* 126–141.

Scott, J. W., & Vaz, E. W. (1963). A perspective on middle-class delinquency. *Canadian Journal of Economics and Political Science, 29,* 324–335.

Scudder, R. G., Blount, W. R., Heide, K. M., & Silverman, I. J. (1993). Important links between child abuse, neglect, and delinquency. *International Journal of Offender Therapy and Comparative Criminology, 37* (4), 310–323.

Sealock, M. D., & Simpson, S. (1998). Unraveling bias in arrest decisions: The role of juvenile offender type-scripts. *Justice Quarterly, 15* (3), 427–457.

Senna, J. J., & Siegal, L. (1994). *Juvenile law: Cases and comments.* 2nd ed. St. Paul, MN: West.

Shaw, C. R., & McKay, H. D. (1942). *Juvenile delinquency and urban areas.* Chicago: University of Chicago Press.

———. (1969). *Juvenile delinquency and urban areas.* rev. ed. Chicago: University of Chicago Press.

Sheehan, T. (2000, September 12). Defense asks judge to exclude juvenile's statements to the police. *The Columbus Dispatch,* p. 3D.

Sheldon, W. H. (1949). *Varieties of delinquent youth: An introduction to constitutional psychiatry.* New York: Harper and Row.

Shelton, T. L., Barkley, R. A., & Crosswait, C. (2000). Multimethod psychoeducational intervention for preschool children with disruptive behavior: Two-year post-treatment follow-up. *Journal of Abnormal Child Psychology, 28* (3), 253–266.

Sherman, L. W., & Weisburd, D. (1995). General deterrent effects of police patrol in crime "hot spots": A randomized study. *Justice Quarterly, 12* (4), 625–640.

Sherman, L. W., Gottfredson, D., MacKenzie, D., Eck, J., Reuter, P., & Bushaway, S. (1997). *Preventing crime: What works, what doesn't, what's promising: A report to the United States Congress.* http://www.ncjrs.org.

Short, J. F., & Nye, F. I. (1958, July-August). Extent of unrecorded juvenile delinquency: Some tentative conclusions. *Journal of Criminal Law, Criminology, and Police Science,* 296–302.

Short, J. F., & Strodbeck, F. (1965). *Group process and gang delinquency.* Chicago: University of Chicago Press.

Shure, M.B. (1999). Preventing violence the problem-solving way. *Juvenile Justice Bulletin. OJJDP.* Washington, D.C.: U.S. Department of Justice.

Sickmund, M., Snyder, H. N., & Poe-Yamagata, E. (1997) *Juvenile offedners and victims: 1997 update on violence.OJJDP.* Washington, D.C.:U.S. Department of Justice.

Siegal, L. J., & Senna, J. J. (1994). *Juvenile justice: Theory, practice, and law.* 5th ed. St. Paul, MN: West.

Simms, S. O. (1997). Restorative juvenile justice: Maryland's legislature reaffirms commitment to juvenile justice reform. *Corrections Today, 59,* 94.

Simonsen, C. E. (1991). *Juvenile justice in America.* 2nd ed. New York: Macmillan.

Simonsen, C. E., & Gordon, M. S. (1982). *Juvenile justice in America.* 2nd ed. New York: MacMillan.

Skinner, B. F. (1953). *Science and human behavior.* New York: Macmillan.

Smart, C. (2000). Reconsidering the recent history of child sexual abuse, 1910–1960. *Journal of Social Policy, 29,* 55–71.

Smith, C. A., & Stern, S. B. (1997). Delinquency and antisocial behavior: A review of family processes and intervention research. *Social Service Review, 71,* 382–420.

Smykla, J. O., & Wills, T. W. (1981). The incidence of learning disabilities and mental retardation in youth under the jurisdiction of the juvenile court. *Journal of Criminal Justice, 9* (3), 219–225.

Snyder, H. N. (2000, December). Juvenile arrests 1999. *Juvenile Justice Bulletin. OJJDP.* Washington, D.C.: U.S. Department of Justice.

Snyder, H. N., & Sickmund, M. (1999, November). *Juvenile offenders and victims: 1999 national report.* Washington, D.C.: U.S. Department of Justice.

———. (2000). *Juvenile transfers to criminal court in the 1990's: Lessons learned from four studies: Report.* Washington, D.C.: U.S. Department of Justice.

Sorrells, J. (1980, April). What can be done about juvenile homicide? *Crime and Delinquency,* 152.

South Dakota Codified Laws Annotated. 1999.

Sprott, J. B. (1998). Understanding public opposition to a separate youth justice system. *Crime and Delinquency, 44,* 399–411.

Stack, B. W. (2001, March 18). Five years of failure: The "adult time" law for juveniles hasn't fulfilled its backers' promises. *Pittsburgh Post-Gazette,* p. A10.

Stanford v. Kentucky, 492 U.S. 361 (1989).

Stark, R. (1987). Deviant places: A theory of the ecology of crime. *Criminology, 25,* 893–909.

Steffensmeier, D. J., & Steffensmeier, R. H. (1980). Trends in female delinquency: An examination of arrest, juvenile court, self-report, and field data. *Criminology, 18* (1), 62–85.

Steinmetz, S. K. (1986). The violent family. In M. Lystad (ed.), *Violence in the home: Interdisciplinary perspectives.* New York: Brunner/Mazel.

Stearns, M., & Garcia, M. (2001, July 29). Law challenges preacher's principles: Religious development's founder defends the way he ministers to children. *The Kansas City Star,* p. A1.

Stern, R. S. (1964). *Delinquent conduct and broken homes.* New Haven, CN: College and University Press.

Steward, M. (1997, June). Promising programs: Missouri implements broad range of programs to meet juveniles' needs. *Corrections Today, 59,* 90–93.

Straus, Murray A., & Richard J. Gelles. (1986). Societal change and change in family violence from 1975–1985 as revealed by two national surveys. *Journal of Marriage and Family, 48,* 465–479.

Streib, V. L. (1998). Moratorium on the death penalty for juveniles. *Law & Contemporary Problems, 61* (4), 55–87.

———. (2000). *The juvenile death penalty today: Death sentences and executions for juvenile crimes, January 1, 1973–June 30, 2000.* Ada, OH: Northern University Clause W. Pettit College of Law.

Stroh, M. (2000, December 10). Rally calls for stay of executions: Death penalty opponents seek state moratorium. *The Baltimore Sun,* p. 3B.

Stroud, D. D., Martens, S. L., & Barker, J. (2000). Criminal investigations of child sexual abuse: A comparison of cases referred to the prosecutor to those not referred. *Child Abuse & Neglect, 24* (5), 689–700.

Sudnow, D. (1965). Normal crimes: Sociological features of the penal code in a public defender office. *Social Problems, 12,* 255–276.

Sutherland, E. H. (1939). *Principles of criminology.* 3rd ed. Philadelphia: J. B. Lippincott.

Sutherland, E. H., & Cressey, D. R. (1978). *Criminology.* 10th ed. New York: J. B. Lippincott.

———, Cressey, D. R., & Luckenbill, D. F. (1992). *Criminology.* 11th ed. Dix Hills, NJ: General Hall.

Sutpen, R., Kurtz, D., & Giddings, M. (1993). The influence of juveniles' race on police decision-making: An exploratory study. *Juvenile and Family Court Journal, 44* (2), 69–76.

Tappan, P. (1949). *Juvenile delinquency.* New York: McGraw-Hill.

Tarpy, C. (1989). Straight: A gloves-off treatment program. *National Geographic, 175* (1), 48–51.

Taylor, J., McGue, M., & Iacono, W. G. (2000). A behavioral genetic analysis of the relationship between the Socialization Scale and self-reported delinquency. *Journal of Personality, 69* (1), 29–50.

Taylor, L. S. (1980, May). The serious juvenile offender: Identification and suggested treatment responses. *The Juvenile and Family Court Journal,* 29.

Taylor, R. L. (1994). Black males and social policy: Breaking the cycle of disadvantage. In R. G. Majors & J. U. Gordon (eds.), *The American black male: His present status and his future* (pp. 148–166). Chicago: Nelson-Hall.

Teepen, T. (2000, April 29). Racial inequities in America's criminal justice system start early. *Star Tribune,* p. 22A.

Terry, R. M. (1967). The screening of juvenile offenders. *Journal of Criminal Law, Criminology, and Police Science, 58* (2), 173–181.

Texas Family Code. 1996.

Thompson v. Oklahoma, 487 U.S. 815 (1988).

Thornberry, T., Moore, M., & Christenson, R. L. (1985). The effects of dropping out of high school on subsequent criminal behavior. *Criminology, 23* (1), 3–18.

Thornton, W. E., Voight, L., & Doerner, W. G. (1987). *Delinquency and justice.* 2nd ed. New York: Random House.

Thrasher, F. M. (1927). *The gang.* Chicago: University of Chicago Press.

Tittle, C., Villemez, W., & Smith, D. (1978). The myth of social class and criminality. *American Sociological Review, 43,* 643–656.

Torbet, P. M. (1996, March). Juvenile probation: The workhorse of the juvenile justice system. *Juvenile Justice Bulletin.* Washington, D.C.: U.S. Department of Justice.

Tower, C. C. (1993). *Understanding child abuse and neglect.* Boston: Allyn and Bacon.

Turk, A. (1969). *Criminality and legal order.* Chicago: Rand McNally.

Turkheimer, E. (1998). Heritability and psychological explanations. *Psychological Review, 105* (4), 782–791.

Twentieth Century Fund Task Force on Sentencing Policy Toward Young Offenders. (1987). *Confronting youth crime: Report of the Twentieth Century Fund Task Force on sentencing policy toward young offenders.* Background paper by Franklin E. Zimring. New York: Holmes & Meier.

Tysver, R. (1999, May 4). Youth drug-arrest rate worries local officials. *Omaha World-Herald,* p. 13.

Uniform Juvenile Court Act. (1968). National Conference of Commissioners on Uniform State Laws. Philadelphia, PA.

University of Maryland Conference. (1996, March). Symposium: Genetics and crime. *Politics & Life Sciences, 15,* 83–109.

U.S. Department of Education. (2000, October). *Indicators of school crime and safety.* Washington, D.C.: U.S. Government Printing Office.

Utah Code Annotated. 1999.

Van Vleet, R. K. (1999). The attack on juvenile justice. *Annals of the American Academy of Political and Social Science, 564,* 203–214.

Venkatesh, S. A. (1997). An invisible community: Inside Chicago's public housing. *American Prospect, 1* (34), 35–40.

Vermont Statutes Annotated. 1991.

Violent Crime in the United States. 1999. (2000). U.S. Department of Justice. Washington, D.C.: U.S. Government Printing Office.

Vold, G. B. (1958). *Theoretical criminology.* New York: Oxford.

Voss, H. L. (1966, Winter). Socioeconomic status and reported delinquent behavior. *Social Problems, 13,* 314–324.

Walker, S. (1998). *Sense and nonsense about crime and drugs: A policy guide.* 4th ed. Belmont, CA: Wadsworth.

Wallerstein, J., & Kelly, J. B. (1980). *Surviving the breakup.* New York: Basic Books.

Walters, P. M. (1993). Community-oriented policing: A blend of strategies. *FBI Law Enforcement Bulletin, 62* (11), 20–23.

Warmbir, S. (2001, May 15). DCFS goes on trial for missing abuse. *Chicago Sun-Times,* p. 16.

Webber, A. M. (1991, May–June). Crime and management: An interview with New York City Police Commissioner Lee P. Brown. *Harvard Business Review,* 110–126.

Wells, E., & Rankin, J. (1991). Families and delinquency: A meta-analysis of the impact of broken homes. *Social Problems, 38,* 71–93.

Welsh, W. N., Jenkins, P. H., & Harris, P. W. (1999). Reducing minority overrepresentation in juvenile justice: Results of community-based delinquency prevention in Harrisburg. *Journal of Research in Crime & Delinquency, 36* (1), 87–110.

Werthman, C., & Piliavin, I. (1967). Gang members and the police. In D. Bordua (ed.), *The police: Six sociological essays.* New York: John Wiley and Sons.

West Virginia Code Annotated. 1999.

Weston, J. (1993). Community policing: An approach to youth gangs in a medium-sized city. *Police Chief, 60* (80), 80–84.

White v. Illinois, 112 S.Ct. 736 (1992).

Whyte, W. F. (1943). *Street corner society.* Chicago: University of Chicago Press.

Wilkins v. Missouri, 492 U.S. 361 (1989).

Wilkinson, R. A. (1997, December). Back to basics. *Corrections Today, 59,* 6–7.

Wilks, J. A. (ed.). (1967). Ecological correlates of crime and delinquency. In *Task force report: Crime and its impact- An assessment.* President's Commission on Law Enforcement and the Administration of Justice. Washington, D.C.: U.S. Government Printing Office: A, 138–156.

Williams, J. H., Ayers, C. D., & Abbott, R. D. (1999). Racial differences in risk factors for delinquency and substance abuse among adolescents. *Social Work Research, 23* (4), 241–256.

Williams, J. M., & Dunlop, L. C. (1999). Pubertal timing and self-reported delinquency among male adolescents. *Journal of Adolescence, 22* (1), 157–171.

Willis, C. L., & Welles, R. H. (1986). The police and child abuse: An analysis of police decisions to report illegal behavior. *Criminology, 26* (4), 695–715.

Willwerth, J. (1993, March 11). Hello? I'm home alone . . . *Time,* 46–47.

Wilson, J. J. (2000, November). *1998 national youth gang survey. OJJDP Summary.* Washington, D.C.: U.S. Department of Justice.

Winner, L., Lanza-Kaduce, L., Bishop, D., & Frazier, C. (1997). The transfer of juveniles to criminal court: Re-examining recidivism over the long term. *Crime & Delinquency, 43,* 548–563.

Winters, C. A. (1997). Learning disabilities, crime, delinquency, and special education placement. *Adolescence, 32,* 451–462.

Wolfe, D. A. (1985). Child-abusive parents: An empirical review and analysis. *Psychological Bulletin, 97,* 462–482.

Wooden, W. S., & Blazak, R. (2001). *Renegade kids, suburban outlaws: From youth culture to delinquency.* Belmont, CA: Wadsworth.

Wright, J. P., & Cullen, F. T. (2001). Parental efficacy and delinquent behavior: Do control and support matter? *Criminology, 39* (3), 677–705.

Wyoming Statutes Annotated. 1987, 1999.

Yablonsky, L., & Haskell, M. (1988). *Juvenile delinquency.* 4th ed. New York: Harper & Row.

Yates, A., & Comerci, G. (1985). Sexual abuse. In V. L. Vivian (ed.). *Child abuse and neglect: A medical community response* (pp. 135–144). Chicago: American Medical Association.

Yogan, L. J. (2000, January). School tracking and student violence. *Annals of the American Academy of Political & Social Science, 567,* 108–122.

Yoo, C. (2000, December 19). State's human resources director resigns. *The Atlanta Journal and Constitution,* p. 1A.

Yoshikawa, H. (1994, January). Prevention as cumulative protection: Effects of early family support and education on chronic delinquency and its risks. *Psychological Bulletin, 115,* 28–54.

Youth Development and Delinquency Prevention Administration, Department of Health, Education, and Welfare. (1971). *National strategy for youth development and delinquency prevention. Memo.* Washington, D.C.: U.S. Government Printing Office.

Zaslaw, J. G., & Balance, G. S. (1996, February). The socio-legal reponse: A new approach to juvenile justice in the '90s. *Corrections Today, 58,* 72.

Zimmerman, J., Rich, W. D., Keilitz, I., & Broder, P. K. (1981). Some observations on the link between learning disabilities and juvenile delinquency. *Journal of Criminal Justice, 9,* 1.

Index